7/16/15
$44.95

Racist America

This third edition of Joe R. Feagin's *Racist America* is significantly revised and updated, with an eye toward racism issues arising regularly in our contemporary era. This edition incorporates more than 200 recent research studies and reports on U.S. racial issues that update and enhance all the last edition's chapters. It expands the discussion and data on concepts such as the white racial frame and systemic racism from research studies by Feagin and his colleagues. The author has further polished the book to make it yet more readable for undergraduates, including eliminating repetitive materials, adding headings and more cross-referencing, and adding new examples, anecdotes, and narratives about contemporary racism.

Joe R. Feagin is Ella C. McFadden Professor in Sociology at Texas A&M University. Feagin has done research on racism and sexism issues for decades. He has written 63 scholarly books and more than 200 scholarly articles in his research areas, and one of his books (*Ghetto Revolts*) was nominated for a Pulitzer Prize. His numerous Routledge books include *Systemic Racism: A Theory of Oppression* (2006), *Two Faced Racism: Whites in the Backstage and Frontstage* (2007), *White Party, White Government: Race, Class, and U.S. Politics* (2012), and *The White Racial Frame* (second edition, 2013).

Feagin is the 2012 recipient of the Soka Gakkai International-USA Social Justice Award, the 2013 American Association for Affirmative Action's Arthur Fletcher Lifetime Achievement Award, and the 2013 American Sociological Association's W. E. B. Du Bois Career of Distinguished Scholarship Award. He was the 1999–2000 president of the American Sociological Association.

TITLES OF RELATED INTEREST

White Party, White Government: Race, Class, and U.S. Politics by Joe R. Feagin

Yes We Can? White Racial Framing and the Obama Presidency, second edition, by Adia Harvey Wingfield and Joe R. Feagin

White Racial Frame: Centuries of Racial Framing and Counter-Framing, second edition, by Joe R. Feagin

Race, Law, and American Society: 1607–Present, second edition, by Gloria J. Browne-Marshall

Forthcoming:

Racial Formation in the United States, third edition, by Michael Omi and Howard Winant

How Blacks Made America Possible, by Joe R. Feagin

Racist America
Roots, Current Realities, and Future Reparations

Third Edition

Joe R. Feagin

Routledge
Taylor & Francis Group
NEW YORK AND LONDON

First published 2014
by Routledge
711 Third Avenue, New York, NY 10017

and by Routledge
2 Park Square, Milton Park, Abingdon, Oxon, OX14 4RN

Routledge is an imprint of the Taylor & Francis Group, an informa business

First edition published by Routledge 2000
Second edition published by Routledge 2010

Library of Congress Cataloging in Publication Data
Feagin, Joe R.
Racist America : roots, current realities, and future reparations / by Joe R. Feagin. – Third edition.
pages cm
    Includes bibliographical references and index.
    1. African Americans–Civil rights. 2. African Americans–Social conditions–1975–
    3. Racism–United States. 4. Race discrimination. 5. United States–Race relations.
    6. African Americans–Reparations. I. Title.
    E185.615.F387 2014
    323.1196'073–dc23   2013031290

ISBN: 978-0-415-70400-7 (hbk)
ISBN: 978-0-415-70401-4 (pbk)
ISBN: 978-0-203-76237-0 (ebk)

Typeset in Minion
by Wearset Ltd, Boldon, Tyne and Wear

Printed and bound in the United States of America by Sheridan Books, Inc. (a Sheridan Group Company).

To Mel Sikes, Roy Brooks, Hernán Vera, Ronald Takaki, and Thomas Pettigrew

Contents

Preface

A few years back the prominent white comedian Michael Richards, who was once part of the television show *Seinfeld*, was caught on camera yelling racist slurs, including "nigger," at black customers in his audience during a comedic performance. According to news reports, Richards yelled at one black audience member: "Shut up! Fifty years ago, we'd have you upside down…" as part of his commentary. Later he apologized, with an explanation that "I work in a very uncontrolled manner onstage. I do a lot of free association."[1]

Some months later popular radio talk-show host Don Imus made similarly blatant racist comments about a successful black women's basketball team. He laughingly called these talented college students "nappy-headed hos." Imus brought harsh emotion-laden framing of black women usually reserved for white locker-room banter into the public frontstage. Imus was briefly fired, but white executives soon had him back on the radio. Surveys indicated that the overwhelming majority of African Americans thought he should have been fired for his remarks, but only 47 percent of whites agreed. Apparently, a large proportion of white Americans do not see such viciously racist public attacks as particularly serious.[2] Blatantly racist incidents still routinely erupt across a country that many people now wishfully describe as "post-racial."

Anthropologist Jane Hill has examined how and why many whites come to define racist outbursts by white celebrities and politicians as not serious, as "gaffes" that do not reveal a deeper racist framing of the protagonists. Her research makes clear the central role of the English language in imbedding and perpetuating the old and very deep white racial framing of U.S. society. The widespread character of this "gaffe" racism, and the way such events get discussed obsessively and circulated extensively around the society, are an indication that the old-fashioned racism of the past has not disappeared and been replaced by a post-racial society.[3]

In verbal attacks on black Americans, these prominent white entertainers used emotion-laden racist words, imagery, and commentary that was taken out of a centuries-old white-racist framing of black Americans. Such views date back to the days of slavery and legal segregation. These views and actions stemming from them today reveal the important aspects of the societal racism examined in this book—the negative images of black men and women dancing in white heads, the white racial framing that legitimates antiblack images, the commonplace discriminatory practices of whites, the arrogance of white power, and white-dominated institutions that allow or encourage such racist practices.

In the United States, racist thought, emotion, and action are structured into the rhythms of everyday life. They are lived, concrete, advantageous for whites, and painful for those who are not white. Each major part of the life of a white person or a person of color is shaped directly or indirectly by this country's systemic racism. Even a person's birth and parents are often shaped by racism, since mate selection is limited by racist pressures against intimate interracial relationships and intermarriage. Where one lives is frequently determined by the racist practices of landlords, bankers, and others in the real-estate profession. The clothes one wears and what one has to eat are affected by access to resources that varies by position in the U.S. racial hierarchy. When one goes off to school, one's education is shaped by contemporary racism—from the composition of the student body to the character of the curriculum. Where one goes to church is often shaped by racism, and it is likely that racism affects who one's political representatives are. Even getting sick, dying, and being buried may be influenced by systemic racism. Every part of the life cycle, and most aspects of one's life, are shaped by the racism that is integral to the foundation and continuing operation of the United States.

One of the great tragedies today is the inability or unwillingness of most white Americans to see clearly and understand fully this racist reality. Among whites, including white elites, there is a commonplace denial of personal, family, and group histories of racism. Most do not see themselves or their families as seriously implicated in racial oppression, in the distant past or the present. Referring to themselves, most will say fervently, "I am not a racist." Referring to ancestors, many will say something like, "My family never owned slaves" or "My family never benefited from segregation." Assuming racial discrimination to be a thing of the past, many assert that African Americans are "paranoid" about racism and often give them firm advice: forget the past and move on, because "slavery happened hundreds of years ago." Most do not wish to honestly discuss issues of contemporary racial framing and discrimination.

Over the last few decades, numerous white commentators have suggested that white racism is no longer a serious problem. Thus, one analysis of white attitudes on public policy matters concludes that "racism is not built-in to the American ethos," while another book boldly proclaims "the end of racism."[4] This line of argument about a post-racial society has become more popular since Barack Obama's pathbreaking election as president in 2008. The "post-racial" perspective now articulated by mainstream commentators often includes the idea that contemporary black politicians like President Obama have an obligation to be racial healers who do not articulate a civil rights enforcement agenda and whose elections prove racism is no longer a serious barrier to societal achievement for Americans of color. Thus, the business newspaper, the *Wall Street Journal,* asserted Obama's election is a "tribute to American opportunity, and it is something that has never happened in another Western democracy—notwithstanding European condescension about 'racist' America." The editorial continued with the assertion that "perhaps we can put to rest the myth of racism as a barrier to achievement in this splendid country."[5]

Such unwillingness to face current racist realities is not healthy for the present or future of the United States. It has been said that a major task for the residents of the former Communist countries of Eastern Europe is to forget the falsified past once taught them and to learn the hard facts about that oppressive past. In this process, old heroes become villains, and old villains become heroes. One can say the same about white (and some other) Americans and U.S. history. Few mainstream media presentations or school textbooks provide full and accurate accounts of the history or current status of racial oppression in the United States.

The great scholar of the African diaspora, C. L. R. James, argued that the oppressive situation of African Americans is the number-one problem of racism in the contemporary world. If the problem of white racism cannot be solved in the U.S., it cannot be solved anywhere.[6] In this book I focus primarily on this critical case of white-on-black oppression in the United States. One reason is practical: given limited space, this focus means I can dig deeper into the development, structure, processes, and likely future of one major case of white-imposed racism. My decision is also theoretically motivated. I will show that white-on-black oppression is in important respects the archetype of racial oppression in North America. For example, African Americans were the only racial group specifically singled out several times in the U.S. Constitution for subordination within the new U.S. nation. James Madison, the leading theorist of the Constitution, openly noted that, from a white point of view, "the case of the black race within our bosom ... is the problem most baffling to the policy of our country."[7]

A few decades later, white-on-black oppression would be central to the bloodiest war in U.S. history, the Civil War. Within this white-dominated society, African Americans have been subordinated and exploited by whites in much larger numbers than any other racial group. Over nearly four centuries, tens of millions of African Americans have had their labor and wealth regularly taken from them. In contrast to other groups, their original languages, cultures, and family ties were substantially obliterated by their being torn from Africa, and the oppression faced under slavery and segregation was extremely dehumanized, racialized, and systematic.

No other racially oppressed group, and there have been numerous others, has been so central to the internal economic, political, and cultural structure and evolution of the North American society—or to the often obsessively racist frame developed by white Americans over many generations. Thus, it is time to put white-on-black oppression fully at the center of a comprehensive study of the development, meaning, and reality of this country.

In this book I assist in the development of an antiracist theory and analysis of the white-on-black oppression that is almost four centuries old. Theory is a set of ideas designed to make sense of the empirical and existential reality around us. Concepts delineating and probing racism need to be clear and honed by everyday experience. Here I accent concepts, in language understandable to the non-specialist, that can be used for an in-depth analysis of this still-racist society. These concepts are designed to help readers probe beneath the many defenses and myths about "race" to our deep and painful racist realities. They are useful in countering inaccurate assessments of the society's racialized history and institutions. A critical theory of racism can help us better understand the numerous racialized dimensions of our everyday lives.

We need an antiracist theory not only to explain the operation of the racist system but also to envision possibilities for change. Antiracist theory attempts to facilitate agency, the movement of human actors to bring change in spite of oppression. Antioppression analysts have long viewed the relationship between structures of oppression and human agency as dialectical. Structures of domination shape everyday existence, but an insightful understanding of these structures and their recurring contradictions can assist people in forcefully resisting racial oppression. It is hard to be optimistic in times of continuing oppression, but some contradictions—especially everyday resistance by those oppressed—can provide a source of optimism because they suggest significant possibilities for human societal change.

Systemic racism is about everyday experience. People are born, live, and die within the racist system. Much recent social science research helps to unmask the workings of the deep structures of this persisting system. My conceptual perspective is informed not only by the research of others but also by numerous field-research projects that I and my colleagues have undertaken in recent years. These projects have entailed more than 500 in-depth interviews with African Americans and other Americans of color in various walks of life about daily encounters with racial hostility and discrimination. Staying in contact with the lived experience of seasoned veterans of racism enables an analyst to move beyond the mental construction of race to the concrete reality, daily trials, and accumulating burdens of everyday racism. Black Americans and other people of color often experience the societal world differently from white Americans, and this experience can be an important guide for conceptualizing the structures, processes, and future of U.S. racism. My colleagues and I have also spent much time interviewing more than 300 white Americans on their racial views and issues of public policy. I also draw on these interviews in understanding white perspectives and actions on racial matters.

Currently, we have theoretical traditions that are relatively well developed in regard to the systems of class and gender oppression in the U.S. and other Western countries. There is a well-developed Marxist tradition with its many important conceptual contributions. The Marxist tradition provides a powerful theory of social oppression centered on such key concepts as class struggle, worker exploitation, and alienation. Marxism identifies the basic social forces undergirding class oppression, shows how human beings are alienated from each other in class relations, and points toward activist remedies for oppression. Similarly, in feminist analysis there is a diverse and well-developed conceptual framework targeting key aspects of gendered oppression. Major approaches accent the social construction of sexuality, the world gender order, and the strategy of consciousness-raising. Feminist theorists and activists have argued that at the heart of institutional sexism is the material reality of human reproduction and sexuality, the latter including how a woman is treated and viewed sexually by men and how she views herself. Systemic sexism is a concept that is now being developed. In the Marxist and feminist traditions, there are also well-developed theories of group resistance and change.

In the case of racist oppression, however, we do not as yet have as strongly agreed-upon concepts and well-developed theoretical traditions as we have for class and gender oppression. Of course, numerous researchers, writers, and activists have focused their analytical and theoretical tools on the deep structure of North American racism now for more than a century. In this book I draw heavily on these important analysts, past and present—including Frederick Douglass, Anna Julia Cooper, Ida B. Wells-Barnett, W. E. B. Du Bois, Oliver Cox, Kwame Ture, and Bob Blauner, among numerous others. Each of these analysts has probed various aspects of this country's racist history and institutions, and some have defined basic concepts for the analysis of institutionalized racism. Beginning more than a century ago, these scholars and activists began a paradigm shift in conceptualizing and analyzing institutional and systemic racism, as well as antiracism. As yet, however, there is no widely used term for this antioppression paradigm, and I propose that we choose terms like "systemic racism," "antiracist theory," and "antiracist strategies" for this growing antioppression tradition.

Today, the dominant social science paradigm, seen in much mainstream scholarship on "race," still views racism as something in decline or as something tacked on to an otherwise healthy American society. One variant of this perspective portrays the problem as one of white bigots betraying egalitarian ideals and institutions—the theme developed well by then-famous Gunnar Myrdal in the 1940s and by his contemporary followers (see Chapter 9, p. 282). Another variant in the mainstream approach accents "intergroup relations" or "race relations," the array of intergroup relations and conflicts in society, with whites seen as only one group among many others having more or less equal impact or resources on an increasingly level playing-field. As I will show, however, the central problem is that, from the beginning, European American institutions were racially hierarchical, white-racist, and undemocratic. To a very substantial degree, they remain so today.

Nicolaus Copernicus started a revolution in astronomy by putting the sun at the center of the solar system. Begun some time ago by African American activists such as David Walker and scholar-activists such as Frederick Douglass, W. E. B. Du Bois, and Ida B. Wells-Barnett, a revolution in the analysis of U.S. racism is gradually developing, one that views the U.S. social system as imbedding white racism at its very core. The conceptual framework developed in this book places the reality, development, and crises of systemic racism at the heart of U.S. history and society. Here I develop a theoretical approach centered on the concept of systemic racism, viewed as a centuries-old foundation of North American society. A systemic racism approach sees white-on-black oppression as the substantial foundation of this society, one in place since the seventeenth century and persisting to the present day. White-on-black oppression, and other white-on-nonwhite oppression, has been the central racial reality of this country for four centuries.

Systemic racism involves both the deep structures and the surface structures of racial oppression. It includes the complex array of antiblack practices, the unjustly gained political-economic power of whites, the continuing economic and other resource inequalities along racial lines, and the emotion-laden racist framing created by whites to maintain and rationalize their privilege and power. Systemic racism thus encompasses the white-racist attitudes, ideologies, emotions, images, actions, and institutions of this society. This racism is a material, social, and ideological reality and is indeed systemic, which means that the racist reality is manifested in all major institutions. If you break a three-dimensional hologram into separate parts and shine a laser through any one part, you can project the whole three-dimensional image again from within that part. Like a hologram, each major part of U.S. society—the economy, politics, education, religion, the family—reflects the fundamental realities of systemic racism.

Many Americans, especially white Americans, view racism as just an individual matter, as something only outspoken bigots engage in. Yet racism is much more that an individual matter. It is both individual and systemic. Systemic racism is perpetuated by a broad social-reproduction process that generates not only the recurring patterns of racial discrimination within institutions and by individuals but also a deeply alienating racist relationship—on the one hand, the racially oppressed, and on the other, the racial oppressors. These two groups are created by the racist system, and thus have different experiences and group interests. The former resists and seeks to overthrow the system, while the latter seeks to maintain it. Thus, in dialectical fashion oppression creates contradictions that can bring change. Everyday oppression and the great inequality of socioeconomic resources across the color line regularly lead to subtle and overt resistance by Americans of color.

While racism directed at Americans of color is a core characteristic of U.S. society, it is not the only major type of institutionalized oppression. I do not claim here that an antiracist theory can explain everything about societal oppression. Indeed, I reject a reductionist analysis that tries to reduce all oppressions to one type. A pluralistic analysis of oppression is necessary. Indeed, class-structured capitalism, sexism, bureaucratic authoritarianism, and heterosexism are all important parts of the webbed package of oppressions internal to U.S. society. As I proceed, I will note some aspects of other oppressions as they intersect and interact with racial oppression at various points in this book.

As we move well into the twenty-first century, people of color are now more than 80 percent of the world's population and are gradually becoming a demographic majority in the U.S. Today, Americans of color constitute more than half the population of four of the country's largest cities—New York, Los Angeles, Chicago, and Houston. They will soon make up more than half the population in large areas of the country, including the largest states. Americans of color are now a majority in California, Texas, Hawaii, New Mexico, and the District of Columbia. By the 2020s the states of Arizona, Nevada, Florida, Georgia, Mississippi, New York, and New Jersey are also predicted to have populations in which whites are a minority. Sometime in the 2040s, whites will likely become a statistical minority in the U.S. population as a whole.[8] These impressive demographic changes will probably bring great pressures for change in the ordinary racist practices and institutions of this country. Moreover, as the world's peoples of color become more influential in international politics and economics, yet other pressures are likely to be put on U.S. political-economic institutions to treat all people of color with greater fairness and justice.

We also need an international perspective on the systemic racism central to the United States. Adopting an international human rights perspective provides a place from which to critically assess human rights, social justice, and racial equality in a powerful nation-state like the United

States. There is a growing international view of what are fundamental human rights, which include rights extending well beyond the civil rights ideally guaranteed by U.S. laws. Drawing on this international viewpoint, one can argue that people are entitled to equal treatment because they are human beings, not because they are members of a particular nation-state. According to the United Nation's 1948 Universal Declaration of Human Rights, which the U.S. government signed, fundamental human rights are rooted in the inherent dignity of each human being, are inalienable and universal, and are acquired by birth by "all members of the human family." This declaration asserts the principle of non-discrimination and equality and lists three fundamental human rights: life, liberty, and personal security. The right to a life free from racial discrimination and oppression is clearly enunciated in international law and morality. Today, the United States stands judged by international human rights doctrine and law as still quite unjust and inegalitarian in its racial structures and contours.[9]

Overview of Revisions to This Edition

Responding to students, teachers, and other readers, I have added throughout this edition many enhancements, revisions, and updates. In all chapters I have updated important statistics and included significant new data and analysis from more than 200 recent research reports and studies relevant to aspects of systemic racism. Although I continue with a central focus on white-on-black oppression, I have added significant research material on how systemic racism affects Latinos, Asian Americans, and Native Americans.

Throughout the chapters I have clarified and expanded important points about how systemic racism operates. For instance, I have significantly enhanced the discussion of how systemic racism is reproduced over the generations. In Chapters 1, 2, and 7, I have drawn on new research showing (1) how most white families have had far greater access to asset and wealth development over many generations than most African American families and many other families of color, and thus (2) how a majority of white families have been able to pass important assets and wealth from one generation to the next. This research-based discussion is central to explaining how racism is indeed systemic and persists even as its powerful reproductive mechanisms rarely make their way into public discussions.

In Chapters 3 and 4, I have added significant materials on the white racial frame's dimensions and operation in many areas, including new research on the racist realities and impacts of popular culture such as video gaming and Internet websites. Chapter 4 also presents new material on the white-framed attacks on President Barack Obama. The increase in research on the operation and institutionalization of racial oppression has been significant, and I have split the old Chapter 5 into two chapters (5 and 6) on the persisting patterns of discrimination in major U.S. institutions. Among other enhancements, Chapter 5 has updated discussions of discrimination against voters of color, racial profiling in police and other agencies, and the persisting school segregation now supported by the Supreme Court. Chapter 6 has new or updated discussions of housing discrimination, racism in college and professional sports, discrimination against administrators of color in higher education, and the role of pro-white favoritism in numerous employment spheres.

In Chapter 7, I have added new data and discussion on the reality and consequences of income and wealth inequality along racial lines. In Chapter 8, I have updated the discussion of the impacts of systemic racism on nonblack Americans of color, including a new section on the white-racist framing of Native Americans and on their concerns in sports mascots controversies.

In Chapter 9, I have enhanced the discussion of antiracist strategies by black Americans and other Americans of color in face of white backtracking in regard to racial justice. I have added discussions of important new research on numerous diversity and antiracism efforts, including concrete examples of successful educational and other antiracist efforts by individuals and organizations committed to significant change. Expanded too is the discussion of the increasing demographic diversity of the United States and the reality and societal impact of whites no longer being a majority of the population in various states, and eventually in the country as a whole.

Acknowledgments

Lives are much like symphonies, with a grand assortment of people having effects on how we develop. I am indebted to my parents Frank and Hanna Feagin for showing me that respect for others was possible as I grew up in a sea of blatant racism in the Jim Crow South. I am grateful to Connie and Preston Williams and Melvin and Zeta Sikes for teaching me what the black experience in the United States means in many of its complexities, pains, frustrations, and joys. I am also indebted to my graduate school professors, Tom Pettigrew and Gordon Allport, who introduced me to the study of U.S. racism.

In the preparation of this book's various editions, I have relied on Hernán Vera, Sharon Rush, Bernice M. Barnett, José Cobas, Gideon Sjoberg, and Roy Brooks for their friendship and encouragement, for vital discussions, and for reviews of various versions of this book. I am especially indebted to Rachel Feinstein, Louwanda Evans, Jennifer Mueller, Brittany Slatton, Rosalind Chou, and Ruth Thompson-Miller for extensive library work and other research assistance that helped me with this book's two revisions. A special thanks to the reviewers:

Alford A. Young, Jr., University of Michigan
Brenda Forster, Elmhurst College
Darwin Fishman, SUNY, Stonybrook
David Leonard, Washington State University
Derrick R. Brooms, University of Louisville
Gloria Martinez, Texas State University
James Fenelon, California State University, San Bernardino
Laura Khoury, University of Wisconsin, Parkside
Doreen Loury, Arcadia University
Michael Johnson, Washington State University
Matthew Nichter, Rollins College
Ralph Bangs University of Pittsburgh
Richard Smith, McDaniel College
Wendy Leo Moore, Texas A&M University
Joyce Bell, University of Pittsburgh

I would also like to thank the following scholars for their willingness to discuss ideas, sources, and research in versions of this manuscript over many years: Jessie Daniels, Edna Chun, Terence Fitzgerald, Aldon Morris, Charles Gallagher, Nestor Rodriguez, Leslie Houts Picca, Juanita Garcia, Glenn Bracey, Sharon Chang, Maria Chávez, Kamesha Spates, Lisa Spanierman, Herb Perkins, Margery Otto, Pinar Batur, Tommy Curry, Leland Saito, Karyn McKinney, John Foster, Michael Regan, Eileen O'Brien, Adia Harvey Wingfield, Athena Griffith, Chris Chambers, Kristen Lavelle, Rodney Coates, Ken Bolton, Charity Clay, Carla Edwards, Jim Button, William Smith, Greg Squires, Ken Nunn, Mel Sikes, Karen Pyke, Earl Smith, Ray Allen, Christiana Otto, Joseph Rahme, T. R. Young, Tim Wise, Michelle Dunlap, Hsiao-Chuan Hsia, Claire Jean Kim, Sidney Willhelm, Steve Rosenthal, Nancy DiTomaso, John Liu, Kerri Vitalo, Margaret Ronkin, and Laurel Tripp.

I would also like to express my gratitude to the hundreds of black women and men, and many other women and men of color, now in two dozen different field studies and many other consultations, who have explained to me and my colleagues just how systemic racism still operates in their everyday lives. One day, perhaps, this country can live up to the liberty-and-justice ideals held so fervently by these courageous Americans.

1
Systemic Racism
A Comprehensive Perspective

We the people of the United States, in order to form a more perfect union, establish justice, insure domestic tranquility, provide for the common defense, promote the general welfare, and secure the blessings of liberty to ourselves and our posterity, do ordain and establish this Constitution for the United States of America.

Preamble, U.S. Constitution

The American idea is the nation's holiday garb, its festive dress, its Sunday best. It covers up an everyday practice of betraying the claims of equality, justice, and democracy.

John Hope Franklin

The year is 1787, the place Philadelphia. Fifty-five men are meeting in summer's heat to write a constitution for what will be called the "first democratic nation." These pathbreaking founders create a document so radical in breaking from monarchy and feudal institutions that it will be condemned and attacked in numerous European countries. These determined radicals are all men of European origin, and most are well off by the standards of their day. Significantly, at least 40 percent have been or are slaveowners, and a significant proportion of the others profit as merchants, shippers, lawyers, and bankers from the trade in slaves, commerce in slave-produced agricultural products, or supplying provisions to slaveholders and slavetraders.[1] The man who pressed hard for this convention and chairs it, George Washington, is one of the very richest men in the colonies because of the hundreds of black men, women, and children he has long held in bondage. Washington and his colleagues create the first "democratic" nation, yet one for whites only. In the preamble to their bold document, the white founders cite prominently "We the People," but this phrase does not encompass the one-fifth of the population that is enslaved or the large indigenous population.

Laying a Racist Foundation: the United States

Many historical analysts have portrayed slavery as only a minor matter at the 1787 Constitutional Convention. Yet slavery was central, as a leading participant, James Madison, made clear in notes on convention debates. Madison accented how the convention was scissored across a slave/not-slave divide among the states.[2] Southern and northern regions were gradually diverging in their politico-economic frameworks. Slavery had once been of some importance in most areas, but by the late 1700s and early 1800s the northern states were moving away from chattel slavery as a part of their local economies, and some were seeing a growing antislavery sentiment. Even so, a great many northern white merchants, shippers, and consumers still depended on products produced by enslaved workers on southern and border-state plantations, and many merchants sold manufactured goods to the plantations. Northern shipbuilders and bankers were also central to the U.S. slavery economy.

Debates Influenced by Slavery

While all delegates to the Constitutional Convention agreed that the new government should protect private property, and thus existing economic inequality, this white male elite had a right wing, a center, and a left wing. The small left wing, with its strong views on class equality and popular revolution, was closest to the general population, and some of its members had dominated the writing of the more radical Declaration of Independence. At the Constitutional Convention, however, the center and the right wing had more influence. The right wing even included numerous delegates who desired some form of monarchy. The left wing and center successfully countered this desire, for that seemed unacceptable to the majority of the population. In numerous provisions the final document was oriented to political liberty: there was agreement on rejecting religious tests for office and an established religion, on protecting freedom of debate in Congress, and on protecting citizens from much arbitrary government. Even so, many conservative and center delegates at the convention were anti-democratic in their thinking, fearing "the masses." Thus, the left wing of this white elite was unable to add a specific list of individual rights to the Constitution, and some states did not ratify the new document until their populations were persuaded that a democratic Bill of Rights would be added.[3]

The trade in, and enslavement of, people of African descent was an important and divisive issue for the convention. Almost all of these prominent, generally well-educated men accepted the view that people of African descent could be the chattel property of others—and were not human beings with citizens' rights. At the heart of the Constitution was protection of the wealth of the affluent bourgeoisie in the new nation. There was near unanimity on the idea, as delegate Gouverneur Morris (New York) put it, that property is the "main object of Society." For these founders, freedom meant the protection of unequal accumulation of property, particularly property that could produce a profit in the emerging capitalist system. This was not just a political gathering with the purpose of creating a new bourgeois-democratic government; it was also a meeting to protect the racial and economic interests of men with substantial wealth in the colonies. As historian Herbert Aptheker has put it, the Constitution was a "bourgeois-democratic document for the governing of a slaveholder-capitalist republic."[4]

The harsh reality of slavery conditions and the often death-dealing slave trade hung over the convention like a demonic specter. Slavery intruded on important debates, including debates over representation in the new Congress. Northern and southern delegates vigorously argued the matter and reached the famous three-fifths compromise on counting those enslaved for the purpose of white representation. Article 1 speaks only of three groups in the new nation: "free persons," "Indians not taxed," and "all other persons." The "other" persons were those enslaved, mostly of African descent. Whether free or enslaved, African Americans were not to be citizens or voters, yet 60 percent of their number could be counted to enlarge *white* representation in the states. Interestingly, the earlier Articles of Confederation had used the term "white" in setting the formula for enumerating the country's population. The new Constitution made use of the Confederation's language in this regard but without the word "white."[5]

One delegate from Pennsylvania, James Wilson, questioned the three-fifths compromise; he did not see

> on what principle the admission of blacks in the proportion of three-fifths could be explained. Are they admitted as Citizens? Then why are they not admitted on an equality with White Citizens? Are they admitted as property? Then why is not other property admitted into the computation?[6]

The answer, however, was clear. Enslaved blacks were to be counted as human beings only when it suited whites to do so. Otherwise, they were just white property. Some framers of the Constitution realized that they were divesting black people of their humanity. After the convention, the *Federalist Papers* supported the compromise thus:

> Let the case of the slaves be considered as it is in truth, a peculiar one. Let the compromising expedient of the Constitution be mutually adopted, which regards them as inhabitants, but as debased by servitude below the equal level of free inhabitants; which regards the slave as *divested of two fifths of the man.*[7]

The new country formed by European Americans in the late eighteenth century was openly viewed as a white republic. These founders sought to build a racially based republic in the face of monarchial opposition and against those on the North American continent that they defined as inferior. James Madison, who himself enslaved many black Americans, put it this way: "Next to the case of the black race within our bosom, that of the red on our borders is the problem most baffling to the policy of our country."[8]

The concerns of slaveholders would appear again and again in debates over taxation, the presidency, commerce, and other matters. For example, there were two days of debates over the importation of enslaved Africans into the colonies. A compromise was reached and placed in Article 1, Section 9. This section allowed the brutal trade to continue until at least 1807.[9] At the convention a few delegates did speak critically of chattel slavery or the slave trade. George Mason, himself a prominent slaveholder, blamed the slave trade on the greed of British merchants. He noted the threat of slave uprisings and argued that slavery made poor whites lazy. As Mason put it, "every master of slaves is born a petty tyrant." Strikingly, however, Mason did not mention slavery's impact on those actually held in chains.[10] He and delegate Elbridge Gerry (Massachusetts) would later refuse to sign the document, in part because of its slavery provisions. Yet their objections were not moral but political. Mason feared that the continuing slave trade would make the new United States "more vulnerable" and less capable of defense.[11] Not one of the 55 delegates advocated that the abolition of slavery and freedom for all Americans should be an integral part of the new Constitution. On key votes most northern delegations voted with southern delegations, in part because the trade in enslaved workers and slave-produced products was generally of economic benefit to northern traders and merchants.

The "Most Prominent Feature"

In one of the vigorous debates touching on slavery, the wealthy Gouverneur Morris noted cogently that "domestic slavery is the most prominent feature in the aristocratic countenance of the proposed Constitution."[12] By the end of the summer of 1787 there were at least seven sections where the framers had the system of slavery clearly in mind:

1. Article 1, Section 2, which counts slaves as three-fifths of a person;
2. Article 1, Sections 2 and 9, which apportion taxes on the states using the three-fifths formula;
3. Article 1, Section 8, which gives Congress authority to suppress slave and other insurrections;

4. Article 1, Section 9, which prevents the slave trade from being abolished before 1808;

5. Article 1, Sections 9 and 10, which exempt goods made by slaves from export duties;

6. Article 4, Section 2, which requires the return of fugitive slaves; and

7. Article 4, Section 4, which stipulates that the federal government must help state governments put down domestic violence, including slave uprisings.[13]

The founders were generally aware of the oppressiveness of the slavery from which they profited. In spite of their freedom to speak, read, and do business in the colonies, they and other whites often described their own sociopolitical condition as one of actual or potential "slavery." Ironically, many publications of the revolutionary period compared whites' colonial conditions under the British king to black enslavement. As early as 1774, George Washington noted the crisis over colonists' rights in this way: "The crisis is arrived when we must assert our rights, or submit to every imposition, that can be heaped upon us, till custom and use shall make us tame and abject slaves, as the blacks we rule over with such arbitrary sway."[14] One convention delegate, John Dickinson, expressed the common view: "*Those* who are *taxed* without their own consent, expressed by themselves or their representatives, are *slaves. We are taxed* without our own consent, expressed by ourselves or our representatives. We are therefore— SLAVES."[15] Dickinson was at one time the largest slaveholder in Philadelphia. Dickinson, Washington, and other white leaders described slavery as creating people who would be cowardly and inferior.

Generally, the white male founders viewed Americans from Africa as slaves by natural law. Natural law was also used to explain why these founders and their compatriots could subordinate two other large groups—white women and Native Americans. White women were not directly mentioned in the Constitution, and their legal rights under local and national laws were limited. In Article 1 of the Constitution, the section dealing with Congress regulating interstate and foreign commerce briefly adds relations with "Indian tribes," indicating that indigenous peoples were not generally seen by the founders as part of their new nation. Until the mid- to late nineteenth century, indigenous societies were mostly viewed as separate nations, with some whites advocating treaty-making, land purchases, and the "civilizing" of indigenous Americans while others pressed for land theft, extermination, or removal of all indigenous Americans to distant western areas.[16]

A House Founded on Racism

Antiblack racism is centrally about the lived experiences and interactions of black and white Americans. Historical events reflect and imbed the tangible realities of everyday life—the means of concrete oppression and the means of symbolizing and thinking about that oppression. Politicians, columnists, teachers, lawyers, executives, and ordinary Americans routinely cite the U.S. Constitution, and the founders' actions, as the glory of U.S. society. The white founders' decisions and understandings still shape our lives in a great many ways.

An "Agreement with Hell"?

The U.S. Constitutional Convention, the first such in the democratic history of the modern world, laid a strong base for the new societal "house" called the United States. Yet, from the beginning, this house's foundation was fundamentally flawed and frequently undemocratic. While most Americans have thought of this document and the sociopolitical structure it created as keeping the new nation together, in fact this structure was created to maintain racial separation and oppression at the time and for the foreseeable future. The elite framers reinforced and legitimated a system of racial oppression that they thought would ensure that whites, especially men of means, would rule for centuries.

The social and political system they created was riddled with contradictions that have surfaced repeatedly over the course of U.S. history. The contradictions were obvious to many Americans. By the 1840s, for example, many black and white abolitionists were protesting slavery and the constitutional document undergirding it. Before this period there had been white antislavery advocates—black Americans, of course, had advocated abolition from the beginning—but large-scale action against the slavery system did not take place until the nineteenth century. At one 1843 meeting of the Massachusetts Antislavery Society, a resolution was adopted: "Resolved, that the Compact which exists between the North and the South is a 'covenant with death, and an agreement with hell'—involving both parties in atrocious criminality—and should be immediately annulled." At a gathering in Massachusetts on July 4, 1854, the eminent abolitionist William Lloyd Garrison burned a copy of the U.S. Constitution, uttering the words: "So perish all compromises with tyranny."[17]

The "Normality" of Slavery

Then, as now, this was not the prevailing view. Indeed, in the first two centuries of the new country most European Americans, in spite of a professed ethic of liberty, implemented or accepted the brutal subordination of black Americans and the driving away or killing of Native Americans. Religious leaders like Cotton Mather, the famous Puritan, and William Penn, a Quaker and founder of Pennsylvania, enslaved black Americans. The founder of U.S. psychiatry, Dr. Benjamin Rush, enslaved a black American. Men of politics like Thomas Jefferson, George Washington, Alexander Hamilton, Patrick Henry, Benjamin Franklin, John Hancock, and Sam Houston enslaved black Americans. Ten U.S. presidents (Washington, Jefferson, James Madison, James Monroe, Andrew Jackson, John Tyler, James Polk, Zachary Taylor, Andrew Johnson, and Ulysses S. Grant) at some point held African Americans in bondage.[18]

Many at the head of the new United States supported, or were not uncomfortable with, the idea of a *permanent* slave society. Even the first Republican president, Abraham Lincoln, often called the "Great Emancipator," was willing to support a constitutional amendment making slavery permanent in the existing southern states if that would prevent a civil war. Such a projected pro-slavery amendment was supported by many Republicans and was actually approved by the U.S. Congress in early 1861. Indeed, from the 1780s to the Civil War period, some slaveholders articulated grand visions of expanding the U.S. slavery system across the continent and the globe.[19]

The combination of white freedom and black enslavement seems radically contradictory. Historian William Wiecek notes that "the paradox dissolves when we recall that North American slavery was racial. White freedom was entirely compatible with black enslavement."[20] Indeed, the work of those enslaved brought the wealth and leisure that many whites, especially in the ruling elite, could use to pursue their own liberty. Various U.S. analysts have argued that it is unfair to judge early white enslavers by contemporary standards. However, not only were there many outspoken black opponents of slavery in this early era, there were numerous opponents of slavery among whites. One of the most wealthy slaveowners, Robert Carter III, freed all 500 of the African Americans he enslaved, for he had come to view slavery as "contrary to the principles of religion and justice."[21] Carter was well known to Thomas Jefferson, James Madison, and George Washington, the most prominent slaveholders among the founders. They ignored the views and examples before them *in their own time.* In addition, the founders sometimes exhibited guilt over slavery. Madison himself argued that it would be wrong to state openly in the Constitution the "idea that there could be property in men."[22] As a result, the words "slave" and "slavery" do not appear, but are replaced with euphemistic terminology in the U.S Constitution's sections dealing with the slavery system.

Into the mid-nineteenth century, most whites—in the elites and among ordinary folk—participated directly in slavery or the economic trade around slavery, or did not object to those who did so. The antihuman savagery of slavery was considered normal in what was assertively seen as a white republic. This point must be understood if one is to probe deeply into the origins, maintenance, and persistence of racist institutions in North America. W. E. B. Du Bois put this forcefully in summing up European **colonialism** in the Americas and elsewhere, saying:

> There was no Nazi atrocity—concentration camps, wholesale maiming and murder, defilement of women and ghastly blasphemy of childhood—which the Christian civilization of Europe had not long been practicing against colored folk in all parts of the world in the name of and for the defense of a Superior Race born to rule the world.[23]

A Continuing Foundation

European colonialism and imperialism eventually reached much of the globe and created a *global racial order*, which has had severe consequences for the world's peoples for centuries. The U.S. Constitution, which embraced slavery and imbedded the global racist order in the United States, remains the nation's legal, political, and—to a substantial degree—moral foundation. Its openly racist provisions, although overridden by later constitutional amendments, have not been deleted. At no point has a new, truly democratic Constitutional Convention been held to replace this document with one created by representatives of all the people, including the great majority of the U.S. population not represented at the 1787 Convention. Moreover, the racist spirit and impact of the original document persist today. Even as they live in, and often maintain, a racist system, most white Americans still do not see slavery, legal segregation, or contemporary racism as part of the country's continuing foundation. At the most, the majority see racist institutions as something in the distant past, something tacked on to a great nation for a short time, and something non-systemic. From this perspective the serious racism that may have once intruded into the U.S. house has been substantially eradicated.

Conceptualizing Systemic Racism

A Rich Conceptual Tradition

In the analysis of racial matters, almost all mainstream social science research principally utilizes individualistic concepts long ago developed almost entirely by white social scientists, many of whom were uninterested in large-scale societal change. These concepts include prejudice, stereotyping, intolerance, bigotry, assimilation, and bigoted discrimination. While these concepts are useful for assessing many racial issues, and I will sometimes use them herein, they are skewed in the direction of an individualistic interpretation of societal racism. In contrast, the black intellectual and activist tradition is a rich source for developing a more accurate and systemic view of this U.S. house of racism. Drawing on analyses of Frederick Douglass, W. E. B. Du Bois, Anna Julia Cooper, Ida B. Wells-Barnett, Oliver Cox, Kwame Ture, among others, I accent here a conceptual framework understanding this white racism as centuries-long, deep-lying, institutionalized, and systemic. Systemic racism includes a diverse assortment of racist practices: the unjustly gained economic and political power of whites; the continuing resource inequalities; the rationalizing white-racist frame; and the major institutions created to preserve white advantage and power.

The brilliant, formerly enslaved, Frederick Douglass was one of the first to develop a conceptual approach accenting the dimensions of institutional racism. In 1881, speaking about the ubiquitous impact of racist prejudice and discrimination, he argued that

> in nearly every department of American life [black Americans] are confronted by this insidious influence. It fills the air. It meets them at the work-shop and factory, when they apply for work. It meets them at the church, at the hotel, at the ballot-box, and worst of all, it meets them in the jury-box … [the black American] has ceased to be a *slave of an individual,* but has in some sense become *the slave of society.*[24]

No longer did only a small group of slaveholders hold African Americans in chains; the total racist society held them in bondage. This broad conception of racism permeated Douglass's later speeches and writings. By the late 1800s and early 1900s, drawing on the black experience and intellectual tradition, W. E. B. Du Bois was working from a conceptual perspective viewing U.S. society as pervaded by racism across major institutions. He was the first social scientist to analyze fully the emergence of the dominant idea of whiteness and of a white-racist order extending beyond the United States. Writing of the years around 1900, Du Bois argued:

> White supremacy was all but world-wide. Africa was dead, India conquered, Japan isolated, and China prostrate…. The using of men for the benefit of masters is no new invention of modern Europe…. But Europe proposed to apply it on a scale and with an elaborateness of detail of which no former world ever dreamed.[25]

In this era numerous black activists and sociological analysts like Du Bois, Anna Julia Cooper, and Ida B. Wells-Barnett had a clear view of the character of white-racist oppression. As the activist-researcher Wells-Barnett put it, black Americans have faced the "unbridled power" of white men for several centuries, power that during Jim Crow segregation showed itself in many "acts of conscience-less outlawry" called lynchings. In a pathbreaking book, Wells-Barnett argued that the anti-lynching crusade of her era, in which she was a leader, will determine

> whether [U.S.] civilization can maintain itself by itself, or whether anarchy shall prevail; Whether this Nation shall write itself down a success at self government, or in deepest humiliation admit its failure complete; whether the precepts and theories of Christianity are professed and practiced by American white people as Golden Rules of thought and action, or adopted as a system of morals to be preached to heathen until they attain to the intelligence which needs the system of Lynch Law.[26]

For at least two centuries, African American activist-scholars have developed an accurate critique of fundamental flaws in Western "civilization."

The first extended social science analysis of U.S. society as a well-institutionalized system of racism was probably that of Oliver C. Cox, who provided in the 1940s a well-researched argument showing how sustained labor exploitation of black Americans created a centuries-old structure of "racial classes." In the case of African Americans, the white elite decided "to proletarianize a whole people—that is to say, the whole people is looked upon as a class—whereas white proletarianization involves only a section of the white people."[27] By the 1960s black activists and scholars were developing the institutional racism perspective further. Drawing on Du Bois and others, the civil rights activist Kwame Ture and the historian Charles Hamilton demonstrated in empirical and theoretical detail the importance of institutionalized racism—patterns of racism built into this society's major institutions, the discriminatory patterns involving much more than actions of scattered bigots. Moreover, by the late 1960s a few white scholars and analysts were also moving in the direction of accenting institutional racism. These race-critical black and white analysts saw racism as more than about demons in white minds, for white racism entails a complex array of racialized relationships developed over many generations and imbedded in all major societal institutions.[28]

Historically, the social science study of racial oppression has often been identified by such terms as "intergroup relations" or "race relations." These somewhat ambiguous phrases are often used by analysts who prefer to view an array of racial groups as more or less responsible for the U.S. "race problem." Such terminology, however, can allow the spotlight to be taken off the elite and ordinary whites who have most centrally created and maintained the system of racism. In the North American case, systemic racism began with European colonists enriching themselves substantially at the expense of indigenous peoples and the Africans they imported for enslavement. This brutally executed enrichment was part of the new society's economic and political foundation.

In the rest of this chapter we will examine briefly some key aspects of systemic racism, including:

1. the patterns of **unjust impoverishment** and **unjust enrichment** and their transmission over time;
2. the resulting vested group interests and the alienating racist relations;
3. the costs and burdens of racism;
4. the important role of white elites;
5. the rationalization of racial oppression in a white-racist framing; and
6. the continuing resistance to racism.

Undeserved Impoverishment and Enrichment

Analyzing Europe's extensive colonization of Africa, Du Bois demonstrated that extreme poverty and degradation in the African colonies was "a main cause of wealth and luxury in Europe. The results of this poverty were disease, ignorance, and crime. Yet these had to be represented as natural characteristics of backward peoples."[29] The unjust and brutal exploitation of African labor and land had long been downplayed in historical accounts of European affluence. Yet this impoverishment was directly linked to European prosperity. A similar connection needs to be made between the immiseration and impoverishment of African Americans and the enrichment and prosperity of European Americans.

A few scholars have suggested extending the idea of *unjust* enrichment, an idea taken from the Anglo-American legal tradition, to discuss the reality of racial oppression.[30] Unjust enrichment is an old legal term associated with relationships between individuals. One legal dictionary defines the concept as "circumstances which give rise to the obligation of restitution, that is, the receiving and retention of property, money, or benefits which in justice and equity belong to another."[31] This legal concept encompasses not only the receiving of benefits that justly belong to another but also the obligation to make restitution for that injustice. This idea can be extended beyond individual relationships envisioned in the traditional legal argument to the *unjust theft of labor or resources* by one group, such as white Americans, from another group, such as black Americans. I have long suggested the parallel idea of *unjust impoverishment* to describe the conditions of those who suffer such racial oppression. For generations the exploitation of African Americans has redistributed much income and wealth earned by them (for example, as slave laborers or segregated workers) to generations of white Americans, leaving the former relatively impoverished as a group and the latter relatively privileged and affluent as a group.

Occasionally, some influential white Americans have been able to see some of the scale of this unjust enrichment. In his Second Inaugural Address in 1865, not long before he was assassinated, Abraham Lincoln made this perceptive commentary on whites' ill-gotten wealth and its consequences. He noted that, at the beginning of the Civil War,

> One-eighth of the whole population were colored slaves ... localized in the southern part of it. These slaves constituted a peculiar and powerful interest. All knew that this interest was somehow the cause of the war.... It may seem strange that any men should dare to ask a just God's assistance in wringing their bread from the sweat of other men's faces, but let us judge not, that we be not judged.[32]

Racial Classes with Vested Group Interests

Understanding how this undeserved impoverishment and enrichment get transmitted and institutionalized over many generations of white and black Americans is an important step in developing an adequate conceptual framework for U.S. racism. Black labor was extensively and unjustly used for building up the wealth and prosperity of whites from the 1600s to at least the 1960s—the slavery and Jim Crow segregation periods.

Today, as in the past, U.S. racial groups occupy different rungs on the society's racial ladder and thus have divergent group interests. Arising in the era of Middle English (1150–1470), the word "interest" (literally "to be between") originally meant a share in something. A *group interest* can now be seen as a relation of being objectively concerned in something, of having a stake in something. Thus, whites are strong *stakeholders* in a centuries-old hierarchical structure of opportunities, wealth, and privileges that stems from a long history of racial exploitation and oppression. The interests of the white racial group have included not only a concrete interest in labor exploitation and other exploitation of black Americans during the slavery and segregation periods, but also a concrete interest later in maintaining the substantial economic and other social privileges often inherited from white ancestors.

The racial hierarchy, initially created by the white ruling class, provided various benefits to most white Americans. From the seventeenth century onward, the farms and plantations run with enslaved laborers brought significant income and wealth to many white Americans, and not just to their owners. These enterprises multiplied economic development for many whites inside and outside the farms' and plantations' immediate geographical areas (see Chapter 2, pp. 37–42). Ordinary whites, for the most part, bought into the racialized identity of whiteness, thereby binding themselves collectively to the white racial group.

Slavery's impact extended well beyond the economy. Each major institutional arena in the country was controlled by whites and was linked to other major arenas. As we have seen, the new Constitution and its "democratic" political system were grounded in racist thinking and practices of white men, many with strong ties to slavery. Those who dominated the economic system crafted the political system. Likewise, the religious, legal, educational, and media systems were interlinked with the slavery economy. Woven through each institutional area was a broad racist framing centered on rationalizing white-on-black domination (and soon the domination of other racial groups) and assertively creating positive views of whites and whiteness.

Alienated Racist Relations

Systemic racism involves recurring and unequal relationships between groups and individuals. At the macro-level, large-scale institutions—with their white-controlled normative structures—routinely perpetuate racial subordination and inequalities. These institutions are created and recreated by routine actions at the everyday micro-level by particular individuals. People do not experience "race" in the abstract but in concrete recurring relationships with one another. Individuals, whether perpetrators of discrimination or recipients of it, are caught in a web of alienating racist relations. These socially imbedded relations distort what could be positive egalitarian relationships into alienated relationships. The racist system categorizes and divides human beings from each other and severely impedes the development of a common consciousness. It fractures human nature by separating those socially defined as the "superior race" against those defined as the "inferior race." Life under a system of racism involves an ongoing struggle between racially defined human communities—one seeking to preserve its unjustly derived status and privileges and the other seeking to resist or overthrow its continuing oppression.[33]

Consider the situation of black workers subordinated by slavery, Jim Crow segregation, or contemporary institutional discrimination. For these black workers, that which should most be their own—control over their lives and work—is that which is substantially taken away from them by systemic racism. There is a parallel here to the alienation described by analysts of class and gender oppression. In Karl Marx's analysis of capitalism, the workers' labor, that which in one sense should most be their own, is that which is most taken away from their control by the capitalist employer. The worker is separated from control over, and thus alienated from, his or her work. In addition, feminist theorists have shown that at the heart of a sexist society is an alienating reality of dehumanized sexuality. Women are generally separated by intentional and institutional sexism from real personal control over how their own sexuality is defined.

To lose significant control over one's own life choices, body definition, future, and even self, is what societal subordination typically imposes. Not surprisingly, thus, racial oppression forces a life-long struggle by black Americans and other Americans of color, as groups and individuals, to attain their inalienable human rights.[34]

In some theorizing about contemporary inequalities, racial matters have been more or less reduced to issues of class, as in some neo-Marxist work, or to issues of socioeconomic status, as in some work of scholars like William Julius Wilson. Many analysts have argued that race and racism are of declining societal importance.[35] These positions have been rigorously contested. For instance, racial formation theorists Michael Omi and Howard Winant have shown with much evidence that "race" cannot be reduced to ethnicity or class, but remains an "autonomous field of social conflict, political organization and cultural/ideological meaning."[36]

However, even among numerous analysts who take contemporary racism seriously, such as Omi and Winant and the British scholar Robert Miles, there is often too much emphasis on the ideological construction of race or the formation of racial meanings and identities.[37] While these are important aspects of systemic racism (see Chapters 3 and 4), they must be directly connected to other very important aspects. The conceptual framework I accent here is grounded in an understanding of the *concrete material advantages* that whites have gained unjustly over several centuries of slavery, segregation, and contemporary racism. Systemic racism is about more than the construction of racial definitions, attitudes, and identities. It is centrally about the creation, development, and maintenance of white privilege, economic wealth, and sociopolitical power over centuries. It is about hierarchical interaction and dominance. The past and present worlds of white-imposed racism include not only racist relations at work but also the racist relations that black Americans and other Americans of color encounter in trying to secure, among other things, adequate housing, consumer goods, and public accommodation for themselves and their families. As the scholar Cornel West has put it, "Categories are constructed. Scars and bruises are felt with human bodies, some of which end up in coffins. Death is not a construct."[38]

Patterns of Undeserved Enrichment and Impoverishment

In the mid-1990s, Senator Bob Dole, a Republican presidential candidate, spoke in an NBC television interview of "displaced" white men who compete with black workers because of **affirmative action**. He said that he was not sure that "people in America" (he meant "whites") should be paying a price for discrimination that occurred "before they were born." He was candid, saying, "We did discriminate. We did suppress people. It was wrong. Slavery was wrong." Yet Dole added that he was not sure any compensation for this unjust and severe damage was now due.[39] Whites' questioning of the relevance of our racist past to our present society is commonplace.

Sources of White Wealth: A Vignette

Consider four young children coming into a North American colony in the early 1700s. An African brother and sister are ripped from their homes and imported in chains into Virginia, the largest slaveholding colony. Their African names being ignored, they are renamed "negro John" and "negro Mary" (no last name) by the white family that purchased them from a slave ship. This white (Smith) family has young twins, William and Priscilla. Their first and last names are those given to them by their parents, and they never wear chains. The enslaved children are seen and named as "black" by the Smith family, while the twins will live as "white."

What do these children and their descendants have to look forward to? Their experiences will be very different as a result of the system of racist oppression. William's and Priscilla's lives may be hard because of the physical environment, but they and their descendants will likely build lives with an array of personal choices and the passing down of significant social resources. As a girl and later as a woman, Priscilla will certainly not have the same privileges as William, but her life is more likely to be economically supported and protected than Mary's. Indeed, John and Mary face a stark, often violent existence, with most of their lives determined by the whims of the slaveholder who has stolen not only their labor but their lives. They will never see their families or home societies again. They can be radically and permanently separated at any time, a fate much less likely for William and Priscilla. From their labor and other enslaved black labor some wealth will be generated for the Smith family and passed to later generations. Unlike the white twins, John and Mary will probably not be allowed to read or write and will be forced to replace their African language with English. Where they work and sleep will be substantially determined by whites. As they grow, major decisions about their personal and family relationships will be made by whites. Mary will face repeated sexual threats, coercion, and violence at the hands of male overseers and slaveholders, perhaps including William. Moreover, if John even looks at Priscilla the wrong way, he is likely to be punished severely.

If John and Mary are later allowed to have spouses and children, they will face a much greater infant mortality rate than whites. And their surviving children may well be taken from them, so that they and later generations may have great difficulty in keeping the full memory of their ancestors, a problem not faced by William and Priscilla. If John or Mary resists oppression, they are likely to be whipped, put in chains, or have an iron bit put in their mouths. If John is rebellious or runs away too much, he may face castration. John and Mary will have to struggle very hard to keep their families together because the slaveholders can destroy them at any moment. Still, together with other black Americans, they build a culture of support and resistance carried from generation to generation in oral traditions. Moreover, for many more generations John's and Mary's descendants will suffer similarly severe conditions as the property of white families. Few if any of their descendants will see freedom until the 1860s.

The end of slavery does not end the large-scale oppression faced by John's and Mary's descendants. For four more generations after 1865 the near-slavery called legal or de facto segregation will confront them, but will not racially restrict the lives of descendants of William and Priscilla. The later black generations will be unable to build up significant resources and wealth; they will have their lives substantially determined by the white enforcers of legal or de facto segregation. Where they can get a job, where they can live, whether and where they can go to school, and how they can travel will still be substantially determined by whites. Many will face brutal beatings or lynchings by whites, especially if they resist oppression. They will likely have inherited no wealth from many generations of enslaved ancestors, and they are unlikely to garner much in the way of resources themselves to pass along to later generations. From the early 1700s to the 1960s, John and Mary and their descendants have been at an extreme economic, political, and social disadvantage compared to William and Priscilla Smith and their descendants. The lives of these African Americans have been significantly shortened, their opportunities severely limited, their inherited resources all but non-existent, and their families pressured by generations of well-organized white oppression.

The desegregation era of the 1960s did renew hopes for major changes in the racist system. But the changes came at a great price. For example, the parents of black children were forced to watch them be spat upon by howling mobs of whites seeking to stop racial desegregation. Since the **civil rights movement** forced an end to legal segregation in the 1960s, John's and Mary's descendants have had more opportunity to control their lives and to garner socioeconomic resources. Yet they too have faced large-scale discrimination in employment, housing, and other societal arenas because the 1960s' civil rights laws have often been unenforced. Descendants of William and Priscilla Smith have not faced such racial discrimination, nor have the many whites whose families came into the country after the end of slavery or legal segregation. Over the many generations since the early 1700s, John's and Mary's descendants have usually been unable to build up the economic, educational, and cultural resources necessary to compete effectively with typical white individuals and the significantly greater socioeconomic resources they mostly enjoy.

From this vignette we can begin to see how racial oppression is economically and systematically constructed over time. Unjust impoverishment for John and Mary and undeserved enrichment for William and Priscilla become bequeathed inheritances for many later generations. Undeserved impoverishment and enrichment are at the heart of colonial land theft from indigenous societies and the brutal slavery system targeting people of African descent. Over time this ill-gotten gain has been used and invested by white colonizers and their descendants to construct a prosperous white-dominated country. Today there is often a denial in the white population that African Americans have contributed substantially to American (or Western) development and civilization. However, the facts are clear: the slavery system provided much stimulus for economic development and generated critical surplus capital for the new nation. As we will see in Chapter 2, without the enslaved labor of millions of black Americans, there might not be a prosperous United States today.

Extorting More Resources: Legal Segregation

Once in place, oppressive institutions have demonstrated great social inertia and persistence. When the Civil War and the Thirteenth Amendment to the U.S. Constitution put an end to African American enslavement, systemic racism soon took the form of officially sanctioned segregation. Like slavery, widespread segregation was implemented under the cover of law. Extensive Jim Crow segregation of free African Americans—in employment, housing, the justice system, and politics had already been socially invented in the north in the 1700s and early 1800s. It was firmly in place there when southern elites adopted it.[40]

The Thirteenth Amendment abolished slavery but did not abolish the new racial barriers faced by those formerly enslaved. After the Civil War, the status of being enslaved by an individual master was replaced by a condition of being a "slave to white society," in the North and the South. Access to significant wealth-building resources was for the most part not open to the technically "free" African Americans. In contrast, whites coming of age in the century between the end of slavery and the 1960s—including recent European immigrants—were mostly able to accumulate significant family resources or individual opportunities, unfairly and very disproportionately, because there was little or no black competition for many important socioeconomic resources and opportunities. As we will see later, these resources and opportunities included, among other things, decent-paying jobs, quality educations, good farm land, oil leases, airline routes, radio and television frequencies, and good housing areas. The new barriers of racial segregation were regularly enforced by individual whites and organized white violence, including police brutality, house burnings, and lynchings.

Contemporary Racism: More Enrichment and Impoverishment

With the end of legal segregation in the 1960s came some changes in the operation of systemic racism. For the first time African Americans had, at least officially, access to many areas of the economy and larger society off-limits to them for centuries. However, the political and legal changes of the contemporary era have by no means eradicated white-imposed racism as the foundation of the U.S. "house." Since the 1960s, oppression has persisted in the form of widespread discrimination against African Americans and numerous other Americans of color—often in violation of civil rights laws. To make matters worse, these laws have often been weakly enforced. Some continuing oppression of black Americans is more covert or subtle than in the past, and this can make racist practices difficult to see for those who are not the targets. Nonetheless, racism is still systemic and webbed across all sectors of this society. Whites still dominate almost every major organization and most major resources, be they economic, political, educational, or legal. Official violence against African Americans can be seen in recurring instances of police brutality and other malpractice.

In Chapters 5–8, I provide much detail on current discrimination targeting African Americans and its advantages for whites. One example will suffice here: Like the legally segregated economy of the 1950s, the contemporary economy channels many black Americans into certain types of jobs and away from other employment. Many do not have access to well-paying jobs—or they face serious unemployment—because of persisting and intentional discrimination in the job market or because of job-screening barriers of employers that reflect the lack of access by black workers to white-dominated job networks or to adequate job training and educational programs. Today, indeed, many low-wage jobs are held by African Americans and other workers of color who regularly service white managers, white employers, or white skilled workers. These service jobs "entail a transfer of energies whereby the servers enhance the status of those served."[41] In addition, black workers who secure well-paying jobs face other discriminatory hurdles such as hostile workplace climates and discrimination in wages, promotions, or benefits. Over time such discrimination, directly or indirectly, has serious consequences that take the form of more undeserved impoverishment for black workers and their families, and more unfair enrichment for white workers and their families. Recent government data indicate that black full-time male workers earn less per week (median weekly earnings) than white full-time male workers, in most of the country's major occupational groups. Black workers (15.8 percent) and Latino workers (11.5 percent) also have significantly higher unemployment rates than white workers (7.9 percent).[42] Today, the mechanisms of discrimination and de facto segregation continue to operate in major societal areas, and the long-term consequences of past and present discrimination can be seen vividly in major economic inequalities dividing this country's white communities from numerous communities of color.

Social Reproduction: Transmitting Wealth over Generations

How does prior wealth and privilege, once gained in an earlier generation, translate into wealth and privilege for later generations? What are the main forms of socioeconomic resources that are transmitted? More generally, how is the *whole societal system* of racial inequality reproduced as a whole? An inter-temporal perspective on racial discrimination and related oppression is essential to a comprehensive understanding of the development and structure of U.S. society. Thus, I accent here the **social reproduction** of oppression.

For systemic racism to persist across many human generations, it must reproduce well and routinely the necessary socioeconomic conditions. These conditions include substantial control by whites of major economic resources and possession of the political, police, and ideological power to dominate subordinated groups. Systemic racism is perpetuated by social processes that reproduce not only racial inequality but also the fundamental racist relation—on the one hand, the racially oppressed, and on the other, the racial oppressors. This alienated relationship, which undergirds the racial hierarchy, is reproduced across most areas of societal life, from one neighborhood to the next and from one generation to the next.

The perpetuation of systemic racism requires an inter-temporal reproducing of a variety of organizational structures and institutional and ideological processes. These structures and processes are critical to sustaining racial inequalities. Reproduced over long periods of time are racially structured institutions, such as the economic institutions that imbed the exploitation of the labor of black Americans and other Americans of color. These institutions also include the legal and government institutions that protect that exploitation and extend racial oppression into other societal arenas. Each new generation of Americans *inherits* the established organizational structures that protect unjust enrichment and unjust impoverishment. Important too is the reproduction from one generation to the next of the interpretive and ideological apparatus, that is, the **white racial frame** (see below, pp. 26–30) that aggressively rationalizes and legitimates racial oppression.

By the 1700s, slavery was well entrenched and profitable for a great many whites, including slaveholders and those servicing or trading with slave farms and plantations. After the initiation of slavery, the next step was its perpetuation and maintenance, not only in terms of meeting the internal requirements but also in terms of countering challenges. Much effort went into reinforcing and expanding this oppressive system. Numerous laws were passed; courts were used to sustain it. Slave insurrections had to be protected against, so white slave patrols were created to police those enslaved. The political system, including its founding documents, was shaped in response to the need to protect this slavery economy. This oppressive political-economic system was succeeded, in the late nineteenth century, by the near-slavery of legal segregation (Jim Crow).

For many generations now, this deeply imbedded system of racial inequality has been regularly reproduced. Today, most whites greatly underestimate the degree to which the United States remains a very racist society. They underestimate the extent of white racial privileges and resources and the degree to which these privileges and resources have been passed down from their predecessors. Social inheritance mechanisms are imbedded in society and disguised to make inter-temporal inheritance appear fair. Each new generation of whites has inherited an array of racial privileges and resources. The full extent of this social inheritance has yet to be recognized. Over time, the majority of whites have inherited at least some economic resources—often in the form of a house equity or family savings—or other social resources such as access to job training or to a good education.

Recent research by sociologist Jennifer Mueller on white families and families of color in a southwestern state has demonstrated in dramatic detail the reality of this highly racialized inheritance process. She found huge racial differences in the acquisition and intergenerational transfer of wealth and social capital over three or more generations, up to and including the present generation:

> White families reported more than six times as many transfers of monetary assets across generations in these families histories—216 transfers of monetary assets reported in the 105 white families histories, compared to a paltry 13 such transfers reported among 39 families of color. Intergenerational inheritances of land, home and businesses were similarly disproportionate.[43]

The social reproduction of assets and wealth across these white generations was greatly facilitated by white-run governmental institutions. As I will demonstrate throughout this book, a great many white families secured their significant family assets as a result of an array of white "affirmative action" programs, including large-scale federal and state homestead acts from the 1860s to the 1930s (see Chapter 2) and an array of federal housing and veterans programs established after World War II (see Chapter 7). For many decades these white-controlled programs were administered so as to exclusively or very disproportionately benefit white families. Significantly, in Mueller's sample the white family histories have five times as many instances of such government-derived assets as do the histories of families of color.

Not surprisingly, thus, the most recent (2010) government Survey of Consumer Finances found huge differentials in family wealth between white families and black and Latino families. White families' median wealth is about eight times that of black and Latino families, and this wealth gap has grown considerably in recent decades. Much of this gap stems from generations of family income inequality and experience with unemployment, but a very important cause lies in the housing equities built up in white families over generations of discrimination limiting access to housing and other socioeconomic resources for families of color. For example, almost all the home mortgages provided on a large scale to soldiers returning after World War II went to white soldiers and their families. This and other mortgage and housing discrimination against black and other families of color was blatant and commonplace until the late 1960s. Much housing discrimination has continued, if often more covertly, since then. The white wealth built up in these housing equities and other forms has often been passed along several generations to the present.[44]

Whiteness itself is also a form of social capital. Even the relatively poor immigrants from southern and eastern Europe who came into the United States in the early 1900s were, within a generation or so, defined as "white." Although they faced initial discrimination, they and their descendants benefited greatly from the far more extensive discrimination then restricting black Americans (and other Americans of color). These new whites often participated in that antiblack discrimination. In a generation or two, they or their descendants were able to move up economically, politically, and socially. This is a striking societal result, given that the average black American then (as now) had ancestors going back *more* generations in this country's history than these relatively new white Americans.[45]

Not only do most whites today benefit from inheritance of some, or a lot of, economic and cultural wealth from their ancestors who profited from slavery or legal segregation, but most also benefit from contemporary racist patterns—job, housing, political, educational, and other discrimination that still gives them and their children significant advantages over black Americans. While white Americans vary by class and gender in the scale and type of **white privileges** and inherited wealth, most in all walks of life have benefited to some degree from white privileges and resources (see Chapter 7, pp. 206–216). Note that the vital resources inherited by a great many whites over time include educational and other cultural wealth. Edward Ball, a slaveholder's descendant, noted, "If we did not inherit money, or land, we received a great fund of cultural capital, including prestige, a chance at an education, self-esteem, a sense of place, mobility, even (in some cases) a flair for giving orders."[46] Ball is one of several white descendants of powerful slaveholding families who have acknowledged the substantial inheritances gained from slaveholding ancestors.

Extraordinary Costs and Burdens of Racism

Unjustly gained wealth and privilege for whites are often linked directly to undeserved immiseration for black Americans. This was true for many past generations, and it remains true for today's generations. What does it cost to be black in the United States? Recent government reports regularly repeat the grim statistics: the average black person has *a life expectancy three to five years (female/male) less* than the average white person. The median black household has *less than 59 percent of the income* of the median white household. The median wealth of black families is only about one eighth of the median wealth of white families. These data spectacularly signal the cumulative cost of many generations of white racial oppression for black Americans.

Acts of oppression are not just immediately harmful, but carry long-term effects. In the social science literature, much has been made of the impact of historical racism on black families, subculture, or values. At least as important is the impact of this systemic racism on the social, economic, political, and educational resources and opportunities available to black individuals and families, now for ten-to-eighteen generations. If the members of a group suffer serious discriminatory bars to securing the resources necessary for achievement and mobility, this restricts their own achievements and shapes the opportunities of their descendants for generations to come.[47]

When men and women of color do not have significant and equivalent access to inherited savings or other economic resources, or to cultural capital such as a good education, or to important job skills because of blatant or subtle discrimination, they usually cannot prosper like more privileged whites. They and their descendants will likely have a serious and persisting disadvantage relative to whites. Researchers have shown that the cumulative lack of wealth for black families often has a serious impact on children. One analysis examined the amount of time the average black, white, or Latino child is likely to spend growing up in a substantially impoverished neighborhood. The average black child spends about half his or her first 18 years in impoverished neighborhoods. This compares to about 40 percent of these years for average Latino children, but only 5 percent of these years for average white children. Being born in an impoverished neighborhood was found to be the most determinative factor for spending much of one's youth there.[48]

The value of having money and other economic resources in hand is very important, for once a group is far ahead in terms of resources it is very difficult for another group without access to those resources, or even with modest new resources, to catch up, even over a substantial period of time. When entry to employment, education, or business is blocked by slavery, legal segregation, or widespread informal discrimination today, African Americans have infinite entry costs. Even if these racial barriers are removed at some later point, and African Americans are finally allowed to enter once exclusively white arenas, they will likely enter with more significant resource and operational problems, including higher personal or business costs, than whites who have not faced massive discrimination in the past or present (see Chapter 7, pp. 219–228). For African Americans and other Americans of color, everyday racism generally involves not only living with fewer socioeconomic resources, but also enduring the consciousness that grows out of and reflects on racially oppressive conditions.

Most theories about U.S. racial matters do not take seriously enough the existential perspective of the oppressed others, their everyday *experiential* intelligence. When black men, women, and children speak of being black in a country largely controlled at the top by whites, they typically do not speak in abstract concepts learned from books, but voice accounts of racialized encounters with whites. Take this account from an interview with a black woman, a dental assistant, who describes a black child's experience:

> [An] incident happened to my girlfriend's daughter about a month or so ago. She's in a Christian school. And the teacher told the kids that black, black children are born with their sin. And the little girl went home and she asked her mother, she said, "Sit down," and told her mother. She said, "I just wish I was white." And she's only nine, she's nine.... And [the] little girl had said what the teacher had said, and she said, "Black people were born of sin, let's pray for the black people." And now the little girl is really scarred, but you don't know how scarred ... and that kind of stuff makes you angry. You take a little child that doesn't know anything about prejudice, and this is the way you plant it ... in all these little white children's heads.[49]

The white teacher in this elementary school appears to be drawing an old fictional explanation of black inferiority, the mythical story of Noah condemning his black son Ham's descendants to be the servants of whites (see Chapter 3, p. 67). We see here the operation of the racialized hierarchy of power—the perhaps unthinking use of a white person's power to cause a black child and the adults who love her much personal damage.

Racism is a *lived* experience. Racist relations recur frequently in the lives of black Americans. Whites generate much pain, frustration, stress, and anger. We see the white-generated alienation of a black child from herself, and perhaps from her community. Racism means that what should be most her own, the control of her own self and identity, is what is often taken away. Theories of racial oppression should take seriously the life experiences and experiential intelligence of Americans of color. They know too well the oppressive world that hits them in the face on a routine basis. This gives them a well-developed knowledge base from which they can develop sophisticated, usually collective, understandings of everyday racism.

White Elites and Ordinary Whites: The Public Wage of Whiteness

In the seventeenth century European and European American elites began the large-scale exploitation of the labor of African Americans and the land of Native Americans. Ever since, white elites have acted forcefully to create or maintain the social, economic, and political organizations and institutions, as well as conceptual framing, that reflect their interests. The actions of white economic elites—originally slaveholders, traders, and merchants, but later industrialists and other entrepreneurs—and political elites are critical for the creation and maintenance of the racist system. White elites crafted and reworked the system at critical junctures in U.S. history, and were central to its rationalization. Significantly, the makeup of those drafting the U.S. Constitution is similar to the demographic makeup of those who still disproportionately dominate the top positions in most sectors of U.S. society today.

For several centuries, most whites not in the elites have accepted the society's racist hierarchy because of their access to the privileges, opportunities, and cultural resources associated with being white and because they have bought heavily into a white-racist framing of society. Thus, white workers have accepted what W. E. B. Du Bois called the "public and **psychological wage**" of whiteness, instead of the greater economic wages and better working conditions they might have had if they had joined in strong unions and other organizations with black workers and other workers of color over the last century.[50] In the United States, unlike in numerous European capitalist countries, class consciousness among white workers has to a substantial degree been lessened by a very strong racial consciousness (see Chapter 7, pp. 209–210).

By the late seventeenth century many in the colonial elites were concerned about the resistance of white laborers and small farmers to elite rule. Critical to the development of the colonial economic system was the problem of labor. At first, the farmers who operated on a large scale made use of significant numbers of property-less European immigrants. These white laborers and servants revolted a number of times against class oppression. Sometimes they were joined by enslaved African Americans, as in Nathaniel Bacon's Rebellion in 1676 against the elite administration of the colonies. The possibility of biracial coalitions was a serious concern among elites. Out of this fear was born, at least in part, the extension to property-less whites of certain privileges of whiteness, as well as an extensive racial framing rationalizing white superiority. The creation of a system in which only Americans of color could be enslaved was coupled with accenting racial solidarity across white social classes.[51]

After the Civil War, the elite-crafted social and ideological arrangements that deflected white workers' class consciousness were threatened by the new freedom for ordinary blacks and small white farmers that emerged with the destruction of slavery and the implementation of more democratic governments in the South during the era called Reconstruction. On occasion, blacks and some whites joined in mutual-aid organizations, such as militant farmers' organizations working for better farming conditions in the late nineteenth century. It was not long, however, before the old elites in the South recovered their positions by aggressively buying off ordinary white farmers and workers with a renewed racist framing of society that made whites of all classes feel racially superior, as well as by use of violence against African Americans and some white activists.[52]

This history is important to understanding how systemic racism was perpetuated over time. To a substantial degree, social-class oppression is obscured by the elites' use of a white-racist framing of society and by white workers' fully accepting that framing and the concrete advantages they viewed as stemming from it. For the most part, white leaders in union movements that expanded from the mid-1800s to the 1960s collaborated in maintaining the system of black workers' exclusion and white workers' racial privileges. Union leaders were often outspoken in their commitment to racially exclusionary barriers. In addition, we should consider some shifts in the last half of the nineteenth century in the views and allegiances of numerous white women who had been active in abolitionist movements and outspoken against slavery. Once slavery was abolished, and the movement for women's rights accelerated in the late nineteenth century, numerous white leaders in this women's movement dismissed the significant concerns of black women (and men) and developed racially segregated political interests and organizations. The majority of these white feminist leaders accepted white racial privileges and the new racist theories of U.S. imperialism at the turn of the twentieth century.[53]

In later chapters we will observe the intensity of white identity and white-racist attitudes in many aspects of U.S. history and society. A common white racial identity has persisted for centuries across class and gender lines. In contrast, there is no similar trans-racial world of workers in which all U.S. workers hold a strong and common class identity and loyalty across the racial line. Nor is there a trans-racial world of gender where all women (or all men) hold a strong common identity and loyalty across the color line. Historically, most white workers and most white women have been uninterested in building unity of identity and protest with, respectively, black workers or black women across the color line of systemic racism.

The White Racial Frame: Legitimating and Rationalizing Oppression

Historically, most whites have not been content to exploit African Americans and other Americans of color and then to just admit candidly that such action is crass exploitation for their own individual and group advantage. Instead, white Americans have developed a strong racial frame that interprets and defends white privileges and advantaged conditions as meritorious and accents white virtues as well as the alleged inferiority and deficiencies of those people of color who are racially oppressed.

In recent decades, cognitive, neurological, and social scientists have developed the idea of a perspectival frame that gets imbedded in individual minds (that is, in the brain's neural networks) and helps people interpret and deal with situations encountered in everyday lives. In their everyday rounds, people use multiple frames, but the one I accent here is the dominant, white-created racial frame that provides an overarching and racialized *worldview* extending across major divisions of class, gender, and age. Since the seventeenth century, this powerful *white racial frame* has provided the vantage point from which whites and others have regularly viewed and interpreted this society. This broad racial framing includes at least these important dimensions:

1. racial **stereotypes** (a verbal–cognitive aspect);
2. racial narratives and interpretations (integrating cognitive aspects);
3. racial images (a visual aspect) and language accents (an auditory aspect);
4. racialized emotions (a "feelings" aspect); and
5. inclinations to discriminatory action.[54]

As we will see in detail in Chapters 3 and 4, this dominant racial frame includes a socially imbedded set of racial stereotypes, images, and emotions that is widely accepted and critical to maintaining white subordination of black Americans and other Americans of color. Over centuries now, this strong framing has had a very positive orientation to whites and whiteness and a negative orientation to the racial "others" who are oppressed. Early on, this overarching framing vigorously accented a very positive view of white superiority, virtue, and moral goodness. Whites have long rationalized this society's dominant racial hierarchy by defining "superior" groups who are "justifiably" dominant and "inferior" groups who "deserve" their lower place in society.

Much historical research we consider in this and later chapters shows well the long history of this dominant, white-created racial frame, one that provides an overarching and generally destructive worldview extending across divisions of class, gender, and age among white Americans. From the seventeenth century to the present, this powerful frame has provided the vantage point from which most white Americans have constantly viewed North American society.

Today, as in the past, this white racial frame is much more than just one more societal frame among many, for it routinely defines a broad perspective on everyday life and provides interpretations that make sense out of society. Let us briefly consider some recent research examining the white racial frame in operation. This contemporary example comes from the diary of a white college student, whom we will call Trevor, at a midwestern college. He provides this account of recurring party joking with other white male students:

> When any two of us are together, no racial comments or jokes are ever made. However, with the full group membership present, anti-Semitic jokes abound, as do racial slurs and vastly derogatory statements.... Various jokes concerning stereotypes ... were also swapped around the gaming table, everything from "How many Hebes fit in a VW beetle?" to "Why did the Jews wander the desert for forty years?" In each case, the punch lines were offensive, even though I'm not Jewish. The answers were "One million (in the ashtray) and four (in the seats)" and "because someone dropped a quarter," respectively. These jokes degraded into a rendition of the song "Yellow," which was re-done to represent the Hiroshima and Nagasaki bombings. It contained lines about the shadows of the people being flash burned into the walls ("and it was all yellow" as the chorus goes in the song).

The racist performances at this party blatantly and negatively frame and target specific groups. Trevor then records some additional racist perform-ances at this college student party:

> A member of the group also decided that he has the perfect idea for a Hallmark card. On the cover it would have a few kittens in a basket with ribbons and lace. On the inside it would simply say "You're a nigger." I found that incredibly offensive. Supposedly, when questioned about it, the idea of the card was to make it as offensive as humanly possible in order to make the maximal juxtaposition between warm

and ice hearted. After a brief conversation about the cards which dealt with just how wrong they were, a small kitten was drawn on a piece of paper and handed to me with a simple, three-word message on the back.... Of course, no group is particularly safe from the group's scathing wit, and the people of Mexico were next to bear the brunt of the jokes. A comment was made about Mexicans driving low-riding cars so they can drive and pick lettuce at the same time. Comments were made about the influx of illegal aliens from Mexico and how fast they produce offspring.[55]

This brief account reveals a broad white racial framing of certain societal groups. The racist performances reveal numerous racial stereotypes and images signaling the inferiority of Americans groups of color. Even Jewish Americans are apparently viewed as not quite authentically white. The racialized images are vivid, as is the song using the "yellow" metaphor. These performances are emotion-laden and are set in a joking format. These students show that they have learned much from friends, relatives, and other sources about white superiority and the racialized others' inferiority.

Clear here is the way that the dominant white frame structures events, which in turn maintain the frame. Different roles are played out. We observe protagonists centrally acting out racialized notions from important subframes within the white frame in a private backstage area where only whites are present. Yet other students act as cheerleading assistants supporting the active protagonists. The student writing up the event may have acted as a passive bystander or mild dissenter showing some awareness of the moral issues here. However, not one of the white men strongly dissents in his recounting.

Note too that there is more to the white racial frame than just its subframes that target people of color. At the center of the dominant white frame is a pro-white subframe accenting white privilege and power, as well as a certain arrogance and certainty of racial judgment. In the past and in the present day, this white frame has accented the right of whites to judge other groups racially and generally with impunity. White arrogance, virtuousness, and sense of righteousness also mean that whites do not need to take seriously the views and perspectives of those racially subordinated– the "unvirtuous" people in society.

For most whites like these students, this dominant racial frame is more than one perspectival frame among many. Indeed, it is a worldview that routinely defines a way of being and acting, a broad perspective on life, and one that provides the language and interpretations that structure, normalize, and make sense out of much in this society. Moreover, almost all Americans (and many people overseas), of various racial and other backgrounds, are indoctrinated to some extent in elements of this white racial frame, usually from their earliest years.

Once it was developed and began to be imbedded in human minds centuries ago, the white racial frame also became a *concrete force* in Western and global history. It precipitates and rationalizes much discriminatory and oppressive action. Today, as in the past, the impoverishment and enrichment stemming from centuries of slavery, legal segregation, and contemporary racism are rationalized by this extensive framing with its racial myths, prejudices, stereotypes, narratives, and images. We have noted previously how the founders' myths about liberty co-existed with the extreme exploitation and subordination of Native Americans and African Americans. White elites have been indispensable for this myth-making process, for they have long created or reformulated the central legitimizing frame by means of the mass media, schools, workplaces, legislatures, and churches.

The Central Idea of Whiteness

In the first extended social science analysis of whiteness, the pioneering book *Darkwater* (1920), the influential sociologist W. E. B. Du Bois noted that

> the discovery of personal whiteness among the world's people is a very modern thing.... The ancient world would have laughed at such a distinction ... we have changed all that, and the world in a sudden, emotional conversion has discovered that it is white and by that token, wonderful![56]

The early articulations of whiteness as a defense of white power and privilege came from slaveholders and others who sought to rationalize slavery. The generally darker skin (early called "black") of Africans was used by white slaveholders and other whites as an early marker of subordinated status. The skin-color imagery was part of a larger conceptual framing among Europeans who had long before viewed most aspects of "blackness" in negative terms, as relating to the devil and darkness. By the late 1600s whiteness, in contrast, stood for "civilization" and advanced "culture" among Europeans and European Americans.[57]

According to Benjamin Franklin, a relatively liberal U.S. founder, the ideal of the virtuous American was grounded in whiteness. "[T]he number of purely white people in the world is proportionably very small," he said. "Why increase the sons of Africa, by planting them in America, where we have so fair an opportunity, by excluding all blacks and tawneys, of increasing the lovely white and red?"[58] Even the political liberals among the founders, including those opposed to importing more enslaved Africans, held strong antiblack (and often anti-Indian) images and saw their preferences for "lovely white" people as quite normal and natural.

Persisting Biological Racism

By the eighteenth century, a virulently racist framing of society had been created, and it came to dominate most white views on "race" for the next two centuries. Images of "lovely whiteness" were soon wedded to a strong biological racism, a deterministic view that saw white Americans as the biologically and intellectually "superior race" and black Americans as the biologically and intellectually "inferior race." Influential scholars and intellectuals like Immanuel Kant in Europe and Thomas Jefferson in the U.S. lent their authority to the "scientific" notion of a hierarchy of "races" (see Chapter 3, pp. 73–74). This reinvigorated biological racism developed by leading Western intellectuals in the late 1700s was spread by newspapers, pamphlets, and pulpits of the day to the general population. Over the course of the eighteenth and nineteenth centuries a strong biological view of a hierarchy of races came to accompany older antiblack views accenting black inferiority in culture, religion, and civilization. As we will see in later chapters, in the early twentieth century the developing motion picture, radio, magazine, and television industries accelerated the spread of this racist framing of African Americans and other Americans of color to all corners of U.S. society and, eventually, to much of the globe.

Today, numerous social scientists and popular analysts view racism as mainly about racial attitudes, as personal prejudices "directed at people because of their race."[59] They focus on the micro-level of the bigoted individual. As I noted previously, this approach is far too individualistic and limited. Although this conventional perspective recognizes some individual and relational aspects of U.S. racism, it usually overlooks or downplays the point that the prejudices and stereotypes held by individuals are rooted firmly in an extensive *system* of racism. As the great African American sociologist Oliver Cox once put it, "race prejudice is not an individual idiosyncrasy; it is a social attribute. Ordinarily the individual is born into it and accepts it unconsciously, like his language, without question." Antiblack prejudices have been socially perpetuated as a way of stigmatizing black Americans "as inferior so that the exploitation of either the group itself or its resources or both may be justified."[60] Today, as in the past, such antiblack attitudes are deeply imbedded in European American culture and are part of the well-developed white-racist framing that has dominated white society now for centuries.

Resisting Systemic Racism

A comprehensive theory of systemic racism should encompass the dialectical idea that oppression creates the seeds of its own destruction. Historical analysis indicates that racist oppression regularly breeds much resistance. Racist structures heavily shape the lives of human beings, but when human agents gain a developed understanding of weaknesses in these structures of oppression, they can and do use that knowledge to rebel, sometimes successfully.

The social process that reproduces systemic racism has major contradictions. One important contradiction is that racially subordinated groups like black Americans have for some time been allowed access to certain limited resources so that they can survive and be useful to the economy. However, when they have secured some resources beyond those necessary for subsistence, they have often increased their individual and collective resistance to racial oppression. Human beings have a unique ability to reflect on their circumstances and create, in association with others, a collective consciousness that can lead to social change efforts. Thus, because black women and men have long been at the center of the racist system, their protest consciousness has great potential for remaking or destroying that onerous system. Periodically, changes in this racist system have been forced by the antiracist consciousness and organizational efforts of African Americans (see Chapter 9, pp. 273–275). We see evidence of this in the many conspiracies to revolt, and periodic insurrections, of enslaved African Americans that took place between the mid-1600s and the 1850s. In addition, in the decades before the Civil War, many thousands of black and white abolitionists organized actively against slavery, thereby helping to bring it down.

Continuing resistance to systemic racism could again be seen a few decades later during the early 1900s in the dramatic rise of the Niagara movement and the National Association for the Advancement of Colored People (NAACP)—organizational efforts by African Americans and their white allies that built a strong tradition of legal action and educational efforts against Jim Crow segregation and other entrenched racial discrimination (see Chapter 9, pp. 274–276). These movements laid the basis for later civil rights movements that brought significant changes in the operation of systemic racism by the 1960s and 1970s. Over their long and arduous history in North America, African Americans have created many resistance efforts and organizations, some of which are still working actively to end systemic racism.

From the beginning, black Americans, as well as other Americans of color, have been theorists of their own experiences with institutional and systemic racism, as they have made clear in a long history of antidiscrimination manifestos and protests. In each period of overt struggle by black Americans against racism, the renewed development of antiracist perspectives is often viewed by white Americans with great alarm. Black protest against oppression has encompassed not only overt confrontation with the dominant group but also the development of a critical and counter-framed perspective on the surrounding racist world, an antiracist framing generated from daily fighting racial domination (see Chapter 9). Nothing is a clearer thread running through the tapestry of

U.S. history than recurring African American struggles against deeply entrenched racial oppression.

Conclusion

From the systemic racism perspective, the United States can be viewed metaphorically as a "house" of racism, one with an economic and political foundation of racial oppression that was firmly built during the first two centuries of colonial development. While many U.S. founders asserted in the Declaration of Independence and elsewhere that "all men are created equal," they did not mean literally what they said. Their equality and liberty framing was conditional and hypocritical, for it excluded black Americans, indigenous peoples, and white women. The real U.S. foundation was crafted to create wealth and privilege for transplanted Europeans and their descendants who stole the lands of indigenous peoples and enslaved African labor. In this process, Europeans and European Americans came to frame themselves and their society as a virtuous "white" republic.

Since this house of racial domination was created, it has periodically been remodeled. We observe remodeling in some reforms of the Reconstruction period after the 1860s Civil War and again during and after the 1950s–1960s civil rights movements. When progressive changes have come in the racist system, white elites—always with debate and divisions among themselves—have typically worked to make the least significant changes necessary under conditions of mass protest. Never have elites been interested in changes that would be substantial enough to build a new non-racist foundation and political-economic structure for the United States. Thus, under pressure from black and white abolitionists, and reacting to the impact of the Civil War, the more liberal wing of the white leadership finally saw to it that slavery was abolished in the 1860s by an amendment to the U.S. Constitution. However, in spite of this constitutional eradication of slavery, no new constitutional convention was called so that a governing document could be democratically written with the participation of all Americans, including those black Americans newly freed from enslavement. Moreover, the white elites created, in the North and South, a new system of near-slavery called legal segregation (Jim Crow). Every major sector of U.S. society—the economy, politics and the law, education, and the media—was still run by and for whites, with the white elites generally making the most important decisions.

When black protest movements in the 1960s forced the white leadership to again consider significant societal changes, this elite made modest changes in the racist system. They passed important civil rights laws and issued major court decisions against formal Jim Crow segregation, but over the next few decades they also made certain that the enforcement of antidiscrimination laws and regulations would mostly be weak.

Legal segregation ended, but little compensation for the massive past oppression of African Americans and other Americans of color was provided, and informal patterns of racial discrimination persisted in most major institutions and on a large scale. Consider, too, that most antidiscrimination programs have only been intended as modest efforts designed to fit some black Americans, other people of color, and white women into the Procrustean bed of historically white institutions. Today, most major U.S. institutions remain, mostly or disproportionately, white-male-controlled in their normative structures and white male in terms of those who hold the top decisionmaking positions.

2
Slavery Unwilling to Die
The Historical Development of Systemic Racism

Historian Charles Joyner graphically describes the Atlantic slave trade as it was regularly experienced by Africans:

> Slaves who were herded into the slave ships, into the dark, landed on unsanded plank floors, chained to their neighbors, their right foot shackled to the left foot of the person to their right. Their left foot shackled to the right foot of the person to their left. About 18 inches or less below, another layer of slaves on another unsanded plank floor. Every time the waves came you could see them and prepare for them, you just slid across these unsanded floors. There was no fresh air, no light. The slaves had no way of knowing where they were going [or] when, if ever, they would get there. And indeed it was a long trip.[1]

This country was born in blood and violence against non-European "others." This grim historical reality must be understood well if we are to comprehend contemporary racism and current interracial relations. As the European colonists gradually established permanent settlements in North America, they intentionally drove off or killed the indigenous inhabitants and routinely took their lands by force or treachery. These colonists and their descendants enriched themselves by what was often a process of **genocide** directed against indigenous peoples. Soon, too, they or their descendants enslaved Africans to work these appropriated lands.

Land Theft and Genocide: Indigenous Americans

Article 2 of the United Nations Convention on the Prevention and Punishment of Genocide defines genocide specifically as "acts committed with intent to destroy, in whole or in part, a national, ethical, racial, or religious group." These acts include "causing serious bodily or mental harm" and "deliberately inflicting on the group conditions of life calculated to bring about its physical destruction in whole or in part."[2] From the late 1400s to the early 1900s, the European colonizers and their descendants periodically, often deliberately, inflicted conditions of life that brought about the physical devastation, in whole or in part, of numerous indigenous societies across the Caribbean and North and South America. The intentional attacks on indigenous peoples—and the devastating effects of European diseases—are estimated to have cost as many as 90 million casualties—the largest case of human destruction in recorded history. The brutal and exploitative practices of whites were not aberrations or occasional; they were common practice in European colonialism.[3]

The English colonists on the Atlantic coast relied on indigenous peoples to survive the first difficult years. Soon, however, these Europeans turned on the indigenous inhabitants. As early as 1637, a war with the indigenous Pequots in New England ended when a white-led force massacred several hundred. The 1675–1676 King Philip's War with the indigenous Wampanoag society and its allies, precipitated by encroachment and other actions of the colonists, resulted in substantial losses on both sides. The Native American leader, Metacom (King Philip), was "captured, drawn, and quartered: his skull remained on view on a pole in Plymouth as late as 1700."[4] Some survivors were sold as slaves by the European colonists who, ironically, saw themselves as a "civilized" people dealing with "savage" peoples. For some time European colonists enslaved some Native Americans in their initial attempts to find exploitable labor.

Later, in the eighteenth century, James Madison commented that the stereotyped "red race" was second only to the "black race" in the racist concerns of whites. What should be done with indigenous societies who stood in the way of European lust for the resources and riches of what came to be called "the Americas"? Few European colonizers made an effort to understand the attempts of indigenous peoples to protect themselves from the invaders. While some white leaders like Benjamin Franklin and Thomas Jefferson occasionally expressed admiration for Indian societies, most whites more than balanced their admiration with great hostility, negative imagery, and savage actions.[5]

Until the mid-nineteenth century, numerous indigenous societies maintained substantial political and cultural autonomy. Europeans were frequently forced by the strength of these societies to negotiate for land and other resources. A process of gradual encroachment became the rule. Europeans would move into Native American lands (often violating agreements or treaties), Native Americans would respond with defensive violence, colonial or U.S. troops would put the rebellion down, and a new treaty securing much or all of the stolen land for whites would be made. There was often some pretense of negotiation and treaty-making. However, by the 1830s—with slaveholding President Andrew Jackson's decision to expel Native American groups from the eastern states by force (the "trail of tears" costing at least 4,000 lives)—Native American societies increasingly faced a policy of overt displacement from white areas to western "reservations" or renewed attacks designed to eliminate whole societies. Even the pretense of legality was gradually disappearing. By 1831 an all-white U.S. Supreme Court had redefined indigenous societies as "domestic dependent nations."[6]

In an infamous 1857 *Dred Scott* decision, this Supreme Court showed that leading whites viewed the situations of Native Americans and African Americans as different. Indians, Chief Justice Roger Taney asserted, had

> formed no part of the colonial communities, and never amalgamated with them in social connections or in government. But although they were uncivilized, they were yet a free and independent people, associated together in nations or tribes, and governed by their own laws ... and if an individual should leave his nation or tribe, and take up his abode among the white population, he would be entitled to all the rights and privileges which would belong to an emigrant from any other foreign people.

Whites, this leading white judge and slaveholder asserted, had long viewed Native American groups as separate nations, although less civilized than whites. In contrast, in this decision about the status of an enslaved black American, Dred Scott, the white judges viewed black Americans not as a nation to be negotiated with, but rather as "beings of an inferior order, and altogether unfit to associate with the white race, either in social or political relations; and so far inferior, that they had no rights which the white man was bound to respect."[7] Whites' racist framing of indigenous societies often allowed them more independence or freedom, albeit as groups only beyond white borders and as individuals only if assimilated. Moreover, over the centuries most Indian societies confronted whites on their own geographical turf, with much strength arising from their own indigenous cultural and geographical resources.

Native Americans lost their ability to make treaties with the U.S. government in 1871. Over the decades, federal policies forced many of the surviving indigenous Americans onto federally supervised reservations. With some oscillation, federal policies allowed whites to take more Native American land and pressured Native Americans to assimilate to white ways. By 1890, with most forced onto reservations, the number of Native Americans had decreased to about 250,000, sharply down from an estimated 15 million people when Europeans first arrived. The bloody actions and consequences of European conquests do often fit the United Nations definition of genocide.

Slavery and Modern Capitalism

In the Spanish colonies in Mexico and South America, indigenous Americans were usually the major source of labor, and were central to the internal development of these colonial societies. This was not true for the English. As Benjamin Ringer notes, "except for the early days when trade with the Indian was important for the survival of the English settler, the Indian played virtually no significant role in the internal functioning of the colonial society, but a crucial role in defining its frontier."[8] Africans, on the other hand, did play a very central role in the functioning of colonial society. By the 1700s people of African descent had become a major source of labor for the white-run colonies.

The North American colonies developed two modes of production. One type was the subsistence economy of small-scale farmers, who were European immigrants or their descendants. Alongside this subsistence farming was a profit-making commercial economy, much of it rooted in the slave trade, slave farms and plantations, and the commercial businesses linked to the slavery economy. Slavery in the Americas became a large-scale commercial and capitalistic, market-centered, racialized operation, which distinguished it from slavery in the ancient world of the Greeks and Romans.[9]

With much farm land available for new European immigrants, colonial entrepreneurs and development companies frequently could not secure enough white laborers, particularly for large-scale agriculture. At first, larger landowners made use of white indentured servants, but these laborers could be difficult to secure or control. Enslavement of African women, men, and children not only stemmed from a desire for profit but also from a concern with developing a scheme of control that maintained bond-labor against the resistance of those enslaved. The color and cultural differences of Africans typically made them easier for whites to identify for purposes of profitable enslavement and sustained control.

The Legal Establishment of Slavery

The first Africans brought into the English colonies were bought by Jamestown colonists from a Dutch-flagged ship in 1619. Laws firmly institutionalizing slavery were not put in place in the English colonies until the mid-seventeenth century. Yet, even during the earliest decade, the 1620s, the Africans were treated differently from English colonists. As early as 1624, one court case made clear that a "negro"—note the early white naming of Africans and lowercase spelling—could testify in court only because he was a convert to Christianity. A "negro" status was already socially and legally inferior to a European colonist's status.[10] Historians have shown that Christianity in this period, as later, was dogmatic and Eurocentric in "**ideology**, organization, and practice."[11] In this 1624 example the Eurocentric viewpoint included the idea that a person must become a Christian to have legal rights. To the present day, many apologists for centuries of enslavement of African Americans have argued that one of the virtues of slavery was bringing this Christianity to those enslaved.

Early on, the human degradation of this slavery was clear. In one 1671 declaration Virginia's General Assembly put "sheep, horses, and cattle" in the same category as "negroes." Colonial laws early attempted to prevent black men and women from running away; there were barbaric laws encompassing the whipping, castration, or killing of those who were rebellious. Slavery meant more than coerced labor. Enslaved black men, women, and children were legally subjugated in or excluded from key areas of all major societal institutions, including economic, legal, and political institutions.[12]

Moreover, in the 1770s and 1780s the white group interest in the slavery system was recognized in the defining documents of the new "democratic" nation. The draft Declaration of Independence, prepared mostly by Thomas Jefferson, originally contained language accusing the British king of pursuing slavery and the slave trade, of waging

> cruel war against human nature itself, violating its most sacred rights of life and liberty in the persons of a distant people who never offended him, captivating them and carrying them into slavery in another hemisphere, or to incur miserable death in the transportation thither.[13]

Such accusations against the British king were hypocritical, since at least half the signatories to the Declaration, including Jefferson, were slaveholders or significantly involved for profit in the slavery economy. Because of pressure from slaveholding interests in the South and slavetrading interests in the North, this critique of slavery was *omitted* from the final Declaration of Independence.

Slavery and Commercial Capitalism

While a number of factors played an important role in the expansion of commercial capitalism in the Americas, slavery was one of the most consequential. Between the 1600s and the 1820s, at least eight million Africans were forcibly brought to the Americas, while in contrast only 850,000 European immigrants came during the same period. For each person put on a slave ship, many others lost their lives while chained and waiting for ships, in slave raids, or from disease. The total number who died is unknown, but has been estimated to be 30 to 50 million. Two-thirds were men, often young men, a reality that caused a sharp decrease in African population growth, and thus in economic development in Africa over subsequent centuries. In many parts of the Americas, enslaved African labor was far more important than European labor in building up the wealth of enslavers and other whites linked to the slavery economy. Involved in this economic growth was an array of European participants on both sides of the Atlantic, including slaveholders, slavetraders and merchants, intellectual apologists, ministers, and government officials. The trade in enslaved Africans was begun by the

Portuguese and Spanish as they early developed overseas empires, but the English (by 1707 the "British") and English American colonists soon joined in the barbaric Atlantic trade in human beings.[14]

A principal objective of English colonization of North America was to secure raw materials and markets for English goods. Once land was taken from indigenous societies, the European colonizers' search for labor soon led to the pre-existing African slave trade, which became critical to exploitation of the land. Larger farms and plantations using enslaved Africans were generally profitable and produced a range of agricultural products for the international market—sugar, tobacco, rice, indigo, and, by the late 1700s, cotton. Plantation owners demanded large numbers of workers, and the number of those enslaved grew rapidly—from about 60,000 in the early 1700s to several million by the 1860s. By the 1770s, about 40 percent of the population in southern areas was African American. In the North there were also significant numbers of enslaved and free African Americans. In the late eighteenth century, African Americans reached their highest proportion of the population (about one-fifth), before or since, in what was by then the United States.[15]

Variations in Plantation Capitalism

In important respects the variant of capitalism developing in southern agricultural areas was different from the capitalism developing in northern urban areas. Jefferson and other southern slaveholders emphasized that an agricultural society was to be preferred to an urban society. The gentleman's life necessitated owning black men, women, and children for status as well as profit. One irony of the slavery system was the accent these "gentlemen" and their "ladies" put on values such as chivalry and personal honor, even as they practiced social barbarism.[16]

In the decade preceding the Civil War, one-quarter of white families in southern and border states legally owned nearly four million black Americans. These families, especially those who enslaved the most African Americans, were influential in controlling the regional economy and politics. Ordinary whites provided the infrastructure of the system—providing transport, growing foodstuffs, policing slaves, running local governments, and providing many of the skilled tradespeople. The slaveholding oligarchy maintained its dominance over the non-slaveholding white majority not only by these critical economic ties but also by propagating a white-supremacist framing of society and by providing certain white privileges to all whites.[17]

What was the position of white women in this system? Whatever their class level, they were usually under the control of husbands and fathers. They had far fewer rights than white men and suffered significantly from patriarchal oppression. Working-class women, the majority of white women, provided most of the household labor that supported male workers and farmers. Women in affluent families also played a direct role in maintaining the racist system. One prominent analysis notes that white

> mistresses, even the kindest, commonly resorted to the whip to maintain order among people who were always supposed to be on call; … among people whose constant presence not merely as servants but as individuals with wills and passions of their own provided constant irritation along with constant, if indifferent, service.[18]

Among social scientists there is debate as to whether the slavery system was capitalistic or just a unique enclave economy imbedded in a larger capitalistic system. However, scholars generally agree on two points: (1) the larger slaveholders were clearly oriented to making profits off their enslaved laborers; and (2) these slaveholders oriented themselves to trading within a capitalistic world-market system. Whatever other values (for example, aristocratic inclinations) they may have held, the larger plantation owners were early capitalists.[19]

Slavery in the North

Northern merchants and manufacturers were often active in the slave trade or had other economic ties to slave plantations. At the time of the American Revolution, the slave trade was, in Lorenzo Greene's detailed analysis, the "very basis of the economic life of New England; about it revolved, and on it depended, most of [the region's] other industries."[20] Thus, Greene lists 160 prominent slaveholding families in the area. Slavery-linked businesses included those dealing in sugar, molasses, and rum, as well as those dealing with shipbuilding and shipping. Numerous northern merchants and industrialists were supporters of southern slaveholders, and most colluded in the slavery system that buttressed their businesses.[21]

Significant numbers of black Americans were enslaved in northern areas. The colony of Massachusetts Bay was the first to legalize slavery, and by the mid-1600s there were strict slavery laws throughout the northern colonies. By the 1720s more than one-fifth of New York City's population was black, and mostly enslaved. New York City's famous Wall Street area was one of the first colonial markets where whites sold enslaved black Americans. This savage business lasted there until 1862.[22]

White northerners often responded to black attempts to break slavery's bonds like white southerners—with barbaric brutality. In 1712 there was a major slave revolt in New York City; in retaliation, whites hung, starved, or roasted to death at least 15 of the estimated 70 African Americans who participated in the revolt. In New York state, where slaves made up 7 percent of the population in 1786, even a partial emancipation statute was not passed until 1799. That statute only freed enslaved children born after July 4, 1799, and only when they reached their mid-twenties. All those enslaved did not become free until the 1850s. In Massachusetts, famous for abolitionists, it was not until the 1780s that certain pressures forced the abolition of slavery. It was not a recognition of black rights but pressure from white workers, who objected to competing with enslaved laborers, that played the major role in forcing slavery's abolition there. Moreover, in northern states where black workers and their families were emancipated, they faced intensive Jim Crow segregation and discrimination in jobs, housing, and public accommodations. The early enslavement of black Americans in the North became part of a deep and early systemic racism that facilitated later patterns of institutional racism there.[23]

Unjust Immiseration: Terrible Costs for Africans and African Americans

The Barbarity of Slavery

Unjust enrichment for whites brought great immiseration for blacks. Considering the number of people killed or maimed, and the scale and time involved, the enslavement of Africans is one of the most savage aspects of European and North American history. The slavery system was hellish and deadly. Once captured, enslaved Africans were often taken to slave corrals in Africa where they were chained, branded, and held for shipping. The horrors of this Atlantic "Middle Passage" included seriously inadequate food and water, beatings, epidemics, and death.[24] On the Atlantic voyage, those enslaved were usually chained in close quarters, and often in death-dealing conditions. Smallwood summarizes the profit-making that came from this horrific trade:

> Slaves became, for the purpose of transatlantic shipment, mere physical units that could be arranged and molded at will—whether folded together spoonlike in rows or flattened side by side in a plane. Because human beings were treated as inanimate objects, the number of bodies stowed aboard a ship was limited only by the physical dimensions and configuration of those bodies.[25]

The conditions of those enslaved at the points of destination in North America were also brutal and oppressive. William Wells Brown, son of a white slaveowner and enslaved black woman, reported on what happened to an assertive black man named Randall. One day a white overseer, Grove Cook, got three friends to help subdue Randall. As Brown explains:

> He refused to go; whereupon he was attacked by the overseer and his companions, when he turned upon them, and laid them, one after

another, prostrated on the ground. [One man] drew out his pistol, and fired at him, and brought him to the ground by a pistol ball. The others rushed upon him with their clubs, and beat him over the head and face, until they succeeded in tying him.... Cook gave him over one hundred lashes with a heavy cowhide, had him washed with salt and water, and left him tied during the day. The next day he was untied, and taken to a blacksmith's shop, and had a ball and chain attached to his leg.[26]

Brown recounts that this brave man was forced to work hard in the fields with the chain on him and that the slaveowner was pleased with the overseer's sadistic cruelty. Brown observed numerous beatings and killings of black men and women by whites during his years of enslavement. The surviving narratives of those enslaved are filled with accounts of white-imposed chains, mutilation, whippings, and starvation.[27]

The Rape of Enslaved Women

Once fully instituted, the arrangements of slavery became much more than a machine for generating wealth. They constituted a well-developed system for the social and sexual control of men and women. During slavery, and later under legal segregation, many African and African American women were sexually coerced and raped by white sailors, slavemasters, overseers, and employers. Sexual violence symbolized white male power. Under the North American system, the children resulting from coerced sexual relations were automatically classified as black, even though they had European ancestry. Indeed, it is estimated today that at least three-quarters of "black" Americans have at least one "white" ancestor.[28] No other U.S. racial group's physical makeup has been so substantially determined by the sexual coercion and depredations of white men. Patricia Williams, a black law professor, has described the case of Austin Miller, the young white lawyer who bought her 11-year-old great-great-grandmother, Sophie. By the time Sophie was 12, Miller had made her pregnant with the child who was Williams's great-grandmother. Sophie's child became a house servant to Miller's white children. Williams's great-great-grandfather was one of a large number of white men who sexually coerced black women or sexually molested black children.[29]

Numerous surviving narratives from enslaved women recount this sexual exploitation. In 1850 a prosperous Missouri farmer, Robert Newsom, bought Celia, then a 14-year-old, and soon attacked her. Over five years, Newsom sexually attacked her many times, fathering children by her. In summer 1855, when Newsom came to Celia's cabin to attack her yet again, she hit him with a stick, and he died. In a travesty of justice, Celia was convicted in a Missouri court of the "crime" and hung in December 1855. Black women typically had no redress for such brutal crimes against them.[30]

Like Miller and Newsom, many white oppressors were respectable men in their communities. Another was Thomas Jefferson. In his forties he coerced the young enslaved teenager Sally Hemings into his bed. That he fathered at least one child with her has been confirmed by DNA testing, and it is likely he fathered her other children as well. Yet in his lifetime Jefferson, a leading racist intellectual, never admitted to this interracial relationship.[31] Indeed, until the DNA evidence showed the likelihood of this exploitative relationship, most white historians and commentators denied that the upright Jefferson could have had children with an enslaved woman. As the first professional biographer of Jefferson, James Parton, put it in 1874, "If Jefferson was wrong, America is wrong. If America is right, Jefferson was right."[32]

One of the most oppressive aspects of U.S. racism lies in this sexual thread, which weaves itself through various manifestations of systemic racism to the present. White men often coerced and raped African American women with impunity during the country's first three centuries. Given that most such men proclaimed themselves virtuous and religious, such sexual attitudes and actions contradicted their expressed morality. Tensions between this image of themselves as virtuous and their sexualized coercive actions toward black women—often coupled with a denial at the conscious level of these feelings—seem to have led to a projection of many white men's sexual desires onto black men, thereby often constructing the latter as "oversexed."[33] Given this early projection of white men's desires onto black men, one can perhaps better understand certain lasting aspects of U.S. racism—the obsession of many white men (and women) with the black man as a rapist (see Chapter 4, pp. 54–55) and the extraordinarily brutal, often sexualized attacks on black men in thousands of lynchings and other violent attacks on black men over the last century and a half of U.S. history.

African Immiseration

Numerous African societies paid a very heavy price for the slave trade. For centuries many of the African continent's young people were ripped from its shores, thereby damaging its future development. Tens of millions were enslaved or died in the slave trade, so some argue that the term "black holocaust" is appropriate for this extraordinarily savage process.[34] Over time, this Atlantic trade in human beings had serious negative effects on institutions in parts of Africa, a destruction that facilitated later European exploitation and colonization of that continent. Recall Du Bois's argument that African colonization is usually downplayed in mainstream histories of European development and affluence. Any serious understanding of the development of European wealth must center on African colonialism, for the labor and mineral resources of Africans were taken to help create European prosperity.

Some scholars and popular writers have accented the role of Africans in this slave trade, often to play down the European role. However, Europeans were not enslaved by Africans, and most Africans enslaved in the Americas were taken from Africa by European slavetraders and sold to Europeans, usually in the Americas. This trade began when European ships arrived seeking commerce with African societies, whose economies were not centered in profit-making from enslavement. As Europeans grew in power, African societies were played off against each other. The European intruders built 600 slave ports for their bloody slave trade, and engaged in at least 300 battles with Africans as part of the enslavement process. In some cases Africans were kidnapped directly by Europeans. In many other cases African social and political leaders, who at first traded African goods for European goods, ran out and, pressed by the Europeans, turned to trading people held in servitude.[35] This theft of millions of able-bodied Africans in the Atlantic slave trade, plus the loss of tens of millions who died in the enslavement process, together with the past and present-day theft of African mineral and other resources, likely account for a significant amount of the poverty and degradation seen across the African continent in recent centuries, indeed to the present day.

A Distinctive Form of Human Slavery

The enslavement of Africans in the Americas was not only more extreme than slavery in most African societies, but also more oppressive than slavery in ancient societies such as the Roman Empire. In the Americas the Europeans applied slavery, as Du Bois reminds us, "on a scale and with an elaborateness of detail of which no former world ever dreamed. The imperial width of the thing—the heaven-defying audacity—makes its modern newness."[36] Unlike Roman slaves, North American slaves were generally forbidden by law to read or write. Those enslaved

> could own nothing; they could make no contracts; they could hold no property; nor traffic in property; they could not hire out; they could not legally marry ... they could not appeal from their master; they could be punished at will.[37]

Even the English language became an important weapon for subordinating enslaved Africans. The latter were from many different societies, but were forced to learn the language of their oppressors. Voluntary immigrants to the United States have generally been allowed to retain more of their home languages and cultures. In the destruction of African languages and their replacement by English we see how extensive the system of racial oppression is. Enforced adaptation to English not only marked the movement of early English colonizers across the lands of conquest, but also marks today—such as in attacks on Spanish or Ebonics—similar attempts to maintain white cultural dominance over those who are racially subordinated.[38]

Ill-gotten Gains: Wealth and Prosperity from Slavery

American slavery was a system created, supported, and financed by a large number of the leading political, business, and intellectual figures in the country's early centuries. Consider just one major enterprise of the early eighteenth century, the famous British South Sea Company. This was an official company set up to transport enslaved Africans overseas. Stockholders included the leading scientist Isaac Newton, major authors like Jonathan Swift and Daniel Defoe, and the founder of the Bank of England, the Earl of Halifax. They included many members of the House of Lords and of the House of Commons.[39] The leading men of Britain were directly and financially involved in the slave trade. Similarly, many leading Americans, including George Washington, Thomas Jefferson, Patrick Henry, George Mason, and James Madison, profited from slavery or the slave trade. These founders saw slavery as an honorable, wealth-generating business activity.

Building the Wealth of Britain and Continental Europe

The British merchants of the eighteenth century recognized the centrality of slavery in building the wealth of their nation. In the 1740s one business pamphleteer wrote about Britain's wealth:

> The most approved Judges of the Commercial Interests of these Kingdoms have ever been of the opinion that our West-India and African Trades are the most nationally beneficial of any we carry on. It is also allowed on all Hands, that the trade to Africa is the Branch which renders our American Colonies and Plantations so advantageous to Great Britain: that Traffic only affording our Planters a constant supply of Negro Servants for the Culture of their Lands in the Produce of Sugars, Tobacco, Rice, Rum, Cotton, Fustick, Pimento, and all other our Plantation Produce: so that the extensive Employment of our Shipping in, to, and from America, the great Brood of Seamen consequent thereupon, and the daily Bread of the most considerable Part of our British Manufactures, are owing primarily to the Labour of Negroes; who, as they were the first happy instruments of raising our Plantations: so their Labour only can support and preserve them, and render them still more

and more profitable to their Mother-Kingdom. The Negroe-Trade therefore, and the natural consequences resulting from it, may be justly esteemed an inexhaustible Fund of Wealth and Naval Power to this Nation.[40]

This summary accurately accents the primary role of the "labour of Negroes" in British shipping and manufacturing, and thus in creating an "inexhaustible fund of wealth" for whites in Britain and its American colonies.

Economic trade generated by British and French plantations in the Americas was the source of much of the capital for the commercial and industrial revolutions of the two countries. British and French industry, shipping, naval and merchant marine development, banking, and insurance were significantly stimulated by or grounded in the labor of enslaved Africans in their respective colonies. From the 1700s to the mid-1800s a large proportion of agricultural exports in world trade was produced by enslaved people of African descent. British port cities became prosperous as centers for the trade in Africans, and British industrial cities became prosperous in part because of the manufacturing of goods with materials from slave plantations. Textile manufacturing was the core industry of the Industrial Revolution, and most cotton was grown by enslaved laborers. Circulating through banking enterprises, the profits from growing international trade— much of it related to the slave trade and trade in slave-produced products—provided a substantial part of the large-scale investments in ever-expanding British industry, growth that led to new technologies and products of the Industrial Revolution.[41]

Slavery and Economic Development in the Americas

It is unlikely that the American colonies and, later, the United States would have seen the dramatic agricultural and industrial development of the eighteenth and nineteenth centuries without the blood and sweat of those enslaved. Much wealth generated between the 1700s and the 1860s came from the slave trade and the labor of enslaved men, women, and children on plantations and in other profit-making enterprises. In the seventeenth century, the famous triangular trade emerged between Europe, Africa, and the North American colonies. Europe and America provided ships and agricultural exports, while Africa provided enslaved laborers. Sugar plantations in the West Indies "became the hub of the British Empire, of immense importance to the grandeur and prosperity of England," and it was African laborers who made the West Indies the "most precious colonies ever recorded in the whole annals of imperialism."[42] A major economic bridge between Europe and overseas colonies was this slave–sugar complex. The Caribbean plantations also spurred mainland development. Much of the oats, corn, flour, fish, lumber, soap, candles, and livestock exported by the continental American colonies went to West Indies plantations. A substantial proportion of the wealth of the New England and Middle Atlantic colonies came from the trade with slave plantations in the southern colonies and the Caribbean.[43]

From the early 1700s to the mid-1800s much of the surplus capital and wealth of North America came directly, or by means of economic multiplier effects, from the slave trade and slave plantations. With the growing demand for textiles, U.S. cotton production expanded between the 1790s and the beginning of the Civil War. Cotton was shipped to British and New England textile mills, greatly spurring the wheels of British, U.S., and international commerce. By the mid-nineteenth century New England cotton mills were industrial leaders in value added, and second in number of employees, in the United States. Without slave labor there would probably not have been a successful textile industry, and without that cotton textile industry—the first major U.S. industry—the United States would have been unlikely to become a major industrial power when it did.[44] In the first half of the nineteenth century northern merchants, bankers, and shipping companies became "closely tied to cotton. New York became both the center of the import trade and the financial center for the cotton trade."[45] Slave-grown cotton became ever-more central to the economy and accounted for about half of all exports, and thus for a large share of the profits generated by exports.

In the North profits from the cotton economy and sale of products to slave plantations stimulated the growth of investment in financial and insurance enterprises, other service industries, and various manufacturing concerns, as well as, by means of taxes, of investment in government infrastructure projects. Cotton-related activities were an important source of economic expansion before the Civil War; most cotton was grown by enslaved Americans. Their agricultural production undergirded national economic development and the U.S. market revolution. One researcher notes there was not a New England "merchant of any prominence who was not then directly or indirectly involved in this trade."[46] As the nineteenth century progressed, descendants of earlier traders in slaves and slave-related products became the economic captains of the textile and other industries in the North.

British and New England manufacturers' demand for cotton fueled the demand for enslaved workers and Native American land. Leading cotton states—Mississippi, Alabama, and South Carolina—were substantially carved out of Native American lands, and as the cotton system expanded westward, the lands of more indigenous societies were taken, usually by force or threat of force. Labor was perhaps the most critical factor in economic production in the eighteenth and nineteenth centuries; enslaved African Americans often filled that demand. In the decade before the Civil War the dollar value of those enslaved was estimated by one planter to be $2 billion—a figure then *exceeding* the total value of all northern factories.[47]

Not only did the southern agricultural system provide cotton for the textile mills of the North, but profits from the cotton trade also helped to generate demand for northern manufactured products and, increasingly, for western foodstuffs. The coerced labor of black men, women, and children built up profits used by many slaveowners for luxurious living, investments in various enterprises, and deposits in banks. Such capital—and capital generated in international trade in slave-produced products—could be used or borrowed by merchants, railroad executives, and other industrialists in the North or South. The economic prosperity and industrial development of Western nations, including the U.S., were grounded to a substantial degree in the slavery system of the Atlantic basin.[48]

The Wealth of Powerful Slaveholders

In the century prior to the Civil War the slaveholding oligarchy of southern and border states controlled a huge share of the resources and riches of this country. By the nineteenth century slaveholders owned much of the country's most productive land and the agricultural produce for export. They owned a large proportion of the livestock, warehouses, plantation buildings, and processing mills, as well as of enslaved workers. The South was the most economically prosperous and politically powerful U.S. region from the mid-1700s to the 1850s.[49]

The theft of Indian land and enslavement of Africans became the foundation of prosperity for many white families. George Washington, chair of the Constitutional Convention and first U.S. president, was one of the wealthiest Americans. Owner of more than 36,000 acres, he held substantial securities in banks and land companies. By 1783 his accounting showed he enslaved 216 black Americans. Reading his records, one sees that he viewed black men, women, and children primarily as economic investments, like farm animals whose purpose was to bring monetary profit. Enslaved workers made possible his luxurious lifestyle. As Hirschfeld has documented:

> Slaves washed his linens, sewed his shirts, polished his boots, saddled his horse, chopped the wood for his fireplaces, powdered his wig, drove his carriage, cooked his meals, served his table, poured his wine, posted his letters, lit the lamps, swept the porch, looked after the guests, planted the flowers in his gardens, trimmed the hedges,

dusted the furniture, cleaned the windows, made the beds, and performed the myriad domestic chores.[50]

Washington said he was opposed to slavery, but the reality contradicted his stated view. His overseers used flogging, and he vigorously pursued enslaved runaways.

The principal author of the Declaration of Independence, Thomas Jefferson, was wealthy because he owned 10,000 acres of land and because, by the 1800s, he held 185 African Americans in bondage. He enslaved hundreds over his lifetime. His extravagant lifestyle was made possible by these workers. While Jefferson was sometimes critical of slavery, he rarely freed those he enslaved. When he held positions of political authority, such as the U.S. presidency, he also did little or nothing to end slavery. The founder still seen as a principal progenitor of U.S. liberty, who penned "all men are created equal," was a major slaveholder. He fathered children with an enslaved woman, children whom he kept enslaved; and he chased down fugitive slaves and had them severely whipped.[51]

Slaveholders and the U.S. Government

Without the capital and wealth generated by enslaved black Americans, it is possible that there would not have been an American Revolution and, thus, a United States in the late eighteenth century. One of history's great ironies is that the Declaration of Independence's "all men are created equal" did not apply to African Americans, yet the American victory in the struggle against Great Britain was possible substantially because the wealth generated by the slavery system and its economic spin-offs was available to help finance the American Revolution. A significant proportion of the money amassed or borrowed to fight that revolution came, directly or indirectly, from capital generated by slave plantations and trade in slaves and slave-produced products. Money borrowed from northern sources often had its ultimate origin in the slavery constellation, as did some money borrowed from overseas. France's involvement in the American Revolution was essential to its outcome, and, as Edmund Morgan has shown, the "single most valuable product with which to purchase assistance was tobacco, produced mainly by slave labor.... To a large degree it may be said that Americans bought their independence with slave labor."[52]

The political structure established after the revolution continued to reflect the elite interest in slavery and controlling African Americans, enslaved or free. The mainstream view of the U.S. government still views it and its actions as set, from the first decades, in the context of "democracy"—as the result of competing group interests jockeying for position through democratic political mechanisms.

A contrasting view sees the early U.S. government as very undemocratic and as central to the creation of systemic racism and the perpetuation of a lasting racial hierarchy. Historically, white male elites have worked through local and federal governments to create institutions serving their interests. In the early development of the government, white women, African Americans, and Native Americans had no direct representation. The white male ruling class created a racialized government, which played a central role in defining who was "black" and "white" and what the benefits of being in each racial group were. For most African Americans—and Native Americans forced onto reservations—this took the form of a type of "police state." The standard dictionary definition of police state is "a political unit characterized by repressive governmental control of political, economic, and social life usually by an arbitrary exercise of power by police."[53]

Slavery dominated U.S. politics in many ways. For 50 of the first 64 years of the new U.S. nation the president was a slaveowner. Chief Justices of the Supreme Court for most of the period up to the Civil War were slaveholders, as were numerous others on that court. In the decades after the U.S. Constitution was put into place, the slavery system continued to shape legal and political decisions in major ways, including the building up of constitutional law in federal court decisions such as the *Dred Scott* decision discussed in Chapter 3. For decades few major decisions made by the federal legislative and judicial branches went against the interests of the slaveholding oligarchy, and foreign and domestic policies generally did not conflict with the interests of major slaveholders. George Washington's administration even loaned money to French slaveholders in Haiti to put down a major slave uprising on that island.[54]

By the 1850s a major schism in the ruling class, between southern planters and growing numbers of northern industrialists with little economic interest in slavery, was becoming clear in political battles over such issues as expansion of slavery into western lands. Fearful of its economic and political future, the South's slaveholding oligarchy eventually moved to secede from the union. The victory of the North in the subsequent Civil War marked the arrival of northern industrialists and merchants as a dominant force in the U.S. economy and government.[55]

The Emergence of Jim Crow: Slavery Unwilling to Die

Group Terrorism by White Americans

After the Civil War, in the late 1860s and early 1870s, the Reconstruction period came to the South as a breath of fresh air. Federally enforced Reconstruction policies were precipitated by southern whites' unwillingness to make major changes in the treatment of freed slaves or to prevent the unrepentant leaders of the old Confederacy from again assuming power. Prior to the 1860s black Americans had not generally been allowed to vote at any level of government. Now the Thirteenth, Fourteenth, and Fifteenth Amendments to the U.S. Constitution abolished slavery, asserted the civil rights of black Americans, and officially guaranteed black men (not women) the right to vote. During Reconstruction new state constitutional conventions included black delegates, although in most states white southerners predominated. For a time southern governments were mostly controlled by ordinary whites who had not been active leaders in the Confederacy, and black Americans gained a measure of personal and political freedom, although considerable Jim Crow segregation already existed. During Reconstruction these biracial state governments brought needed political reforms to the South, including the first public education.[56]

Today there is little recognition, in the media or many history textbooks, of the scale and barbarousness of the white terrorism that brought an end to the often progressive Reconstruction governments and, with that, any hope for political or economic equality for black Americans. Sometimes, this southern terrorism has actually received positive coverage. The early 1900s movie *The Birth of a Nation*, still considered a classic by movie experts, celebrates the very hostile and racist Ku Klux Klan view of Reconstruction. Moreover, the recurring release of certain beloved pro-slavery movies (for example, the 1930s *Gone with the Wind* movie is periodically re-released) signals how unconcerned or ill-informed the white majority still is about the country's sometimes savagely racist history.

What mainstream U.S. movies should cover, but never have, is how the South's white elite, often with the collusion of northern elites, established an extensive terrorist campaign against Reconstruction state governments and newly freed black southerners. A leading Confederate general, Nathan Bedford Forrest, was the first "Grand Dragon" of the new Ku Klux Klan, and the famous General Robert E. Lee pledged his "invisible" support to the violent Klan. White terrorism destroyed the often progressive southern governments, and thousands of men, women, and children were severely beaten, raped, or killed by the Klan and other white-supremacist groups. The Confederacy lost the four-year war, but fought on for "twelve more years—using every weapon at its disposal, including the ultimate one of mass terrorism—until the nation finally acceded to most of the Confederacy's modified war aims."[57]

After a few years of this white terrorism, northern interest in the South waned. Northern leaders were not interested in punishing those who led the rebellion. The so-called Hayes Compromise of 1877 removed the few remaining federal troops and eliminated much federal protection of black southerners. Leaders of the old Confederacy had finally won most of their political and economic goals. This arch-conservative revolution ended most attempts to provide the newly freed black Americans with substantial civil rights protection and economic help. As the white anti-Klan researcher, Stetson Kennedy, has explained, black southerners were "sold back down the river into virtual enslavement, and all three of the new constitutional amendments—so far as blacks were concerned—were rendered dead letters for a century to come."[58] The Thirteenth, Fourteenth, and Fifteenth Amendments officially gave African Americans citizenship rights, but most of these new rights were effectively denied by southern legislatures, federal courts, and presidential or congressional action until the civil rights revolution of the 1950s–1960s. Whites in the North and the South joined in solidarity on behalf of the white group interest in preserving systemic racism.

The Continuing Badges and Disabilities of Slavery

In a dissenting opinion to the important 1883 Civil Rights Cases, then Supreme Court Justice John Marshall Harlan argued:

> That there are burdens and disabilities which constitute badges of slavery and servitude, and that the power to enforce by appropriate legislation the Thirteenth Amendment may be exerted by legislation of a direct and primary character, for the eradication, not simply of the institution, but of its badges and incidents, are propositions which ought to be deemed indisputable.[59]

Harlan was arguing that the federal government had a right to intervene and dismantle the many serious and lingering effects of African American slavery, and not just slavery itself.

Yet the end of slavery did not bring an end to the many devastating badges, burdens, or disabilities of slavery. Comprehensive Jim Crow patterns became a reality soon after Reconstruction, as extensive segregation laws and informal segregation practices kept African Americans from voting, attending good schools, and using public accommodations. By the 1880s and 1890s legal segregation was linked to the elite's successful attempt to disenfranchise black voters and reassert the power of the Democratic Party against inroads made during Reconstruction by the Republican Party. Elite-controlled, authoritarian political regimes dominated southern states, and these regimes worked with white planters and southern industrialists to insure control of black workers in agriculture and new industries. By the 1900s, officially and informally enforced Jim Crow segregation was the rule throughout southern and border states, and even in some parts of northern and western states.[60]

A major Supreme Court decision, *Plessy v. Ferguson* (1896), involved segregation of Louisiana railroad cars, which was challenged by a man whose ancestry was one-eighth African and seven-eighths European.

The court's decision delivered a major blow to the idea of civic equality by upholding the legality of so-called "separate but equal" facilities for white and black Americans. Following the tradition of white-supremacist thinking, this all-white Supreme Court reasoned, with one lone dissenter, that racism was natural and that

> legislation is powerless to eradicate racial instincts or to abolish distinctions based upon physical differences, and the attempt to do so can only result in accentuating the difficulties of the present situation.... If one race be inferior to the other socially, the Constitution of the United States cannot put them upon the same plane.

The racial privileges of whites as a group were maintained. Justice John Marshall Harlan, again the dissenter, argued that

> the arbitrary separation of citizens, on the basis of race, while they are on a public highway, is a badge of servitude wholly inconsistent with the civil freedom and the equality before the law established by the Constitution. It cannot be justified upon any legal grounds.[61]

The long-term effect of this *Plessy* decision and similar federal court cases upholding Jim Crow segregation was to bar African Americans from fair access to major political, economic, and social institutions for decades.

By the early 1900s authoritarian police-state conditions in southern and border states shaped the lives of the more than 80 percent of African Americans who lived there. Most public facilities were segregated, including buses, water fountains, public toilets, parks, theaters, hospitals, colleges, churches, and cemeteries. Black southerners were also forcibly denied electoral influence in most areas.

Maintaining Jim Crow Segregation with Violence

White violence undergirded the growing edifice of legal segregation. A central aspect of these arrangements was the omnipresent lynching, usually of a black man thought to have spoken against, organized against, committed a crime against, or insulted his white oppressors. The accusation was often fictional or greatly exaggerated. Some 3,513 lynchings of black men and 76 of black women were recorded for the years 1882 to 1927, but many more did not get recorded. Between the Civil War and the present, perhaps as many as 6,000 lynchings of black men and women have been perpetrated in the southern states and in certain areas of the northern and border states. Many thousands of other violent white attacks on African Americans have also gone unrecorded.[62]

Lynchings were savage events often with a strongly ritualized character. Over the years from the late 1860s to recent times, thousands of whites have participated in them. One lynching account from the 1940s involved a black man accused of trying to rape a white woman. A participant told the story of a white mob's actions:

> I ain't tellin' nobody just what we done to that nigger but we used a broken bottle just where it'd do the most damage, and any time you want to see a nigger ear all you gotta do is go to see old man Smith and ast him for a peep at one.... Yes, ma'am, we done things I never knowed could be done and things I certainly ain't mentionin' to no lady.

After being cut, the black victim was doused in kerosene and burned, with the ending being that "the groanin' got lower and lower and finely it was just little gasps and then it wasn't nothin' a tall." The white mob next tied him to a tree, leaving him for relatives to take down.[63]

In most lynching episodes there was no legal trial. At the heart of this ritualized barbarism was whites' concern that dominance must be maintained. These whites felt that antiblack violence would make black residents afraid to challenge Jim Crow customs. Many lynchings involved large turnouts by white men, women, and children who cheered the killings. In many cases black victims were tortured, and pieces of bodies were gladly taken as souvenirs. Sexual mutilations of black victims, as well as the emotional (often unfounded) accusations of rape against them, signal again the importance of the strong and irrational sexual thread in the history of white racism.

Segregation's Economic Impact

Legal segregation had a severe impact on economic opportunities. Once slavery was ended, black families were promised productive land by certain federal officials. Those newly freed pressed for "forty acres and a mule" with which to begin a new life. Some federal generals initially gave confiscated Confederate lands to African Americans. Yet most lost this land when the new president, Andrew Johnson, a white-supremacist slaveholder, overruled them. Property had to be protected, even if it belonged to treasonous slaveholders who fought against the United States. The common interest of white southerners and northerners in protecting unjustly gained property and resources was stronger than stated commitments to social justice.[64]

Black southerners were ineligible for public land given away by the first Homestead Act (1862), and by the time the Southern Homestead Act came to be (1866), they were unable to take full advantage of it because of widespread discrimination, intimidation, and violence against them. Those who were able to overcome these odds often found the land they secured to be poor for farming or lost it later to white force or threats of force.[65] Savvy black leaders like W. E. B. Du Bois argued thus: "To have given each one of the million Negro free families a forty-acre freehold would have made a basis of real democracy in the United States that might easily have transformed the modern world."[66]

In contrast, white families benefited greatly from government homestead acts. From the 1860s to the 1930s the federal government provided about 246 million acres of land at low or no cost for about 1.5 million farm homesteads. Almost all recipients were white. The large number of black families in these areas at that time could have worked and benefited from that land, but were excluded by various forms of racial discrimination, including Klan-type violence. Working these homesteads, many white families, including European immigrants, built up substantial wealth in the initial generation and subsequent generations. Drawing on careful demographic projections, one researcher's data suggest that as many as 46 million white Americans are current descendants of the white homestead families and are thus substantial inheritors and beneficiaries of this major wealth-generating government program.[67] Recall too the research of Jennifer Mueller in Chapter 1, which showed that the histories of contemporary white families reveal *five times* more family access to such government-derived assets as those of contemporary families of color.

After slavery came a period of renewed enrichment and capital accumulation by the larger white farmers and merchants in southern and border states. They made their fortunes from the labor of theoretically free black laborers, tenant farmers, and sharecroppers. Booker T. Washington described the conditions that free blacks faced on the large farms and plantations as "a kind of slavery that is in one sense as bad as the slavery of antebellum days."[68] In theory, tenant farmers and sharecroppers could sell their share of the crops, pay off debts, and buy land. Yet most were unable to make enough to escape the cycle of indebtedness to white landowners and merchants. When large-scale industrialization finally came to the South, black workers were virtually excluded, except for the lowest-wage segregated positions.

Long before the Civil War, Jim Crow laws in the North had enforced racial segregation in employment, public transportation, hospitals, jails, schools, churches, and cemeteries. The first Jim Crow railroad cars were established on Massachusetts railroads. In northern cities whites enforced housing segregation. Into the 1930s not only did the 11 southern states have Jim Crow laws, but all the border states did as well—from Delaware and Maryland to Missouri and Oklahoma. Northern states like Kansas and Indiana had towns and cities with racial segregation statutes. Into the late 1940s numerous northern and western states, including Michigan, Colorado, Oregon, and California, had laws banning marriages between white and black Americans. Beyond these laws, white northerners openly enforced racial segregation in housing and employment by various informal means (de facto segregation).[69]

Persisting Patterns of Legal Segregation

Racist Barriers: 1910s to the 1930s

In 1910 more than 80 percent of black Americans, most of them descendants of those recently enslaved, resided in the southern states. Most were in agricultural areas with little access to productive farmland and faced segregation in most aspects of their lives. As a result, they began to migrate North in significant numbers. There, too, they met large-scale racial discrimination and exclusion.

In the North many southern migrants were concentrated in low-wage domestic and service positions; they were routinely excluded by employers and unions from better-paying jobs in industrial settings. Black workers were often displaced by new immigrant workers from southern and eastern Europe.[70] Without this white-racist exclusion and discrimination, the black Harlems and South Chicagos "might have become solid working-class and middle-class communities with the economic and social resources to absorb and aid the incoming masses of Southerners."[71] This time the unjust impoverishment of black workers and enrichment of white workers stemmed from white control over better-paying jobs and jobs with the potential for mobility. Whites who arrived after the slavery period—and their many descendants—thus benefited greatly from legal and informal racial segregation in employment. Once again, whites had more or less exclusive access to the economic, housing, and political resources that enabled them and their children and grandchildren to move up the socioeconomic ladder.

Whites sometimes used violence to enforce traditional patterns of racial discrimination. During one white-generated riot in 1900 in New York, a mostly Irish American police force encouraged whites to attack black men, women, and children. One major riot occurred in 1917 in East St. Louis. White workers, viewing black immigrants from the South as a job threat, violently attacked a black community. Thirty-nine black residents and nine white attackers were killed. This was followed in 1919 by white riots in cities from Chicago to Charleston. In the North and South, millions of white men, and half a million white women, belonged to the Ku Klux Klan or voted for its political candidates. During the years 1910 to 1930 numerous state and national politicians belonged to the white-supremacist Klan, and dozens of members of the Senate and House of Representatives were elected with its help. Prior to becoming president, Warren Harding was closely tied to the Klan. Before he was a leading Supreme Court justice, Justice Hugo Black had been a member. Klan activities included marches and thousands of cross-burnings, assaults, and lynchings in towns and cities across the country—actions often winked at by white police and other government officials.[72]

Racist Barriers: The 1930s to the 1950s

During the 1930s most black men, women, and children still lived in the South's near-slavery of Jim Crow segregation, a subjugation that did not allow the build-up of significant economic or educational resources for most black families. Segregation, with its racist etiquette, was very much in place. Though the Supreme Court in 1915 had begun to invalidate a few restrictions on black voters, most were still not permitted to vote. In agricultural areas most worked as wage laborers, domestic workers, or sharecroppers. In the North black workers likewise remained mostly in low-wage jobs as unskilled workers, domestics, and laborers.[73]

During the Great Depression of the 1930s, unemployed whites frequently pushed black workers out of menial jobs. Whites in Atlanta organized under the slogan of "No Jobs for Niggers Until Every White Man Has a Job." By 1932 half of black workers in cities were unemployed. Extreme hunger or starvation was often their lot.[74] Moreover, as federally funded employment programs began to put some black job seekers back to work and provide some economic support, black voters shifted from a solidly Republican vote in 1932 to a solidly Democratic vote in 1936. Nonetheless, black workers continued to suffer much discrimination from the whites who administered New Deal agencies, especially in the South. In most federal relief programs black workers got lower wages than whites, were employed only as unskilled laborers, and were employed only after whites were. New Deal housing programs increased residential segregation by restricting the new federally guaranteed home loans to homes in segregated areas and by locating public housing so that it would be segregated. President Franklin Roosevelt and most of his advisors were unwilling to press for anti-lynching legislation because they feared losing white votes. Federal government agencies were also openly segregationist in many of their policies.[75]

During the long era of legal segregation from the 1880s to the 1960s African Americans, and numerous other Americans of color, endured many types of overt racial discrimination in employment, housing, medical care, education, and everyday etiquette. David Brown and Clive Webb have noted how the "provision of medical care for African Americans was far inferior to that for whites." In addition, fearing that education might encourage black resistance and operating out of the white-racist frame that viewed black Americans as unintelligent and undeserving, white-run governments provided meager support for black public schools:

In 1910, South Carolina, for instance, spent an average of $5.95 per black pupil, compared with $40.68 for the average white pupil.... Schools were forced to close during the harvest season so that every hand was available to work in the fields.[76]

Public schools thus reinforced a highly coercive and racialized southern employment system.

In addition, extreme *deference rituals* were forced on black men, women, and children. They were required to show deference to whites by stepping off sidewalks, bowing heads, or pretending ignorance. In everyday interactions most whites did not address black Americans with the normal "Mr.," "Mrs.," or "Miss" and insisted on using their first names. Most used such denigrating language as "nigger," "boy," "girl," and "uncle" for black Americans they knew.[77] These racist actions were implemented to ensure that whites in all classes benefited from a strong sense of racial superiority—what sociologist W. E. B. Du Bois called the "public and psychological wage of whiteness."[78]

Workers Become an Economic Surplus

During World War I white immigration from Europe to the United States subsided, but workers were still badly needed to produce war goods. Some opportunities for employment in formerly all-white, male job sectors were opened up for black workers. During World War II the worker shortage again allowed black workers into some skilled blue-collar jobs for the first time. Similarly, the 1950s Korean War permitted some expanded black employment in better-paying jobs. However, after the end of each war the employment situation for black men and women changed for the worse. White veterans and other white workers poured into many cities after World War II, usually taking the better-paying jobs. The jobs that remained for black workers were mostly menial and low-paying.[79]

During the 1960s Vietnam War there was significant black mobility into better-paying jobs, with assistance this time not only from that war and associated economic growth but also from the renewed civil rights movement. In spite of this, however, black workers were farther behind whites in income, occupation, and unemployment in the 1960s than they had been in 1945. Thus, in 1962 black workers in the prime working-age group had an unemployment rate three times that of whites. While formal segregation laws were dismantled by the civil rights acts of the 1960s, large-scale informal discrimination persisted.[80]

Since the 1960s large-scale automation and corporate investments overseas have often created a harsh reality of substantial unemployment, underemployment, or lower real wages for many workers. By the late

1960s substantial automation had created a situation where many of the country's black blue-collar workers were no longer needed as much by white employers in numerous sectors of the economy. Significantly, it was not until this black labor surplus became a conspicuous economic reality in the 1960s that many white employers and other whites were finally willing to consider the abolition of coercive legal segregation. Many employers no longer sought out the large numbers of black workers upon whom they had formerly depended so heavily for necessary labor. A country that had long built much of its prosperity off the backs of black workers was gradually abandoning many of them to a life of recurring unemployment or underemployment.[81]

Conclusion

A central feature of the systemic racism perspective is an accent on these "deep context" understandings. Few whites today are truly knowledgeable about the racialized past of this society, and indeed of their own families, and how that historical context profoundly shapes the racialized present. This lack of an accurate contextual memory and understanding is central to the dominant white framing of society. Indeed, collective forgetting seems essential to the dominant-group morality of systems of oppression. In contrast, those Americans who are oppressed often remember more of that deep context and history accurately, even though they do not control mainstream history-making resources. They frequently rely on oral histories and scrapbooks or on their own group's historical recorders whose work is published outside the mainstream. There are some things most human beings are constantly aware of—for example, the obvious immensity of space or the impact of regular weather patterns—because those contextual realities are immediately observable in contemporary environments. However, the deep historical context of systemic racism is not so immediately evident to most white Americans, and usually because the powerful tellers of our history in the dominant group have intentionally suppressed, distorted, or fictionalized that racialized history. As I show in later chapters, most whites today resist even trying to better understand the harsh racist realities and meanings of our historical past and present.

Clearly, the United States was originally built as a *white* republic. It was a principal part of the world racist order created by European colonialism and imperialism to enrich Europeans and impoverish indigenous peoples. The white-racist institutions established during the slavery period and undergirded by the U.S. Constitution have generated, enhanced, and/or reproduced the privileges and prosperity of most white Americans for many generations.

Today, there are many indirect and direct connections between the generation of white resources and wealth in the eras of slavery and legal segregation and the resources and prosperity of contemporary white individuals and families. The current racial situation is very much the legacy of black enslavement, and the "badges and disabilities" of slavery still lie heavily on black Americans. This reality is recognized, albeit only occasionally, at the highest levels of the justice system. In a pioneering 1968 Supreme Court case, *Jones et ux. v. Alfred H. Mayer Co.*, the U.S. Supreme Court considered blatant housing discrimination in St. Louis. In that perceptive decision the liberal majority of the court ruled that

> just as the Black Codes, enacted after the Civil War to restrict the free exercise of those rights, were substitutes for the slave system, so the exclusion of Negroes from white communities became a substitute for the Black Codes. And when racial discrimination herds men into ghettos and makes their ability to buy property turn on the color of their skin, then it too is a relic of slavery.[82]

For a brief period in the Supreme Court's long history, in the 1960s and early 1970s, a majority of the white justices recognized that persisting racial discrimination and informal racial segregation were relics of the old slavery system and, thus, of the country's centuries-old systemic racism.

In a dramatic concurring opinion in this major Supreme Court case, the progressive white Justice William O. Douglas enumerated the ways in which persisting racial discrimination is connected in a direct line back to slavery:

> Some badges of slavery remain today. While the institution has been outlawed, it has remained in the minds and hearts of many white men. Cases which have come to this Court depict a spectacle of slavery unwilling to die. We have seen contrivances by States designed to thwart Negro voting.... Negroes have been excluded over and again from juries solely on account of their race ... or have been forced to sit in segregated seats in courtrooms.... They have been made to attend segregated and inferior schools ... or been denied entrance to colleges or graduate schools because of their color.... Negroes have been prosecuted for marrying whites.... They have been forced to live in segregated residential districts ... and residents of white neighborhoods have denied them entrance.[83]

Few white justices have ever demonstrated such a deep understanding of systemic racism. Douglas recognized that legally or informally institutionalized segregation, like slavery, was a masterful societal machine designed to protect white privilege and whites' unjust enrichment. Today, slavery's badges and disabilities persist because they are perpetuated by the racist framing and discriminatory practices of a great many whites, as well as by the less obvious, macro-level processes of U.S. institutions that constantly reproduce white power and privilege.

3
The White Racial Frame
A Social Force

Our third president, the prominent theorist of liberty and equality Thomas Jefferson, wrote in his only major book, *Notes on the State of Virginia*, that black Americans are racially inferior to whites in reasoning, imagination, and beauty. Furthermore, in his view blacks are more adventuresome than whites because they have a "want of forethought," are unreflective, and even feel life's pain less than whites. In an extreme animalizing statement, Jefferson further asserted that even black Americans favor white beauty, "as uniformly as is the preference of the Oranootan [Orangutan] for the black women over those of his own species." Blacks are also alleged to have produced no important thinkers, musicians, or intellectuals. Improvement in black minds comes only when there is a "mixture with whites," which Jefferson argues "proves that their inferiority is not the effect merely of their condition of life."[1] As our first major secular intellectual and a major slaveholder, Thomas Jefferson played a central role in the early development of racial rationalizations for the enslavement of black Americans, especially including this dominant white-racist framing of U.S. society.

Creating a White Racial Frame

The expansion of European countries from the 1400s to the early 1900s brought colonial exploitation to more than 80 percent of the globe. The resulting exploitation and resource inequalities stemmed, as Du Bois noted, from letting a "single tradition of culture suddenly have thrust into its hands the power to bleed the world of its brawn and wealth, and the willingness to do this."[2] For the colonizing Europeans it was not enough to bleed the world of labor and resources. Colonizers were not content to exploit indigenous American and African peoples and view that exploitation simply as "might makes right." Instead, most saw themselves as virtuous Christians and justified what they had done for themselves and their descendants. Gradually, a broad racial framing like that illustrated by Thomas Jefferson's commentaries early rationalized this extensive oppression and thereby reduced its conscious moral cost for Europeans and European Americans.

Much historical research demonstrates there has long been in North America and elsewhere a dominant, white-created racial frame that provides an overarching and generally destructive worldview, one that extends across divisions of class, gender, and age. Since its full development over the course of the seventeenth century, this powerful frame has provided the vantage point from which most whites have constantly viewed North American society. Its centrality in white minds is what makes it a dominant frame throughout the country and, indeed, the Western world. Over time, this powerful frame has been elaborated by, and imposed on, the minds of most Americans, becoming thereby the country's dominant "frame of mind" and "frame of reference" in regard to racial matters.

Recall from Chapter 1 (pp. 26–27) that in this broad racial framing white Americans have combined at least these important features: racial stereotypes; racial narratives and interpretations; racial images and language accents; racialized emotions; and inclinations to discriminate. In this chapter we will touch on all of these, but focus on the first three. Typically, for a broad social frame like this, its deeply imbedded beliefs and attitudes are constantly reflected in the talk and actions of everyday life. One need not know or accept the entire frame for it to have a substantial impact on thought and action. Each person may utilize selected elements of the dominant frame.

The perpetuation of systemic racism has required an intergenerational reproducing not only of racist institutions but also of the white racial frame that buttresses them. The early exploitative relationships that whites developed in regard to African and Native Americans were soon rationalized, and they became enduring racist relationships. From the beginning, white-imposed racism has been webbed into most arenas of North American life, including places of work and residence, and activities as diverse as eating, procreating, and childrearing. Racist practices in these everyday life worlds create, and are in turn shaped by, basic racist categories, stereotypes, images, and emotions in the minds of Americans, especially white Americans. The white racial frame is an overarching umbrella frame that includes all such racist material, in regard to both Americans of color and white Americans. In later sections we will examine in detail the overarching white framing of our past and present, with an emphasis on the role of elites in framing and perpetuating antiblack and other elements of that broad and long-dominant racial frame. In Chapter 4 we will look at the present day, and focus on the array of specific antiblack stereotypes, images, emotions, and interpretations that persist in that frame, with an emphasis on the views of ordinary white Americans.

Major societal frames are typically created, codified, and maintained by those at the top of a society, although this construction and perpetuation takes place in routine and ongoing interaction with the views and practices of ordinary citizens. Those with the greater power typically have the greater ability to impose their social frames on others. As Karl Marx and Friedrich Engels long ago pointed out, "the ideas of the ruling class are in every epoch the ruling ideas: i.e. the class, which is the ruling material force of society, is at the same time its ruling intellectual force."[3] White elites have dominated the creation, discussion, and dissemination of a system-rationalizing racist frame in institutional arenas such as business, the media, politics, education, churches, and government. While there is much popularly generated racist stereotyping, imagery, and interpretation, even this is usually codified and embellished by the white elites.

As with most important societal frames, if the elites had been opposed to the development of the dominant racist framing, they would have actively combated it, and it would likely have declined in social importance. In a detailed analysis of the racist ideas and actions of presidents from George Washington to Bill Clinton, researcher Kenneth O'Reilly has shown that conventional wisdom about presidents *following* a racist populace is wrongheaded. The historical evidence shows that most of the powerful white men who have controlled U.S. political institutions at the top have worked hard "to nurture and support the nation's racism."[4] The dominant racist framing did not arise accidentally. It was, and still is, actively developed and insistently propagated by whites in all social classes.

Eurocentric Framing: Early Views

For several centuries white religious leaders, businesspeople, political leaders, academics, scientists, and media analysts have developed and disseminated to all people a complex and variegated white-racist framing that defends the theft of land and labor from people of color. The antiblack elements of the old white racial frame are perhaps the most developed and have long included various religious, scientific, and psychosexual rationalizations for oppression. Although the dominant frame has been elaborated and changed somewhat over time, in all its variations it has operated to rationalize, sustain, and script white power and privilege.

Negative Images of Colonized Peoples

By the mid-1400s the Portuguese were sailing regularly to Africa and exporting Africans in chains. Views of European superiority were fostered in the first imperialistic countries, Portugal and Spain, as they exploited the resources of indigenous peoples. For a time, a few Catholic priests and theologians opposed the ruthless exploitation of indigenous populations, including the often genocidal operations of Spanish colonizers such as those led by Christopher Columbus against indigenous peoples in the Americas in the fifteenth and early sixteenth centuries. However, in a 1550 debate Spanish theologian Gaines de Sepulveda argued that it was lawful to enslave indigenous populations because of their heathen, sinful, and uncivilized natures, which obligated the latter to serve those (the Spanish) with the superior culture. De Sepulveda represented the increasingly dominant European view and was perhaps the first European thinker to defend the barbarity of colonialism in comprehensive cultural terms.[5]

The English soon followed. Prior to English colonization of North America and much of the globe, negative ideas about non-English peoples overseas were current in England, probably coming from other European explorers. In 1611, a few years before English colonists brought Africans into the Jamestown colony, William Shakespeare's play *The Tempest* had featured the sinister figure of Caliban. Caliban is portrayed as the dark other, as a "savage and deformed slave." His mother is said to be from Africa. Caliban is portrayed as physically threatening to Prospero, a European man of intellect. Already, the English had some negative images of certain cultural others before their overseas conquests were well underway.[6]

Virtuous "Christians" versus the "Uncivilized Others"

From the 1600s to the 1800s the English and other European Protestants dominated the religious scene on the Atlantic coast of North America, and from the beginning their religious views incorporated notions of group superiority and inferiority. Early English Protestants regarded themselves as Christian and civilized, but those they conquered as unchristian and savage.

Very important to the emergence of European imperialism and colonialism was the early development of a strong acquisitive and predatory ethic, an ethic coupled with a zeal convinced of the superiority of European civilization. At the center of European imperialism was a powerful drive to dominate the world at whatever human cost, for economic and cultural gain. By the 1500s and 1600s the ever-spreading acquisitiveness of the north European bourgeoisie was reinforced by the values of their religious groups. Their individualistic Protestant ethic fostered certain values associated with capitalism, including a greedy individualism that contrasted with the collectivistic values of most of the world's indigenous peoples.[7]

European colonists coming to the Americas saw themselves as Christian people of good virtue and advanced civilization. From the first century of colonization these Europeans portrayed themselves as, to use Ronald Takaki's phrase, "virtuous republicans." They did not, or should not, have the instinctual qualities of the "creatures of darkness," the "black" and "red" Calibans of the invaded areas that they saw in their stereotyped framing. Europeans were rational, ascetic, self-governing, and sexually controlled, while the Native American and African others were irrational, uncivilized, instinctual, and uncontrolled.[8] The first non-Europeans with whom European colonists came into contact were Native Americans. Rationalizing the destruction of indigenous societies, European colonists early developed negative images and stereotypes of those they conquered. Native Americans were often framed as "uncivilized savages" to be killed off or pushed well beyond the boundaries of European American society. Significantly, much white thinking about indigenous peoples alternated between great hostility, such as can be seen in the Declaration of Independence's complaint about "merciless Indian savages," and the paternalism seen in the image of a "noble savage" in much Western literature.[9]

In Europe and the Americas, a commonplace European or European American explanation for the exploitation and enslavement of other groups, especially people of African descent, drew on an old myth based on the biblical story of Noah and his sons (Genesis 9–10). This old story relates how a drunken Noah was encountered by three sons. Two of them, Shem and Japheth, did not look on him but covered his nakedness. Noah's son Ham looked but did not cover him. As a result, Ham's son Canaan was cursed by Noah and told that he would be the servant of his brethren. A later version of this myth views Ham as African and suffering the divine punishment of his descendants being made servants to other peoples, the descendants of Ham's brothers. However, in the Christian Bible there is *nothing* about Ham's African characteristics. It was later, in the Talmudic and Midrashic (Jewish) religious tradition, that Ham (or Canaan) was said to have "darkened the faces of mankind," and thus was asserted to be father to the African peoples. This Ham myth was picked up in Christian communities by the 1500s, and the story was used by European colonists to justify the subjugation and enslavement of Africans and African Americans.[10]

A religious theory of black subordination and separation remained strong throughout the slavery and legal segregation periods, and some of it can still be found today. For centuries such religious myths about people of African descent have been retold as part of the dominant racial framing by members of white ruling elites, including ministers, business leaders, political officials, and judges, as well as by ordinary whites.[11]

Early Color Coding: The Link to Slavery

In the early seventeenth century English American colonists first used terms like "Christians" for themselves and "negroes" for Africans and African Americans. "Negro" referred to African descent. This conceptualization was moving in the direction of a full-fledged biologized racism, for the colonists were paying increasing attention to skin color and the purity of their ancestry ("blood"). Indeed, as early as 1614, Reverend Samuel Purchas spoke of the "black Negroe" and the "whiter European."[12] Moreover, many Europeans and European Americans were arguing that there was a God-ordained hierarchy of human beings. It was thus part of the hierarchical nature of being defined as "black" to suffer discrimination. One was only "black" in relationship to those self-defined as "white" in this hierarchical thinking.

In the process of English colonialism and the African slave trade some of the world's lightest-skinned people came into contact with some of the world's darkest-skinned people. Gradually, color and other physical characteristics became central to a dominant racial framing that tenaciously rationalized and sustained this intensive exploitation and oppression. In the prevailing European view, which was verbalized and emotion-laden, the enslaved status of most African Americans was natural: They were inferior because they were enslaved, and they were enslaved because they were inferior. The expansion of enslavement and color typing developed side-by-side, thereby reinforcing each other. By the late 1600s colonial accounts refer to the unusual "complexion" of the slaves as making an impression on the "white" mind. The word "white" was increasingly used alongside "Christian" and "English" by the colonists to distinguish themselves from "negroes," who had no role in this naming process. By means of the slave trade and slavery European colonists had created a new group consisting of people from different African societies, one sharply differentiated from whites in rights and privileges. Enslaved Africans and their descendants became a major point of reference for the construction of the newly defined whiteness. In 1709 an English official noted in his diary that a Spaniard had petitioned the Massachusetts Council for his freedom and that a certain Captain Teat had alleged that "all of that [dark] Color were Slaves."[13] Darker skin color was early on taken by whites as the visible badge of enslavement.

The controlling language in the new nation was that of the English colonists. They had power to shape the everyday terminology used in interaction with one another and with those they oppressed. Increasingly, skin color was linked to older color meanings in English. In Old English, the word "black" meant sooted, while the word "white" meant to gleam brightly, as for a candle. In line with earlier Christian usage, the word "black" was used by the English colonists to describe sin and the devil. Old images of darkness and blackness as sinister were transferred to the darker-skinned peoples exploited in the system of slavery. European colonists—usually some shade of tan, brown, or pink in skin color—must have seen that Africans also varied greatly in skin color, with the majority being some shade of brown, and not actually black.[14]

In the first century of North American slavery the pro-white framing and antiblack framing were becoming ever-more developed and comprehensive. This racial framing increasingly focused not only on the negative blackness of the others but also on the virtuous whiteness of Europeans. Africans and African Americans were viewed as physically, aesthetically, morally, and mentally inferior to whites—differences regarded as more or less permanent. "Whiteness" was created by self-named whites in opposition to "blackness," in comparison to which whiteness was not only different but quite superior. Significantly, the antiblack framing was not "out there," but rather in the white mind (brain) and riddled with racialized emotions.[15]

Legal and Educational Underpinnings

At an early historical stage, the antiblack perspective of white Americans was imbedded in the legal and political institutions undergirding slavery. By the 1670s slavery was firmly enshrined in colonial laws defining Africans as chattel property. From that time to the 1860s Civil War much lawmaking, North and South, supported the barbaric institution. Consider the central colony in the first century and a half—Virginia. In that area could be found about 40 percent of all those enslaved, as well as many prominent whites who were speaking out on issues of their own liberty. Thomas Jefferson published the cases of Virginia's General Court for the years 1730 to 1772. More than half involved legal matters of concern to slaveholders "such as testamentary disposition of slaves, creditors' rights in a debtor's slaves, warranty in the sale of slaves, life estates in and mortgages of slaves, dower in slaves, and entailed slaves."[16] From the 1600s to the 1800s many court decisions revealed the centrality of slavery to the new country.

The U.S. Constitution recognized the slavery economy and implicitly incorporated strong white-supremacist ideas in such provisions as the one that counted an African American as only three-fifths of a person. After the new nation was created, the unifying of ever-growing numbers of immigrants from various European countries was done in part through legal and political doctrines buttressing white privilege and superiority. In the first naturalization law in 1790, the new Congress made the earliest political statement on citizenship. Naturalization was restricted to "white persons." Whiteness thereby became an official category; only European immigrants could qualify to become U.S. citizens. In contrast, African Americans who had ancestors going back several generations were *not* citizens.[17]

From the colonial era to the present, educational institutions have also been critical to the transmission of the dominant antiblack framing. Elites have long maintained power in part by controlling processes of knowledge dissemination through schooling and other means of public education. Early in colonial history, one New England minister, Samuel Hopkins, noted why whites see blacks so negatively:

We have been used to look on them in a mean, contemptible light; and *our education* has filled us with *strong prejudices* against them, and led us to consider them, not as our brethren, or in any degree on a level with us; but as quite another species of animals, made only to serve us and our children; and as happy in bondage, as in any other state.[18]

Historically, whites have learned much racial stereotyping, racial prejudice, and other racial framing at school, at home, in church, and from the mass media.

Emotional Underpinnings

From the seventeenth century to the present, the white framing that justifies antiblack oppression, while overtly verbal-cognitive and legally enshrined, has had a very strong *emotional* character. Antiblack stereotyping, images, and actions have long been linked to such emotions as hate, fear, guilt, repulsion, and greed.

For example, for generations many whites have been emotionally obsessed with what they term "racial mixing." Strong and irrational emotions are evident in taboos and laws against interracial sex and marriage, which have long been racially framed as "unnatural" by many whites. In 1662 the colony of Virginia established the first explicit law against interracial sex, and in 1691 a law against interracial marriage was enforced by banishment.[19] Mixed-ancestry Americans were viewed not only as inferior but also as degrading what Benjamin Franklin called the "lovely" whiteness: White "amalgamation with the other color produces a degradation to which no lover of his country, no lover of excellence in the human character can innocently consent."[20] Like most whites of the era, Franklin had developed some fear of black Americans. A slaveholder for several decades, then an abolitionist later in life, Franklin appeared to oppose slavery not so much because of its inhumanity, but because of its negative impact on the white population. Ironically, for most of U.S. history it was white men who were by far the most likely to cross the color line, and thus force sexual relations on enslaved or free black women.

Strong emotions are evident in the white violence that has long targeted black Americans. While most bloodthirsty lynchings of black Americans took place after the Civil War, they were preceded before that war by barbaric beatings, rape, torture, and mutilation of Africans and African Americans on slave ships, farms, and plantations. The early white framing of African Americans as "dangerous savages" and "degenerate beasts" played a role in rationalizing this violence. To deserve such treatment "the black man presumably had to be as vicious as the racists claimed; otherwise many whites would have had to accept an intolerable burden of guilt for perpetrating or tolerating the most horrendous cruelties and injustices."[21] After slavery, the white racial frame legitimated lynchings, whose sadistic character suggests deep and shared white emotions of guilt, hatred, or fear.

Fear is central to the white-racist framing woven through the system of antiblack oppression. Significantly, of the three large-scale systems of social oppression—racism, sexism, and classism—only racism involves the dominant group having a deeply rooted and often obsessively emotional fear of the subordinated group. Why do many whites often react negatively and viscerally to the presence or image of the black body, especially that of black men? Joel Kovel has speculated that many whites dislike black bodies because they project onto them their own psychological fears, which are often rooted in childhood fears. As they are socialized, young whites often learn, directly and indirectly, consciously and unconsciously, that the dark otherness of black Americans somehow symbolizes degradation, danger, sinfulness, or the unknown—imagery dating back centuries and still present in many whites' imaginings. Over a lifetime many antiblack actions are strongly shaped by images in whites' conscious and unconscious minds.[22]

Developing a More Explicit Framing of "Race"

A we/they **ethnocentrism** and Eurocentrism existed long before Europeans built their colonial empires, but a well-developed exploitative, and soon to be fully racist, frame emerged only with European domination of peoples overseas. As Oliver Cox has noted, the modern racist perspective did not arise out of some "abstract, natural, immemorial feeling of mutual antipathy between groups," but rather grew out of the exploitative relationships of colonialism.[23] Indeed, there are significant variations across societies. Some do not develop the high level of xenophobia that others do. Historically, many indigenous societies showed a friendliness (xenophilia) toward Europeans when the latter first came into their areas.

The racial framing that rationalized European exploitation was gradually elaborated as European colonialism expanded globally. Initially, the "others" were primarily viewed as religiously and culturally inferior— the early accent on a hierarchy of inferior and superior groups. A little later, those oppressed were seen as distinctive "races" that were inferior in physical, biological, and intellectual terms to Europeans. A fully developed concept of "race" as a pseudo-biological category was developed by Europeans and European Americans in the late 1600s and 1700s and was codified in the work of leading European and American intellectuals around the time of the American Revolution.

By the late 1700s these hierarchical relations were increasingly explained in overtly bio-racial terms. This biological determinism read existing

European prejudices back into human biology; then it read that biology as rationalizing social hierarchy. Those at the bottom were less than human; they were alleged to have inferior brains. The concept of "race" in the dominant racial frame had at least these three important elements:

1. an accent on physically and biologically distinctive categories called "races";
2. an emphasis on "race" as the primary determinant of a group's essential personality and cultural traits; and
3. a hierarchy of superior and inferior racial groups.[24]

Early White Leaders and Intellectuals

Anthropologist Audrey Smedley has argued that "race was, from its inception, a folk classification, a product of popular beliefs about human differences that evolved from the sixteenth through the nineteenth centuries."[25] However, much of the effort to create a societal frame accenting a distinctive hierarchy of races has come from *white elites*. While most people tend to sort others into social categories, elites actively codify and propagate certain strong versions of social categorization. From the beginning, European and European American elites have worked hard to defend imperialism and its oppression. By the mid- to late eighteenth century, white intellectuals and political leaders were explicitly arguing that "negroes" were a biologically different "race" from Europeans. In his book, *The History of Jamaica* (1774), prominent judge Edward Long, a slaveholder, argued that Africans were a "truly bestial" species. Long's book was published in the United States in 1788.[26]

About this time our important early theorist of equality and liberty, Thomas Jefferson, contended that black Americans were an inferior "race," a word he helped to make central to the racialized framing of his day. In his influential book *Notes on the State of Virginia*, published in the late eighteenth century, Jefferson articulated the first well-honed and extensive arguments by a North American intellectual for black racial inferiority. As I noted previously, he viewed African Americans as inferior to whites in reasoning, imagination, beauty, and numerous other important qualities.[27] Over his lifetime Jefferson was a major slaveholder who owned hundreds of African Americans, even though he periodically, and hypocritically, asserted that he disliked slavery. Among his famous words on the subject are those inscribed on the Jefferson Memorial in Washington, DC: "Nothing is more certainly written in the book of fate than that these people are to be free." Significantly, his critical words that *follow* this quoted sentence are (probably intentionally) omitted on this famous monument: "Nor is it less certain that the two races, equally free, cannot live in the same government." For this explicit reason, Jefferson was a supporter of exporting African Americans back to Africa, should they ever become free.[28]

During the eighteenth and nineteenth centuries white American leaders in business, politics, and academia were greatly influenced by European intellectuals and writers, many of whom held openly antiblack views. The latter, in turn, were significantly influenced by reports from the colonies in the Americas. The major Western philosopher of the late eighteenth century, Immanuel Kant, produced the first developed theory of "race" in modern terms. Many people have long viewed Kant as the leading philosopher of the West, a pure philosopher uncontaminated by racist thought. However, for decades Kant taught some of the first courses on the geography and anthropology of race. At the heart of his influential thinking was an attempt to define humanity, and in his view one must be *white* to be fully human, for "humanity exists in its greatest perfection in the white race."[29]

During the 1770s, Kant wrote of the hierarchy of "races of mankind," one of the early uses of the term "races" in the sense of biologically distinct, hierarchical categories. In one document Kant delineated a hierarchy, with whites at the top:

> STEM GENUS, white brunette.
> First race, very blond (northern Europe), of damp cold.
> Second race, Copper-Red (America), of dry cold.
> Third race, Black (Senegambia), of dry heat.
> Fourth race, Olive-Yellow (Indians), of dry heat.[30]

In his view the black "race" was quite inferior. At this point in Western history, even the most advanced European philosophy and philosophical anthropology were grounded in ideas about the supremacy of the white race and Western civilization.

Scientific Racism

From the mid-eighteenth century to the mid-twentieth century, the ever-expanding physical and social sciences were regularly used to defend and racially frame the oppression of Americans of color. Leading scientists developed a scientific view of black Americans and other people of color as innately inferior and thus deserving of subordination. Such ideological racism is not something that comes only out of the margins of Western societies, but rather from their intellectual and cultural centers.

For instance, between the 1770s and the 1790s the very prominent German anatomist and anthropologist Johann Blumenbach worked out a detailed racial classification that became very influential. At the top of his ladder-like list of "races" were what he called the "Caucasians"

(Europeans), a term coined because in his judgment the people of the Caucasus were the most beautiful of the European peoples. Lower on the list were the Mongolians (Asians), the Ethiopians (Africans), the Americans (Native Americans), and the Malays (Polynesians).[31]

The new scientific racism determinedly asserted the notion of specific races with different physical characteristics, a belief that these characteristics were hereditary, and the notion of a natural hierarchy of inferior and superior races. In its broad sweep this assertively racist framing was not supported by careful scientific observations of all human societies, but rather was buttressed with racially slanted reports gleaned by European missionaries, travelers, and sea captains from their experiences with selected non-European societies. Most scientists of the late eighteenth and nineteenth centuries, while presenting themselves as objective observers, tried to marshal evidence for human differences that the European imperialists' perspective had already decided were important to highlight.[32]

Celebrating and Expanding the Racist Frame: The 1830s to the 1930s

The International Industry of Racist Framing

By the mid-nineteenth century the propagation of antiblack and other racist ideas and images had become a major industry in Europe and the United States. From then to now, literally thousands of articles and books have been written, as well as speeches given, as part of a racist framing machine that constantly defends white supremacy and racial oppression, especially antiblack oppression.

Historically, this dominant racial framing has frequently been challenged when those who are oppressed fight back—such as in slave rebellions, abolitionist movements, and civil rights movements (see Chapter 9, pp. 273–276). However, when white interests have been seriously challenged, whites, especially those in the elite, have attempted to deflect or destroy all major challenges. The elite must constantly combat the counter-framed insights and actions of these movements, insights into the real nature of the oppressive racist reality that its members have fostered and maintained. For example, during the mid-decades of the nineteenth century the growing antislavery movement in Britain and the United States spurred an elite reaction that was extensive and combative. Not surprisingly, an even more developed and formalized racist framing was created in a vigorous attempt to defend slavery against this growing abolitionism.[33]

Many U.S. and European intellectuals intensified arguments for white supremacy and African or African American inferiority. In his 1830 lectures the leading German philosopher G. W. F. Hegel spoke about the "Negro" as "natural man in his wild and untamed nature" and argued that there is "nothing remotely humanized in the Negro's character." Black people were not human beings with a civilized history and human consciousness. He too based his ill-informed judgments on the racist reports of numerous European travelers. Drawing on similar biased sources, leading British authors as diverse as Thomas Carlyle, William Makepeace Thackeray, and Charles Dickens defended racist ideas or the enslavement of Africans.[34]

Count Joseph Arthur de Gobineau, a French diplomat and important racist thinker of the nineteenth century, argued that whites are

> gifted with reflective energy, or rather with an energetic intelligence.... They have a remarkable, even extreme love of liberty, and are openly hostile to the formalism under which the Chinese are glad to vegetate, as well as the strict despotism which is the only way of governing the Negro.[35]

In his extensive writings Gobineau articulated a developed white-racist framing and, once translated, his writings became very influential in the United States and other countries. Later, Gobineau's ideas would be drawn on by German Nazi thinkers and officials, indicating again how powerful the white-racist frame has been across the globe. Pre-eminent physical scientists also emphasized notions of white supremacy. In the nineteenth century the leading French anatomist Paul Broca broke new ground in understanding how the brain works. Nonetheless, Broca was a leading racist thinker who argued that variations in human head shape were linked to significant mental differences among racial groups. Black skin and wooly hair were associated with inferior intelligence, while white skin and straight hair were the "equipment of the highest groups."[36] While Broca later retracted these views, many scientists and popular writers of the era persistently spread his idea of head form being linked to "race" and character.

Political Elites and Racial Framing

In the United States distinguished lawyers, judges, and political leaders promoted scientific racism and its white-supremacist assumptions. In the first half of the nineteenth century whites with an economic interest in slavery dominated the U.S. political and legal system. This influence was conspicuous in the previously mentioned *Dred Scott v. John F. A. Sandford* (1857) decision (see p. 37). Replying to the petition of an enslaved black American, a substantial majority of the Supreme Court ruled that Scott was not a citizen under the Constitution. Chief Justice Roger Taney argued that African Americans had, since long before the making of the U.S. Constitution,

> been regarded as beings of an inferior order, and altogether unfit to associate with the white race, either in social or political relations; and so far inferior, that they had no rights which the white man was bound to respect; and that the negro might justly and lawfully

be reduced to slavery for his benefit. He was bought and sold, and treated as an ordinary article of merchandise and traffic, whenever a profit could be made by it. This opinion was at that time fixed and universal in the civilized portion of the white race.[37]

This important *Dred Scott* decision showed that the dominant racial frame was well established: all black Americans, whether slave or technically "free," were inferior racialized beings with no rights, and white supremacy was asserted to be part of the law of the land.

U.S. senators and presidents played a role in spreading this dominant white frame. President James Buchanan, a northerner, urged the country to support the racist thinking of *Dred Scott*. Before he became president, in a debate with Senator Stephen A. Douglas, Abraham Lincoln had argued that the physical difference between racial groups was insuperable, saying:

> I am not nor ever have been in favor of the social and political equality of the white and black races: that I am not nor ever have been in favor of making voters of the free negroes, or jurors, or qualifying them to hold office or having them to marry with white people.... I as much as any other man am in favor of the superior position being assigned to the white man.[38]

Lincoln, soon called the "Great Emancipator," had made his white-supremacist views very clear, views later cited by southern officials in their 1960s struggle to protect legal segregation. Indeed, today Lincoln's racist views are still quoted by white-supremacist groups in their literature and on their sometimes influential Internet websites.

The demise of slavery in the 1860s did not end the pervasiveness of the strong white-supremacist version of the dominant racial frame. Many whites pressed for a system of legal segregation. They had the support of President Andrew Johnson, who in 1867 commented on what he called the "naked savages," saying "It is vain to deny that they [black Americans] are an inferior race—very far inferior to the European variety. They have learned in slavery all that they know in civilization."[39] Numerous white members of Congress also used the new racist science to argue for the continuing racial subordination of black Americans.[40]

With the end of Reconstruction in 1877 came comprehensive Jim Crow segregation in the South and other areas. Distinguished judges, including on the Supreme Court, played a key role in solidifying this legal segregation and in unifying racially framed defenses of it. Recall that in *Plessy v. Ferguson* (1896) a nearly unanimous Supreme Court legitimated the fiction of "separate but equal" for white and black Americans in a case dealing with segregated railroad cars. This "separate but equal" fiction was legal for more than half a century, until the 1954 *Brown v. Board of Education of Topeka* decision desegregated some Jim Crow schools, and until broken down further by 1960s' civil rights laws. Until then, there had been widespread agreement in the white elite and the white population about the desirability of thorough racial segregation for black men, women, and children. Even whites opposed to official segregation articulated a belief in white superiority. Justice John Marshall Harlan, the lone dissenter in *Plessy v. Ferguson,* noted in his opinion that "the white race deems itself to be the dominant race in this country. And so it is, in prestige, in achievements, in education, in wealth and in power. So, I doubt not, it will continue to be for all time."[41] Two sentences later, Harlan added that "our Constitution is colorblind, and neither knows nor tolerates classes among citizens." Harlan was among the first to publicly articulate the mythical view that the U.S. Constitution is colorblind.

The open assertion of white-supremacist views was commonplace for government officials in the nineteenth and early twentieth centuries. Given increasing immigration in this period from non-European countries, these officials gave much attention to who was, or was not, "white." Between 1878 and 1923 a series of federal court cases decided that the following Americans were not white and thus were ineligible for citizenship: Chinese Americans, native Hawaiians, those half-Asian, those half-Indian, Burmese Americans, Japanese Americans, Filipino Americans, those three-quarters Filipino, and Korean Americans. They were placed, by white judges and other whites, toward the "black end" of the white-to-black racial desirability continuum that has long been common in white minds (see Chapter 8, pp. 236–241). Indeed, whiteness as an official criterion for immigrants to become U.S. citizens was not officially changed until the 1952 Immigration and Nationality Act.[42]

Social Darwinism

In his influential writings the English scientist Charles Darwin applied the important evolutionary idea of "natural selection" not only to animal development but also to the development of human "races." In spite of his pathbreaking idea of human evolution, he was unable to escape the white-racist framing common among scientists of his day. He saw natural selection at work in the killing of indigenous peoples in Australia by the British, wrote of black people as a category between whites and gorillas, and spoke against government social programs for the "weak" because they permitted the least desirable people to survive. The "civilized races" would eventually replace "savage races throughout the world."[43]

During the late 1800s and early 1900s an elite perspective called "social Darwinism" argued aggressively that racially "inferior races" were less evolved, less human, and more ape-like than the "superior races." Prominent social scientists like Herbert Spencer and William Graham

Sumner argued that social life was a life-and-death struggle in which the best individuals would win out over inferior individuals. Sumner argued that wealthy Americans, who were almost entirely white at the time, were products of natural selection and essential to the advance of civilization. Black Americans were seen by many of these racist analysts as a "degenerate race" whose alleged "immorality" was a natural trait. Significantly, some consciously connected their racist doctrines with defenses of other societal oppression, particularly sexism and class oppression. In the late nineteenth century one white author, M. G. Delaney, argued that the races at the bottom of the ladder were inferior and female-dominated, while those at the top of the ladder were superior and male-dominated. From this perspective a strong patriarchal system was a clear sign of the "better races."[44]

By the late 1800s a eugenics movement was spreading among scientists and other intellectuals in Europe and the United States. Eugenicists accented the importance of breeding the "right" types of human groups. Britain's famous scientist Francis Galton argued for improving the superior race by human intervention. Like Galton, U.S. eugenicists opposed "racial mixing" because it destroyed the racial purity of whites. Allowing "unfit races" to survive would destroy the "superior race" of northern Europeans. Those from the lesser races, it was decided, should be sterilized or excluded from the country. Such views were not on the far-out fringe, but had the weight of established scientists, leading politicians, and major business leaders. For example, in 1893 Nathaniel S. Shaler, a prominent Harvard University dean, publicly argued that black Americans were inferior, uncivilized, and an "alien folk" with no place in the U.S. body politic—and destined for eventual extinction under ongoing processes of the laws of nature.[45]

In the first decades of the twentieth century most social scientists and intellectuals accepted scientific racism. In 1923 Carl Brigham, a Princeton psychologist who would later play a central role in developing college entrance tests, argued pugnaciously for the intellectual inferiority of various racial groups, using data from psychometric tests given to World War I draftees. Low psychometric test scores by Italian and Russian immigrants, as well as black Americans, were explained by Brigham and other elite scientists (of north European ancestry) in terms of their "inferior racial stocks."[46]

Madison Grant, another influential intellectual, developed racist ideas in *The Passing of the Great Race*. In four editions between 1916 and 1923, Grant wrote that the new immigrant groups from southern and eastern Europe would interbreed and destroy the superior "Nordic race."[47] In 1920 Lothrop Stoddard, a Harvard-educated lawyer and historian, wrote in another influential book, entitled *The Rising Tide of Color: Against White World-Supremacy*, of the "overwhelming preponderance of the white race in the ordering of the world's affairs ... the indisputable master of the planet."[48] Like many of his white contemporaries, as well as many commentators today (see below, p. 82), Stoddard feared that in the future whites would be overwhelmed by very large numbers of black Americans and other Americans of color. Grant and Stoddard were influential among white scientists and administrators at colleges and universities, as well as among celebrated politicians.

More Politicians and Presidents

Scientific racism was periodically used by white members of Congress to support passage of discriminatory legislation, including the openly racist 1924 immigration law, which excluded most immigrants other than northern Europeans. In this period overtly racist ideas were advocated by U.S. presidents. President Theodore Roosevelt liked scientific racism and praised Madison Grant's book for its "grasp of the facts our people need to realize."[49] President Woodrow Wilson was well known as an advocate of the superiority of European civilization over all others, including those of Africa. As president, Wilson increased the racial segregation of the federal government. Significantly, no less a racist leader than Adolf Hitler would later report having been influenced by Wilson's racist writings.[50] (The first modern use of the term "racism" was apparently in a 1933 German book by Magnus Hirschfeld, who sought to counter the Nazis' and other European racists' notions of a biologically determined hierarchy of races.[51])

In 1921 President Warren G. Harding, who had been linked to the Klan, rejected any "suggestion of social equality" between whites and blacks, citing Stoddard's book as evidence that the "race problem" was global. Before he became president, Calvin Coolidge wrote in *Good Housekeeping* magazine, "Biological laws tell us that certain divergent people will not mix or blend. The Nordics propagate themselves successfully. With other races, the outcome shows deterioration on both sides."[52] Ideas of white supremacy and rigid segregation were openly advocated by white political leaders.

With the expansion of European and U.S. colonialism into Asia and Africa in the last half of the nineteenth century, new emphases were added to the prevailing racial frame. One relatively new emphasis was "teleological racism"—the view that non-European peoples, including Africans, had been created as inferior so that they could serve, and be civilized by, whites. A famous statement is Rudyard Kipling's 1899 poem, "The White Man's Burden" ("Take up the White Man's burden / Send forth the best ye breed"). From Kipling's perspective whites had a missionary obligation to help "inferior races," termed in the paternalistic poem as "half devil, half child."[53] These white-racist formulations not only explained the character and conditions of those oppressed but also celebrated whites as especially civilized, Christian, powerful, and generous toward those conquered. Variations on this old racist framing have long rationalized the oppressive policies directed by Western corporations and governments at peoples of color across the globe, to the present day.

Immigrants Becoming "White"

What the white elites have propagated as a white racial framing of society, the white majority has usually accepted, often with their own adaptations. The transmission of the racist framing from one social group and generation to the next is a critical mechanism in the social reproduction of racism. Most ordinary whites have come to look at their social worlds in white-racist terms and accepted the "psychological wage of whiteness" and racist ideas propagated by elites.

For example, from the 1830s to the early 1900s millions of European immigrants accepted the dominant racial frame as a way to gain white privileges. Take the case of poor Irish immigrants who came in substantial numbers in the 1830s and 1840s. These Irish immigrants did not initially view themselves as "white," but identified with their home country. Once in the U.S., however, they were taught in overt and subtle ways that they were white by already established white ministers, priests, teachers, business people, newspaper editors, and political leaders with whom they interacted. They were pressured and manipulated by British American elites and their own leaders into accepting the dominant racial framing that privileged whiteness and denigrated blackness. Over the course of the nineteenth century most came to envision themselves as white and deserving of white privileges in regard to jobs and living conditions. Often coupled with this move to whiteness was active participation in efforts to drive black workers out of the better-paying jobs in numerous U.S. cities.[54] Other European immigrant groups such as Italian and Jewish Americans also soon defined themselves as white (see Chapter 7, pp. 210–211). Many European groups accepted a comfortable place in a socially constructed "white race" whose privileges included such things as greater personal liberty, better-paying jobs, and the right to vote. They too developed a strong antiblack perspective. Their general acceptance of the dominant racist frame—such as that reflected in performances at blackface minstrel shows seen by many thousands of European immigrants in the decades around 1900—created a "sense of popular whiteness among workers across lines of ethnicity, religion, and skill."[55]

Perpetuating the Racial Frame: The Contemporary United States

Periodically, the dominant racial framing developed in the first century of North American development has been added to, subtracted from, or rearranged in its emphases. Powerful whites have periodically dressed it up differently for changing circumstances, although much of its racist reality has remained the same. New ideas or interpretations have been added to deal with pressures for change from those oppressed, particularly with regard to government antidiscrimination policies. After World War II, for example, certain aspects of the dominant racial framing were altered somewhat to fit the new circumstances of the 1950s and 1960s, during which era black Americans increasingly challenged established patterns of legal segregation.

Continuing Elite Control: The Importance of the Media

In recent decades white elites have continued to dominate the construction and transmission of new or refurbished racist ideas, images, and narratives designed to buttress the system of racial inequality, and they have used ever-more powerful means to accomplish their social ends. The U.S. mass media now include not only the radio, movies, and print media used in the past, but television, music videos, satellite transmissions, Internet websites, and social media.

Today, for the most part, the mainstream media are still controlled by whites. The overwhelming majority of full-time news reporters, supervisors, and editors at more mainstream newspapers and magazines are white. On major television networks whites usually are over-represented in managerial jobs and often as on-air reporters; they are greatly over-represented as "experts" in the mainstream media. In these media Americans of color typically have a token or modest presence in the choice and shaping of news reports and popular entertainment. The concentration of media control in a few corporations has increased dramatically in recent decades. In the twenty-first century fewer than two dozen corporations control much of the U.S. media. One 2012 Federal Communications Commission study calculated from available data that less than 1 percent of full power commercial television stations are owned by African Americans, and that less than 5 percent are owned by Americans of color. The latter are also very underrepresented among the owners of full-time commercial radio stations. Americans of color currently make up about 37 percent of the U.S. population.[56]

Today, the mainstream media are substantially supported by corporate advertisers. Directly or indirectly, these advertisers have significant command over programming. Information about racial matters is usually filtered through a variety of elite-controlled organizations. This filtering is not necessarily coordinated, but reflects the choices of powerful whites socialized to the dominant value system in regard to racial issues. Looking for stories, reporters and journalists typically seek out established government, business, and think-tank experts, who are very disproportionately white.

Historically, the right-wing of the elite, a large segment, has been committed to a more obvious racist perspective and has often pressed for curtailment of citizen protests against societal oppression. In contrast, historically, the more liberal wing of the elite has been smaller and more attuned to popular movements. It has been willing to liberalize society to some degree—for example, getting rid of legal segregation—and make some concessions to those protesting against racial oppression, for the sake of preserving societal order. The center of the elite has waffled between the two poles. Recent decades have seen periodic shifts in the influence of these sectors of the white elite. During the late 1960s and 1970s many political and social science experts consulted by top executives in government and the media came from think tanks espousing views of those in the center or liberal wing of the elite. In the 1970s wealthy conservatives funded right-wing think tanks and pressed conservative white-framed views on universities, politicians, and media owners. Right-wing think tanks— including the American Enterprise Institute, the Manhattan Institute, and the Heritage Foundation—have been successful in getting numerous, and disproportionately white, right-wing commentators into the media as "experts." Working alongside other conservative intellectuals, media experts, and activists, right-wing think tanks continue to be successful in what is an indoctrination campaign aimed at conservatively shaping public views on racial matters in a pro-white direction.[57]

Most Americans get their news from commercial television, radio programs, and mainstream websites. Using local and national media, white elites generally have the capability to mobilize a mass consensus on elite-generated ideas and views; this consensus provides an illusion of democracy. Elites encourage collective ignorance by allowing little systematic, fully analyzed information deeply critical of the existing, often undemocratic, social and political system to be circulated through the mainstream media to the general population.[58] Given this dominance, and the generally weak history and other social science courses in schools, most Americans are uninformed about many aspects of U.S. society. One survey of political knowledge found that less than a quarter knew the names of their U.S. senators; four in ten could not name the vice-president. In another survey, most respondents did not know elementary facts about U.S. history. A Department of Education survey of high school seniors also found that six in ten lacked a knowledge of simple historical facts.[59] Even those Americans who think they know U.S. history often adhere to many misconceptions taught in school. Current high-school textbooks communicate much in the way of inaccurate, distorted, or elliptical views of that history, including in regard to important issues of racism and interracial conflicts.[60]

Because of this pervasive ignorance, white elites can more easily persuade, create confusion in, or foster apathy in the population.

Television has often circulated racist stereotypes straight out of the dominant racial frame. These stereotypes create or reinforce negative racial images in many minds. For example, one study found that television viewing had an important effect on white viewers' negative stereotypes of U.S. Latinos—especially when these viewers felt that they had learned important information about Latinos from watching television. In contrast, those who said that they had talked with, or had positive contacts with, Latinos were more likely to hold positive views of Latinos.[61]

Thus, with our national racial order firmly in place, most white Americans, from childhood on, have generally adopted the racially framed views, assumptions, and proclivities of previous generations, established white authorities, and/or the mainstream media. In this manner important aspects of systemic racism are routinely reproduced from one generation to the next.

Increased Equality and Opportunity Rhetoric

Since the 1960s some significant changes in whites' discriminatory practices and in the rationalizing white frame have taken place. Consider briefly some history. By the 1940s and 1950s African American protests against Jim Crow segregation were growing and having a very negative impact on the U.S. image abroad. Legal segregation and protests against it created international problems for a U.S. government trying to fight Nazi Germany and, after World War II, contending with the Soviet Union for the allegiance of non-European nations. As early as 1952, U.S. Secretary of State Dean Acheson gave the Supreme Court a statement proclaiming that "the continuation of racial discrimination is a source of constant embarrassment to this government … and it jeopardizes the effective maintenance of our moral leadership of the free and democratic nations of the world."[62] A U.S. attorney general commented on the 1954 *Brown* school desegregation case (see p. 84) to the effect that Jim Crow segregation in schooling must be eradicated because it "furnishes grist for Communist propaganda mills." Constitutional scholar Derrick Bell suggested that, historically, white elites have acted to improve the conditions of black Americans only when whites themselves can benefit in the process—what Bell termed the process of racial-group "interest convergence."[63]

By the 1950s, and accelerating in the 1960s, the liberal wing of the white elite was pressing for a softening of blatantly racist prejudices and for new group-based remedies such as school desegregation and affirmative action, the latter aimed at integrating some men and women of color (and white women) into historically white-male-dominated employment, educational, and other societal settings. For a time, a more liberal approach rejecting Jim Crow segregation and accenting civil rights laws and affirmative action was successful in bringing some societal desegregation. From the

1950s to the 1970s federal courts ordered racial desegregation in various institutions. Reversing the earlier white-supremacist Supreme Court position in *Plessy v. Ferguson* (1896), a more liberal high court handed down *Brown v. Board of Education* (1954)—a unanimous ruling that "in the field of public education the doctrine of 'separate but equal' has no place."[64] Group-based remedies were increasingly used to implement significant school desegregation. In the face of black, Latino, and other protests in the streets some white executives in multinational corporations decided not only to provide the civil rights movement with funds but also to support political liberals in efforts to expand government efforts against some discrimination. The liberal and centrist members of the elite were concerned with the U.S. image abroad and with regaining what they saw as "social order" after civil rights protests at home.[65]

From the 1960s onward the rhetoric of equality of opportunity grew in volume among the elite, including presidents and members of Congress. Black protests and protests by other Americans of color in the 1950s and 1960s had an important effect in eradicating legal Jim Crow segregation and most public defenses of overt discrimination in the white leadership. Since the 1960s most political and economic leaders have proclaimed at least the rhetoric of racial and ethnic equality. For example, a major advisor of leading business and political officials, the late conservative Harvard professor Samuel Huntington, asserted in the influential policy journal *Foreign Affairs* that U.S. identity is centered in a widely accepted "set of universal ideas and principles articulated in the founding documents by American leaders: liberty, equality, democracy, constitutionalism, liberalism, limited government, private enterprise."[66]

By the late 1960s, moreover, a few white leaders and researchers were moved by the antiracist protests of Americans of color to reject some white-racist ideas and practices in yet stronger terms. An example of this critical perspective is the report of the 1968 Kerner Commission, established by President Lyndon Johnson to investigate urban rioting. In a bold report this commission, most of whose members were white, concluded the United States was "moving toward two societies, one black, one white—separate and unequal." The report asserted that "white racism is essentially responsible for the explosive mixture which has been accumulating in our cities since the end of World War II."[67] However, this view, while accurate, was considered too radical by most white leaders, and the pathbreaking report was soon forgotten.

The structural dismantling of a large-scale system of compulsory Jim Crow segregation from the 1950s to the 1970s brought a renewed emphasis on equal opportunity rhetoric in much public commentary. Nonetheless, while the everyday relationships and interactions of white and black Americans often changed somewhat, or significantly, with the demise of legal segregation, most whites in the elites and general public were not interested in giving up most white power and privilege in historically white institutions. Real racial equality was not even remotely on the agenda of societal change for most whites. As a result, even with an end to Jim Crow segregation, the dominant white racial frame continued to incorporate many of its old antiblack and other racist features. It continued to rationalize persisting white power and privileges, but now under conditions of official racial desegregation.

The dominant racial frame was altered in some significant ways, especially by softening some racist imagery and re-emphasizing notions of equal opportunity and fairness that had actually been part of some versions of that frame for decades. Indeed, throughout the long Jim Crow era, most whites in segregated areas insisted that black Americans were usually treated fairly and had significant opportunities to succeed. Since the 1960s, moreover, accentuated notions of equality of opportunity and colorblindness have been moved to the forefront of common versions of the contemporary white frame. However, as I demonstrate later, the more open professing by the white elite and public of at least the principles of **equal opportunity** and official desegregation of public schools, workplaces, and public accommodations has not meant that black Americans now have true equality of institutional access and societal opportunity. It also does not mean that most whites desire the federal government to implement large-scale racial integration of our major white-dominated institutions.

A Conservative Shift

As a result of this elite and public orientation, beginning around 1969 with the arrival of Richard Nixon's presidential administration, the rhetoric of "equal opportunity" and "colorblindness" was increasingly accompanied by a federal government that was backing away from commitments to desegregation and enforcement of civil rights laws. At the local level, there was increased police repression of militant dissent in the black community, such as the illegal attacks on the Black Panthers and other militant groups by police and FBI agents. Old racially framed images of "dangerous blacks" were emphasized by prominent white leaders and media commentators who often simultaneously proclaimed this rhetoric of equal opportunity.[68]

Moreover, over the decades since the 1960s white conservative organizations have worked tirelessly in pressing Congress, the courts, and the private sector to weaken or eliminate antidiscrimination programs such as affirmative action, as well as other government programs designed to help the oppressed and impoverished (see Chapter 9, pp. 282–284). This organizational effort signaled the increasing influence on national government policy of a conservative Republican Party that mainly represented the interests of white Americans. Even at the top of the

Democratic Party there was some shift to the right, which could be seen in the relatively modest antidiscrimination policies of the 1970s Jimmy Carter administration and the 1990s Bill Clinton administration.

The federal courts provide another example of this conservative shift. In the decades from the 1970s to the present, numerous conservative, mostly white, judges have ruled that group-remedy programs for racial discrimination violate the U.S. Constitution, which they assert only recognizes the rights of individuals, not groups. For instance, in 1989 a conservative Supreme Court handed down a still-cited major decision, *City of Richmond, Virginia v. J. A. Croson Co.*, which knocked down a Richmond city program designed to remedy some past discrimination against black and other minority businesses with modest business set-asides (contracts).[69] The high court ruled in favor of a white-run construction company, the plaintiff, which argued that the municipal government had unconstitutionally set aside a modest number of local government contracts for small minority companies. The mostly white court ruled that the Richmond government had not made a compelling case for remedying antiblack discrimination, even though the government defendant's statistics showed that in a city whose population was one-half black, *less than 1 percent* of city government business went to black-owned firms. Similar philosophical and legal arguments against significant remedial action for systemic racism have been reiterated by the (usually white) plaintiffs and justices in other federal court cases since this important case. Subsequent federal court cases have built on this precedent and others to weaken or eliminate even the, mostly modest, affirmative action programs seeking to remedy some of the contemporary effects of 350 years of slavery and Jim Crow segregation in this country.

To this day, and in spite of common beliefs to the contrary, the appropriate government agencies, including the Supreme Court, have *never* pursued aggressive and comprehensive enforcement of civil rights laws in major areas, including housing and employment, primarily because of white resistance. Over recent decades the conservative justices in the majority on the Supreme Court have intentionally and severely limited the reach of our civil rights laws by rejecting the legal relevance of plaintiffs' arguments showing institutionalized racism and by narrowing the legal definition of discrimination to cover only discriminatory incidents where a defendant can clearly prove that specific (usually white) actors discriminated because of intentional racial prejudice.[70]

Since the 1970s, in the major sectors of society, including federal and state courts, many white officials have portrayed major institutions as now "colorblind." Recall nineteenth-century Supreme Court Justice John Marshall Harlan's view that the "Constitution is colorblind." Harlan's colorblind view did not become commonplace among the elite until the

1960s. Since then, white adherents of the colorblind perspective have come to the forefront. They view racial discrimination at the hands of judges and other government officials as rare and see U.S. legal and political institutions as operating in a colorblind fashion—in spite of much research evidence indicating that this is only a convenient fiction from the dominant white frame.

Still Arguing for Biological "Races"

For much of the nineteenth and twentieth centuries the commonplace view among whites, including scientists and others in the academic elite, of the difficult social and economic conditions faced by African Americans was that those conditions resulted from blacks' inferior biological and cultural heritages. However, by the 1940s numerous leading scientists were questioning conventional wisdom on biological racism, and by the 1960s many had rejected the old biological determinism.

Still, there were many physical scientists who persisted in holding to the idea of real biological races. As late as the 1980s, one survey found that 50 percent of physical anthropologists and 73 percent of animal behaviorists believed there were biologically differentiated "races" within the species *Homo sapiens.* However, a substantial majority of the cultural anthropologists and sociologists surveyed disagreed. By that time, the majority of social scientists no longer accepted traditional biological determinism, with most likely accepting the idea that "race" was just a social construction.[71]

Nonetheless, in recent decades a few social and physical scientists at major universities, such as Arthur Jensen at the University of California and Richard Herrnstein at Harvard University, have continued to argue that racial-group differences in average scores on the so-called "IQ" (intelligence quotient) tests reveal genetic differences in intelligence between whites and certain Americans of color. In 1969 the *Harvard Educational Review* lent its prestige to an article by Jensen. His arguments there and over the next two decades received national attention, including stories in major magazines and newspapers. Jensen argued that on average black Americans are born with less intelligence than whites, and that "IQ" test data support this contention. Another widely read example of biological determinism was a 1990s book, *The Bell Curve*, which sold more than half a million copies. Well into the twenty-first century, this book is still being read and cited. Like Jensen, the authors of *The Bell Curve*— Richard Herrnstein and Charles Murray—argued that the "IQ" test data show that black and Hispanic Americans are inferior in intelligence to whites. Though the authors had no training in genetics, they suggested that this supposed inferiority in intelligence results substantially from genetic differences.[72] The fact that the book sold well and was widely discussed in the media—in spite of overwhelming evidence against its arguments—strongly suggests that biologically oriented racist thinking remains commonplace.

Indeed, in 2013 Jason Richwine created a similar controversy. A Heritage Foundation report that he co-authored argued that immigration law reform assisting Hispanic immigrants would be very costly for the United States. In an earlier PhD dissertation Richwine had argued that, because Hispanics average lower scores on the "IQ" tests than whites, they are less "intelligent"—and, like Herrnstein and Murray, that there is likely a genetic component to this. In his view this differential is likely to persist over generations of descendants of Hispanic immigrants, which makes their admission to the country problematical. Instead, he suggested that immigrants be admitted substantially on the basis of "IQ." One of Richwine's advisors in this racist research was Charles Murray.[73]

Also relatively recently, James Watson, the co-discoverer of the structure of DNA and a Nobel prize winner in science, has argued that the "IQ" test data indicate black people are less intelligent than whites: "All our social policies are based on the fact that their intelligence is the same as ours—whereas all the testing says not really."[74] It is significant that white scholars and popular analysts who continue to make such ill-informed arguments about "IQ" and racial groups do not recognize that they are thinking out of an uncritical white frame of reference. They write as though there is no other way to view the group data on these conventional *skills* tests (inaccurately named "intelligence" tests) of children, other than their racist framing of the supposedly lesser intelligence of children of color. They do not critically analyze the fact that these skills tests have mostly been created by and/or normed on whites, and they do not acknowledge that much of the substance of these tests reflects the knowledge and culture of those (mostly white) middle-class analysts who have traditionally made up these tests. Indeed, these "IQ" tests are actually skills tests that measure children's differential access to educational and economic resources, access that is still affected greatly by well-institutionalized racism.

Racist arguments about contemporary intelligence levels are grounded in nearly 400 years of viewing black Americans and other Americans of color as having an intelligence inferior to that of white Americans. Today, such views are much more than just an academic matter. Over recent decades versions of these racialized intelligence arguments have periodically been used by white members of Congress and other officials to argue against antidiscrimination and other government programs that benefit Americans of color.

Today, renewed forms of biologically oriented racist thinking are appearing in yet other important settings. In numerous medical circles, for example, there are uncritical discussions of disease rates and physiological variations among the "races," as though these groups have fixed genetic or other biological realities and boundaries. According to health researchers Daniels and Schulz, some human genome scientists make uncritical use of racist categorizations in studying group disease issues—the scientists' argument often being that it is easier "to categorize people based on phenotypically based notions of 'race' rather than to look exclusively at individual genetic composition for prevention, diagnosis, and treatment of disease."[75] These and other biological researchers argue that their research on genetic links to diseases confirms the typology of Caucasian, African, Asian, Pacific Islander, and Native American—a flagrantly racialized typology first developed in the eighteenth century.

Even though a century of physical and social science has shown how socially constructed and useless for assessing real biological ancestry and health issues these old racist categories are, their dominance in Western culture is so strong that some physical scientists cannot resist using them. Daniels and Schulz argue that one reason for this persisting racist conceptualization in genome and other biological research is that these researchers ignore voluminous social science research that shows the many ways that racial categories are socially variable and instead rely uncritically on the centuries-old racist typology of Johann Blumenbach and Thomas Jefferson. Such racist interpretations of health inequalities enable these genetic researchers to avoid dealing with the systemic causes of the health inequalities they find between racial groups, and thus to blame such inequalities on something other than the institutionalized racism that often generates or reinforces them. Moreover, their use of discredited "biological race" categories helps to perpetuate the age-old racist framing of society.[76]

The Cultural Critique: More Stereotyping

Another aspect of older racist views that can be found in new dress today is what one might call the racial–cultural critique—the view that black Americans have done less well than white Americans because of their allegedly deficient culture with its weak work ethic and family values. This is not new racist framing. By the early seventeenth century, African Americans were seen by European Americans as inferior in civilization and morality. On a regular basis, these blame-the-victim views have been resuscitated among the white elites and passed along to ordinary whites and others as a way of explaining the often difficult economic and other social conditions faced by African Americans.

The common accent on inferior family and personal values among black Americans got a major boost in a 1960s government report called *The Negro Family*, which focused on social pathologies in black communities. Social scientist and later U.S. senator Daniel Patrick Moynihan there argued that "the deterioration of the fabric of Negro society" was mainly because of black family problems, and he emphasized what he called the "tangle of pathology" and crumbling social relations he saw in many black communities.[77]

Since this famous Moynihan report, many leading magazines and scholarly journals have periodically published articles accenting a strong version of this white-framed perspective on what some have called the "black underclass." This perspective accents the allegedly deficient morality and lifestyle of many black Americans. For example, an article in the *Chronicle of Higher Education* surveyed research on the black poor and underclass, noting that

> the lives of the ghetto poor are marked by a dense fabric of what experts call "social pathologies"—teenage pregnancies, out-of-wedlock births, single-parent families, poor educational achievement, chronic unemployment, welfare dependency, drug abuse, and crime—that, taken separately or together, seem impervious to change.[78]

To the present day, similar reports and stories designed to explain black problems in cultural terms regularly appear in the local and national mass media, as well as in an array of books on "what is wrong with black America."

Indeed, influential books by a few relatively conservative African Americans—such as *Enough* (2007) by media commentator Juan Williams and *Come On People* (2007) by comedian Bill Cosby and psychiatrist Alvin Poussaint—have accented these perennial problems of impoverishment in many black communities and blamed them centrally on internal cultural issues. They call on poor black Americans to pick themselves up by their bootstraps and break out of these impoverished conditions. While these authors are operating from a sympathetic perspective and within the larger black community, even they adopt significant aspects of the old *white* racial framing of poor African Americans.[79] Conservative analysts, white or black, generally blame the victims for their plight, but usually without dealing in depth with the systemic racism that is much more central to explaining well the difficult economic and family conditions faced by these impoverished Americans. They do not examine systematically the individual and institutional *discrimination* still faced by these and other black Americans in employment, housing, and numerous other societal arenas—discrimination that usually sets up prohibitive barriers to significant socioeconomic mobility. Clearly, too, they do not provide a thorough analysis of the aggressive government actions necessary to eradicate such structural racial barriers, as well as to compensate those Americans of color whose recent and distant ancestors were massively prevented by centuries of slavery and Jim Crow segregation from passing along significant socioeconomic resources to their descendants.

Much underclass theorizing and morals preaching by whites barely disguise the racist fears, assumptions, and biases about black bodies and lives long held by many whites. The legal scholar Anthony Farley has argued that poor black communities in cities are often seen by whites as "urban Bantustans" that export a type of deviant pleasure by displaying themselves as the negation of white middle-class culture. Many whites can thus feel superior as "virtuous republicans" because of the negative view they hold of black culture and communities. At the same time, however, some whites view these areas as dark seductive places where they can go for forbidden pleasures such as securing illegal drugs or prostitutes.[80]

Denying Racism, Asserting Innocence

Most whites at all class levels have long held a fairly rosy view of U.S. history. Today, as in the past, there is a strong impulse to break the historical linkage between the genocidal and enslaving past and the conditions faced by Americans of color today. An important aspect of the contemporary white frame buttressing systemic racism is the omnipresent notion of white innocence and virtue. Today, many whites deny the seriousness of antiblack racism in the past and present history of this country. In interviews with powerful members of the white elite, my colleagues and I have found that many view racism as having declined greatly in importance. For that reason they often argue that certain types of government action, such as affirmative action programs, are no longer needed as remedies for racial discrimination.[81] Optimistic views of an allegedly sharp decline in U.S. racism are also common among ordinary whites. For example, research involving white Californians has shown that their constructions of racial realities "are not a rational, unbiased reflection of available evidence, but instead reflect strong motivations to *deny* the impact of racism."[82] The whites in this study minimized racism—except under special conditions where their defensive motivations were reduced in an experiment, in which case they were more likely to see contemporary racism as a problem.

White defensiveness about racism is seen today in numerous assertions that the United States is a "post-racial" society. These assertions have become commonplace since Barack Obama was elected president. Recall that after his initial election the prominent business newspaper the *Wall Street Journal* editorialized that a "man of mixed race" being president was a "tribute to American opportunity, and it is something that has never happened in another Western democracy—notwithstanding European condescension about 'racist' America." After this assertion of U.S. moral superiority, this white-framed piece continued: "One promise of his victory is that perhaps we can put to rest the myth of racism as a barrier to achievement."[83] Recall too comments made by presidential candidate Bob Dole about contemporary white innocence and lack of responsibility (p. 14). Like many whites, Dole tried to break the connection between the racial past and present, in his temporizing on the question of compensatory **reparations** for damages inflicted by whites during the slavery and Jim Crow eras. Powerful whites like Dole still control a majority of major organizations and institutions today, which is one key reason that this common framing of contemporary white innocence and lack of remedial responsibility in regard to past racial discrimination remains so strong.

A key factor in how the white racial frame operates today involves what Hernán Vera and I term whites' "social alexithymia," that is, the *inability* of a great many whites to understand where African Americans and other Americans of color are coming from and what their racialized experiences are like. This social alexithymia involves a significant lack of cross-racial empathy and understanding. Recently, some psychologists interviewed white college students and found significant variation in their awareness of the reality of white racism and in their affective, social, and cognitive responses to it. Significantly, and in spite of this variation, *most* students "experienced some level of distortion and denial of race, racism, or White privilege. In other words, students who demonstrated higher levels of racial awareness also expressed some distortion and/or denial of racism in the interviews."[84] This finding is unsurprising given the intensity and extent of most whites' early and continuing socialization in U.S. society's dominant racial frame. Indeed, only one of these white students was strongly antiracist and empathetic in regard to racism faced by black Americans. She was isolated on her historically white campus because she could not connect with most whites, who had at best shallow understandings of racism.

As leading anthropologist Jane Hill suggests, the commonplace lack of white empathy often entails a line of mindful reasoning about white innocence something like this:

> I am a good and normal mainstream sort of White person. I am not a racist, because racists are bad and marginal people. Therefore, if you understood my words to be racist, you must be mistaken. I may have used language that would be racist in the mouth of a racist person, but if I did so, I was joking. If you understood my meaning to be racist, not only do you insult me, but you lack a sense of humor, and you are oversensitive.[85]

Hill adds that this "reasoning makes the speaker the sole authority" over what her or his racist commentaries mean. Operating out of the often arrogant pro-white center of the white racial frame, many whites are today unwilling even to listen to the views of those Americans regularly targeted by white racism—even to their views about the reality, character, harm, and pain of that everyday mistreatment. Because of their dominance, whites generally get to be the final judges of what gets to be successfully called out as "racism."

Sincere Fictions: Romanticizing the Past

Associated with a rosy view of U.S. society and the assertion of white innocence is a romanticizing of the racist past. This romanticizing can be seen in the long tradition of Hollywood movies dealing with U.S. history. Only rarely has a mainstream movie dealt honestly with slavery or Jim Crow segregation, and then almost never with much depth or concern for the authentic perspective of Americans of color. Nonetheless, Hollywood movies dealing with racial matters have evolved in a more positive direction since the early 1900s. In the famous 1915 movie *The Birth of a Nation*, the pioneering film-maker D. W. Griffith used cinematic advances to spread a viciously racist, Klan-inspired image of black southerners during the Reconstruction period. In this epic white-supremacist movie, black Americans are portrayed as savages, corrupt legislators, and uneducated officials. In contrast, white southerners are shown as gracious, brave, and honest. White virtue is generally celebrated. There is no hint that in the Civil War unvirtuous white southerners were fighting for one of history's most oppressive systems. If we move to the 1930s–1950s era, we observe more racist images of black Americans in classic white-supremacist movies such as some Shirley Temple movies (for example, *The Littlest Rebel*) and *Gone with the Wind*, the latter still periodically reissued and still treasured by a great many people around the globe. The images of black Americans therein are not as vicious as in *The Birth of a Nation*, but they include highly stereotyped black figures such as a "mammy" and obsequious enslaved servants. Most whites are still gallant, gracious, or brave figures, and there is no hint of something being wrong with a society grounded in a bloody slavery system. Again we see the **sincere fictions** of the virtuous white self. *Gone with the Wind* is only one of many such white-supremacist portraits. Between the 1920s and the 1940s more than 75 films portrayed the Old South favorably and presented slavery as unproblematic and/or mostly benevolent. By the 1930s almost all the national mass media's accounts touching on the history of U.S. racism were regularly romanticized and sanitized.[86]

Other movies made since the early decades of the twentieth century have often portrayed Africans as savages and whites as saviors, such as in the old Tarzan movies still shown across the globe. The same is true for old cowboy-and-Indian movies, with indigenous Americans therein usually portrayed as savages. Today on television and in documentaries, a "wild

Africa" or "untamed" image is frequently portrayed by media producers as they accent Africa's distinctive animals and savannahs much more than its complex and critical history or diverse and creative peoples.

More recent Hollywood movies dealing with U.S. racial history, such as *Glory* (1989) and *Amistad* (1997), have portrayed black Americans in a substantially less stereotyped and more humane light. While these more recent movies touching on racial issues have sometimes presented a white person as villainous, such images are usually more than balanced by those of whites who are honorable or heroic. In recent mainstream films we mostly see positive stereotypes of whites—as good, civilized, and the central heroes even in stories that are mostly about black people. As Hernán Vera and Andrew Gordon put it

> The portrayal of whites in *Birth of a Nation* is almost identical to their portrayal in *Glory* and in *Amistad*. What we have found in our analysis is a persistence across time in representations of the ideal white American self, which is constructed as powerful, brave, cordial, kind, firm, good-looking, and generous: a natural-born leader.[87]

In these and even more recent movies like *Gran Torino* (2008), *The Blind Side* (2009), and *Django Unchained* (2012), which do offer a more human and less stereotyped portrait of Americans of color, there is no serious indication that the broader white-controlled society has long been deeply grounded in pervasive and institutionalized racism. A thorough and unromanticized movie on the systemic character, deeper sociopolitical significance, and human destruction of slavery, Jim Crow segregation, or contemporary racism has yet to be made by the mainstream movie studios.

In recent years numerous writers, journalists, and politicians have written accounts of U.S. history designed to preserve the white sense of innocence and of inculpability for the genocide, slavery, and segregation so central to that history. In a best-selling book one conservative journalist has argued not only that antiblack racism has come to an end but also that the historical background of white oppression of black Americans has been misperceived. In his view the enslavement of black Americans had good features such as bringing Africans to real "civilization."[88] Numerous conservative politicians have articulated ideas like these, usually again to assert white innocence or virtuousness. For example, in 2013 a prominent white Republican in the Arkansas House of Representatives self-published a book in which he insisted that slavery was "a blessing" for African Americans because they were brought into the "greatest nation ever established."[89] White defenders of black enslavement have articulated this whitewashed view from the earliest days of colonialism. Such arguments do not take seriously the extraordinarily barbaric character of

Atlantic-basin slavery and its devastating slave trade. There is no serious discussion of the many millions who died in the mostly European-controlled slave trade, nor of the severe destruction of African societies by that trade and later European imperialism, nor of the continuing negative impact of this historical white plundering of Africa's human resources and natural resources on *contemporary* African development (see Chapter 2, pp. 35–46).

Indeed, the extreme oppressiveness of U.S. slavery has not been taken seriously by a great many whites, in the past or the present. Not surprisingly perhaps, brochures circulated by numerous local and state government officials, especially in the South, still provide a distorted view of U.S. history. One South Carolina brochure provided to visitors at the state's travel centers has a two-page history of the state from the 1500s to the present, with not one mention of slaves or slavery being there. Yet slavery was central to that state's economy for a very long period. A research study in North Carolina examined the way that slavery has been portrayed at 20 slave plantations that are now tourist sites. Seven of the plantation websites do not note the presence of slavery, and only three make serious efforts to present the oppressed experiences of those enslaved. The other 17 sites accent such things as house furnishings and the lives of the white families. Some play down the brutality of slavery and project images of "happy slaves." The lead researcher, Derek Alderman, accents the point that "plantations were not just about their white owners. As we come to terms with the legacy of racism in the United States, we have to recognize … that there was brutality that happened in the Old South."[90]

A Whitewashed Worldview

Seen comprehensively, all the mental images, prejudiced attitudes, stereotypes, sincere fictions, emotions, racist explanations, and rationalizations that link to systemic racism make up a white racial frame, a racist worldview, one deeply imbedded in the dominant U.S. culture and institutions. The system of racism is not something that only affects Americans of color, for it is central to the lives of white Americans as well. It determines how whites think about themselves, their ideals, and their country.

We saw earlier how European immigrants to the U.S. in the early 1900s came to accept this worldview and its assumption that being "American" meant being white. Today the word "American" still frequently means "white"—at least for a great many white Americans, and apparently for many others in the U.S. and across the globe. One can pick up major magazines or read major news websites and find "American" or "Americans" commonly used in a way that clearly references or accents *white* Americans. Take this sentence from a news writer in a Florida newspaper: "The American Public isn't giving government or police officers the blind trust it once did."[91] Unmistakably, "American" here means "white American," for a majority of black Americans (and probably of other Americans of color) have never blindly trusted the police.

One social science analysis examined all articles in 65 major English-language newspapers for a six-month period and estimated that there were thousands of references to "black Americans" or "African Americans" in the articles. However, in the same newspapers there were only 46 mentions of "white Americans." In almost every case these mentions by newspaper writers occurred in connection with "black Americans," "blacks," or "African Americans." A similar pattern was found for major magazines. Not once was the term "white Americans" used alone in an article; if used, it was always used in relation to another racial category. The same study examined how congressional candidates were described in news articles in the two weeks prior to a November election. In every case white congressional candidates were *not* described as "white," but black congressional candidates were always noted as being "black."[92] In the United States, blackness is usually salient and noted, while whiteness generally goes unmentioned, except when reference is specifically made to white connections to other racial groups.

Being American still means, in the minds of many, including editors and writers in the mainstream media, being white. This need not be conscious. For centuries most whites have probably not seen the routines of their everyday lives as framed in white. "Race" is often not visible when one is at the top of the racial hierarchy. Today, major social institutions, those originally created by whites centuries ago, are still dominated by whites. Yet from the white standpoint they are not white, just *normal* and *customary*. They are not seen for what they actually are—white-dominated institutions reflecting in many of their aspects the history, privileges, norms, values, and interests of white Americans. Thus, when whites operate in these customary institutional arrangements, they need not think in overtly racist terms. However, when whites move into settings where they interact with people of color, in the United States or elsewhere, they usually foreground their whiteness, whether consciously or unconsciously.

The sense of white entitlement is often passed along in relatively subtle ways. Edward Ball, a descendant of one of South Carolina's prominent slaveholding families, has underscored the sense of privilege and superiority passed along from old slave plantation days to many whites today. He notes that

> inwardly the plantations lived on. In childhood, I remember feeling an intangible sense of worth that might be linked to the old days. Part of the feeling came from the normal encouragements of parents who wanted their children to rise, an equal part came from

an awareness that long ago our family had lived like lords, and that world could still be divided into the pedigreed and the rootless.[93]

Fear of a Multiracial Future

Recall the influential racist writers who in the 1910s and 1920s feared that whites were becoming a minority (p. 79). Today, many white media analysts, other commentators, and conservative political officials similarly view "Western civilization" as under threat from groups that are not white or European. Racist framing involves more than just rationalizing racial oppression, for it often represents an emotional and defensive response, a fear of losing power. In recent years many influential advocates of white superiority have directed their attacks at the values or cultures of new immigrants of color coming to the United States, such as those from Mexico, as well as at black Americans. In one interview study we did, numerous elite white men expressed some fear of the growth of Americans of color in the United States, sometimes seeing Western civilization as under great threat.[94]

We observe examples of this fear among contemporary politicians, commentators, and intellectuals. For example, in his frequent speeches, articles, and books, Patrick Buchanan, one-time candidate for the Republican presidential nomination, has argued that "our Judeo-Christian values are going to be preserved and our Western heritage is going to be handed down to future generations and not dumped on some landfill called multiculturalism."[95] Again we see the linkage between Christian religion and a strong sense of European supremacy. We also see a concern for the reproduction of the white-dominated system from current to future generations. In addition, Buchanan told one interviewer that

> if we had to take a million immigrants in, say, Zulus next year or Englishmen, and put them in Virginia, what group would be easier to assimilate and would cause less problems for the people of Virginia? There is nothing wrong with us sitting down and arguing that issue that we are a European country, [an] English-speaking country.[96]

The Zulus, who are Africans, seem to represent in his white framing the specter of savage hordes who would not assimilate well into the country. Ironically, Africans have been in the country longer than Buchanan's Irish ancestors, and Virginia has been home to a great many African Americans for nearly four centuries. During the 2008 presidential election, Buchanan continued this accent on the centrality of whiteness with an article called "A Brief for Whitey," in which he adopted a strong version of the old white-racist frame, one again asserting the notion that African Americans should be grateful for having been enslaved and Christianized by Europeans. He insistently criticized then-Senator Barack Obama in a stereotyped way—for example, by only calling him "Barack," the traditional segregationists' way of naming black Americans without using last names. Buchanan agreed with Obama on the need for a new national conversation on race, but one that gives supposedly "silent" white Americans "a voice." Considering that whites have long controlled most major media outlets and other means of national communication, this is an uninformed and unreflective perspective on contemporary U.S. society.[97]

Similarly, *Forbes* editor Peter Brimelow lays out white fears for Western civilization in a book, *Alien Nation*. For him, the "American nation has always had a specific ethnic core. And that core has been white." Back in the 1950s, most Americans "looked like me. That is, they were of European stock. And in those days, they had another name for this thing dismissed so contemptuously as 'the racial hegemony of white Americans.' They called it 'America.'"[98] An immigrant from Britain himself, Brimelow is a founder of a far-right Internet website that has pressed to sharply reduce contemporary immigration, a website that has also published openly racist analyses. In addition, influential Harvard professor Samuel Huntington once argued that "[i]f multiculturalism prevails and if the consensus on liberal democracy disintegrates, the United States could join the Soviet Union on the ash heap of history."[99] Today, great concern for white Western cultural supremacy is periodically evident in the views of numerous white editors, scholars, and politicians.

Conclusion

The systemic racism that is still part of the base of U.S. society is interwoven with a strong racial framing that has been partially reworked at various points in U.S. history, but which has remained a well-institutionalized set of emotion-laden attitudes, concepts, images, and narratives defending the subordination to whites of black Americans and other Americans of color. Until the late 1940s, U.S. commitment to a white-supremacist view was proud, openly held, and very insistent. Most whites in the U.S. and Europe, led by elites, took pride in forthrightly professing racist perspectives on others and racist rationalizations for imperialistic adventures. Brutal discrimination and overt exploitation were routinely implemented. Whites' global domination was "seen as proof of white racial superiority."[100]

Beginning in the 1940s, however, open expression of a white-supremacist perspective was made difficult by a growing U.S. awareness of actions of the racist regime in Nazi Germany. By the 1950s and 1960s civil rights protests against U.S. racism—with their counter-framing of real freedom and justice—and the U.S. struggle with the (former) Soviet Union made the open expression of a strong white-supremacist ideology less acceptable, at least in public. The dominant racist framing changed slowly to reflect these conditions, with a renewed if often rhetorical accent on equality of opportunity, and there was more white support for moderate government programs to break down certain segregated institutions (see Chapter 4, p. 104). Still, many important aspects of the old white racial frame, sometimes dressed up in a new guise, have persisted to the present day. From the beginning, the age-old idea of the superiority of white (Western) culture and institutions has been basic in the dominant frame that rationalizes continuing racial discrimination and related oppression.

Control over a society's ideas and discourse includes control over its central conceptual metaphors. Powerful whites usually decide what the dominant images and metaphors are, and thus what is or is not seen as true. Metaphors are integral to such conceptual frameworks.[101] For some time now, elite whites and most other whites have viewed the last few centuries of societal development in terms of a broad imagery equating the engine of "human progress" with Western civilization. We hear phrases like "Western civilization is an engine generating great progress for the world" or "Africans have only seen advancement because of contacts with Western civilization." Western imperialism's bringing of "civilization" or "democracy" to other peoples is made to appear as an engine of great progress. However, this equating of "progress" with European civilization conceals the devastating consequences of European and U.S. imperialism and colonialism. Moreover, when whites speak of Western civilization as equivalent to great human progress, they are talking about the creation of white-dominated societal systems that do not take into serious consideration the interests and views of the indigenous, enslaved, and exploited peoples of color whose resources and labor have often been ripped from them, whose societies have been harmed or destroyed, and whose lives have been cut short.

4
Contemporary Racial Framing
White Americans

Periodically, researchers have found a strong association in some white minds of ape images with images of black Americans. In one social science study, white and other nonblack college students who were exposed to black faces were quicker in recognizing hazy drawings of apes than those not exposed to black faces. Another study discovered that whites subliminally primed with ape images later paid more attention to black faces than to white faces, while those not primed paid more attention to white faces. Even more dramatic was the finding that white students' blacks-as-apes mental connections, primed by ape-related words, tended to shape their willingness to accept more police violence against a black criminal suspect than against a similar white suspect when these students were shown videos of police violence. Images of black Americans as ape-like or somehow ape-linked date back to the seventeenth and eighteenth centuries, including as we saw in an earlier chapter (p. 63) back to Thomas Jefferson. Such ape imagery seems to be yet another way of symbolizing black Americans as inferior, animalistic, or threatening to whites.[1]

For most whites and many other nonblack Americans, specific antiblack views are part of a broader racial framing of society. As we have seen, this dominant white-created framing of society includes racial stereotypes, images, emotions, interpretations, and other important elements that legitimate racial discrimination. The elements of this broad framing have changed in some important ways over the centuries, but today many elements bear a significant similarity to those of earlier eras. This pervasive, elite-fostered framing provides a racialized overview of our social worlds. It organizes and makes coherent the racial views of elite and ordinary whites, buttresses white power and privilege, and generates discriminatory practices.

Persisting antiblack attitudes, images, and emotions represent much more than a matter of a few scattered bigots; they are the pervasive and continuing legacy of the material exploitation and racist framing that emerged with slavery and legal segregation. The "everydayness" of contemporary racist framing among whites means that it operates in

101

many situations of intergroup contact and regularly gets translated into alienated racial relations—that is, into relationships of white-on-black discrimination. Thus, we see yet another important aspect of the societal reproduction and transmission of the centuries-old racist system. The perpetuation of systemic racism requires an inter-temporal reproducing not only of racist institutions and structures but also of its rationalizing racial frame.

Racial Prejudice and Stereotyping: Dimensions of the White Frame

Too often the realities of individual stereotyping and prejudice have been disconnected from the larger racial framing and from widespread discriminatory practices. Stereotyping and prejudice are part of a much larger social scaffolding. Antiblack stereotyping and prejudice are part of an expansive racial framing and are rooted in the everyday defense of white power and privilege. As Herbert Blumer put it, prejudice is "rooted in a sense of group position."[2] Racial prejudice has been defined as antipathy toward a racial other based on a faulty generalization. Such prejudice can be directed toward a group as a whole, or toward an individual as a member of that group. Typically, racial prejudice has an emotional and a belief dimension. It usually includes a negative feeling about a racial out-group as well as a negative belief. The belief aspect is often termed a "stereotype." As false or exaggerated generalizations, stereotypes commonly serve as rationalizers of discriminatory behavior.[3]

Today racist thinking and feeling attach great significance to physical characteristics such as skin color, which remains a badge of oppression for black Americans and many other Americans of color. This persistence is an example of the legacy of the highly oppressive past, of the marks and burdens of a "slavery unwilling to die." While many whites now reject, at least publicly or on a conscious level, a blatantly biologized racism, they still hold without misgiving many of the negative conceptions and images of black men and women that have been long associated with a biologized racism accenting certain "inferior races" and "superior races." Racist attitudes tend to distort the targeted group's origins, physical appearance, values, or culture. In the case of white views of black Americans, general principles and notions from the broad racial framing get imbedded in specific racist attitudes and stereotypes. In regard to ideas about group origin, for example, during the first two centuries of slave importation whites regarded Africans and African Americans as foreign, uncivilized, and unchristian. While some aspects of this older framing have disappeared, other aspects can currently be found in a variety of white views and images that center on the alleged dangers of black men. Today, they are often framed by whites as deviant, dangerous, or violent. In regard to appearance, black men and women are still thought to have a distinctive and, for a great many whites, undesirable or ugly appearance. They are also often stereotyped and imaged as lazy, criminal, or immoral.

Antiblack attitudes and images are revealed and reproduced constantly in the everyday discourse, commentaries, and writings of whites (and often other nonblacks) at all class levels. Framing black Americans in negative terms and framing whites in positive terms are perspectives shaped by elite indoctrination, such as through the media, but they also constitute the way a majority of ordinary whites regularly communicate with each other about racial matters. These racist views have been perpetuated over the generations by means of everyday communication. Racist attitudes and images are constantly available to virtually all whites, including the very young, by means of presentations in daily discourse, as well as in the media, through the writings of intellectuals, and in the speeches of politicians and business leaders. Such attitudes and images are adapted and used as the social situation warrants, and they vary in expression or impact depending on the situation and the persons involved. Over centuries now, these racially framed views have had a severely negative impact on their human targets (see Chapter 7, pp. 216–228). Racist ways of thinking and feeling can be conscious and directly stimulative of discriminatory action, or they can be unconscious and implicit in that damaging action. Indeed, most racial stereotyping and prejudice not only portray the racial others negatively but also imbed a learned predisposition to act in a negative way toward the racialized others.

Racist Images and Attitudes: The Recent Past and the Present

Historical data on white images of and attitudes toward black Americans suggest that for centuries the overwhelming majority of whites have been openly and unapologetically racist. While there were no national opinion surveys before the 1930s, we can infer strongly antiblack attitudes from the omnipresent and unreservedly racist letters, speeches, actions, jokes, popular entertainments, and organizations of the slavery and legal segregation eras.

For example, in the decades before the Civil War there was an increase in popularly expressed racism, including racist images, attitudes, and invectives. One place this can be seen is in the growing popularity, especially among white workers, of whites-in-blackface minstrel shows. In front of large crowds, composed mostly of white working-class men, white performers made up in blackface did musical numbers and other comedy skits on stage. Extreme caricatures and mimicking of black Americans were centerpieces of these shows, which featured a vocabulary of racist epithets (such as "coon," "nigger," and "buck"), a mocking of black English speakers, and a portrayal of fantasies and fictions held in white heads (for example, the white-male fantasy of the oversexed black woman).

By presenting black people in very negative terms, the virtues of whites and whiteness were highlighted. Whites were generally seen as smart, courageous, and civilized, while blacks were presented as dumb, cowardly, deviant, oversexed, and uncivilized. The shows were very popular with white workers, including new European immigrants then seeking to be accepted as "white." The shows were eagerly attended by members of the elite, including presidents John Tyler and Abraham Lincoln, as well as novelists like Mark Twain. These highly racialized public entertainments continued well into the 1900s as a major form of mass entertainment.[4]

The Recent Past

National opinion surveys in the 1930s showed strong white support for overtly racist and segregationist views. A late 1930s Roper poll reported that eight in ten respondents thought that blacks should be kept out of white residential areas. In the late 1940s a Gallup poll found that 43 percent of those polled thought there should be racially segregated trains and buses. The majority opposed whites and blacks living and working together in the armed forces. (Ironically, this strong opposition was expressed just before President Harry Truman dramatically desegregated the U.S. armed forces.) A 1944 opinion survey found that half of the respondents thought "white people should have the first chance at any kind of job." Just under half thought restaurants should not serve both blacks and whites, and a similar proportion said they would not like having a black nurse in a hospital.[5] These national surveys probably included some Americans of color—these poll data are not reported by racial group—so it is likely that an even larger proportion of whites than of the total sample supported enforced racial segregation in restaurants, hospitals, housing, workplaces, and the armed forces.

By the 1960s publicly expressed support for legal segregation was waning, although whites' negative views of blacks were still strong. In a 1963 national Harris poll a majority of whites admitted to a pollster that they agreed with negative statements about black Americans: they "tend to have less ambition," "smell different," and "have looser morals." Four in ten thought that blacks "have less native intelligence," and more than one-third thought that they "breed crime." In the 1960s, the era when some older white leaders today received early racial socialization, a majority of whites still indicated quite openly that they held blatantly racist prejudices and stereotypes. Nonetheless, publicly expressed attitudes toward equal opportunity and public desegregation—at least in principle—were changing, for 57 percent of the white respondents said they approved of a federal voting rights law, and 62 percent said they approved of a fair employment practices law. Still, according to the 1963 national survey white attitudes about personal contacts with blacks were often negative. Half said they would object to a black family moving next door, and 84 percent were opposed to a close friend or relative marrying a black person.[6]

White Racial Framing Today

In recent decades much has been made of the reported reduction among whites of certain racist attitudes. Some longitudinal data show that whites have become less likely to give openly racist answers to pollsters and survey researchers than in earlier decades. While a 1942 survey had found that only 47 percent of whites thought blacks were "as intelligent as white people," that proportion increased to 77 percent by 1968. In recent decades, thus, many journalists and other analysts have taken such poll findings to mean that a majority of the white population is today no longer significantly racist in attitudes, opinions, and images of black Americans. They frequently argue the U.S. is now a "post-racial society," or that there is an "end to racism." Such notions are badly mistaken, and often naive or disingenuous. A significant decrease in overtly expressed segregationist or other blatantly racist attitudes does not necessarily mean that most whites are no longer substantially racist in some or much of their thinking about or imaging of black Americans and other Americans of color.[7]

One review of the social science literature on whites' racial views and attitudes found that opinion surveys of whites indicate that most publicly support, when given abstract questions, equality of opportunity and equality of treatment and oppose racial discrimination. However, at the same time, the majority do not believe there is major and widespread racial discrimination across this society, and they also do not believe that governments should actively intervene to secure further racial equality. Drawing on this literature review, Lincoln Quillian suggests that most contemporary whites, like earlier whites, reconcile the continuing reality of racial inequality with their beliefs about little discrimination by blaming people of color for their lack of effort. Thus, "even among persons who hold a sincere belief in race blindness, images and depictions of members of racial groups learned beginning in childhood are influential in their thinking."[8] We observe much other evidence for this conclusion throughout this book.

Responses to opinion surveys on racial matters can often be superficial and misleading. Typical surveys involve very brief questions and answers, and these are also seriously limited by the fact that many people give pollsters socially desirable answers, which often disguise their true views. Assessed from this perspective, the apparent decrease in certain antiblack images, prejudices, and stereotypes among whites from the 1930s to the present likely reflects to a significant degree increased concern for social acceptability.[9] Clearly, it is less socially acceptable to publicly avow strong racist attitudes today, so many whites reserve many of their more blatantly racist comments for the private spheres of home, locker-room, club, or bar. Researchers who probe more deeply into the white mindset have found that indirect and subtle research measures (as well as in-depth interviewing) often reveal that antiblack views and other aspects of the old white racial frame are still very common among whites.[10]

For instance, research on white students at three major college campuses found racial attitudes expressed on short-answer survey items were often different from those expressed in response to similar interview questions requiring more detailed responses. On one brief survey item, for example, 80 percent of 451 white college students approved of marriages between blacks and whites. When a smaller group of comparable students were interviewed in depth this figure dropped to about one-third. Given time to explain, the majority expressed reservations about intermarriage. A similar pattern was found for a question about affirmative action. Numerous whites used a variety of hedging phrases (for instance, "I agree and disagree"), often apparently to downplay racist views. In-depth interviews indicated that a majority held significantly negative racial attitudes on issues like intermarriage.[11]

In opinion polls a majority of whites now appear, like these students, to be unopposed to interracial marriages on brief survey questions. However, when allowed more time to develop their views, they too frequently reveal significant hedging or outright resistance to actual intermarriage within their families. In a pathbreaking study by Brittany Slatton of the views of 134 white men, one well-educated respondent recently commented in detail on a questionnaire that, while he worked with black men and women, he was negative in his view of intermarriage: "There are many areas in which I am pleased to interact with persons of any ethnicity, but marriage is not one of them. I don't like many aspects of black culture, music, family structure, etc. Not necessarily wrong, just not for me. Some aspects of black culture are inferior."[12] In such commonplace white views, we observe a racial framing of black families and "black culture," much of it likely drawn from stereotyped depictions of black Americans in the mainstream media. Such racialized framing prevents whites like this respondent from an accurate understanding of the character and situations of black families and communities—again a type of social alexithymia (see p. 92).

Social psychologists have found that, when given a test of subtle or unconscious racial stereotyping such as the implicit association test, most whites quickly associate black faces (photos) with *negative* words and traits (for instance, with evil character traits or failure). Most whites have more difficulty in linking black faces to pleasant words and positive traits than they do for white faces. Analyses of thousands of such facial-response tests at psychology websites have shown that the overwhelming majority of whites signal an antiblack, pro-white bias in such face-reaction tests. Moreover, in research projects where whites have been shown black faces, even for milliseconds, key areas of their brains that respond to *perceived threats* have tended to light up automatically under brain scans. In these studies the more racial stereotyping that white subjects revealed on paper-and-pencil psychological tests, the greater their brains' threat responses were when they were shown black facial photos.[13] This type of research suggests that black photos and visages generate not only cognitive stereotyping in minds but also racialized emotions.

In another study using the implicit association test, researchers found that young white children showed a pro-white and antiblack bias in connecting white and black faces to good or bad words, but also that their self-reported racial attitudes showed a similar overt racial bias. But older white children and adults who were tested revealed a comparable implicit racial bias in matching white and black faces to good or bad words, yet showed less (or no) racial stereotyping on more overt psychological tests.[14]

Other contemporary research on white thought and behavior also shows the persistence of strong white-racist attitudes about black Americans and other Americans of color. One 2012 Associated Press national survey found that just over half of the respondents admitted they held antiblack views, an increase over the previous four years. This proportion would doubtless have been higher if only whites had been included in the survey.[15] Moreover, in numerous studies of white racial views that I and my colleagues have done, we have found that whites often engage in racist commentaries and other performances, especially in backstage settings where only other whites, such as friends and relatives, are present. In one major study 626 white students at numerous colleges and universities kept journals for a few weeks about racial events, discussions, and performances they encountered. They recorded a large number, nearly 7,000 instances, of clearly racist events. Many of these were in backstage settings with white relatives or acquaintances, but others were in settings with a racially diverse group of people present. The diaries strongly indicate that racist commentaries, joking, and actions are commonplace among younger, better-educated whites. African Americans appear in a substantial majority of the racist commentaries, jokes, and performances reported by students in various regions. Other racial groups, such as Native Americans, Latinos, and Asian Americans, are periodically targeted, but verbal and other attacks on them make up a minority of the events recorded.[16]

Antiblack Attitudes and Images: Key Examples

The specific attitudes that whites hold toward themselves and toward black Americans often take the form of, on the one hand, a model of white virtue, merit, and superior morality and, on the other, an "antimodel" of black deficiency, pathology, and threat. Both are essential parts of the dominant white racial frame in this society. The positive model encompasses a range of sincere fictions about the white self, such as the images of white innocence and nobility discussed in Chapter 3 (pp. 91–94). The antimodel encompasses a range of images and attitudes, including the often inherited views of black men and women as lazy workers, criminals, dumb athletes, or welfare cheaters. An example of this overarching antimodel can be found in this comment by a well-educated white respondent in a recent online questionnaire study: "I find the 'black' race to be, in general, morally corrupt as well as culturally and intellectually defunct."[17] Not surprisingly, this antiblack framing not only causes much daily pain and harm to black Americans but also corrupts the minds and understandings of white Americans—and thus is very damaging to this society.

Attributions of Laziness

Specific negative representations of African Americans are critical parts of the contemporary racial framing. One particularly strong and age-old representation is that of black laziness. The old Protestant ethic, with its accent on individual acquisitiveness, was important for early European colonists. Enslaved Africans who resisted in any way the very long hours of work imposed on them were often judged by this ethic to be "lazy," even though they did much of the hard work that lay behind growing white prosperity. Similar white attitudes about black laziness persisted during the system of Jim Crow segregation, although again a disproportionate amount of the hardest work in southern and border state economies was done by these maligned black workers.

Descending through decades of U.S. history, the racist image of lazy men and women is still commonplace today. One 1990s national survey asked whites to evaluate on a scale just how work-oriented blacks are. Only a small percentage, 16 percent, ranked blacks at the hardworking end; just under half put blacks at the lazy end of the spectrum. A more recent study at a western university found that black employees, especially black men, were viewed as "lazy, irresponsible, and not serious about work"—characteristics that negatively influence white employers' employment and hiring decisions. Other recent studies have found similar patterns.[18] Moreover, such views of the black work ethic are manifested in common white comments about lazy black welfare recipients. Notions of laziness are so strong as to overcome countering evidence. Researchers Lewis and Jhally had white subjects watch *The Cosby Show*, a popular television show from the 1980s and still seen in reruns. Whites generally liked the high-achieving black family (the Huxtables) portrayed on the show, yet many processed the images to fit with their pre-existing racist attitudes. Explicitly or implicitly viewing black

Americans as a lazy group, these whites continued to view black Americans as inferior, and thus saw the success of the Huxtables as evidence that any black person could succeed if he or she would just work harder.[19]

Some psychological research indicates that people with strong stereotypes of an out-group often attribute negative behavior by individual members of that out-group to alleged group characteristics ("That's the way they are"). In contrast, when they see positive actions or accomplishments by individuals in the out-group, they often attribute those to the uniqueness of the situation rather than group characteristics. They will argue in the latter case that the person is an exception to the group, that they had a special advantage or luck, that anyone in the situation could have done well, or that it took exceptional motivation and effort to overcome the inherent weaknesses of the person's group. For instance, comedian Bill Cosby and President Barack Obama are often viewed as "exceptions to their race." Many whites tend to view negative actions by individual black Americans as tied to the group, to its defective biology or culture, while positive achievements are frequently linked only to the individual or situational aspects of the case at hand—and not to the general values and perspectives, and efforts, of black communities.[20]

Images of Black Women

We can underscore here what scholars call *intersectionality*—in this case, the way in which racism plays out somewhat differently for key gender groups within the African American population. Consider the white-racist framing of African American women, who have been the targets of this framing for centuries. Reviewing U.S. history, Patricia Hill Collins has noted that "portraying African American women as stereotypical mammies, matriarchs, welfare recipients, and hot mommas has been essential to the political economy of domination fostering Black women's oppression."[21] One chronic image, long reproduced on the packaging of commercial products and in reissued movies like *Gone with the Wind*, is the Aunt Jemima image—that of the corpulent "mammy" borrowed from the racist past. In the dominant U.S. and European cultures images of black women are often negative, intense, and visual. For many decades highly stereotyped and caricatured negative images of black women (and men) were very common in popular art, ads, movies, television, and on postcards. Even today, "mammy" dolls and black female and male figurines with exaggerated physical features such as big lips can be found in antique shops in the United States. Racist dolls and figurines are popular with some whites. Indeed, they are still manufactured and can be found for sale in countries across the globe.[22]

In the aforementioned research involving mostly college-educated white men in many states, Slatton found that *80 percent* operated from a racist framing of black women, much of it focusing on negative images of their bodies or lifestyles. Like a substantial majority of her sample, this middle-class respondent in the Midwest was emotional in his highly stereotyped evaluation: "I think black women's features are too extreme; they are too dark, and they usually are much too large for my tastes. The black women I have know[n] are very aggressive and have terrible attitudes." Numerous interviewees used hostile framing for black women. They are variously described as "ghetto, loud, obnoxious"; having "disproportionate bodies, like some sort of mutants, stove pipe noses"; having a "bad attitude, nasty in-your-face, neck breaking"; or "being opposed to a soft femininity because it is 'weak.'"[23] In the frequently vicious stereotyping of these men, we observe a mix of negative images of black bodies and strategies for living in a racist society. Nowhere in Slatton's interviews was there a serious attempt to understand the contemporary conditions of racism that black women and men face.

A recurring white framing of black families is that of a large *welfare* family with a woman in charge. This is a popular example of the underclass imagery of black Americans we examined as part of the contemporary black framing propagated by some intellectuals (see Chapter 3, pp. 89–91). A 1990s CBS News/*New York Times* poll found that the majority of those questioned thought that most poor people were black and that most welfare recipients were black. (In both cases, majorities were not black at the time, and still are not today.) Moreover, recent research continues to show this stereotyping pattern, with the common face of mothers getting public assistance still being that of a woman of color. Media and other popular images of black women and other women of color cheating off government assistance remain commonplace.[24] Not surprisingly, thus, in the interview study by Slatton one college-educated white northerner recently asserted such negative views of black women, again drawing uncritically on racially framed images of welfare recipients:

> I see a large number of black women, young and old, simply unable and unwilling to form relationships with men that last more than a few months to a few years ... I do see it as a major contributor to a continuing "state welfare" lifestyle where they believe they are entitled to a monthly paycheck, and all the trimmings, so long as they keep churning out children ... actual fathers are unnecessary.[25]

Not only does he parrot old white-framed stereotypes about black women, families, and welfare, but next in his interview he takes it upon himself as a white man to give unsolicited advice to black Americans who have long been oppressed by whites. Again, we observe how central white arrogance about what is "reality" for Americans of color and about the white right to control and dominate is to the contemporary white framing.

In fact, the welfare reforms of the 1990s cut down sharply on the number of public assistance recipients, but did not alter the racist images of them. Thus, one study found that whites' negative views of black Americans still hinder their willingness to spend money even on the strict and limited government welfare programs we still have, and that whites' "welfare attitudes are as strongly racialized [today] … as they were a decade earlier."[26]

A major source of various welfare and poverty stereotypes is the mainstream media. Research has shown that network television and news magazines exaggerate greatly the black presence among the country's poor. Another common stereotype found in the media and elsewhere is that of black Americans not wanting to have traditional two-parent families. Many white commentators seem to assume that black adults have different family values from whites. However, in one survey hundreds of black adults were asked what their view of the ideal marriage partner was. These respondents preferred "well-educated, financially stable, monogamous, and affluent partners who are spiritual, religious, self-confident, and reliable." This listing is what a majority of white adults would probably list. The central difficulty for many black families lies not in their values but in the difficult economic and other social circumstances this racist society constantly creates for them.[27]

Black women face yet other serious forms of gendered racism—the double burden of suffering racist framing because they are both black *and* female. One example is the imaging of black women as "jungle bunnies." Since at least the 1600s, this white stereotype has accented black women's allegedly exotic sexuality. Researcher Diane Roberts has shown how white notions of blackness have frequently been loaded with sexuality. European books, beginning in the 1600s, portrayed black women and men naked and with exaggerated sexual organs. "The white world drew the black woman's body as excessively and flagrantly sexual, quite different from the emerging ideology of purity and modesty which defined the white woman's body."[28] This view has persisted over the centuries. Greatly influenced by and perpetuating such racist images, numerous white men during the slavery and Jim Crow eras sexually molested and/or raped black women. Today, much social science research continues to show that some white men still image and seek out black women as exotic sex objects. In this manner, gendered racism is regularly inscribed in the bodies of black women.[29]

Even the dominant societal preferences for female body type are racialized in a manner that is usually biased against black women. From the seventeenth to the twenty-first century not only white politicians and missionaries, but also those whites developing the sciences of medicine, biology, and ethnography and those developing the mainstream media have set typical whites' skin, hair, and body type as the traditional standards for aesthetic superiority. For centuries white men have been the standard for male handsomeness, as well as masculinity and manly virtue. White women—in recent decades, especially those who are fair-haired and relatively slender— have long been the standard for female beauty. Thus, whites have frequently viewed black women in terms that stereotype them as having "ugly" physical characteristics, including hair that is too "wooly" and or skin color that is too dark. Recently, a white female Louisiana state representative referred to a black female NAACP president as "buckwheat," an old white-racist term for black Americans that often accents "ugly" hair characteristics.[30] Not surprisingly, such negative images of black women create serious problems not only for women but also for young girls. As one young black woman put it in an interview: "I went through a long, long time thinking I was like the ugliest thing on the earth.... It's so hard to get a sense of self in this country, in this society, where ... every role of femininity looks like a Barbie doll."[31]

Even so, this dominant gendered–racist imagery regularly generates resistance by black Americans. Research by Adia Wingfield on black beauty-salon owners found that such businesses are places where *black beauty* is defined, honored, and enhanced, often in resistance to the dominant framing. While these are places where black hair is often straightened to conform to a certain white-framed image of good hair, since the 1960s "black is beautiful" movements, many shops have expanded hairstyling services to include more natural hair styles with African and Caribbean origins, such as braided cornrows, other braiding, afros, and dreadlocks. Adopting natural styles is viewed by many as openly rejecting white-oriented images of beauty or style.[32]

In contrast to this negative framing of black women by whites is the reality of black women's creativity and, as sociologist Kamesha Spates puts it, their subtle resistance and "coping mechanisms that act as protective barriers" against life's stresses. In her study of the *low* suicide rate of black women, Spates did interviews with black women of varying class levels. They often dealt with racism and other life stresses by accenting their family and community responsibilities, by drawing heavily on religious faith, and by a counter-framing that included a sense of blacks' resilience against racism and other barriers. Her respondents associated suicide with people who had racial or gender privilege, especially whites (and white men)—privilege that in their view weakened the latter's ability to deal well with certain difficult life conditions. Very rarely have white media commentators or researchers accented these important insights and *strengths* of black women, men, and communities.[33]

Images of Black Men

African American men represent another key example of race–gender intersectionality, and the white framing of them is riddled with an array of racist stereotypes, images, emotions, and narratives. For example, in recent interviews with pilots at major airlines, sociologist Louwanda Evans got this commentary on the discriminatory impact of white framing in the everyday lives of two senior black pilots:

> At the hotel, I can be standing there waiting for the van to take us to the airport and [white] passengers have come up and dropped their bags at my feet on more than one occasion. I was flying with a black captain and we were waiting in the lobby, in full uniform, and a white guy walked up to him and said, "Can you get my cab for me?" The captain looked at him and said, "The only thing we know how to do is fly airplanes." The man said, "I understand that, but can you get my cab for me?" He just couldn't get it through his mind that he was talking to a pilot.[34]

In this setting a white man acts out of his racially stereotyped framing. Ignoring the obvious uniforms of these airline pilots, he "sees" only black men and assumes they are black service workers ("skycaps") at his command. After being corrected, the white interlocutor still does not "get it." His assertive racist framing is firmly fixed in mind.

Another common white stereotype is that of the dangerous black man. This is a staple of much white thinking and imaging, including that of white leaders and intellectuals speaking or writing about the black poor. Many whites, including media commentators, seem to view the typical street criminal as a black man. During the first centuries of colonial development, whites constructed a view of enslaved men as dangerous "beasts," a stereotyped view that has rationalized much racial oppression over the centuries. The beast-like image was then, as now, put into words, but it was also held at a deeper, more visceral and emotional level. As with black women, the bodies of black men are culturally stigmatized and routinely trigger antiblack stereotypes and images in white minds—which, in turn, often generate defensive or other discriminatory actions.[35]

Members of the white elite not only play a key role in creating and maintaining the common racist framing, but also themselves operate out of stereotypes and images from that framing. Take the example of Dwight D. Eisenhower, a U.S. general who served as president during the 1950s. While President Eisenhower did not publicly advocate the inferiority of black Americans, he did speak in racially framed terms in private. Earl Warren, then chief justice of the Supreme Court, reported that Eisenhower told him at a 1954 dinner that white southerners opposed to school desegregation were "not bad people. All they are concerned about is to see that their sweet little girls are not required to sit in school alongside some big overgrown Negroes."[36] He referenced black boys. Then as now, white stereotyping of black boys and men often exaggerates their size or other physical characteristics. To describe ordinary school boys as "big overgrown Negroes" is reminiscent of the scary images of black men some white parents have used to discipline their children. Most strikingly, Eisenhower did not even mention the severe impact of the often violent white opposition to school desegregation on the lives of black boys and girls, and their parents.

Today, this image of black people (especially men) as especially dangerous and criminal remains an important part of the racist framing in many white minds, including those of the elite. In 2013 a group of civil rights organizations filed a judicial misconduct complaint against a federal appellate court judge for her comments to a Pennsylvania law school audience early that year. According to five college students and an attorney present at the talk, who gave signed affidavits, the judge is alleged to have said that "racial groups like African-Americans and Hispanics are predisposed to crime" and are "prone to commit acts of violence" more so than other groups.[37] In another example of such framing, William Bennett, a former U.S. Secretary of Education, asserted on a talk show that, "if you really wanted to reduce crime, you could—if that were your sole purpose—you could abort every black baby in this country and your crime rate would go down." Bennett then backed off, saying such actions would be "an impossibly ridiculous and morally reprehensible … but your crime rate would go down." Bennett insisted he only conjured up a hypothetical notion, but we observe again how *firmly* imbedded in white minds this connection between African Americans and crime remains.[38]

As a result of these common images of criminality, many whites (and other nonblack people) regularly have fearful reactions to a black man encountered on streets, in public transport, or in elevators. In interview studies, black men often report aversive reactions taken by whites when they are walking the streets of towns or cities. Many whites take special defensive precautions when a black man is near. The reality of being framed and targeted as a dangerous black man by nonblack Americans was emphasized by the president of the United States, Barack Obama, in comments to the press at the White House in July 2013. Responding to the not-guilty jury verdict for a man who killed an unarmed black teenager (Trayvon Martin) walking in a predominantly white neighborhood where his father lived, Obama underscored the life-long, painful black experience:

> When Trayvon Martin was first shot I said that this could have been my son. Another way of saying that is Trayvon Martin could

have been me 35 years ago. And when you think about why, in the African American community at least, there's a lot of pain around what happened here, I think it's important to recognize that the African American community is looking at this issue through a set of experiences and a history that doesn't go away. There are very few African American men in this country who haven't had the experience of being followed when they were shopping in a department store. That includes me. There are very few African American men who haven't had the experience of walking across the street and hearing the locks click on the doors of cars. That happens to me—at least before I was a senator. There are very few African Americans who haven't had the experience of getting on an elevator and a woman clutching her purse nervously and holding her breath until she had a chance to get off. That happens often.[39]

It is hard to imagine a leading white official making the point that Obama did. Likely for political reasons, he did not say enough about this white racism, but his commentary was pathbreaking, especially for a white population often in denial about this everyday racism.

Some conservative commentators have asserted that such white defensive actions are "rational" because of the high black crime rate.[40] These commentators, like many ordinary whites, seem to assume that the majority of criminals who attack whites are black. However, most violent crime affecting whites is carried out by *white* criminals, most typically white men. Yet most whites do not routinely take similar defensive precautions when they are in the presence of ordinary white men.

The emotionally freighted images of black men are often crafted in childhood. In the past and present, some white parents have threatened disobedient children with fearful images of black bogeymen. In an interview conducted by one of my students, a clerical worker described her mother's method of discipline:

> "The niggers would come in the night and steal us away and use us for their pleasure," that's what my mother told us. What an awful thing to do, don't you think, frightening little children like that.... She scared us to death. The first time I ever saw a colored person I just about had hysterics.[41]

This emotionally loaded language of the white racial framing becomes what psychologist Lev Vygotsky called *inner speech*, the mind's language in considering and relating to racial issues. Racist words learned as children can carry many complex understandings beyond their apparent meaning. Later on, such racialized language frequently triggers psychological linkages and understandings in minds, and thus can shape numerous discriminatory actions.[42]

Today, a major source of negative images of black men, as for black women, is the mainstream media. Many people watch local television news programs several nights a week. These programs, a major source of everyday information, often accent violent crimes. One study of many cities found that crime was the subject of one-third or more of local news programming. In addition, a study of local news in Los Angeles found that while violent crimes got extensive coverage, non-violent crimes such as fraud and embezzlement got little. News stories about violent crime mentioning a suspect also featured black suspects, usually men, in a much higher proportion than their arrest rate indicated would be accurate.[43]

Several other research studies have found similar patterns for other cities. One recent examination of news stories in Pittsburgh's newspapers and television media found that the largest block of reports on African American boys and men were about crime—36 percent of stories in the daily newspapers and 86 percent of stories in television newscasts. Quality-of-life issues involving black boys and men in such areas as the arts, education, employment, and leadership got much less attention. A follow-up Pew study found a similar pattern of local media accenting of crime stories, but also found another major category of sports stories. Neither study found there was adequate attention to black community issues beyond crime and sports. An associated online survey of hundreds of black residents found that almost all "expressed deep dissatisfaction with what they perceived to be the media's negative focus on African Americans in connection to crime and indicated that they want a change."[44]

Some communications researchers have examined Los Angeles television news and found that black residents were not only more likely to be portrayed as criminals, but also less likely to be portrayed as victims, than white residents. Black suspects were over-represented relative to actual arrest rates, while the opposite was true for whites. The researchers suggested that this media imagery likely influenced the way many whites viewed their own chances of being crime victims, as well as the way they might decide guilt if on juries in cases involving black defendants. In addition, a Los Angeles survey of 506 English-speaking respondents by Dixon found that a person's time spent viewing local news programs' over-representation of black criminals, as well as attention to crime news and trust of news, predicted well the person's likelihood of holding traditional racial stereotypes of black people as criminals. (This was true after controls were applied for neighborhood diversity and crime rates.) Those who paid the most attention to crime news were the most likely to be obsessed with local crime and give harsher culpability ratings to hypothetical black suspects as compared to hypothetical white suspects. The amount of television exposure was also found to be directly related to racially stereotyped images of black people as violent.[45]

The media "cultivation theory" argues that heavy exposure to television content about the social world tends to influence how people view the outside society, even if that outside world is not at all like the television programming. Exposure to television images of crime tends to increase white exaggeration of actual black crime involvement, thereby reinforcing pre-existing black criminality images from the old white-racist frame.[46] From his recent studies, Dixon has concluded that "News viewing may be part of a process that makes the construct or cognitive linkage between Blacks and criminality frequently activated and therefore chronically accessible."[47] In this manner television viewing—and, likely, similar viewing of Internet news and other websites—constantly reinforces antiblack stereotypes from the old white racial frame.

In addition, for centuries many white Americans have crafted images of black Americans, especially black men, as ape-like. This is a provocative way to symbolize them as threatening. Recall the research that found a strong association in white minds of ape images with black images, including the finding that ape–black stereotypes held by white college students shaped their willingness later on to accept police violence against a black suspect. In addition to the studies mentioned previously, another research study did a content analysis of hundreds of newspaper articles discussing death-eligible criminal defendants and found that words eliciting ape-like images in people's minds were more likely to have been used by newspaper writers for black than white defendants. Such animalistic imagery is part of the dominant white framing that likely helps to legitimate whites' targeting black Americans for much discrimination, including discriminatory policing.[48]

Negative media imagery has action consequences, as we just saw in the case of the aforesaid newspaper writers. Another striking example can be seen in public reports by whites of black men attacking them, when in fact *no* such attack took place. One major study has documented dozens of these false reports by whites in recent decades. Racial hoaxes continue to the present, often to cover up socially deviant actions by whites making such faked accusations.[49] In addition, in one experimental study researchers found that showing white, Asian, and Latino research subjects local crime news videos increased their punitiveness in regard to criminals—much more so when they were shown black perpetrators than when they were shown white perpetrators of crime. Another recent experimental study also found that exposing white subjects to news portrayals of white and black perpetrators of rape crimes resulted in more punitive judgments about black than white perpetrators.[50] Such harsh white predispositions may well affect various actions that whites and other nonblacks take in relation to black people while on the street, at the workplace, or as members of juries.

Images of Drugs and Deviance

Many whites and some other nonblack Americans seem to think that the majority of the poor, the homeless, drug-users, and drug-dealers are black Americans. As we have already suggested, one reason for this stereotyped framing is obvious: The mainstream media tend to greatly exaggerate the role of black Americans in poverty, homelessness, and drug use. This biased media coverage contributes to greatly exaggerated and stereotyped images of "deviant" black Americans in many minds. Yet much of the available data paint a different picture. For example, white youth are more likely than black youth to smoke cigarettes, drink alcohol, and use illegal drugs. Surveys of high school students find that whites routinely indicate they are more likely to use illegal drugs than blacks. Research also shows that rates of drug abuse (also of child abuse) are higher for single-parent white families than for similar black families. Moreover, periodic surveys of white and black adults indicate variable percentages of illegal drug use, but the percentages are roughly similar.[51]

White and other nonblack Americans account for seven out of eight illegal drug-users, yet black Americans have become the national symbols of drug-users and dealers. This racially stereotyped framing affects white actions in serious ways. For instance, black drug-users are disproportionately targeted by the police (see Chapter 5, pp. 157–158). Blacks and Latinos make up most of those Americans put in jail for illegal drug use. In contrast, white drug-using and drug-dealing get much less police surveillance and prosecution—even though a majority of drug-dealers are white and there is much drug-selling on predominantly white college campuses and in white suburban areas. This drug-using and drug-dealing reality reveals the substantial racial bias in the operation of policing and judicial systems. As we will document more in the next chapter, numerous aspects of our policing and judicial systems reflect significant racial discrimination.[52]

Views of Black Athletes

Many whites seem to assume that they are not racist because they cheer for black athletes on their favorite teams. They may also feel that society is no longer racist because black players are common on college and professional football and basketball teams. However, much research suggests that black male athletes are frequently framed negatively by whites in and outside the mainstream media—for example, as less intelligent and more thug-like or animal-like than white male athletes. James Rada studied televised pro-football games on major television networks. In his sample of comments by on-air announcers, black athletes got most of the positive comments relating to physical talents. In regard to comments on cognitive abilities and intelligence, however, white athletes got most of the positive comments. All comments of sympathy were for white players. On-air commentaries also tended to portray white players in more friendly and intimate terms. Black men were portrayed as less intelligent and more animal-like than white men, while the latter were shown as the "thinking men" on the field. A later study by Rada and Wulfemeyer found these discriminatory patterns yet again. This time they examined how their sample of on-air announcers periodically distinguished between the player as athlete and the player as person. "When it came time to describe the African American players as people, the announcers' criticism knew no bounds. Of the 18 negative statements made about a player's off-field intelligence, character, or personal interest stories, all 18 were directed toward African Americans. White players, in contrast, received only positive comments across these categories."[53] In addition, a recent study of the images of professional baseball players in many articles in the two leading U.S. sports magazines found much more negative racial stereotyping and other racial framing for black players than for U.S.-born white players."[54]

An important study by Abby Ferber compared the subculture of white-supremacist groups and the general sports subculture in regard to their depictions of black men. She found remarkable similarities in the portrayals of black men as typically violent, hyper-aggressive, hypersexual, and inferior to white men. Today, black male athletes are often viewed as acceptable, but only so long as they are "good" and under control of white owners or coaches. Many whites still frame black athletes in general as having an "inherently violent, aggressive nature lying just beneath the surface, threatening to spring forth at any time." In addition, by especially celebrating black athletes who play by the white rules and fully accept white owners' or coaches' control, "Whites can tell themselves they are not racist, and they can blame African Americans for their own failures."[55] As long as they stay "good" and "well behaved," black male athletes can be viewed by whites as "exceptions to their race," the common perspective from the white-racist framing we have noted previously.

Exaggerating the Black Presence

The focus on black men and women as physically dominant, deviant, or dangerous in the media and in various other public and private discussions appears to create in many white minds the impression that there are more black Americans than there actually are. President Eisenhower's "big overgrown Negroes" image seems to extend to exaggerations about the black population. Over the last decade or two several surveys of whites have shown that they substantially overestimate the size and proportion of the black population. Regularly, a majority of whites have estimated that black Americans make up at least 30 percent of the U.S. population, nearly two-and-a-half times their actual percentage.[56] This perhaps suggests an old emotion-laden conception, dating back to at least early founders like Thomas Jefferson, that there are too many African Americans, a demographic situation many whites still view as threatening. Apparently, many white Americans periodically view their societal position in relation to the presence of black Americans.

Sociologist Charles Gallagher has explored the reasons for these contemporary overestimations of the black population. In interviews with whites he found that a major source of exaggerated estimations is, yet again, the mainstream mass media. For example, whites who watched a lot of sports programs saw many black athletes and concluded the country has a high percentage of black Americans. Whites were also found to exaggerate the black presence because blacks seem so "vocal" about issues such as civil rights in the media. At least as important in shaping these overestimates is the impact of local crime news. The constant barrage of stories about black criminals in the local news gives most whites, as well as many others, the impression that the country has a much larger black population than it does. Again, we observe the profound impact of the media, and yet the media's exaggerated images and interpretations usually go unchallenged.[57]

Mocking Black Americans

Today, many white and other nonblack Americans reveal their negative views and images in the ways they mock or joke about black Americans. Sometimes this mocking is overtly racist, as in the many antiblack jokes told across the country on any given day. Among friends in the workplace, at a bar, on the Internet, or at home many whites tell stories and engage in racist conversations that mock alleged black mannerisms, morals, or speech. Indeed, many whites still seem to enjoy blatantly racist joking. In addition, in our research on white actions, in private backstage and public frontstage settings, we have found that few whites object when white friends, relatives, acquaintances, or strangers engage in blatantly racist performances.[58]

Whites, including those in the elite, have crafted racist jokes about African Americans for centuries. Typical of elite and other white jokes is the one told back in the 1970s by Earl Butz, a former university dean and powerful secretary of agriculture. Joking about what the Republican Party could offer to African Americans, he joked that all a black man really wants is loose shoes, warm toilet facilities, and sex. For many whites at all class levels, ridiculing black Americans or other Americans of color in joking commentaries is commonplace, and apparently considered innocuous by most who do it.[59]

Associated with racist joking is the mocking of speech that many whites engage in when discussing black Americans. What whites believe to be a common black way of speaking is frequently mocked through imitative language. This is done at all levels of society. For example, in March 1970, President Richard Nixon and Vice-President Spiro Agnew performed a piano duet at an elite Gridiron Club dinner. After a series of jokes about Nixon's "southern strategy" (the strategy to win politically by racist appeals to southern white voters) by luminaries on the program, Nixon and Agnew played two pianos. Nixon asked Agnew, "What about this 'southern strategy' we hear so often?" In counterpoint Agnew answered in mock black dialect, "Yes Suh, Mr. President, ah agree with you completely on yoah southern strategy." Nixon then played some favorite songs of Democratic presidents, while Agnew drowned him out with a vigorous rendition of "Dixie." The almost entirely white audience of the Washington, DC, elite laughed and enjoyed the racialized performances. In addition, we now know that President Nixon privately spoke in stereotyped terms of black Americans, for instance as genetically inferior to whites, according to a former top advisor.[60]

Various members of the elite engage in racialized joking. For example, in 2012 a federal judge emailed acquaintances an animalizing "joke" in which President Obama's mother jokes to a young Obama that his mixed-racial ancestry might have been linked to her having wild party sex, joking that alluded to potential sex with a dog. Whites have long mongrelized black Americans in such conventional racist framing. When called out in public, the judge was defensive, said he was not "a racist," meant this joke only for white friends, and apologized. Moreover, in 2011 a California Republican official sent acquaintances a photo of President Obama's face on a chimpanzee, with a caption saying "Now you know why—No birth certificate!" Like many people who have made similar jokes, she insisted that she was only joking and was indeed "not a racist."[61]

Vicious mocking of black language and culture seems to be spreading, especially on the Internet. On the Internet, whites have developed a great number of websites that feature crude, hostile, and racist parodies of what their creators consider black speech. For example, here is the opening of a mocking translation of a speech by Socrates: "How ya' gots felt, O dudes o' Athens, a hearin' de speeches o' mah accusers." Such mocking is linked on these sites to a broad range of antiblack stereotypes, jokes, and images. The site with the Socrates speech listed events at a fictional "Ebonic Olympic Games": the "torching of the Olympic City" and the "Gang Colors Parade."[62] Antiblack websites spread racist images globally; there is at least one antiblack site in Russian! The Internet's anonymity and connectedness allow the spread of racist framing and opinions no longer acceptable for expression in most other public settings to millions globally.

In millions of online searches each year, Americans use common antiblack epithets in their searches. One recent study of millions of

Google searches of the Internet in all U.S. regions discovered a great many (presumably mostly white) Americans had searched for the word "nigger," a significant proportion of which were clearly searches for racist jokes and other antiblack humor. Numerous other racist epithets for black men, women, and children are also common search terms on Google and other search engines. For most whites who do such searches, this type of racist joking appears to be about racist entertainment or a comforting reinforcement of their racist framing of black Americans, or both.[63]

In movies, on television, and in newspaper and magazine columns, well-educated whites are often those who mock black language or behavior. In Hollywood films the "good guys" often speak prestigious versions of the English language, while those portrayed as "bad guys," including black Americans, Latinos, and other Americans of color, frequently speak some negatively stigmatized version of English. Cartoon movies have made use of mock black English and other mock English accents, even for animals in these movies. In this manner language is mapped onto a particular group, as part of an aural stereotyping process, and old racist understandings are perpetuated in new forms. Jane Hill has studied mock Spanish, which is common in the United States. Otherwise monolingual whites (and others) use made-up terms such as *no problemo, el cheapo,* and *hasty banana,* and phrases like *hasta la vista, baby.* Mock Spanish can be found on billboards and in movies, and on cards and other items in various gift shops, especially in the Southwest. Such ridicule reveals underlying stereotyping of Latinos among whites who might reject more openly racist comments or practices. Mocking speech is again often seen as fun and justifiable.[64] There is also much language mocking by whites in the media and in more private settings of the speech of Asian and Native Americans. While it may appear harmless to whites, language mocking supports traditional hierarchies of racial privilege and racial degradation without seeming to be too blatantly racist. Many whites have denied that such mocking is racist or harmful, ignoring the many people of color who have pointed out the harm language mocking actually causes for them and their communities.

Such ridicule of language or speech is racist because it has significant meaning only if one knows the underlying racist framing, the racial stereotypes and images, of the groups of color that are targeted. Indeed, language mocking and subordination are not about standards for speaking as much as they are about determining that some people are not worth listening to and not worth treating as social equals.[65]

The Language of Racism

Culture shapes language, and language fosters or facilitates many aspects of thought. The concepts and categories we learn as children shape how we experience the world around us, and these concepts and categories—including racial stereotypes and images—are mostly delineated in sets of words and phrases. When racially framed language is imbedded in minds, it and its associated concepts often guide everyday thinking and behavior.

Today, antiblack racism is deeply imbedded in spoken and written English. Many whites still use epithets like "nigger," "coon," "spook," or "pickaninny" for African Americans, especially in private settings with friends and relatives and increasingly, as just noted, on white-oriented Internet sites. Some whites still use terms like "boy" for a black man, as happened with President Barack Obama in his two presidential campaigns. Others persist in using other diminutive terms, such as replacing a black man's name that is William with "Willie." While in recent decades there has been a significant decline in white use of openly racist terms, at least in most public settings, numerous terms used in the media and the everyday public conversations of whites have barely hidden racial meanings. For many whites, terms like *gangs, gangbangers, ghetto, inner city, the poor, the economically disadvantaged, welfare recipients, violent criminals, public housing*, and *drug pushers* symbolize black Americans or other dark-skinned Americans. Much white-racist commentary now uses such code words because they communicate (wink-wink) racist framing or inclinations without actually using more blatantly racist terms. A white person, including a media commentator, can use these terms to target or denigrate black Americans but still appear unprejudiced, at least to most other whites.[66]

Even in cases where color words and phrases were not crafted as intentionally racist, they can subtly reinforce antiblack framing. Thus, there are many phrases in English that use the words "black" and "white." Some may be racial in origin, but many seem linked to the old European tradition that associates negative concepts such as evil and the devil with darkness and blackness, and positive concepts such as purity and goodness with whiteness. The conceptual framework underlying these words and phrases accents black in negative ways and white in positive ways. In a standard dictionary the adjective "black" is listed as having these conventional meanings, in addition to color: dirty, soiled, wicked, sinister, connected with magic, gloomy, calamitous, marked with disaster, sullen, grim, and distorted. In contrast, the adjective "white" has these conventional meanings, in addition to color: marked by upright fairness, free of blemish, innocent, not intended to cause harm, fortunate, and favorable. In addition, the negative tone of many phrases using "black" can be seen in the following: to do a black deed; to be a black sheep; to tell a black lie; to indulge in the black arts (magic); to blacken one's name; to blackball someone; to be black-hearted; to have a black outlook; to be a blackguard (scoundrel); to have a Black Monday; to be on a black list;

to give a black mark; to be blackmailed; and to be a black day. In contrast, we have the following: to be a white knight; to tell a white lie; to white list; to be the white hope; to be free, white, and 21; and to say "That's very white of you."[67] While many such white–black distinctions in English are older than antiblack racism, they are commonplace in U.S. English conversations and thus can operate to subtly reinforce dichotomous, racial, or antiblack thinking.

Moreover, in numerous writings and presentations the positive achievements of whites may be put in the active tense, while those achievements of blacks may be put in the passive tense. Thus, Thomas Greenfield reports visiting Thomas Jefferson's Virginia slave plantation, where he was told by his guide, who was referring to large well-made doors that had operated since 1809 without need of repair, that "Mr. Jefferson designed these doors," and also that "the doors were installed in 1809." The enslaved African American workers who actually put up the well-crafted doors remained anonymous and in the passive tense.[68] Numerous slave plantations are now popular tourist sites that play down or ignore the enslaved workers who labored there. Only recently have the public tours at, and written brochures about, some slave plantations begun to give meaningful attention to the intelligence and agency of enslaved workers.

Moreover, today in many organizations a black man or woman who gets a very good job or position often is still said by whites to have gotten it through special consideration or affirmative action and not because of merit. In other cases, there is a *playing down* of black agency. Whites may recognize that blacks have achieved something, but run it down as flawed. For example, many whites have disparaged the innovative character of the music that has often come out of black communities, such as jazz in the early decades of the twentieth century or rap music in recent decades. There is also the strategy of viewing a black achievement as an *anomaly*. As we discussed previously (see p. 109), major success is something individual blacks do achieve, such as President Barack Obama's successful election, but it is seen by many whites as an exception to the negative rule.[69]

The Nobel novelist Toni Morrison has suggested an even deeper point—that black Americans frequently function in important ways as a key metaphor and referent for white Americans in public discourse and in literature. Black Americans often seem to be an overt or hidden referent for much white thought and action.[70] We have seen previously how black Americans constitute a major reference point for whites—in crafting the Constitution, in the Civil War period, in creating wealth and prosperity, in law and politics, and in structuring residential areas in cities. In this and later chapters we observe black Americans as a key referent in many areas of contemporary life—in debates over schools, the criminal justice system, government welfare programs, housing and urban development, and political representation. Moreover, subtle use of the black referent even extends to the definition of what is "American."

White Emotions, White Rage

White ideas and understandings of racial matters are rooted in deep-lying emotions, which are central to the dominant white frame. For centuries many whites have been obsessed with blackness and have seen black people as fear-inspiring or dangerous. Whites have often been particularly emotional about such matters as interracial sex or marriage. However, the level of white emotional involvement in racist thinking and action varies considerably on an individual basis and in regard to a particular issue.

Consider the comments in this anonymous hate letter I received, apparently from a white man. The writer is familiar with extreme white-supremacist thinking and activities. The letter attacked a brief quote from me in a New Jersey newspaper article about current societal trends in regard to discrimination. Handwritten on a New Jersey city's superintendent of schools stationery, the letter read as follows:

> So we should give privileges to placate filthy dirty subhuman coons, your nuts. Never! Never! I'm telling you.... Whites such as myself are just itching to take to the streets and exterminate every dirty nigger ape as well as every white nigger loving commie dog (such as your self). [O. J.] Simpson is the catalyst that will finally awaken the latent, dormant nigger hatred extant in this county. There will be no compromise, no quarter given.... First we elect Buchanan types, next suspend habeus corpis [sic]. Third disenfranchise and resegregate niggers. Then either deportation or extermination. Sound familiar? You white liberal swine are cancers even worse that filthy coons. When the reckoning comes, it will be curtains for them too. The only good nigger is a dead nigger.
>
> ([Signed] WHITE RAGE[71])

Judging from the school letterhead and the vocabulary, this letter seems to be from a well-educated white person. Note old white images of black people as dirty and subhuman. Note too the concern with "nigger-loving" whites. This type of racist venom extends beyond crude epithets and images to the goal of extermination. Perhaps most clear is the high level of emotion.

While the letter is extreme in its racist terminology, some of these themes have long been articulated, if in more restrained language, by many elite and ordinary whites. As I have shown earlier, racist images and attitudes are strongly held by powerful whites. From time to time influential whites air blatantly racist views openly. For instance, in the 1990s Marge Schott, owner of the Cincinnati Reds baseball team, remarked to an employee, "I'd rather have a trained monkey working for me than a nigger." She was reported to have called black players "million-dollar niggers."[72] She is not unusual in such behavior, some of it bursting forth in public settings. Recall discussions of racist performances in public settings by major entertainment and media figures like Michael Richards and Don Imus.

Denying Discrimination and Racism: The White Public

In Chapter 3 we examined how elite whites, including media commentators and officials, have downplayed persisting racism and accented the image of a society where equality of opportunity and colorblindness are supposedly the reality. These "colorblind" themes are common in some current incarnations of the dominant white framing among white elites and the white public. As Damon Williams has underscored, some versions of this contemporary racial framing even include classic terms from the 1960s civil rights movement, yet this use of "terms like protection, individual rights, and nondiscrimination … [sows] confusion among members of the media and public." In this way whites have co-opted civil rights language for the purpose of actually "attacking diversity change movements."[73] Additionally, national surveys indicate that today a majority of ordinary white Americans see "equality of opportunity" as the societal reality. Included in this colorblind perspective is the idea that racial discrimination is no longer widespread and that Americans of color who complain of it are wrongheaded.

Soon after the 1960s civil rights movement declined in intensity, most whites were already moving toward the view that discrimination is no longer an important problem. In a 1976 survey a substantial majority (71 percent) agreed that "blacks and other minorities no longer face unfair employment conditions. In fact they are favored in many training and job programs." In contest, a meager 12 percent then agreed with the statement that "discrimination affects all black people. The only way to handle it is for blacks to organize together." In surveys of this era, most black Americans had a quite different view, instead accenting the large-scale discrimination they faced.[74]

In more recent surveys, white and black Americans still differ dramatically in how they view contemporary discrimination. One Pew survey found that more than 80 percent of the black respondents reported widespread racial discrimination in at least one major societal area. Two-thirds reported that African Americans always or often face discrimination in jobs or in seeking housing; 50 percent said the same for shopping and restaurants. Also significant was the finding that a majority of whites again denied the black view of significant discrimination.[75] In addition, a recent CNN national survey on antiblack discrimination showed a similar pattern, with 87 percent of black respondents reporting that discrimination remains a serious national problem. Another CNN/ORC poll found that 61 percent of black respondents felt that antiblack discrimination was serious in their local area, compared to just 25 percent of whites.[76]

Moreover, a *Newsweek* opinion survey of white registered voters found that only 18 percent of whites thought that discrimination was the main reason why many black Americans cannot get ahead in the country. As whites have done in the past, most opted instead for mainly blaming black Americans for their current socioeconomic conditions. Whites tend to greatly overestimate the progress the African Americans have made. One CNN/ORC survey found that nearly two-thirds of white respondents agreed that the quality of life for black Americans had gotten significantly better over the last ten years, yet 61 percent of the black respondents disagreed, reporting that the quality of life had stayed the same or gotten worse. Interestingly, another ABC News/Post survey found that more than 84 percent of both black and white respondents reported having heard someone make an insulting or insensitive remark about African Americans.[77] Evidently, most whites know there are frequent racist commentaries being made by whites, yet do not want to see that as evidence of serious racism in society.

Today, a majority of whites do not see the United States as having a problem of widespread discrimination. Most do not view themselves as significantly racist in thought or action, often asserting something like "I am not a racist." In recent years many have made such statements as "My family never owned slaves" or "My family did not segregate lunch counters." Many will say to black Americans something like, "Slavery happened hundreds of years ago—just get over it." They do not know, or pretend they do not know, that official slavery ended in 1865, only about 150 years prior to their statements. Whites making such historically oriented assertions usually do not admit that they and their ancestors have likely benefited greatly from slavery, segregation, and/or present-day discrimination.[78]

Many whites seem to mix negative views of black Americans with images of white innocence, thereby giving expression to elements of a broader racial framing. Take this example of a white college student's reply to a question about her first experience with black Americans, in this case children:

> I switched from a private school which had no blacks to a public school, and I was thrown in the middle of a bunch of apes, no I'm just kidding.... And I don't know, my parents have always instilled in me that blacks aren't equal, because we are from [the Deep South].

In her interview she continues in this vein, making negative comments about African Americans. Then at the end of her interview, she adds:

> I don't consider myself racist. I, when I think of the word racist, I think of KKK, people in white robes burning black people on crosses and stuff, or I think of the Skinheads or some exaggerated form of racism.[79]

We see here a strong imaging of a white self in positive terms. Research by Eduardo Bonilla-Silva and others has demonstrated the array of rhetorical devices that many whites use in everyday conversations and interactions, especially with strangers, to try to portray themselves as "colorblind" and "not racist." Recently, researchers have found this strategy to be common for whites at all educational levels, including those involved in psychological counseling and other helping professions.[80]

It seems that many whites assert that they are not racist because they view racism as only something that *other* whites do, or have done in the past. Jerome Culp has summarized this reality:

> To many white people, not being racist means having less racial animosity than their parents (something almost all can at least claim); having less racial animosity than someone they know (something all can claim); or not belonging to a white supremacist group.... For many white people, unless they believe overwhelmingly in the inferiority of black people, they are not collaborators with racism and are not racist.[81]

As we observe in white views of some black athletes or entertainment figures like Oprah Winfrey, many whites do hold positive views of selected black people. However, these often superficial positive views reduce the ability of whites to see their own culpability in ongoing personal and institutional racism.

Historical changes in racism have also been misperceived by most whites. When the legal segregation era came to an end with the passage of civil rights laws in the 1960s, most apparently concluded that serious racism was being rapidly extinguished. Today, most whites, like the woman above, seem to view what racism that remains as a matter of isolated individual bigotry and not as systemic racism cutting across major institutions. As a result, they do not see, or do not wish to admit, their own participation in this continuing racism. Moreover, the level at which racist attitudes are held varies in degree of consciousness. Psychologist Patricia Devine has suggested that those whites who reject overtly prejudiced views can still hold less conscious prejudices that exist because of prior racial socialization. For many this deep-lying attitudinal racism is a persisting bad habit that keeps breaking out into their everyday behavior.[82]

White Views on Government Action against Discrimination

If antiblack discrimination is no longer regarded as a major or well-institutionalized problem by the white majority, then it is not surprising that these whites see less need, or no need, for strong antidiscrimination efforts by local, state, and federal governments. From this perspective black Americans and others pressing for continuing or enhanced antidiscrimination programs, such as aggressive affirmative action, are making illegitimate demands.

Symbolic and Laissez-Faire Racism

Researchers like David Sears have described a contemporary white perspective called "symbolic racism." Whites often combine the notion of declining overt racism with the idea that blacks are now making illegitimate demands for societal changes. As these researchers view the current situation, a majority of whites have shifted away from old-fashioned, blatantly racist ideas and accepted modest desegregation while strongly resisting forceful government action for large-scale desegregation. What they term "symbolic racism" or "modern racism" is grounded in white resistance to substantial changes in the racial status quo. Central to white concerns is a fear that whites have of losing status and power because of black attempts to bring more societal change. Deep-lying antiblack views—especially views of blacks violating traditional American work values—are still present, but white resentment of pressures for substantial change is central to the current racist framing. This symbolic racism perspective does capture some important elements of contemporary white perspectives, but it has been criticized for playing down too much the old-fashioned blatant racism. The latter still exists among many whites and is directly connected to negative views of substantial government programs to eradicate discrimination.[83]

Lawrence Bobo, James Kluegel, and Ryan Smith have suggested a more historical approach. Since the 1950s, and shaped by structural changes in the society, white attitudes have shifted from an accent on strict racial segregation and very overt bigotry to a "laissez-faire racism," by which Bobo, Kluegel, and Smith mean whites' continuing negative stereotyping of blacks and blaming of blacks for their socioeconomic problems. Whites still strive to maintain white privilege in now informally segregated settings. Survey data since the 1960s, as noted previously, indicate a substantial discrepancy between white views on the *principle* of desegregation versus white views on government *implementation* of desegregation. While surveys in the mid-1960s indicated that nearly two-thirds of whites accepted integrated schooling in principle, just 38 percent then accepted a role for government in pressing for more racial integration.[84]

Today this pattern persists. White support for the *principle* of school integration is well above 90 percent, while endorsement of strong government intervention to insure racial integration is far less. Recent survey data indicate similar discrepancies in white views of job and housing integration along racial lines. Recall the review by Quillian of opinion surveys of whites that show the majority publicly support equality of opportunity for Americans of color, yet also do not believe there is major discrimination in society and, thus, do not support major government intervention to secure further racial equality. Acceptance of the principle of racial integration does not mean that most whites wish to see government intervene forcefully to guarantee racial fairness or equality, or that they wish to personally have significantly more contact with black Americans.[85]

Negative Views on Affirmative Action

Affirmative action is a major example of a remedial program designed to deal with contemporary racial discrimination. Most whites, including most political leaders, have been opposed to aggressive affirmative action since it was first proposed in the 1960s. In a 1970s survey of mostly white local and national leaders in business, farming, unions, the media, and academia, most were then overwhelmingly *opposed* to specific affirmative action for black Americans in school admissions and jobs. A substantial majority thought that equality of opportunity, not of results, was the best way to eradicate inequality. The white public agreed with these white leaders.[86]

In surveys, then as now, the generality of the question wording can make a major difference in white responses. One 2013 national survey asked respondents if they supported "programs which make special efforts to help blacks and other minorities get ahead." Sixty-one percent of whites agreed with this rather general statement, compared with 81 percent of blacks. However, when asked in the survey if "blacks and other minorities should receive preference in college admissions to make up for past inequalities," just 21 percent of whites then agreed—compared with 57 percent of blacks.[87] This and other surveys have revealed that far more than half of whites do not believe that government and private agencies should be making extensive remedial and reparative efforts on behalf of Americans of color that might interfere with white privileges. A *Newsweek* survey of white voters found that nearly three-quarters disapproved of giving "preferences to blacks and other minorities … [in] hirings, promotions, and college admissions." Three-quarters felt that such preferences had resulted in less-qualified people being hired, promoted, or admitted. In addition, 39 percent indicated that they thought the United States had gone too far in "pushing equal rights."[88] Indeed, today many whites believe that they are likely to be victims of government affirmative action. One Pennsylvania survey asked a question about how likely it would be that a white worker might lose a job or a promotion to a less-qualified black worker. Most black respondents thought this was unlikely, while most whites thought it was likely. National polls using such a question have gotten similar responses.[89]

As in the past, many whites still comment on the socioeconomic problems of black Americans with such statements as, "Why can't they be like us?" One common notion is that if "they" will just work harder, then normal societal processes will enable them to have greater economic mobility. One survey asked whether respondents agreed with this statement: "The Irish, Italians, and many other groups overcame prejudice and worked their way up, African-Americans and other minorities should do the same without any special help from the government." Most whites agreed.[90] Moreover, many whites argue that they oppose affirmative action because such programs unfairly benefit some at the expense of others. Yet, firmly racist views appear to lie beneath the surface of such views for many whites. For example, one experimental study examined why white conservatives were opposed to affirmative action for African Americans and found that the intensity of their racist framing of African Americans predicted the character of their opposition to remedial programs for racial discrimination.[91]

Imaging the White Self

As we have previously noted, the dominant racist framing held in white minds encompasses much more than antiblack views. Among the important elements are very positive views of white superiority, virtue, and merit. The broad white racial frame views the white-dominated history of the United States as mostly meritorious and unproblematic for the present day. Today, as in the past, group merit and individual merit are judged by standards created by the white majority. In Chapter 3 we noted the common images of white superiority and virtue that recur in Hollywood films (pp. 93–94). From the first years of movie-making to the present, when racial matters have been portrayed, whites as a group have almost always been portrayed as morally superior, intellectually superior, or otherwise meritorious. In older movies and more recent ones, there may be a few white bigots, but white society is not portrayed as institutionally racist. Typically, some white person is a central hero ("white savior"), even in movies substantially about people of color (for example, in *Gran Torino*, *The Blind Side*, and even science fiction movies like *Avatar*).

Among the elites and in the general public, whites have developed numerous sincere fictions about whites and whiteness that reproduce aspects of the dominant racial frame at an everyday level. Such sincere fictions frequently describe whites as "not racist" and as "good people" even as the same whites take part in discriminatory actions or express obviously racist views. This moral privileging of whiteness may be conscious, or it can be half-conscious or unconscious. One older California study found evidence of this unconsciousness in research on white women; whiteness was difficult for most of the white Californians to even conceptualize and name. More recent research by Karyn McKinney using white student biographies found a similarly unreflective response to questions of whiteness for most whites.[92] According to this and other studies, most whites do not think much about being white, or about the society's white-created racial hierarchy. And when they do, that thinking is often in response to the strong presence of black Americans or other people of color. Being white, one might say, means rarely or never having to think about it.

Moreover, one survey found that nearly two-thirds of white respondents did not think that whites as a group had benefited from past and present discrimination against black Americans.[93] As we have noted before, many whites have asserted their innocence with a torrent of comments such as "My family never owned slaves" and "My family never segregated any lunch counters." This white sense of guiltlessness in regard to past and present racism is professed at various levels, including by one-time presidential candidates like Pat Buchanan. Indeed, many whites now believe that whites actually suffer more than blacks from racial bias. One recent psychological study of 209 whites found that most believed that antiwhite bias had increased sharply since the 1950s. These whites' average rating of the current level of antiwhite bias (4.7 on a scale from 1 to 10) was *higher* than the same whites' average rating of what they saw as the current level of antiblack bias (3.6). The researchers concluded that "Whites think more progress has been made toward equality than do blacks, but whites also now believe that this progress is linked to a new inequality—at their expense."[94]

Fostering and Learning Racist Attitudes

In Chapter 3 we examined how white elites and their assistants have insistently fostered a racial framing rationalizing the everyday realities of unjust impoverishment and enrichment across the color line. This effort is a major source of the racist framing held in the minds of the non-elite population. Over the centuries, and through various means, elites have regularly pressured and manipulated ordinary whites to accept important elements of the dominant racist framing. After the major elements of an era's white racial framing and structural arrangements are in place, ordinary whites need less pressuring, for they generally understand what is in their group interest. Ordinary whites often generate new permutations on old racist ideas, innovations that in their turn reinforce or enhance the old racist framing.

The often hidden power of the elite works through propagating the dominant racial frame by means of the mainstream media and the educational system, as well as in workplaces and churches. For several centuries newspapers, magazines, advertisements, and, more recently, media like television and the Internet have played a central part not only in generating the dominant racial frame, but also in creating specific racist images that are the implemented features of that white-imposed frame.

For example, in the century after the Civil War many racially stereotyped images of black Americans were widely circulated in what was then the relatively new means of commercial advertising. "Black faces were used to sell everything from tooth paste to pancakes. Distorted images appeared on boxes and tubes, and even on vaudeville stages, to make white people laugh."[95] By the twentieth century the great expansion of the mass media—especially newspapers, magazines, and radio—provided many more avenues for the circulation of antiblack and other racist images. In addition, the emergence of Hollywood movie-making on a large scale, and then television in the middle decades of the twentieth century, created or reinforced many negative images of Americans of color in millions of minds. We have noted previously the impact of racist movies like *Gone with the Wind*, as well as the impact of racial stereotyping in more recent movies that are less blatantly racist.

Today, as we have often seen already, many negative racial images of black Americans and other Americans of color are still generated and circulated rapidly in the U.S. media, especially on television and cable networks, on radio talk shows, and on many Internet websites. Old-fashioned antiblack images are still found on some consumer goods, like candy bars and toothpaste, sold in various countries across the globe. However, in the United States almost all the old blatantly racist images on mainstream consumer goods have disappeared, or images like those of Aunt Jemima and Uncle Ben in product packaging have gradually been altered to appear much less stereotypical. Still, in capitalistic societies like the United States consumerism is based not only on the consumption of material goods but also on the consumption of important beliefs, images, and narratives, which have long included substantial elements from the dominant racial frame.

The Role of Conformity

Some analysts have viewed racial prejudice as a sort of demon in an individual, indeed often as a type of psychological abnormality. Frustration–aggression and authoritarian–personality theories of prejudice focus on the externalization function of prejudice—the transfer of a person's internal psychological problems to an external object, such as a racial other, as an attempted personal solution for a serious and internal psychological problem. From this psychological viewpoint, those who are racially prejudiced are seriously "sick" individuals. There are certainly whites who fit this interpretation, some of whom belong to white-supremacist groups. However, much social science research indicates that social *conformity* is a much more important factor in shaping the racial views and prejudices of a majority of people, including a majority of whites. Most whites loyally accept the social contexts in which they are socialized and usually hold to many of the racial prejudices taught at home and school or through the mainstream media.[96] Drawing on recent research with white college students, sociologist John Foster has concluded that

> individual whites act as "optimistic robots" when addressing racial issues or racialized social systems, and their actions are bureaucratic in form. Their ... optimism towards race relations in U.S. society assists in the legitimization of the status quo. Similar to loyal bureaucrats of an organization, they engage in impression management for the institutions that provide whites their privileges, while in turn those institutions speak glowingly of the "lily white," which often is defined and affirmed through the defined inferiority of the nonwhite Other.[97]

In this society the white self is typically shaped through interaction with other people. Much learning about the superiority of whites and inferiority of racialized others comes from informal lessons learned as children at home and school and as adults socializing with relatives and friends. White images of people of color are typically passed along family lines of communication. Conformity to views of important relatives and friends is a central source of routinized racist framing. Most racial views are not the result of individual pathologies but reflect shared social definitions and narratives. In this way racial prejudices and other elements from the dominant racial frame function as a means of social adjustment to the views of an important in-group. In general, as several scholars have noted, "our most private thoughts and feelings arise out of a constant feedback and flow-through of the thoughts and feelings of others who have influenced us. Our individuality is decidedly a part of a collective movement."[98] Thus, sociologist Maurice Halbwachs suggested that our personal understandings about society are not just in some nook of our minds to which only we have access. Our racial understandings, and the dominant racial framing we use, are regularly reinforced and recalled to us externally within the social groups of which we are part. In this way a particular person's understandings, images, knowledge, and framing hang together because they are part of the "totality of thoughts common to a group."[99] Negative images of people of color are often old and are deeply imbedded in white communities; they become part of a particular evolving white self, but one emerging in important collective contexts.

Some psychological research indicates that people frequently do not think through what they are doing in everyday behavior but proceed as if they are on automatic pilot; they tend to operate in line with the routinized scripts they have learned from their important socialization settings. Given that racist images, attitudes, and inclinations are generally well-learned elements imbedded in individual and collective memories, much racist behavior on the part of whites thus has an automatic and routinized character.[100]

For most whites the earliest socialization in racist attitudes begins in the family. A CBS poll of high school students found that half of those whose parents made overtly racist comments admitted that they too had made such comments. Consider this interview with a white father, who responds to a hypothetical question about an adult child dating a black person thus:

> I'd be sick to my stomach. I would feel like, that I failed along the way.... I'd feel like I probably failed as a father, if that was to happen. And it's something that I could never accept.... It would truly be a problem in my family because I could never handle that, and I don't know what would happen because I couldn't handle that, ever.[101]

This man's comments signal more than negative attitudes toward and images of the black out-group; they point to his emotion-laden view of his white self and to how he views being a white father. The comments highlight the family context of racist ideas. Quite evident is the substantial emotion being expressed. While more strongly stated than some, his views are in line with the interracial dating and marriage views often expressed in other research studies by a great many whites.[102]

Mainstream theories of the cognitive development of children have often suggested that most do not form clear ideas on racial matters until they are at least five or six years old. Until that age, egocentricity is said to be the child's natural state. However, recent research using photos of white and black faces and good/bad word associations has found that even white preschoolers already tend "to categorize racially ambiguous angry faces as black rather than white; they did not do so for happy faces."[103] In addition, one major ethnographic study of numerous white children in a preschool setting found that three-, four-, and five-year-olds periodically interacted with children of other racial groups using sophisticated understandings of racist ideas and epithets. One example in this study was the use by young white children of the word "nigger" for black Americans, and the white children's also indicating that they had some understanding of the racist *meanings* associated with that vicious epithet. They were not just unreflectively imitating what they had heard white adults say. In that field study white children regularly used a white racial framing and its terms to define themselves as white and to exclude or exert power over children of color. Recall too the socio-psychological research discussed earlier that showed that, as children age, they usually learn to hide their racist views from strangers (p. 107).[104]

We should note too that while most children are initially socialized into racist thinking in family groups, they also learn subtle and blatant racist ideas and images from their neighborhood and school peer groups, from children's books and school books, and from the media.

Learning Racism through Popular Culture: Video Gaming

We do not have the space to discuss in detail the numerous avenues of contemporary socialization of older children and adults into the dominant racial frame, but we can briefly discuss some relatively recent additions to this socialization process. Consider, for example, the video gaming subculture and its numerous examples of racial framing of whites and people of color. More than 170 million people are estimated to play video games in the U.S. alone, and the most dedicated players and the game-makers are very disproportionately white and male. Reviewing existing research, Daniels and Lalone have concluded that over recent decades the gaming world has been heavily white-oriented not only in the makeup of players and game-makers but also in the "procedures or systems included in the games themselves."[105]

Because of their dramatic impact, and how often they are played, an array of popular video games constantly reproduce the dominance of whites, especially white men, in the society's racial framing and associated racial hierarchies. In some cases openly white-supremacist video games have been circulated. One example is the game *Border Patrol*, in which players "shoot the spics" (one white-racist epithet for Latinos). This game is played by many whites, not just white supremacists, on home and office computers and other devices. Moreover, the frequent pro-white and anti-racial-others framing of ordinary video games is yet more problematical because of the much larger audiences that play them—and thus their much more extensive socialization effects. Studying the popular *Grand Theft Auto* video games, Daniels and Lalone have shown how the mostly white male game-makers incorporate an array of racist stereotypes of Americans of color, such as making most black and Latino characters a "gang banger."[106]

At least as serious as this racist framing of characters of color is the openly racist commentary, including much antiblack commentary, carried on by the white players as they play this and other popular video games. When criticized for their openly racist framing and language, the white gamers and other defenders of these video games will often assert the typical defenses of white innocence, such as "I am not racist" or "I am only joking, can't you take a joke?" Such responses also signal, once again, that whites frequently find racist joking and activities to be entertaining. In the end, it is almost always *whites* who get to decide what is racially offensive in the video games or commentaries in which whites engage. This white gaming subculture's dismissive attitude toward critiques of the racism in and around the games reveals how powerful the white racial frame remains in society. The racialized gaming also demonstrates how that white racial frame is constantly reinforced and propagated in the larger society, especially in the next generation of young people.[107]

Group Isolation and Its Consequences

Recent research continues to show most U.S. neighborhoods are still highly segregated. One survey found that most white respondents reported "many whites" living in their area, while two-thirds of black respondents and six in ten of the Latino respondents said the same about the dominance of their own groups in their residential areas. While this question was rather vague, the results confirm what demographic analyses show—a majority of Americans still live in racially segregated communities, and whites are by far the most racially segregated of the major racial groups today.[108]

Residential segregation is a fundamental part of the societal process whereby systemic racism is reproduced from one generation to the next (see Chapter 6). Residential segregation breeds significant social and mental isolation. Thus, the absence of equal-status experiences with black families in relatively segregated neighborhoods contributes materially to white unfamiliarity with and stereotyping of black Americans. This is also true for many other families of color. Some years back, several *New York Times* journalists did important field research on the impact of Chicago's residential segregation in regard to cross-racial attitudes. They interviewed residents in adjacent working-class suburbs, one predominantly white and one predominantly black. Whites were found to be very isolated and mostly living out their lives "without ever getting to know a black person." In both communities there were fears and suspicions of the other group. However, black suburbanites were "fearful because much of their contact with white people was negative," while "whites were fearful because they had little or no contact" with similar black Chicagoans.[109]

Because of the racial demography and spatial ecology of everyday life, the majority of blacks spend much more time interacting with whites than the majority of whites spend interacting with blacks. Most black Americans work or shop with large numbers of whites, whereas relatively few whites do the same with large numbers of blacks. The racial views of most white Americans are not likely to be shaped by numerous equal-status contacts with black Americans. The sense of white superiority is reinforced by the continuing process in which most whites live separated from black Americans or other Americans of color.

Children living in isolation can be significantly affected. One study of intergroup attitudes examined white first- and fourth-graders attending heavily white schools where they had very little contact with African Americans. In contrast to studies of white children at more racially diverse schools, these white children revealed much more racial bias in rating hypothetical interracial encounters. The children were asked to rate white and black children in ambiguous situations on picture cards where interactions between the children could be interpreted as one child having, or not having, negative intentions toward the other child. ("Either a child meant to push the other off the swing or the child fell on his own.") These very segregated white children were more likely to attribute negative intentions in ambiguous situations to blacks than to whites. The tested children indicated that they felt that wrongdoing by a black child was likely to prevent interracial friendships, whereas similar wrongdoing by a white child was less likely to affect friendships. The racial bias of the white children in the very homogeneous, segregated schools was shown to be significant as measured in terms of hypothetical interracial interactions.[110]

Psychological studies reveal that whites who are asked to describe a black person often see fewer descriptive aspects of that person than when they are asked to describe a white person. Members of an in-group tend to see the people in their group in more complex and differentiated terms than they see people in an out-group. Isolation increases bonding and conformity to the norms of the in-group, and the stronger one's attachment to the in-group, the greater the likelihood of prejudice and stereotyping directed at out-groups. This general phenomenon is especially serious when members of a particular group, like white Americans, have great privilege and power over other groups in society.[111]

Activating Antiblack Prejudices and Stereotypes

Racist prejudices, stereotypes, and emotions in the white racial frame are serious not just in themselves, but because they motivate concrete actions implementing and reinforcing the dominant racial hierarchy. White Americans vary in how important their racist framing is in their everyday understandings and practices. Some are so overtly racist in thinking and emotions that they are completely taken over by their internalized racism. They may join white-supremacist groups and target people of color for assault and other violence. In significant contrast, other whites recognize their racist upbringing and proclivities and join groups working against white racism.

Social science research reveals a significant link between racial attitudes and discriminatory actions. One review of 57 research studies found a consistent but moderate relationship between measured attitudes and discrimination. The researchers also found that measures of emotional prejudices were more strongly related to measures of discrimination than were measures of racial stereotypes and beliefs. Especially revealing was that the measures of emotional prejudices were significantly related to "both observed and self-reported discrimination," while the racial stereotype and belief measures were "related only to self-reported discrimination." These data suggest that some people are hiding their true racial views on explicit measures of stereotypes and prejudice and that "we now know that what they do is substantially related to how they feel, and somewhat related to how they think."[112]

Other recent research has found that people who show an implicit racial bias on measures like the implicit association test (associating white and black faces with positive and negative words) are more likely to engage in overtly racist actions. Researchers at Rutgers University found that white and other nonblack subjects who revealed greater implicit bias toward black Americans were more likely than other subjects to report engaging in discrimination, such as hurling racist slurs, excluding black people, and threatening physical harm to black people. In assessing hypothetical university situations, white students with strong racial biases were also more likely than other whites to recommend budget cuts for black, Asian, and Jewish student organizations (that is, potential economic discrimination).[113]

Racist thought or action against black Americans is frequently precipitated by a visual or verbal cue. Perhaps the most common cue is the black body itself. When whites perceive someone to fit their internalized criteria for blackness—which can be skin color, other physical characteristics, and/or speech—their minds may generate negative attitudes or images, and they may act according to those negative attitudes or images. Psychologists have researched several possible responses. Some whites do *not* automatically activate an antiblack stereotype when they encounter a black person. They may activate a positive image and generally act in antiracist ways. Another group of whites react routinely and consciously to racial cues with an overtly negative evaluation and actively express negative views in discriminatory action. For a third group, their negative evaluations are also activated in response to racial cues, but they are not clearly aware of these evaluations. They act on racist views but unconsciously. Yet another group of whites is like the previous one, but they are aware of the negative evaluations and will try to counter them, to varying degrees. Sometimes this countering is because of a personal distaste for the racist reaction, but in other cases it may be only a desire to be seen as socially acceptable to others.[114]

These four types of responses overlap in many lives. Depending on the time in a person's life or the social situation, an individual may react to particular racial cues in different ways. Under certain circumstances, many whites who hold strong racist prejudices and stereotypes will not act on them out of concern for social acceptability. In contrast, many whites with strong racist views will express their negative views in settings, such as in backstage settings with only white friends and relatives, where they do not feel social pressures to act in non-racist ways. Location and context are often important in the expression of racist framing and actions.[115]

Conclusion

Racist stereotypes, images, emotions, and interpretations—all part of the dominant white racial frame—are central to the operation of systemic racism in the contemporary United States. This framing lies behind most discriminatory action taken by whites against Americans of color. Among whites this framing is reinforced and perpetuated by millions of taken-for-granted comments, stories, and actions that target Americans of color every day in public and private settings.

White-racist images and attitudes do not stop at U.S. borders. At any given moment, white Americans working overseas are making racist comments to people around the globe, or television stations across the globe are playing racist U.S. television programs and movies, such as *Gone With the Wind*, old Tarzan and cowboy-and-Indian classics, or more recent movies like *Gran Torino*, *The Blind Side*, and *Avatar* with their more subtle racist notions and imagery. U.S. media corporations have long played a major role in circulating the white frame's negative images overseas. Increasing numbers of people around the world get much information and entertainment from U.S. movies, syndicated television programs, and movie and game videos, as well as directly from such sources as U.S. armed forces radio and television broadcasts.[116]

Currently, all but one of the eight or so international corporations that dominate the world's global media market are U.S.-based. These corporations not only control the production of media products such as movies and television shows, but also control many media outlets such as major television networks and publishing facilities. A few other corporations—just below these dominant companies in size, and from the United States, Europe, and Japan—assist in this concentrated corporate dominance of the world's mass media. These large international corporations have often invested in local mass media, thereby reshaping local popular cultures and traditional music and art. Several times in recent years, representatives of countries such as Brazil, Mexico, Sweden, and the Ivory Coast have held conferences to try to stop the Western media from destroying local popular cultures. However, in spite of such efforts to keep local control, the trend over recent decades has been more corporate mergers building very large media companies and to Western (and Japanese) control of the mass media in many countries. This process of increasing Western control over local media is not new, but has been going on since the nineteenth-century spread of European and U.S. imperialism.[117]

As a result of contemporary globalization, U.S. media corporations are perhaps the most important force shaping the white-racist framing, including racist stereotyping and imaging, that has spread around the world. For example, one study of the impact of U.S. media on educated groups in Turkey has shown that powerful images of whiteness and blackness are brought to that country by U.S. movies and new magazines.[118] Antiblack images are now common in many countries. Researchers in rural Japan gave implicit and explicit attitudinal tests to children and adults who had little or no contact with Americans and found significantly negative views of black Americans. In addition, a survey of Japanese students in the United States found that they too often held very negative views of African Americans, views influenced by whether they had seen positive or negative portrayals of African Americans in the U.S. media.[119]

A study of 15 rural Taiwanese found that the respondents sometimes realized that the U.S. media they enjoyed watching did engage in racist stereotyping, yet most still held negative views of black Americans. They often thought black Americans were self-destructive, dirty, lazy, unintelligent, criminal, violent, or ugly. Negative images were usually gleaned from U.S. television shows, movies, and music videos the respondents had seen in Taiwan.[120] In addition, a recent survey of 345 mainland Chinese high school students found that, the greater their use of U.S. print media, television, and movies, the more negative were their stereotypes of African Americans. In contrast, the greater their use of Chinese television and print media, the more likely they were to have positive images of African Americans, although this relationship was not as strong as for the negative effects of the U.S. media on their stereotyping. The researchers interpreted their findings as reflecting the reality of the U.S. media still portraying African Americans in disproportionately negative terms, while the Chinese media do not have this generally negative portrayal. The Chinese media mostly portray African Americans as impoverished citizens, as protesting for their rights, and as attractive sports figures.[121]

Drawing on informal interviews with immigrants from Central America, sociologist Nestor Rodriguez has concluded that the U.S. media are creating negative views of black Americans in Latin America. "I have traveled to Guatemala and seen theaters showing the same violent, racist movies we show here," he says. "When I asked one migrant in Houston why some migrants have antiblack attitudes, he responded that they first learn about blacks from U.S. movies."[122] In part the result of the globalizing U.S. media, antiblack images and attitudes are often carried by Asian, Latino, and other immigrants coming into the United States. This negative racial framing frequently generates negative attitudes toward, and negative interactions with, black Americans, from the earliest days of interpersonal contact. From this experience, black Americans in their turn may develop negative views of certain immigrants. Thus, the negative attitudes of Asian or Latino immigrants toward African Americans—and the negative attitudes of African Americans toward Asian or Latino Americans—are frequently part of the much larger system of globally circulated, white-generated racial framing and other white-managed racism, which these particular groups had no role in initiating.

5
Racial Oppression Today
Everyday Practice

Researchers at the Massachusetts Institute of Technology (MIT) sent applications to an array of job ads made by Chicago and Boston employers. Using made-up names that sound (especially to whites) like typically white or black names, they found that applicants with "white-sounding" names were 50 percent more likely to be contacted by employers than those with "black-sounding" names. When these researchers increased the job credentials of the tester-applicants, this was far more likely to get the whites a callback from employers than the blacks. Being black with eight years of job experience was necessary to get the same treatment as a white applicant *with no experience.*[1]

To many white observers racial discrimination and other racial oppression no longer seem important because they are no longer matters of official discrimination and legal segregation. Racism is often asserted by whites to be gone or sharply declining in this "post-racial society" because there are at least a few African Americans or other people of color in numerous professional or managerial positions in historically white organizations. Yet, one can recognize social changes in whites' racial domination in the United States without downplaying the still-strong relationship between being a black person or other person of color and being a target of serious racial discrimination, as from the employers in the study above. In one way or another, virtually all Americans of color continue to suffer significant discrimination today because white racial framing and domination of Americans of color remain major organizing features of our group life. The enduring racial hierarchy is still well supported by this racial framing, and it is perpetuated most centrally by the racial discrimination still carried out by a great many whites on a recurring basis in most areas of this society. In this and the next chapter we will examine many examples of persisting individual and institutional discrimination.

The Heart of Racism: Discriminatory Practices

Mainstream social scientists have often examined the paired ideas of racial prejudice and discrimination. A common perspective has been one of individual bigots acting out racial attitudes in discriminatory ways.

In recent decades, as we have seen, some critical analysts and researchers have argued for a different emphasis in looking at racial prejudice and discrimination. They accent the *institutional* and *systemic* racism that undergirds individual acts of discrimination. In its origin, this institutional racism viewpoint mostly stems from a long line of African American scholars and activists, going back centuries. As I underscored in Chapter 1, thinker-activists like Frederick Douglass and W. E. B. Du Bois long ago put white society and its societal institutions at the center of critical analysis of white racism. The 1960s civil rights movement brought a renewed emphasis among black intellectuals and activists on the institutional contexts of individual discrimination.[2]

While in recent years numerous mainstream analysts have rejected a critical institutional-racism perspective, it remains the most important approach to understanding the depths of the U.S. system of racial hostility and discrimination. Today, Americans of color generally experience discrimination not just as the actions of individual whites in one social arena, but rather as the everyday, recurring actions of white actors across many of life's arenas—actions backed by a multifaceted and powerful system of institutionalized white power and privilege. While all racial discrimination is carried out by individuals, the social context is very important, for that is where the framing, norms, and proclivities perpetuating discrimination are institutionalized. Individual discrimination activates the underlying hierarchical relations of power in which whites generally dominate Americans of color.[3]

Over recent decades the international attack on all racial and ethnic discrimination has accelerated. The United Nations International Convention on the Elimination of All Forms of Racial Discrimination, implemented in 1969, defines discrimination as:

> any distinction, exclusion, restriction or preference based on race, colour, descent or national or ethnic origin which has the purpose or effect of nullifying or impairing the recognition, enjoyment or exercise, on an equal footing, of human rights and fundamental freedoms.

This broad view accents not only distinctions on the basis of racial grouping, but also institutionalized restrictions, preferences, and exclusion aimed at impairing human rights. It underscores the costs associated with being the target of discrimination. In another passage, the Convention adds that the "existence of racial barriers is repugnant to the ideals of any human society." The U.S. government did *not* ratify this convention until 1994, although numerous nations had ratified long before.[4] Governments that signed on *agreed* to adopt "all necessary measures for speedily eliminating racial discrimination in all its forms and manifestations," yet U.S. officials have *not* yet undertaken such measures. Moreover, since the early 2000s the United Nations has had two important world conferences dealing with international racism, including issues of reparations for U.S. slavery and colonialism. Top U.S. officials have declined to participate in either conference.

The Social Context of Racist Practices

Contemporary patterns of discrimination are grounded in the benefits that whites have historically secured from four centuries of racial oppression in North America. Most contemporary forms of racial discrimination transmit the legacy of the oppressive past of slavery and Jim Crow. Today discriminatory practices reproduce the unjust impoverishment and enrichment of the past. Discrimination reflects and perpetuates the age-old racist frame, with its associated array of antiblack attitudes, images, and emotions. When black Americans encounter whites in contemporary settings, they often meet negative beliefs about and interpretations of their abilities, values, and orientations. Racial barriers persist because a substantial majority of whites still harbor some antiblack stereotypes, prejudices, images, and interpretations, and because a large minority are very negative in their perspectives. Research indicates that when most whites interact with black Americans at work, in restaurants, on the street, at school, or in the media they tend to think about the latter, either consciously or unconsciously, in terms of racist stereotypes or other racial framing inherited from the past and constantly reiterated and reinforced in the present. Such socially triggered framing often leads to some type of discrimination.

As we observed previously, the translation of antiblack attitudes into actual discrimination is shaped not only by this racial framing but also by social norms, such as by what other people might think, and by perceived behavioral controls, such as what the other's responses to discrimination might be. Routinized discrimination in housing, employment, politics, and public accommodations is carried out by whites acting alone or in groups. The social norms guiding racial discrimination can be formal or legal, but most norms today are unwritten and informal. Moreover, much antiblack action is not sporadic but is carried out repeatedly and routinely by numerous dominant-group members influenced by the important norms of their social networks. Whites have the power to discriminate as individuals, but much of their power to harm comes from their positions in traditionally white networks and white-controlled organizations.

Everyday Racism: Subtle, Covert, and Blatant

The character of everyday discrimination varies significantly. Whites may actively persecute people of color, or they may engage in an array of avoidance behaviors. Discrimination can be self-consciously motivated, or it can be half-conscious or unconscious and deeply imbedded in an actor's core beliefs. At the level of everyday interaction with black Americans and other Americans of color, most whites can create racial tensions and barriers even without conscious awareness they are doing so. Examples of this include when white men lock their car doors as a black man walks by on the street or when white women step out or pull their purses close to them when a black man comes into an elevator they are on. Stereotyped images of black men as criminals probably motivate this and similar types of defensive action.

Experiencing white racism is not about one or two incidents, but rather it is a lifetime experience from which one cannot ordinarily escape. It involves discrimination in most areas of life and over lifetimes. In one recent California study researchers conducted six focus group interviews with 40 black working-class and middle-class women of childbearing age. Echoing previous studies, these women described numerous instances of discrimination from the time they were children to the present. They noted interpersonal and institutional racism: "Racism was experienced in … work and school settings, in everyday social interactions such as shopping and in other settings defined by public space, and when interacting with health care, justice, and housing systems." The women discussed the impact whites' racism had on them, the stress that it caused, as well as the ways in which they dealt with it daily:

> The women maintained a pervasive sense of vigilance in anticipation of future racism events for themselves and their children, preparing themselves behaviorally, cognitively, and emotionally for potential racism encounters: "It's the skin you're in," verbalized by one woman, seemed to capture the inescapable sense of pervasive awareness and vigilance that women in all the focus groups described experiencing on a chronic basis.[5]

Today, our system of racial oppression is sustained by thousands of everyday acts of mistreatment of Americans of color by white Americans, incidents that range from the subtle and hard to observe to the blatant and easy to notice. These acts can be non-verbal or verbal, non-violent or violent. Many racist actions that crash in on everyday life are, from the injured victim's viewpoint, unpredictable. Such actions are commonplace, recurring, and cumulative in their negative impacts. They are, as one retired black teacher in her eighties put it, "little murders" that happen to her every day.[6]

In a specific setting, such as a workplace, a white person in authority may select another white person over an equally or better qualified person of color because of a preconceived notion that whites are more competent or just because of discomfort with people perceived from the old white-racist frame as too different. This latter type of subtle discrimination includes, in John Calmore's words, "the unconscious failure to extend to a minority the same recognition of humanity, and hence the same sympathy and care, given as a matter of course to one's own group." The selectivity results "often unconsciously—from our tendency to sympathize most readily with those who seem most like ourselves."[7]

The racist system is made even more complex by its reinforcement in many other aspects of the everyday behavior of white Americans. When whites make racist comments to other whites, or when they think or say racist things when watching television by themselves or with their families, they also reinforce and maintain the white-racist system, even though no people of color are present.

Who Does the Discriminating?

Discrimination targeting African Americans and other Americans of color comes from all levels and categories of white Americans. Most are involved in some subtle, covert, or blatant way in creating, reinforcing, or maintaining the racist reality of U.S. society. Depending on the situation and opportunity to discriminate, large numbers of whites actively discriminate. Judging from housing audit studies, roughly half of all whites are inclined to discriminate in some fashion, whether subtly or blatantly, in situations where they have housing to rent or sell to black individuals or families. It may well be that whites discriminate at similarly high levels in other major institutional arenas, although this is an area where more research is needed.

There are of course actively antiracist whites, who regularly speak out against white racism, even to the point of risking injury, friendships, or jobs. However, in regard to contemporary discriminatory practices, most whites seem to fall into three other categories of everyday choices. One large group of whites regularly engages in overtly discriminatory and other racist behavior. Some are greatly consumed by racist hatred, as can be seen in many **hate crimes**. A second, much larger, group of whites discriminate against black Americans and other Americans of color in various ways, as the occasion arises, but frequently discriminate in less overt or more subtle ways and may often not be consciously aware of their discrimination. A third group of whites are consistently bystanders, engaging in less direct discrimination but knowingly providing support for those who do. Whites in the latter two groups commonly reject the blatant discrimination in which some whites in the first group engage, even as they themselves engage in subtle or covert discrimination. In addition, most whites in these three latter groups routinely think in white-framed terms when choosing mates, neighborhoods, schools, or business partners. The racist system is thereby reinforced in daily interactions. Research studies also suggest that a sense of white superiority, however dim, is part of the consciousness of most whites, including those who are relatively liberal on racial matters.

In addition, much research suggests that a substantial majority of whites, including those who are liberal, typically do not see the overtly racist actions of other whites as serious enough for them to intervene—or as serious enough to deter their relationships with those who engage in overtly racist behavior. One study examined how 120 college-educated whites reacted to a racist act. Recruited for a psychology study, the students faced an experimental set-up that, unknown to them, had a black actor and a white actor playing out a scenario in which the black person gently bumped the white person on leaving the room. The experimenters varied what the white actor said after the bump: (1) nothing; (2) blurted out, "I hate when black people do that"; (3) said "nigger." After the incident the researcher came in to start the "study" and asked each white student to pick the white person or the black person as a partner. The fact that the white person had made racist comments did not upset most of the white students or deter most from picking the white actor as a partner.[8] These researchers made an educated guess that such white reactions in choosing a white-racist partner over a black partner reflected unconscious racial biases. Apparently, many whites still react the way numerous white students did because they in fact think in consciously and blatantly racist terms about black people, or because they do not find the racist actions of other whites to be serious enough to intervene in or to risk losing a friend or acquaintance.

Recall our research that involved gathering brief semester journals from 626 white students at various colleges and universities. Recording racial events observed in their daily lives, these students reported thousands of clearly racist events. In these many accounts there is not one describing whites who are very assertively protesting racist actions by whites in a diverse frontstage setting. Only rarely in the journal accounts (about 1–2 percent) do we even observe white students or other whites engaging in assertive dissent to racist commentaries and actions by friends, acquaintances, and relatives even in all-white backstage settings. This lack of assertive confrontation was true for the journal writers, even when they later said that they should have intervened. Numerous students commented in their diaries that they recognized their friends and relatives were doing racist stuff, but added that they were still "nice people" to be with. These student journals indicate that even whites who make extremely racist comments or engage in highly racist actions are often viewed by other whites as doing something relatively harmless.[9]

Interestingly, when issues of racism are discussed in the mainstream media, it is often working-class whites (sometimes stereotyped as "rednecks") who get tagged as the most serious racists by media commentators. Blue-collar violence against black Americans or other Americans of color does get some news attention. Elite and middle-class whites are less frequently the focus of serious attention in media discussions of racial problems, and media discussions of discrimination that involve a few middle-class or elite discriminators usually avoid making connections to broader issues of systemic racism. In contrast, the portrait of discriminatory practice that emerges from much social science research is different. Judging from the college student diaries noted above and the many interviews that I and my colleagues have conducted with white Americans and Americans of color over the last two decades, as well as from numerous other field studies of discrimination in housing, employment, and public accommodations cited in this and other chapters, the majority of whites who do this more serious discriminating are those with significant power to bring harm, such as white employers, managers, teachers, social workers, real-estate agents, lenders, landlords and apartment managers, and police officers.[10]

Middle-income and upper-income whites are heavily implicated in contemporary discrimination, although it is likely that in many major institutional areas, such as corporate promotions and urban policing, white men account for the lion's share of the discrimination. Generally, middle-income and upper-income whites are the ones in a position to most significantly affect the lives of a great many black Americans and other Americans of color. Nonetheless, given the right circumstances, most whites in all income groups have the ability to put Americans of color "in their place," to frustrate or sabotage their lives for an array of racist reasons.

Lifetimes of Racial Discrimination: The Harsh Reality

Whether subtle, covert, or blatant, discriminatory practices are commonplace and recurring in a great variety of social settings, ranging from public accommodations to educational facilities, business arenas, workplaces, and neighborhoods. How frequent is the discrimination faced by its targets? What forms does this discrimination take? As we have already observed, whites often play down these harsh racial realities.

National opinion surveys reveal that black Americans face much discrimination, in the present and over their lives. In a 2012 Pew national survey some 43 percent of the black respondents indicated on a general question that black Americans still faced a lot of discrimination, while just 13 percent of the whites in the survey agreed. A very small percentage (14 percent) of the black respondents also reported that they had confidence that local police treated black residents as fairly as whites.[11] An earlier Gallup survey on how black residents are treated in local communities found that the majority said that blacks were not treated equally, which contrasted with the three-quarters of whites who thought blacks were treated the same. More detailed questions revealed significant differences in how black and white respondents viewed blacks' treatment by local police, employers, and store clerks. Another Gallup survey asked black respondents if they had experienced discrimination at work, dining out, shopping, with the police, or in public transportation just during the last month. Nearly half (47 percent) said that they had suffered discrimination in one or more of these areas in this short period.[12] Yet another national survey of African Americans in 2013 found that many faced racially negative encounters several times a year. These included "being threatened or harassed, being treated as if they weren't smart, receiving poorer service at restaurants or stores, having people act afraid of them, or being treated with less courtesy or respect than others."[13]

In addition, a Harvard survey of 202 black Bostonians found that 80 percent viewed discrimination there as significant. The overwhelming majority felt that black Americans lose out on good housing in the area because of fear of how they will be received in white communities. Substantial percentages reported facing discrimination from the police or in workplaces, and nearly half felt they were unwelcome in shopping areas or restaurants in the metropolitan area.[14]

We should note that most opinion survey questions on racial issues are quite brief and customarily deal with only a few of the many types of racial mistreatment that black Americans and other Americans of color face. More detailed questioning would likely reveal a more substantial portrait of discrimination. In addition, there are other reasons why the existing survey data do not adequately describe the reality of everyday racism found in more in-depth studies. For example, most Americans are taught by parents, peers, and clergy to focus on individual reasons for their personal barriers. The reasoning behind such socialization seems to be that a system–blame orientation makes a person seem weak. Thus, some Americans of color who suffer from much discrimination may feel that talking too much about these barriers suggests that they are incapable of dealing with everyday difficulties. In addition, the terminology used in most surveys likely leads to many underestimates. We have found in our research interviews with African Americans that the term "discrimination" itself is reserved by some only for very serious abuse by whites. Lesser forms of mistreatment, because they are so commonplace, may not be characterized as discrimination. For example, a black college professor explained to me that he does not ordinarily think of certain everyday examples of differential treatment—such as white cashiers not putting money in his hand because they do not want to touch a black person—as "racial discrimination." It is only the more serious incidents that he would recall if asked a question by a pollster about having encountered racial discrimination recently.

Racial obstacles are so much a part of most black lives that they generally become a part of the societal woodwork. This everydayness of racist barriers means that for many black Americans a researcher's brief question about discrimination will bring quickly to mind primarily the more serious incidents that stay at the front of the mind—and sometimes not the many intrusions of more subtle racism that occur in one's life. Yet, not recalling some discriminatory incidents when questioned briefly does not mean these encounters are of little consequence. In order to survive in a racist society, Americans of color cannot attend consciously to all the racist incidents that intrude on their lives. The personal and family cost of too-close attention to much discrimination is too great.

To my knowledge, there is no research on the frequency of the incidents and events of discrimination faced by individual black Americans over their lifetimes. In a few exploratory interviews with black respondents, I have asked them a question about frequency and gotten large estimates. I asked a retired printer from New York City how often he had faced discrimination over his eight decades of life. After reflection, he estimated that he confronts at least 250 significant incidents of discrimination from whites each year, if he only includes the incidents he consciously notices. Judging from my field studies and those of my students that have used in-depth interviews with African Americans, this man's experience seems representative. Over the course of a typical lifetime, a black man or woman likely faces *thousands* of instances of blatant, covert, or subtle discrimination at the hands of whites.

Patterns of Discrimination: Political and Legal Institutions

For centuries now, local, state, and federal governments have been proactive in protecting or expanding the system of racial discrimination. Most of these governments are undemocratic in the sense of not having major shaping input in regard to their major structures and operations from Americans of color, historically or currently. While some social science theories, including racial formation theory, play up the importance of "the state" as a relatively impersonal or unbiased terrain over which numerous racial groups compete for political and social power, that is not the empirical reality for the United States, in the past or in the present.[15] As we have seen in Chapter 1, from the beginning the U.S. government has been firmly shaped in terms of the racial interests and framing of the white (male) elite, and that government has mostly been run by a very disproportionately white elite to the present day.

White government officials and programs have often favored the racial and political-economic interests of white Americans. Thus, government programs historically provided much access to homesteading land and numerous other valuable resources exclusively or very disproportionately to white Americans. Coupled with this age-old "affirmative action" for whites, governments created and reinforced extensive patterns of racial exclusion targeting Americans of color. Over centuries, white-dominated legislative, executive, and judicial branches of local, state, and federal governments routinely upheld slavery and Jim Crow segregation.

Discrimination in Voting and Representation

Some 128 years of this country's existence passed before the U.S. Supreme Court (in 1915) finally began to knock down a few state Jim Crow laws severely discriminating against black voters. Increases in political representation still came slowly. Finally, the 1960s civil rights movement forced legislative changes, including passage of the 1965 Voting Rights Act. By the 1970s, in part because of this act, millions of black citizens were finally voting in the South. As a result, the number of black elected officials has increased from a few dozen in the 1960s to several thousand today. Nonetheless, in many areas black voters are still unable to elect black officials in representative numbers. Where they are able to elect some representatives, the latter are often unable to make their voices heeded in still white-dominated legislative bodies.

Today, commonplace voter-restriction actions by political operatives, most of them white conservatives, signal intentional and continuing discrimination against voters of color. Until the 1960s most efforts aimed at reducing the number of voters of color were by operatives connected to the Democratic Party. Yet, in the 1960s' Barry Goldwater and Richard Nixon campaigns voter-restriction activities were increasingly undertaken by Republican operatives. In recent decades these voter-restriction activities have continued to be part of local, state, and federal campaigns. Researchers have identified a disturbing array of blocking strategies used by some white officials to reduce black (and Latino) representation or voting: gerrymandering political districts, changing elective offices into appointive offices, adding new qualifications for office, purging voter-registration rolls, suddenly changing the location of polling places, creating difficult registration procedures, and using numerous other strategies to dilute the black (and Latino) vote. One geographical vote dilution strategy consists of intentionally setting up or continuing at-large electoral systems, instead of utilizing elections by smaller electoral districts. This enables white voters, who dominate a very large political unit, to determine who will be all the political representatives within that political unit, even if it includes a large minority of voters who are not white.[16]

Among the most common of these voter-restriction efforts today are "ballot security" programs of Republican operatives. One major research report explains that these security programs focus almost entirely on voters of color, usually with weak or no evidence of voter fraud to justify them. (Researchers have found very little intentional voter fraud across the country.)[17] In recent elections these voter-restriction programs have involved "intimidating Republican poll watchers or challengers who may slow down voting lines and embarrass potential voters by asking them humiliating questions," "people in official-looking uniforms with badges and side arms who question voters about their citizenship or their registration," "warning signs ... posted near the polls," and "radio ads ... targeted to minority listeners containing dire threats of prison terms for people who are not properly registered—messages that seem designed to put minority voters on the defensive." Some political operatives have mailed false information about voting qualifications to deter black and Latino voters.[18] One mostly Republican strategy involving poll challengers utilizes aggressive "vote caging," a process in which operatives send letters to voters in an area with many Democratic voters just to find out if they will be returned unopened. The returned letters are assumed to be for people who have moved and are no longer living at their voter-registration addresses—people who are challenged by Republican poll watchers at election time. Excessive challenging for minor issues slows down voting for all voters, most of whom are assumed to be voting for the other party.[19]

In recent decades numerous campaigns by members of the Republican and Democratic parties have made use of specific racial appeals to white voters. Recall Nixon's so-called southern strategy, which used racist appeals to attract white southerners from the Democratic Party to the Republican Party. In recent years, some in the Republican Party (see Chapter 9, p. 272) seem to have decided that the party should become primarily one for whites, with mostly token appeals to Americans of color. Indeed, since the 1960s the Republican Party has shown little interest in civil rights issues. While the Democratic Party has had far more participation by Americans of color in its deliberations, elections, and policies, since the 1980s its majority-white elected officials have often failed to increase the input of citizens of color in regard to important state and national policymaking to a truly representative level.

Recently, the conservative Republican majority on the U.S. Supreme Court severely weakened the U.S. Voting Rights Act by, in effect, removing special federal surveillance over political jurisdictions with demonstrated histories of creating barriers for black voters and other voters of color.[20] Today, more than 140 years after African Americans officially gained access to the political process through the post-Civil War amendments to the Constitution, historic promises of truly representative political participation remain substantially unfulfilled. The election of an African American president has not changed most of that general pattern.

White Racism and the U.S. Supreme Court

We saw earlier the critical role of the U.S. Supreme Court in maintaining white dominance in such cases as *Dred Scott v. Sandford*, which upheld slavery and the overwhelming degradation of black Americans, and *Plessy v. Ferguson,* which legitimated the new Jim Crow segregation after the Civil War. This is our historical legacy. Today, whites as a group still benefit greatly from a legal system of their own making, one that often favors the broad group interests of whites. It is not sufficient, as the white founders made very clear in their harsh criticisms of authoritarian British rule, for there only to be equality in access to the law. There must also be fair representation in the creation of all major laws. This is not yet a reality for all Americans. At the top of the legal system black Americans constitute a very small percentage of state attorney generals, district attorneys, leading civil and criminal lawyers, and judges in major state and federal courts. Other Americans of color are also greatly underrepresented in such powerful positions. Given the fact that a greatly disproportionate share of decisionmakers at the top of the judicial and political system are white, it is not surprising that white assumptions and group interests usually predominate. The assumptions of most whites in control of these institutions include: (1) the idea that racial inequality is no longer a serious societal problem needing significant government intervention; and (2) the notion that the legal system currently operates in a generally fair and non-racist fashion.

Recall the white-framed Supreme Court case discussed in Chapter 3, *City of Richmond, Virginia v. J. A. Croson Co.* (1989). A white-run construction company argued that a Richmond program setting aside a little government business for formerly excluded minority companies was unconstitutional. Knocking down this modest set-aside program, a majority of the court ruled that city officials had not demonstrated the continuing reality of racial discrimination. However, city officials had shown that, in a city whose population was half black, less than 1 percent of city business went to black-owned firms. The court dismissed data and testimony from city officials that legal segregation had for decades been the rule in the city and that discrimination in construction contracting was still commonplace. Arguments that large-scale racial discrepancies in business development indicated a high probability of discriminatory practices by white businesses in the present were rejected by that court's white majority.[21]

Justice Sandra Day O'Connor, writing for the plurality, did note "the sorry history of both private and public discrimination in this country" and recognized the reality of "past societal discrimination." Yet she accented the "past," not the present, in her white-framed analysis and described societal discrimination as "amorphous" and having no clear link to the present-day reality of black business conditions in contemporary Richmond. As one critic put it, the use of "amorphous" here means that for the court's majority societal discrimination is "something sporadic, erratic, and diffuse— something that leaves no clearly demarcated traces and produces no readily ascertainable direct effects."[22] Yet the impacts of past discrimination in any

U.S. city, as the data in this book repeatedly demonstrate, are typically major, evident, systemic, and anything but sporadic.

The white majority accented the old white-racist framing that the problems of black Americans are substantially the result of personal choices: "There are numerous explanations for this dearth of minority participation [in construction businesses], including … black and white career and entrepreneurial choices. Blacks may be disproportionately attracted to industries other than construction."[23] The majority suggested that black Americans—who have much experience as construction workers—do not go into construction contracting businesses just because of personal preferences. In making such an unreflective argument the judges provided no evidence of such black inclinations.[24] In a stinging dissent, the court's only black justice up to that point in U.S. history, Justice Thurgood Marshall, concluded that a

> majority of this Court signals that it regards racial discrimination as largely a phenomenon of the past, and that government bodies need no longer preoccupy themselves with rectifying racial injustice. I, however, do not believe this Nation is anywhere close to eradicating racial discrimination or its vestiges.[25]

The legal scholar Jerome Culp has described white justices' assumptions in cases like this as "white supremacist," in that the "interests of black Americans are not considered important enough to be examined or put into the constitutional calculus—the interest blindness assumption."[26]

In recent years, mostly white federal judges and other federal officials have joined with local officials to end even voluntary desegregation and other antidiscrimination programs. President George W. Bush's conservative white appointments to the Supreme Court, working with other conservatives, have regularly weakened local and federal civil rights and desegregation policies and efforts. For instance, in a 2007 decision the high court's conservative majority greatly weakened the 1954 *Brown v. Board of Education* decision by deciding that the local school systems in Seattle and Louisville could *not* make use of any racial markers along with several other factors to increase the desegregation of de facto segregated high schools on a voluntary basis. Liberal Supreme Court Justice Stephen Breyer countered the majority's white-framed ruling with this important point: The

> school board plans before us resemble many others adopted in the last 50 years by primary and secondary schools throughout the Nation. All of those plans represent local efforts to bring about the kind of racially integrated education that *Brown v. Board of Education* … long ago promised.

Breyer emphasized how school desegregation had stalled and how numerous local white officials had often played a significant role in continuing racial segregation. The modest programs in Seattle and Louisville were, in his view, quite constitutional:

> If one examines the context more specifically, one finds that the districts' plans reflect efforts to overcome a history of segregation, embody the results of broad experience and community consultation, seek to expand student choice while reducing the need for mandatory busing, and use race-conscious criteria in highly limited ways that diminish the use of race compared to preceding integration efforts.

Breyer argued that these local plans were fully in line with the goals of the 1954 *Brown* decision: "To invalidate the plans under review is to threaten the promise of *Brown*."[27] Indeed, since 1991 the conservative majority of the Supreme Court has effectively destroyed the promise of *Brown* by rejecting major school desegregation plans. Recent research reports from the prestigious UCLA Civil Rights Project have demonstrated that in most areas black and Latino children still experience great, if not increasing, school segregation.[28]

Police Malpractice

The persisting U.S. racial hierarchy is reproduced by numerous actions of an array of government agents. For instance, white police officers have historically played, and many still often play, a major role in the subordination of black Americans, including those who seek to protest. Data on police violence in U.S. history are chilling. During the years 1920–1932 substantially *more than half* of all African Americans killed by whites were killed by white officers. Police were regularly implicated in the estimated 6,000 bloody lynchings of black men and women from the 1870s to the 1960s. In recent decades, police harassment and violence have continued, and have been openly resisted by black Americans. Analysis of black community "riots" for the years 1943–1972 indicates that the immediate precipitating event of many of these community uprisings was the killing or harassment of black urbanites by white officers. Black residents openly protested police malpractice. This community reaction to police harassment or killings has also been seen in more recent rebellions by black citizens in Los Angeles and Miami in the 1980s and 1990s, and since that time protests of various types against police malpractice have been engaged in by Americans of color in several other cities (for example, Cincinnati in 2001; Toledo in 2005).[29]

In spite of periodic improvements in policing, police violence and other mistreatment have continued to oppress black Americans and their communities. One Gallup poll found that one-fifth of the black respondents reported that they had suffered discrimination at the hands of police officers, a proportion that has increased a little in surveys over recent years. Another Gallup poll found that 42 percent of black respondents (three-quarters of young men) indicated that they had experienced racial profiling by police officers over their lifetimes.[30]

Since 1994 the federal government has been required to collect data on police brutality, but the Congresses in power after that date have failed to appropriate money to collect these data. One social science study analyzed 130 accounts of police brutality in several cities. In these cases the targets of police malpractice were almost always black or Latino. Yet more than 90 percent of the officers involved were white.[31] Police brutality still usually involves white-on-black or white-on-Latino violence. Moreover, some police harassment targeting Americans of color seems to be linked to maintaining certain aspects of residential segregation. Even today, if black or Latino men have to be in historically white residential areas, they often run the risk of pursuit or harassment by public police officers or private security personnel.

In recent years many law-enforcement agencies have used a policy of screening and stopping motorists solely or primarily because of their racial characteristics—what black Americans call the offense of "driving while black" (DWB). One American Civil Liberties Union (ACLU) report has summarized racial-profiling studies involving numerous police departments as showing "large differences in the rate of stops and searches for African Americans and Latinos, and often, Indians (Native Americans) and Asians, even though these groups are less likely to have contraband."[32]

Recently, the Center for Constitutional Rights and two law firms have filed a class action lawsuit against the New York City police department's racial profiling and suspicion-less stops-and-frisks. A research study for the lawsuit by a Columbia University professor found that in the years 2010–2012

> Blacks and Latinos are significantly more likely to be stopped than Whites ... 84% of the stops, a far higher percentage than their proportion of the city's population. Even after controlling for crime, local social conditions and the concentration of police officers in particular areas ... [they] are significantly more likely to be stopped than Whites.[33]

A very small percentage (6 percent) resulted in arrests. This expert's analysis indicated that 95,000 of the stop-and-frisk reports by officers did not involve "reasonable, articulable suspicion," a violation of the Fourth Amendment. Other researchers have shown the extremely discriminatory rates of arrest in New York City for marijuana use by black and Latino residents, in comparison with that for the great many marijuana-using whites in the area.

State judges in California, Rhode Island, New Jersey, and Minnesota have periodically issued orders against such racial profiling. One California study showed that Latinos and African Americans were far more likely to be searched by highway patrol officers for no obvious reason than whites.[34] In 2008 the ACLU and other plaintiffs settled a class action lawsuit on racial profiling by Maryland State Police (MSP) officers in the Interstate 95 corridor. Studies over a long period showed that motorists of color were disproportionately stopped and searched without good reason. An ACLU report notes that the settlement agreement includes a "requirement that the MSP retain an independent consultant to assess its progress towards eliminating the practice of racial profiling" and a statement "condemning racial profiling."[35]

Since many whites are predisposed to view blacks and Latinos out of the white racial frame as inherently criminal, the racial profiling and suspicion-less stop-and-frisk patterns, which often focus on illegal drugs, are unsurprising and have engendered little white protest. In spite of the popularity of racialized drug-courier profiling, no government agency has shown that drug profiles accenting people of color are valid. Such policing is sometimes defended as statistical, or rational, discrimination. But this is another erroneous rationalization for discrimination. Recall from Chapter 4 that black youth use drugs and alcohol somewhat less often than white youth. In addition, whites make up about 70 percent of illegal drug-users. In addition, the majority of drug couriers are likely to be white, as are the majority of drug pushers.[36] This extensive white drug-using and drug-dealing get far less police surveillance and prosecution, yet more evidence of discrimination in the policing and judicial systems.

For several years, including again in 2013, some U.S. representatives and senators have periodically introduced the End Racial Profiling Act, which prohibits racial profiling and requires law-enforcement departments to have effective training procedures and ensure that those abused have a right to sue. This legislation has yet to be passed, although it is supported by 140 civil and legal rights organizations.[37] In 2008 even the United Nations Special Rapporteur on racism spoke out against continuing racial inequality in the U.S. justice system and called on the Congress to pass racial profiling legislation.[38]

More Discrimination: The Criminal Justice System

Racial discrimination extends beyond policing to the numerous aspects of the criminal justice system. In many areas relatively few judges are black, and many white judges appear to have little understanding of the lives of the black Americans—mostly working-class people—that they often face. These judges generally do not come from the same community backgrounds as black defendants, and as a result some discriminate, in subtle or blatant ways, against those in their courtrooms. For example, in the 1990s one New Haven study of more than 1,000 arrests did a statistical analysis of bail-related variables and found that "after controlling for 11 variables relating to the severity of the alleged offense, bail amounts set for black male defendants [by judges] were 35 percent higher than those set for their white male counterparts." In contrast, local bond dealers, operating more realistically, charged significantly lower bonding rates for black than white defendants. A more recent study in North Carolina has found a similar pattern of higher bail amounts being set for blacks than whites.[39]

There is much recent evidence of racial discrimination. We noted previously the impact that the racist framing of black Americans as distinctive illegal drug-users has on how they are treated in the justice system. Consider the policing of marijuana laws. Between 2001 and 2010 police made no fewer than 8.2 million arrests for marijuana crimes, about 88 percent for simple possession. Over this period there was a significant increase in arrests—which accounted for 46 percent of all drug arrests. Huge government expenditures are invested in enforcing the marijuana possession laws—about $3.6 billion in just one recent year.[40]

Once again, the laws are enforced with a dramatic racial bias. A 2013 ACLU research study concluded that

A Black person is 3.73 times more likely to be arrested for marijuana possession than a white person, even though Blacks and whites use marijuana at similar rates. Such racial disparities in marijuana possession arrests exist … in counties large and small, urban and rural, wealthy and poor, and with large and small Black populations…. In the worst offending counties across the country, Blacks were over 10, 15, even 30 times more likely to be arrested than white residents in the same county. These glaring racial disparities in marijuana arrests are not a northern or southern phenomenon, nor a rural or urban phenomenon, but rather a national one.[41]

Research studies indicate that white and black Americans use marijuana at roughly equal rates, with some showing greater use for white youth. The impact of these arrests (and convictions) for marijuana possession are usually devastating, since those arrested and/or convicted often lose jobs and access to programs like student financial aid or public housing. Because of the extreme discrimination, this impact is much greater in black (and Latino) communities than in white communities, and it is an impact extending much beyond the individuals involved.

Consider other drug use as well. In spite of congressional concern and minor tinkering with cocaine drug laws, there is still significant differential punishment for two types of cocaine use. One knowledgeable lawyer has explained:

Powder cocaine is a drug of the affluent suburbs, while crack is used and sold in the inner cities. Since 1986, people convicted in federal court of possessing just five grams of crack cocaine ... face a mandatory sentence of at least five years in prison—and when you get five years of federal time, you do almost all of it. But those caught with powder cocaine must be in possession of 500 grams to get the same five-year sentence.... And day after day, black men are moved out of their homes and communities to serve stiffer sentences than their white, powder-using counterparts.[42]

The 2010 Fair Sentencing Act belatedly moved the minimum amount of crack cocaine to 28 grams, yet still far less than for powder cocaine. There has been only a little change in harsh mandatory sentencing laws in spite of evidence they are obviously discriminatory. (Pressures from the U.S. Sentencing Commission have gotten Congress to reduce possible court sentences, but not to eliminate the underlying cause of this racial differential.) The Obama administration has pressed for elimination of discrimination in the sentencing guidelines, but they have not yet been changed. Some data show that only 9 percent of those arrested for crack cocaine use are white, while 82 percent are black. Yet whites account for a majority of those arrested for using powder cocaine. While illegal drug use is roughly as common among white men as among black men, black men are far more likely than white men to be arrested for illegal drug crimes. This is a major reason why there are disproportionately large numbers of black men in prisons.[43]

The Discriminatory Death Penalty

Institutional racism has long been evident in the application of the death penalty. A recent report of the Death Penalty Information Center revealed that since the 1988 reinstatement of the federal death penalty, federal authorities have "authorized seeking the death penalty against 382 defendants. Of the 382 approved prosecutions, 278 (73%) were against minority defendants."[44] Some 59 percent of those currently on the federal death row are people of color. In addition, a review of death penalty cases involving homicides in California found that those who had killed whites were much more likely to get the death penalty than those whose victims were not white. Apparently, many of those in control of the criminal justice system often value the lives of white Americans more highly than the lives of other Americans.[45] One Philadelphia study found that black defendants were four times as likely as white defendants to get the death penalty for murder, even when the severity of the crimes was considered. A 2008 study of 500 capital punishment trials in Texas's largest county, that surrounding Houston, found black defendants in capital cases were more likely to get the death penalty than similar white defendants, even more so than whites who had committed more heinous murders.[46] Moreover, the racial bias is linked to a regional bias, for 82 percent of death penalty convictions are in the South.

Over the last few decades hundreds of people convicted of serious crimes, including murder, have been shown by DNA tests and other evidence to be innocent. Since the 1970s more than 140 people sentenced to death, mostly people of color, have been freed. Numerous examinations of murder cases across the country have revealed a significant racial bias directed against defendants of color. Because of racial and associated class bias in many court decisions, since 2000 several states have abolished the death penalty, and the total number of death sentences in the United States has dropped by half.[47] The white framing of certain people of color as especially criminal can result in differential policing, unfair but deadly punishments for similar crimes, and false convictions of the innocent for major crimes.

Significantly, in most areas those who decide on pursuing the death penalty and other major prosecution issues—district attorneys and similar state officials—are mostly white. In one study the overwhelming majority of the nearly 1,900 such government officials were white. About 98 percent of prosecutors, nationally, are white. As of 2012, about 83 percent of federal judges are white. States with large black populations, such as Alabama, often have very few, or no, higher-level judges and prosecutors who are black. In addition, according to Amnesty International, a great many juries across the country that try defendants of color for death-penalty crimes are all white or nearly so.[48]

District attorneys and other high-level justice officials control who gets tried, what the charge is, how the trial will proceed, and often what the punishment will be. In numerous areas black jurors are knocked out of jury pools by the racialized use of peremptory challenges by prosecutors, in clear violation of a Supreme Court decision requiring race-neutral reasons for exclusion. White district attorneys desire this exclusion for racial reasons, as one training video for Philadelphia prosecutors makes clear. "Let's face it," the video says, "the blacks from low-income areas are less likely to convict. There's a resentment to law enforcement."[49] In addition, surveys of public defenders and metropolitan judges in Minnesota found that about half of each group thought that the (mostly white) prosecutors there discriminate against potential jurors of color in their peremptory challenges. In this manner—and in spite of a weak Supreme Court decision (*Batson v. Kentucky* 1986) attempting to restrict such practices—potential jurors of color who might disagree with the interpretations of white authorities or who bring an unrepresented real-life perspective to court cases are often excluded from fair participation in the workings of the criminal justice system. Clearly we do not actually have a criminal "justice" system in which all Americans are fairly represented in critical decisionmaking.[50]

Violence against African Americans

The Long History

For centuries whites used extensive violence—from chains and whippings to lynchings—to keep African Americans racially subordinated. Such violence was a recurring part of enslavement and Jim Crow subordination. Violent practices were perpetrated by elite and ordinary whites, including the founders Thomas Jefferson, George Washington, and James Madison. After the Civil War, whites were fearful of freed black Americans and engaged in large-scale violence to create legal segregation. The emerging system of Jim Crow segregation was enforced with private and police violence. Well into the 1990s some white southerners serving proudly in the U.S. Congress had earlier been outspoken advocates of violence-enforced segregation.

Today, many whites exhibit naiveté or willing ignorance about this brutal history of enforced segregation and violence. One caller to a radio show assessing public reaction to a jury's decision that black athlete O. J. Simpson was not guilty of murder suggested half-jokingly that whites should riot. The talk-show host concluded "white people don't riot."[51] However, these whites showed an ignorance of U.S. history. Virtually all U.S. racial riots from the 1840s to the 1930s—and there were many—were characterized by whites attacking black Americans or other Americans of color. In 1863, during the Civil War, white workers in New York City rioted for days over new draft laws and the use of black workers to break a strike. In that rioting more than 100 people, including numerous black Americans, were killed—the largest for any riot in U.S. history. The decades after the Civil War saw many killings of black men, women, and children by white mobs, including lynchings.

In the early 1900s there were many more riots by whites targeting African Americans. There were several major riots by whites just in 1919—in Longview, Texas; Phillips County, Arkansas; Washington, DC; Chicago, Illinois; Knoxville, Tennessee; and Omaha, Nebraska. The growing competition between white and black workers was often an underlying factor in white rioting, and all-white police forces usually did nothing or took the side of white rioters. As late as the 1960s, white mob violence against non-violent civil rights demonstrators could be seen regularly on television.[52]

Recent Violence and Hate Crimes

White attacks and other hate crimes against black Americans and numerous other Americans of color are still part of the U.S. landscape. The most recent (2012) FBI report on single-bias hate crimes noted there had been 3,645 victims of racially motivated crimes in the previous year. Seven in ten were targeted because of an apparent antiblack bias—with Native Americans, Asian Americans (and Pacific Islanders), and Latinos also being victims of significant racialized crimes. (The report states that "victim may refer to a person, business, institution," but most are individuals.[53]) These numbers are serious underestimates because most of the more than 17,000 police jurisdictions did not report their hate crimes, reported for only part of a year, or reported zero hate crimes. A 2013 report by the Southern Poverty Law Center (SPLC) noted that these hate crime "incidents include only a fraction of the approximately 195,000 reported and unreported hate crimes that a 2011 Bureau of Justice Statistics report estimated occurred annually between 2003 and 2009."[54] Although African Americans are still major targets, according to the SPLC much of the recent increase in hate-based crimes has involved immigrants of color, especially those from Latin America. The number of racist hate groups, such as Klan and neo-Nazi groups, has also grown dramatically in recent years.

Some hate incidents have ranged from the placement of threatening nooses on doors and the scrawling of racist graffiti on homes and cars, to aggressive verbal harassment of pedestrians and coworkers, to more violent attacks including killings. In the late 1990s, a black man, James Byrd, Jr., was walking down a Jasper, Texas, road. Three white men, with ties to white-supremacist groups, tied him to a pickup and dragged him until his head was severed. One reportedly said to the others, "We're starting *The Turner Diaries* early," referring to large-scale violence against the U.S. government by white supremacists in that very racist novel. The Jasper lynching triggered copycat crimes in other cities.[55] Violent hate crimes are still commonplace. One fairly recent hate crime took place in West Virginia, where a black woman was reportedly raped and tortured for days by six whites. According to press reports, these whites raped her and constantly called her "nigger." One who assaulted her said, "That's what we do to niggers around here."[56]

In recent decades many whites have engaged in using hangman's nooses as a threat against Americans of color. A series of noose incidents were reported in Hempstead, New York, including a noose drawn on the locker of a black sanitation employee and nooses placed around the police department. Black employees filed complaints charging "intolerable work conditions."[57] The *New York Times* reported a rash of noose incidents a few months before the Hempstead events and also noted that an interracial couple in Suffolk County, New York, had a Klan-type cross burning on their lawn. Hanging nooses and burning crosses are serious because they conjure up images of mobs' engaged in brutal lynchings, especially in the minds of many black Americans who themselves, or whose immediate ancestors, suffered such incidents under the legal segregation that only ended in the 1960s.[58]

Periodically, some whites in the growing number of white-supremacist and racial-nationalist groups have threatened large-scale violence against Americans of color or government agencies viewed as supporting people of color. For example, the 1995 bombing of the Oklahoma City federal building by antigovernment terrorists, who were white supremacists, killed 169 people. Somewhat later, other bomb plots were uncovered, one targeting the Southern Poverty Law Center in Montgomery, Alabama, and others targeting federal buildings. In recent years white militia and supremacy groups have stockpiled explosives and prepared bombing ventures.[59]

For some years now, numerous human rights activists have researched the national and international growth of a renewed white-supremacist movement. In the United States there are many extreme white-nationalist groups, including Ku Klux Klan groups and a variety of neo-Nazi groups and armed white militias. Nationally, in 2013, the Southern Poverty Law Center counted 1,007 known hate groups operating actively across the U.S., a great many of them Klan and other white supremacists, neo-Nazis, racist skinheads, and border vigilante organizations, with at least 300,000 whites as active or passive supporters. This number has grown in recent years, in substantial part because of white extremists' concerns over the increase in Latino and Asian immigration, the expanding racial diversity of the population, and the election of a black president.[60]

Members of these white-nationalist groups, as well as thousands of others who read their literature, sometimes engage in racially motivated crimes. After the 2008 presidential election there were at least 200 incidents of hate-based vandalism, as well as threats of violence against President-elect Obama, more than for any previous U.S. president. Death threats have continued throughout Obama's presidency, many of them likely being racially motivated. White-supremacist leaders have viewed the election of an African American as a recruiting tool to bring new whites into their organizations. David Duke, former Klan leader, gave a press conference at which he reportedly asserted that the election is a "shock to me and it should be a shock to the community that European Americans now have to fight for our rights, in I guess Obama's 'New America.' ... do whites have rights? ... I don't see him as our President."[61]

White Racism and the Internet

Since the late twentieth century, white-supremacist and other hate-based organizations in the U.S. and overseas have grown significantly in number and impact. One contemporary activity involves creating major Internet websites. The Council of Europe (COE) has estimated there are about 4,000 hate-based websites worldwide, with 2,500 originating out of the U.S. Estimates of hate-based websites vary greatly, ranging from hundreds to thousands. Nonetheless, it is clear that there are at least several hundred active websites originating from the United States which insistently spread a white-supremacist ideology and encourage violence or other discriminatory actions based on that ideology. One reason for U.S. dominance in setting up the majority of influential white-supremacist websites is the way that the First Amendment to the U.S. Constitution is usually interpreted to protect racist hate speech. Most other countries—including Austria, Brazil, Canada, France, Germany, Great Britain, Italy, and the Netherlands—significantly restrict white-supremacist and other hate-based speech, yet most U.S. policymakers stand behind the notion that extreme white-supremacist speech should be constitutionally protected. This position ensures that it is difficult to combat white-supremacist speech globally and makes the U.S. an easy place to print extremely racist materials and to create white-supremacist websites.[62]

Researcher Jessie Daniels has shown there are two forms of racist-right and other hate-speech websites on the Internet, websites that many people treat as important sources of information. One type openly showcases "racist propaganda for those outside the organization, including youth; and for those within, use the 'private web' of encrypted messages for communication, command and control." Even more sinister are "cloaked" websites, which present themselves as being about the "truth" of racial issues and may seem moderate or pro-civil rights, yet are working for "a hidden white-supremacist agenda. These sites use a combination of carefully chosen domain names, deceptive graphic user interfaces (GUI), and subtly racist rhetoric that pose a pernicious epistemological threat to racial equality."[63] This growth in racist websites is challenging for those seeking to reduce white-supremacist framing and extreme racist activities in the U.S. and other countries. More so than much other controversial speech, hate-based speech is likely to link to discriminatory action. Historical analyses reveal that the U.S. and other countries have long histories of this hate-based speech motivating much physical violence and other discrimination.[64]

Daniels has further concluded that

> old forms of racism have moved onto the Internet and exist alongside newer forms, such as cloaked websites that seek to disguise racist propaganda. The threat ... is less one of potential recruitment to social movement organizations (although that is possible), but rather the shifting epistemological ground on which politically hard-won ideals of racial equality are based.[65]

These sites help to perpetuate and reinforce the old white-racist framing against which human rights movements have struggled very actively since at least the 1960s' civil rights movements.

Note too that there is frequently significant overlapping in the way in which whites inside extremist groups and numerous other whites who are opposed to such extremist groups racially frame the social worlds in which they live. Whites of different backgrounds and politics periodically make use of similar racist stereotypes, images, or other features of the dominant white frame. In addition, occasionally, a member of a white-nationalist group becomes visible as a member of a mainstream organization. For example, an outspoken white supremacist became a member of the Republican Party's Executive Committee in Palm Beach County, Florida.[66]

Racial Attacks on President Barack Obama

During both the 2008 and the 2012 presidential campaigns, many racist attacks, verbal and otherwise, were made on Obama and his candidacy by those participating in various capacities in the Republican political campaign. Some attacks were similar to the hate crimes perpetrated by the white supremacists just discussed, while others were not hate crimes but reflected an aggressive white-racist framing that overlapped in some ways with the framing common in white extremist groups. In 2008 numerous white supporters of Senator John McCain used racist epithets at presidential campaign events. At a Des Moines rally one woman yelled "He's a nigger!" at the mention of Obama. At other rallies whites had racist signs with messages like "Vote Right, Vote White" or held up racist dolls, racist effigies of Obama, or monkey dolls with Obama's name on them.[67] At one conservative forum, activists bought boxes of waffle mix that racially caricatured Obama with a stereotypically Arab headdress and Mexican dress. Other white conservatives printed mock food stamps portraying a mule with Obama's face on it and pictures of watermelon and ribs. In Washington state a Republican Party official had to apologize for his group's selling at a state fair "$3 bills" showing Senator Obama in Arab dress with a camel and mocking "black speech."[68] The former prominent conservative activist, Frank Schaeffer, supported Obama's candidacy and called on McCain to end the hate-filled actions of some participants in his campaign.[69]

Much racist commentary and action continued to pursue Obama during his 2012 electoral campaign and thereafter. Recall from Chapter 4 the racist joke about Obama's ancestry circulated by a prominent federal judge during the 2012 campaign. During the campaign, and often since, many white Tea Party and other conservatives have asserted the idea that "their country" is being taken over by Americans of color. One Tea Party faction's email emphasized the end of the "White Anglo-Saxon Protestant" race because of growth in the population of color.[70] During that campaign there was much racist mocking of Obama by whites associated with various Tea Party factions. Researchers at the Institute for Research and

Education on Human Rights examined the views of Tea Party activists, almost all white, and found that they frequently operated out of a harsh white framing and made use of racist epithets, distorted racist images of Obama, and Confederate battle flags at political events.[71] This Confederate battle flag, as political writer Ed Kilgore has sarcastically put it, is not problematical as a contemporary symbol for "southern pride" (or "white pride") aside from its "association with a violent revolution against the United States in the cause of human bondage, and aside from its long association with Jim Crow, and aside from its twentieth-century revival as the emblem of hard-core resistance to measures of basic decency."[72]

Conclusion

Being black in U.S. society means always having to be prepared for antiblack actions by whites—in most places and at many times of the day, week, month, or year. Being black means living with various types of racial discrimination and their often severe impacts, from cradle to grave. This *lifetime* reality is also true for most other Americans of color. We observe constantly in the examples of discrimination in this chapter the array of whites, from the elite to working-class whites, who perpetuate the aspects of racial oppression in its many forms—individual and institutional, informal and formal, unofficial and official.

Throughout all these examples of discriminatory practices in the contemporary United States, we observe the great and persisting power of the centuries-old white racial frame. Today, as in the past, this dominant racial frame lies behind most of the recurring racial discrimination at all levels of this society. Some white discriminators act out of it consciously and openly, while others operate out of it half-consciously or unconsciously, for it has become normalized "common sense" for most whites. Clearly, until whites quit racially framing society and regularly acting out of it in racist ways—and thereby maintaining whites' racial privilege and power—the centuries-old system of racial oppression will persist.

In this chapter we have examined just some of the patterns of racial discrimination today—especially in politics, the courts, and policing. We will now turn to other examples of persisting racial discrimination in yet other areas, including housing, employment, business, education, and health care.

6

More Racial Oppression
Other Institutional Sectors

The Spatial Basis of Systemic Racism: Housing Segregation

Today, black Americans often live separately from white Americans, and the latter are often significantly separated from other Americans of color as well. If we look closely at our town and city patterns, we see whites and blacks moving about their daily routines, but find that black residents are more likely to cross the major racial–territorial boundaries of towns and cities than are white residents. Typically, blacks spend proportionately more time interacting with whites than whites spend interacting with blacks. There is a strong racial topography to our towns and cities.

Most metropolitan areas in the North and South continue to have a high degree of residential segregation. The last (2010) census revealed that cities remain very segregated, especially in regard to the segregation of whites from blacks. One statistical measure of residential segregation, the index of dissimilarity, has decreased slowly for white–black segregation over recent decades, though not for certain other groups. Nonetheless, an average black American still lives in a large urban census area that is only about 35 percent white, about the same as *for the 1940s.* Moreover, Asian and Latino Americans are less segregated from whites than blacks are, but their significant residential segregation from whites has not changed since the 1980s. Today, an average white American lives in a much less diverse neighborhood than an average African, Asian, or Latino American.[1]

In a recent report demographers Logan and Stults underscored some persisting reasons for substantial levels of residential segregation:

Part of the answer is that systematic discrimination in the housing market has not ended, and for the most part it is not prosecuted. Fair housing laws by and large are enforced only when minority home seekers can document discrimination and pursue a civil court case without assistance from public officials. Yet studies that track the experience of minority persons in the rental or homeowner market continue to find that they are treated differently than comparable whites. Another part of the answer is urban history.... Changes have been greater in metropolitan areas with historically fewer black residents, but very slow in the old Ghetto Belt—places like New York, Chicago, Newark and Detroit.[2]

Another major reason linked to systemic racism that they note is the inequality and discrimination in public services, such as poor public schools, that many communities of color must endure. Given this lack of good services, few white families, even those willing to live in a diverse area, will consider moving there. When black or Latino families move into historically white areas, white families frequently begin to flee, thereby increasing residential segregation there. Even more consequential, of course, is the impact that inadequate public services and poor environmental conditions have on residents of color. One recent study concluded that the urban environments of whites and people of color are very unequal in numerous ways. Black and Latino urbanites, especially in more segregated larger cities, are much more likely than white urbanites there to have neighbors with meager socioeconomic resources, to endure inferior city services, and to deal with street crime on a recurring basis.[3]

In addition, African Americans are almost as segregated within *suburban* areas now as a few decades back, and Latino and Asian American populations there are more segregated than in the recent past. Racial enclaves are becoming commonplace in suburban areas. Middle-class African Americans often suffer significantly from racial and class segregation. Even when middle-class black Americans have some white residents in their neighborhoods, these whites tend to be less well off than middle-class blacks. Their middle-class neighborhoods tend to be more economically troubled and have weaker public services than typical white middle-class neighborhoods.[4]

Segregation as Slavery Unwilling to Die

Systemic racism has long involved white control of much rural and urban space and territory. Since the 1600s, being defined and treated as "black" has meant limitations on where one can work, live, and travel. During slavery, the majority of African Americans were separated from whites, often in slave quarters; spatial movements were greatly controlled by law and institutionalized violence. After slavery, southern and border state elites created an extensive system of Jim Crow segregation, following the lead of northern elites. Firmly in place by the early 1900s, the rigid segregation, by law or custom, of whites from blacks in housing and other institutional areas could be seen across the country.

Today, housing segregation provides empirical evidence of the impact of past and present racial oppression. In residential segregation we observe what the Supreme Court, in a 1968 decision, *Jones et ux. v. Alfred H. Mayer Co.*, called "a relic of slavery." Ruling on a housing discrimination in St. Louis, the court majority argued that current discrimination is a long-term consequence of centuries of black enslavement:

> This Court recognized long ago that, whatever else they may have encompassed, the badges and incidents of slavery—its "burdens and disabilities"—included restraints upon "those fundamental rights which are the essence of civil freedom, namely, the same right ... to inherit, purchase, lease, sell and convey property, as is enjoyed by white citizens."[5]

In a concurring opinion, Justice William O. Douglas used stronger language, concluding that

> the true curse of slavery is not what it did to the black man, but what it has done to the white man. For the existence of the institution produced the notion that the white man was of superior character, intelligence, and morality.... Some badges of slavery remain today. While the institution has been outlawed, it has remained in the minds and hearts of many white men. Cases which have come to this Court depict a spectacle of slavery unwilling to die.[6]

Douglas then listed the many types of discrimination faced by African Americans.

As we have frequently seen, each generation of whites inherits an array of racialized privileges, including the ability to enter residential areas and job settings reserved more or less for whites—and thereby the ability to build up family assets in the form of access to buying a nice house, and thus a housing equity. In parallel with the intergenerational transmission of white privileges is the transmission of discriminatory barriers for black Americans and other Americans of color.

Many areas that black families have moved into have had deteriorating housing and neighborhoods. Yet few whites are aware of the racial and other political-economic factors involved in such housing and neighborhood decay. Many African Americans have had to rent where the rents are relatively low, and thus where public and private services are typically quite inadequate. Those who have bought houses often have faced similarly serious transportation, economic, health care, educational, and other private and public services limitations. Many critics of black housing situations or communities have ignored the "fact that discrimination in employment, in money lending, and in choice of neighborhood often ensured that the only houses African Americans could afford would be older properties in already declining areas."[7] Variable access to significant socioeconomic resources over centuries of systemic racism has long meant unjust enrichment for a majority of whites and unjust impoverishment for a majority of African Americans, generation after generation.

Patterns of Housing Discrimination Today

For the first 350 years of colonial and U.S. development, residential segregation was often legally or otherwise overtly imposed by whites. After the 1968 Civil Rights Act went into effect, residential segregation across the color line became unofficial and informal, as it remains today. One factor maintaining this segregation is the array of racist attitudes, images, and emotions still in many white minds. Negative views of African Americans as neighbors are usually grounded in age-old stereotypes, such as notions of black families being much more into drugs. Many whites get fearful when the black percentage of their neighborhood or community reaches even a modest level. Research has shown that, when a predominantly white area becomes more than about 8 percent black, some whites consider moving out. As the percentage reaches about 20 percent in what was once an all-white or nearly all-white residential neighborhood, many whites will not consider moving in. Persisting residential segregation is frequently enforced by the hostility of white homeowners and by whites deciding not to move into already integrated areas, as well as by the racial steering and other, mostly subtle, discriminatory practices of many in the real-estate industry.[8] Intentional discrimination is reinforced by the institutionalized reality of unequal assets and incomes across the color line, again stemming from centuries of unjust enrichment for white Americans and unjust impoverishment for black Americans.

Today, housing discrimination cuts across a variety of institutions and includes a range of white discriminators—landlords, homeowners, bankers, realtors, and government officials. Numerous research studies indicate that many whites in each group will discriminate under certain circumstances. One major reason for racially segregated housing is the continuing discrimination by rental housing owners, managers, and real-estate salespeople. Since the 1990s numerous housing audit studies, using white and black testers (and sometimes Asian and Latino testers) have demonstrated that racial barriers in regard to rental housing and purchased housing are commonplace in metropolitan areas.[9] For example, a study after Hurricane Katrina (2005) using black and white testers in southern states discovered much discrimination in rental housing. As one knowledgeable National Fair Housing Alliance official has explained, their researchers

> measured what the apartment seekers were told about unit availability,
> ... security deposit, rental rates, discounts for evacuees, and other terms

and conditions of apartment leasing. In 66 percent of these tests—43 of 65 instances—White callers were favored over African-American callers. This is an extremely high rate of discrimination.[10]

A 2013 government report on housing discrimination also reported research using large-scale paired-testing (a white tester and a tester of color) in 28 metropolitan areas. Researchers found that black, Latino, and Asian American homeseekers were more likely than similarly qualified white homeseekers to be shown fewer rental units and houses. One finding was revealing about the impact of perceived identity on housing experiences:

> Specifically, black and Asian renters whose race is readily identifiable based on name and speech are significantly more likely to be denied an appointment than minorities perceived to be white. During an in-person visit, renters who are identifiably black, Hispanic, or Asian are shown fewer units than minorities who are perceived to be white.[11]

In addition, an innovative research project in Los Angeles found substantial discrimination in initial responses of landlords to rental housing inquiries. Researchers sent out 1,115 email messages inquiring about vacant rental housing. To each message they randomly assigned what the researchers viewed as a distinctive African American, Arab American, or white American name. Inquiries using African American and Arab American names got significantly fewer positive responses than white names, with African American names getting the worst response. Landlords were discriminating against African Americans and Arab Americans even before they gained information about the potential renters' incomes, credit, or references.[12]

Another study of rental and home-buying discrimination examined 2,176 cases of racial discrimination filed with the Ohio Civil Rights Commission. Some 80 percent of these involved African Americans, even though they make up only 18 percent of the population. Black women were the most likely to report discrimination, with half of the mistreatment occurring up front as exclusionary discrimination and half coming after black individuals or families had moved in. The exclusionary cases mostly cited landlords and owners as the discriminators. These cases usually involved a direct refusal to rent or sell (including use of racist slurs) or covert discrimination in the form of lying about housing availability or of using racially differential standards for renter or buyer qualification. Real-estate agents, bankers, and insurance companies played a discriminatory role in some cases. Once housed, some African American renters and homebuyers faced racially differential treatment in regard to pets or rental conditions, or they faced racial harassment by whites. Most discrimination was perpetrated by white landlords and owners, but some was done by white agents at banks and insurance agencies or by white neighbors.[13]

While the very blatant door-slamming discrimination of a few decades back is less often reported, more subtle and covert discriminatory practices limit housing options and significantly increase the personal costs involved in finding adequate housing. Gaining evidence of such discrimination often necessitates looking at the *pattern* of housing decisions, what is termed the racially "discriminatory impact." As Tanya House, with the Lawyers' Committee for Civil Rights Under Law, has noted:

> Blatant bigoted behavior has been reduced over the years because those who discriminate act more discreetly, making evidence of discriminatory intent harder to find. But this does not mean that racial discrimination has disappeared and this is a key reason why courts have consistently found discrimination can be proved through a discriminatory impact standard that does not require a finding of intent to discriminate.[14]

Note too that several studies show that white homeowners play an important role in housing discrimination. A significant percentage openly assert that they should still be *allowed* to discriminate. One survey found that 27 percent of white respondents were willing to publicly admit that they felt there should be a law that allows a (white) homeowner to discriminate against African Americans in the sale of a house. Many others may have felt the same way, but were unwilling to say so to a pollster.[15]

Many whites, including conservative scholars, argue that African Americans are segregated because *they choose* to be segregated—that is, "blacks prefer to live with their kind."[16] Yet, black families often do try to improve housing situations and services by seeking an apartment or home in predominantly white or racially integrated areas, yet frequently run into subtle or covert white opposition. Maria Krysan and Reynolds Farley examined responses of 2,000 black respondents in several cities to questions about neighborhood-mix preferences. The average black respondent was open to living in a diverse neighborhood, indeed preferring a 50–50 black–white mix, but willing to consider any residential mix with a visible black presence. Most did not prefer living in mostly black communities.[17] Certainly, many African Americans do not wish to be among the first families in a predominantly white area. Because of continuing white acts of overt antiblack hostility and some violence—with periodic violent acts against black homeowners and renters, including cross-burnings, recorded in the last few decades—black Americans are often unwilling to be pioneers in moving into historically white areas.[18]

Insurance Agents and Lenders

For many years federal regulations openly fostered racial discrimination in lending. Only since the 1960s have federal regulations sought to ban lending discrimination. The 1968 Civil Rights Act and the Equal Credit Opportunity Act officially prohibit mortgage and other lending discrimination. Nonetheless, research shows continuing and significant discrimination by lending institutions against black Americans and other Americans of color who seek housing mortgages and loans. Many white-run insurance companies also create housing barriers for Americans of color. One study used black, Latino, and white testers, who presented themselves as homeowners seeking insurance to three major insurance companies' offices in nine cities. Researchers found the overall rate of racial discrimination to be 53 percent in regard to such things as insurance coverage and price. Being white increased insurance options and saved money.[19]

Some lending discrimination appears to be motivated by a concern for what are termed "sound business practices," and thus does not appear to be intentionally discriminatory. Numerous lenders and property insurers frequently refuse to provide services, or do provide services but on unfavorable terms, for people seeking to buy older homes in residential areas where home valuations are lower. Such lending practices can have a negative impact on homebuyers from groups with long histories of facing institutional racism. As housing expert Gregory Squires has noted:

> many of those underwriters and sales agents who follow these rules really do believe they are acting on the basis of sound business practice.... Obviously, racism went into the formulation of such rules, and these industries no doubt have as many racists as any other. But such institutionalized practices, with severely discriminatory effects, are often carried out by people who simply are not thinking about race.[20]

The routinization of racially oriented decisions in the housing industry is such that some whites who practice it may not be consciously aware of it. Americans of color have seldom been consulted by white-run insurance companies and banking organizations that determine the rules often favoring white homeseekers.

A significant aspect of the major recession of 2008–2010 involved white lending officials' discriminatory lending practices. One of these practices was to regularly channel black and Latino homeowners into subprime (high-interest) home loans when they would have qualified for regular-interest, less risky loans. Some Federal Home Mortgage Disclosure Act reports indicate black and Latino homebuyers were more than twice as likely as white homebuyers to receive expensive subprime mortgages from lenders—even after loan amounts and household incomes were taken into account. This was true when residential areas were otherwise economically similar. One study of a 97 percent white working-class suburb and a 97 percent black working-class suburb in the Detroit area, with similar family income distributions, found that a substantial majority of home loans in the black suburb had high interest rates, compared to just 17 percent in the comparable white suburb.[21]

One investigative report has described how mostly white bankers, who were often not at the time making much money on conventional home loans, worked with officials in the George W. Bush administration to expand loans to families of color whom lenders knew would have trouble repaying, and in the process making substantial profits. Although the official rationale was that subprime mortgages would "increase homeownership," most of these high-interest loans were not for first mortgages, but for second mortgages insistently peddled by lenders to unsuspecting customers with the argument that the latter could use their home equities for important needs such as paying medical bills. A *majority* of families of color conned into these problematical loans had credit scores that should have enabled them to get loans with more favorable interest rates and conditions, which they did not receive from the mostly white lenders. Significant racialized thinking appears to lie behind many such discriminatory loans. As a result, the NAACP filed a lawsuit against several firms that made these racially predatory loans.[22]

In February 2013, as the economy was beginning to rebound with some people buying and selling foreclosed properties and other urban real estate, the influential magazine *Bloomberg Businessweek*, associated with New York City's mayor, ran a cover with racist caricatures of black and Latino homeowners flush with money in association with a feature story on this housing rebound. The National Fair Housing Alliance reacted to the cover in this way:

> We were shocked and dismayed by a Jim Crow era cover and its depiction of homeowners of color. It is … difficult to know what this newsmagazine was trying to convey. A more accurate cover would have depicted Big Bank CEOs and Wall Street moguls who provided monetary incentives to push predatory loans.[23]

These cover caricatures were drawn from old and blatantly racist framing of black and Latino urbanites.

Actually, the results of these racially predatory loan decisions have been catastrophic for many families and communities of color. Because of the loss of jobs and other negative impacts of the 2008–2010 recession, many black and Latino homeowners lost their homes to foreclosures. That meant a loss of many billions of dollars in assets. Most families of color have their modest assets, if any, in home equities, so this economic loss has been devastating for many communities.[24] In addition, during and after the recession another problem of racial discrimination has arisen. Lenders and investors holding these repossessed houses have let many of them deteriorate in communities of color, while usually maintaining those in white areas. As the National Fair Housing Alliance points out, the Fair Housing Act "requires banks, investors, servicers ... to maintain and market properties that are for sale or rent without regard to the race or national origin of the residents of a neighborhood."[25] Clearly, because predatory subprime lending and the associated foreclosure crisis have hit communities of color much harder than white communities, there has also been a disproportionately negative impact in the form of illegally deteriorating houses—which have had, in turn, a major impact on the quality of life in the former communities.

Moreover, for decades, using a variety of urban redevelopment approaches, white politicians and business leaders across the country have tried to rebuild central cities, and in the process have frequently further segregated black families and destroyed older black communities. Private and public urban redevelopment projects have often taken neighborhoods inhabited by working-class or poor Americans of color and converted them into business districts or gentrified residential areas, many of them mostly for affluent whites.[26]

Today in the United States there is no national watchdog organization that proactively and persistently seeks out and punishes the still commonplace housing discrimination. The federal Department of Housing and Urban Development is doing a better job these days in handling individual complaints, although its enforcement program is very underfunded. State housing agencies vary greatly in processing of complaints; when complaints are brought by victims of discrimination, they often get no redress. A recent report of the National Commission on Fair Housing found that federal and state laws banning racial discrimination in rental and sales housing are at best weakly enforced in many areas.[27] Moreover, two-thirds of the housing discrimination complaints (fewer than 30,000 annually for all protected classes) are in fact investigated by *private* fair housing organizations. (They also do most of the education of consumers and businesses on fair housing laws.) One housing expert has estimated that less than one-third of the housing discrimination complaints filed annually are actually resolved in a way that is satisfactory for the complainant. Even these resolutions usually do not involve stiff penalties for the discriminators, penalties that might discourage further discrimination. Thus, if one considers the estimated four million acts of housing discrimination each year (for all protected classes), less than 1 percent are actually processed to the satisfaction of the targets of that discrimination.[28]

Discrimination in Employment

Spatial Mismatch—Exclusion from Jobs

Residential segregation makes possible, or strongly reinforces, numerous other types of racial exclusion, discrimination, and subordination. In the decades after World War II racial polarization across the geographical expanse of metropolitan areas increased with the government-subsidized movement of white middle-income families to suburbs, often leaving behind a mostly working-class and poor population of color in central cities. Over the decades this large-scale suburban migration has been greatly stimulated by investment decisions of corporations, banks, and developers, and has been greatly assisted by federal government subsidies for home mortgages and for public services such as highways. (In contrast, many white-controlled suburban communities have laws or regulations designed to restrict housing developments for moderate-income residents, especially those of color.) Much employment has decentralized, and many suburbs have seen growing numbers of jobs for their often predominantly white populations. While the numbers of blacks and Latinos moving to suburban areas has increased in the last few decades, the decades-old creation of better-paying jobs away from central cities has made it difficult for the majority of blacks and Latinos still in central cities to have as reasonable access to much good-paying employment as whites.[29] Recent research demonstrates that this spatial mismatch accounts for at least one-third, and perhaps half, of the significant differences in employment and unemployment between white workers and black or Latino workers in various urban areas.[30]

Some of this exclusion from good jobs results from intentional discrimination by business executives. One major study examined the situation of workers of color in Atlanta, Boston, Detroit, and Los Angeles. Researchers again found that the movement of jobs from central cities to suburban areas by employers had a serious impact on black employment opportunities. Significantly, numerous employers admitted that their job-creation decisions and/or hiring decisions involved racist stereotypes about the personality traits, attitudes, and behaviors of black workers and other workers of color.[31]

What many people do not realize is that the economy generally loses from continuing residential segregation and the spatial mismatch between jobs and residents. One recent longitudinal study of metropolitan areas again demonstrated the serious impact of this spatial mismatch in jobs and residence for workers of color. Interestingly, this study showed too that there was a major negative impact from persisting segregation in housing on *overall* metropolitan economic growth—for white residents in suburbs and residents of color in central cities—in the short run and long run.[32]

In addition, many U.S. jobs, especially the less-skilled, have been moved overseas by capitalistic employers seeking lower-wage labor, less regulation, and higher profits. These overseas investment strategies have contributed to higher unemployment and underemployment for workers of color within the United States. One study examined outsourcing of blue-collar and white-collar jobs overseas and found that black workers were especially hard hit by the loss of blue-collar jobs, even more so than Latino or white workers. More than five million U.S. manufacturing jobs have been lost since 1979, about half of these so far in the twenty-first century. Black workers were more concentrated in these jobs, and these employment losses help to explain why in recent years the unemployment rate for blacks, especially black men, has often risen faster than for whites and certain other groups. Today, moreover, some lower-paying white-collar (for example, clerical) jobs disproportionately held by black female and male workers are similarly endangered by the increasing export of jobs by U.S. employers.[33]

Racial Discrimination in Hiring

Today, subtle, covert, and blatant discrimination in employment remains an important aspect of the everyday reality for Americans of color. Many experience differential treatment in attempts to secure their families' needs. Each year numerous lawsuits are filed charging racial discrimination against employers, and thousands of employment discrimination complaints are filed annually with state agencies and the federal Equal Employment Opportunity Commission (EEOC). Over the last ten years the number of race-based complaints filed annually with the EEOC has been in the 28,000–36,000 range. This is only the tip of the iceberg, however. In periodic national surveys African Americans report significant personal and group discrimination, which data suggest the reality of a much higher level of actual employment discrimination just for African Americans each year.[34] Some of this discriminatory treatment occurs at the point of hiring, while other mistreatment is encountered later on. Many corporate executives and their subordinate managers make little effort to recruit and hire black employees or other employees of color, especially for higher-level positions. There is significant variability, however. Studies using government records have found that many U.S. companies hire far fewer workers of color than other comparable companies drawing from the *same* labor pools, a result suggesting some routinized discrimination in the former companies.[35]

Research studies have examined racial discrimination in this hiring process from different angles. Recall the MIT study in which applicants with "white-sounding" names were much more likely to be contacted by employers than those with "black-sounding" names (see p. 143).

Another recent study used a similar naming procedure, but for two sets of black applicants for sales positions whose employment credentials were evaluated by a national panel of 192 white sales professionals. The researchers found that the black applicants with white-Anglicized names got more favorable pre-interview evaluations from these white professionals than did black applicants with black "ethnic names," and also that this differential was greater for outside-sales jobs than inside-sales jobs. They concluded that the findings show "how job-irrelevant factors or characteristics associated with racial cues can affect the employment prospects of Black applicants.... When faced with limited information ... it appears that White sales professionals may subconsciously stereotype ethnic-named Black job applicants."[36]

In addition, a Milwaukee study matched pairs of black and white male applicants, with similar job credentials and self-presentations, and had them apply for 350 less-skilled jobs. Some 34 percent of the white applicants were called back, but just 14 percent of the equally qualified black applicants. A subgroup of the white applicants who indicated to employers they had been in prison were *more likely* to be called back than the black applicants with no criminal record. Employers likely drew on negative stereotypes of black men in screening them out of their hiring pools. A survey of these employers a few months later actually found them saying that they would not discriminate between white and black ex-offenders, leading the researchers to conclude that such employer surveys are probably not good ways to assess discrimination.[37]

Researcher Marc Bendick, Jr., reviewed 16 situational-testing studies involving racial and national-origin discrimination in employment. In research using white testers and testers of color, white applicants have been found to be favored over applicants of color (African Americans or Latinos) at net rates of discrimination averaging about 20 percent of the time. Note that black and Latino employees typically face such discrimination not just once, but repeatedly over many years of work. There is a significant cumulative racial differential over time, as whites use earlier job advantages to build on and move up later on. In addition, employees of color, unlike their white peers, usually face much discrimination in other areas of their lives, which makes dealing with employment discrimination even more difficult.[38]

As we have seen, research shows that in the hiring process African American workers are less likely to obtain jobs than whites with equivalent credentials. This has been found to be true for a few other competitions among groups for certain jobs. One study of Los Angeles hotel employers found that almost all preferred immigrant Latino workers to native-born black workers for maid jobs. These mostly white employers, accenting what many call "soft skills," insisted that immigrant workers had a better work ethic, attitude, and communication skills. However, the researchers found that these racially stereotyped codewords covered up the major reason for employers' preference for immigrants—they were less likely to protest exploitative work conditions and thus were more controllable. Employers also provided little evidence for their contentions about soft skills.[39]

Discrimination has also been found for an array of better-paying jobs. One study of hiring at upscale restaurants in New York City found a relatively high rate of discrimination against applicants. Using pairs of applicants involving a white tester and a black, Asian American, or Latino tester—matched for age, appearance, gender, and mannerisms— the researchers sent them to more than 100 restaurants offering jobs. The applicants of color were less likely than their white partners to be interviewed for the open position, and were a little more than half as likely to get an offer of employment as the white tester. In addition, employers did not examine the previous employment experience of white testers as carefully as they did for the testers of color.[40]

Clearly, much field research shows that many white (and some other) employers view certain groups of workers as much more acceptable than others, and individual applicants are periodically judged by perceived racial characteristics. Yet white employers often argue that they choose white over black workers only because they know whites as a group are better qualified, and they may defend such choices by recourse to the notion that this is really "rational" discrimination. However, the workers they deem unacceptable, such as black workers, are often just as qualified as, or better qualified than, whites who are chosen, as we observe repeatedly in employment testing studies.

More Discrimination in Hiring: Major Sports Teams

In major professional sports, where in recent decades there have been many black players, there is also much subtle, covert, and blatant discrimination in hiring, recruitment, and workplace conditions. The number of black players and other players of color is often taken, by white sports commentators and fans, as a sign that racism is no longer a problem in certain professional and college sports. Yet, numerous recent studies have demonstrated continuing discrimination against well-qualified black (and often Latino) athletes and other applicants when it comes to entry into coaching and other management ranks in Major League Baseball (MLB), the National Football League (NFL), and National Collegiate Athletic Association (NCAA) major sports divisions.[41] For instance, one recent analysis summed up the situation for the major college football division, where black players are about half of all players but there are few black head coaches:

whereas athletic directors, boosters, and other persons of decision-making authority implicitly acknowledge Black student-athletes' athletic prowess, the institution of college athletics has historically devalued Black coaches' capacity to guide a team.... Due to this conceived incapableness, Black coaches are analogous to individuals in lower stratums of caste-like societies.[42]

Professional sports are receiving much more attention these days from researchers. For example, recent research has demonstrated that subtle and overt discriminatory processes have led to a significant underrepresentation of black Americans among athletic agents in the professional sports industry.[43] In addition, a social science study of the NFL's hiring practices utilized field observations and interviews with college players who had been through the NFL screening and hiring process. The researchers found that players of color experienced a number of types of discrimination, including significantly greater scrutiny of their individual and family histories than whites faced. Most athletes applying for NFL positions are young people of color, yet "older white men make up most of the primary decision-makers in terms of hiring." The researchers suggest that these and other data indicate that professional sports are "not the bastion of racial equality popular accounts would suggest; instead, the overt racism reported in many previous examinations of sport may have 'gone underground.'"[44] In addition, the New York Times sports columnist William Rhoden has done his own research on discriminatory patterns in the recruitment and treatment of black football, baseball, and basketball athletes by owners of major sports teams. He demonstrates how a national white-run "conveyor belt" brings talented black youngsters "from inner cities and small towns to big-time programs, where they're cut off from their roots and exploited by team owners, sports agents, and the media."[45]

Not surprisingly, employment discrimination in the hiring stages results in significant underrepresentation for people of color in numerous white-collar workplaces, including those that are sports-related. In recent years, for instance, the number and percentage of journalists and editors who are black or other people of color in the major news media—including in the area of sports media—has declined. Today there are very few black sports editors at news corporations.[46] This is one likely reason for the persistence of more negative framing of black athletes than of white athletes in much of the mainstream media (see Chapter 4). In general, too, the mainstream media have a problem with underrepresentation of people of color in numerous other employment areas.[47]

White Networking and Employment Discrimination

As the aforementioned studies suggest, an array of racial barriers face black workers and other workers of color seeking employment. A number of these barriers are rarely discussed in the mainstream media, but are very important in today's job markets. For example, private employment agencies control a significant part of the applicant flow into white-collar jobs. One study found that "screening out 'undesirable' applicants is one of the services many employment agencies provide to their client firms."[48] These include certain applicants of color. In addition to such direct discrimination against workers of color, there are other screening mechanisms that involve well-institutionalized favoritism for many white employees. Because of centuries of systemic racism, job information and hiring networks are commonly segregated along racial lines, and such network segregation frequently has a serious impact on workers of color. A major reason for the job mismatch problem mentioned previously is that workers of color are often segregated away from critical social networks that are essential to finding good jobs.[49]

Conducting hundreds of interviews, Nancy DiTomaso has recently demonstrated important networking patterns that reproduce systemic racial inequalities in employment. Her white respondents reported that they have long used acquaintances, friends, and family—their personal networks—to find *most* of the jobs secured over lifetimes of job hunting. These findings contradict the colorblind view of the employment world held by many Americans, including most white Americans—that is, that in U.S. employment sectors jobs are secured mainly or only because of personal "skills, qualifications, and merit." However, wherever they can, most white job-seekers tend to avoid real market competition and secure jobs by using their racially segregated social relationships and networks. Indeed, not one white respondent ever openly expressed concern about their use of this unjust system, which system DiTomaso calls "opportunity hoarding" and "unequal opportunity."[50]

Over several centuries white Americans have controlled most of this country's important job markets, and thereby have been unjustly privileged and enriched in their "socio-racial capital," including important employment-related social networks. As a result, they are much more likely to have access to many better-paying and more attractive jobs today— including those with better benefits and advancement opportunities. Even new white immigrants to the United States generally get at least some of the significant privileges of whiteness, which include access to these white-controlled networks. In contrast, lack of access to these networks typically has a very negative impact for workers of color when it comes to finding good jobs. For example, one research study demonstrated that, compared to comparable white male workers, black male workers must spend significantly *more* time and effort looking for work.[51]

In addition to DiTomaso's general research on networks, other researchers have found patterns of institutionalized favoritism in specific job-seeking settings. Deirdre Royster examined white and black students at a technical college and found that, even though on average they worked harder and did better in their training, the black graduates of the program had much more difficulty in finding decent jobs than did the white students. Pre-existing white social networks very often gave white students much better job opportunities than the black students.[52] Additionally, a recent study by Christopher Boulton of the advertising industry involved observational studies and interviews with interns and practitioners at major advertising agencies. He found much favoritism for white applicants and employees, including the use of established and exclusionary white networks to secure employment in the industry. He also found a strong concern among those doing the hiring about how a new employee might fit into existing white work groups.[53] Not surprisingly, another research study of advertising agencies, many of them part of large global firms, found that African Americans made up just 5.3 percent of all advertising managers and professionals. The relevant Census Bureau and EEOC data suggest this percentage should reasonably be in the neighborhood of 9.6 percent.[54]

One important finding from this study of black white-collar employees in advertising agencies applies to numerous other employers. Many employers, in both the private and the public sectors, complain they cannot find enough "qualified" employees of color. If they take any remedial action in this regard, they tend to emphasize educational strategies to improve future job situations for workers of color. However, as Bendick and Egan point out, this is *not* the main reason for low percentages of black employees in advertising and many other employment settings. One more important reason is "persistent unwillingness by mainstream advertising agencies to hire, assign, advance, and retain already-available Black talent."[55] There is indeed much well-educated black talent available. This unwillingness to hire, and its associated practices of white favoritism, are usually rooted in a racist framing of black Americans in general and as employees, as well as in the positive preferences of white employers for employees who look like they do. Not just in the advertising industry, but in many other employment sectors, a central problem is the common practice of white managers operating out of the traditional white frame and using predominantly white networks to hire or advance white managers and professionals like themselves. They thereby "ignore the availability of *tens of thousands* of African Americans with educational and experience backgrounds comparable to whites routinely hired in their industry."[56]

Discrimination within the Workplace

Once hired, employees of color continue to face much discrimination, some of it subtle and some of it blatant or covert. The overwhelming majority of employment complaints made to the Equal Employment Opportunity Commission (EEOC) on racial–ethnic grounds are for barriers beyond the hiring stage. In some cases, white workers are given better access than black workers or other workers of color to job assignments and training programs enabling them to climb the employment ladder. In other cases white employees get better mentoring and continued access to important white networking. In yet other situations employees of color face significant discrimination when seeking promotions and job mobility.[57]

A number of studies have recently assessed the overall level of discrimination faced by black employees and other employees of color in different workplaces. For example, one research study examined problems of discrimination in the U.S. military. A representative survey of active-duty service members of the U.S. Army found substantial reports of racial discrimination. Some 27 percent of black and Latino officers had faced discrimination in their military units, and among enlisted personnel surveyed 24 percent of blacks and 19 percent of Latinos had faced discrimination too. In addition, a majority of white officers and enlisted personnel thought there was less discrimination in the military than in the civilian sector, but less than a majority of black and Latino enlisted personnel agreed with this view. Not surprisingly, given that the overwhelming majority of senior officers are white, the senior leadership

> may not recognize the frequency with which minorities encounter discrimination. In sum, they are comfortably colorblind—unaware of the true prevalence of discrimination and therefore of the belief that the challenges minorities face in the military are because of their own inability to survive in an egalitarian environment.[58]

Those employees who are well educated are at least as likely as the less well educated to report workplace discrimination. One Los Angeles study of 1,000 black workers found that about 80 percent of those with a college degree and almost all of those with a graduate-level education reported workplace discrimination, compared to just under half of those with less than a high school education. A majority of highly educated Asian and Latino workers also reported workplace discrimination.[59] Then there is the recent survey of 366 professionals of color who had gone through the National Urban Fellows (NUF) leadership program at the City University of New York and were now working in important professional and managerial positions in government agencies or other non-profit organizations. When asked about workplace discrimination, a substantial majority replied that they had experienced some type of racial, gender, or other discrimination. Racial discrimination was the most common type. About 80 percent of the black men and 78 percent of the black women replied that they had faced workplace discrimination. Significant proportions of the Asian and Hispanic American professionals also reported discrimination: Hispanic men, 66 percent; Hispanic women, 71 percent; Asian American men, 57 percent; Asian American women, 46 percent. These respondents noted that this racial discrimination included blocked promotions, racially biased comments, lack of professional opportunities, unequal pay, and a lack of proper acknowledgment of them or their work.[60]

Negative Workplace Climates

Numerous research and legal reports indicate a negative work climate at many government and corporate workplaces. One recent review of complaints of racial harassment in the workplace that were filed with the EEOC found that the number has sharply increased since about 1990. Most of these complaints of workplace harassment—including such things as racist slurs, hangman's nooses, blocked access to job resources, and physical threats—have been filed by African American workers. The study also examined data for 245 employees in several workplaces and found that African American workers were more likely to be aware of racial harassment in the workplace than white workers, including those in the same workplaces. African American employees who saw the racial climate at work as negative had more job turnover, less work satisfaction, and more work-related health problems.[61]

Moreover, in an array of contemporary employment settings white senior executives, middle-level managers, and other supervisory employees make use of overtly marginalizing language. Black employees and other employees of color may periodically or routinely be categorized and marginalized as "you people" or "one of them," especially in mostly or all-white decisionmaking settings.[62] Even when employees of color are a small or token presence in such settings, the still-dominant privileges of white men may reveal themselves. One black professional in the National Urban Fellows program recently described the way this privilege affected her current workplace:

> There is this thing about white male privilege, like who gets paid attention to. Let's say we are [in a meeting]. We are all key players, but in terms of who is listened to, whose idea is taken … it is going to go to the white males around the table. I can't believe that … is still happening.[63]

Lack of Promotions and Issues of Tracking

Managerial employees of color, female and male, in corporate and educational workplaces frequently find their promotion avenues restricted. One review of the research literature summed up the contemporary employment situation this way:

> In the corporate and academic worlds, whites are promoted in due course, sometimes ... even when they do not fully meet the standard. Blacks must be twice as qualified to demonstrate that they are only as qualified as whites for the same promotion.[64]

Some research on corporate advancement shows that women of color have not done well in terms of being promoted to the upper ranks of corporate executives. One large-scale study found that barely 1 percent of senior corporate executives were black women, compared to about 3 percent for black men and 77 percent for white men. Interviews with many senior executives by the Executive Leadership Council found that they said they valued having racial diversity among the managers of their companies. However, when asked for reasons for this serious underrepresentation of black women among senior managers, they cited poor efforts by the women involved, a perception gap, and other vague factors. Only 15 percent cited actual discrimination. Most tended to blame black employees themselves and suggested that they should take on more challenging assignments, plan careers better, or take better advantage of job feedback.[65] Apparently, they rarely blamed higher-level white executives for poor mentoring and other subtle or overt discrimination. Indeed, other research has shown that in various corporate workplaces, the white executives and managers who make hiring and promotion decisions often harbor a conventional white racial framing of employees of color (for example, "blacks are not as hardworking"), a framing that makes these executives and managers less comfortable with, and less likely to promote, employees of color.[66]

Many Americans seem to assume that high educational achievement makes for a secure American-dream life of respect and satisfying achievement. However, a recent interview study of 43 black, Hispanic, Asian American, and other administrators at major public and private universities found that most have not achieved this heralded American dream. Most still face subtle and overt discriminatory barriers. Among the barriers is a recurring tracking of administrators of color into a limited number of administrative (often "diversity") staff positions at universities. (In contrast, national data on top administrative positions in such universities reveal them to be very disproportionately white and male.) Compared with comparable white administrators, the administrators of color reported a significant lack of decisionmaking authority with regard to the scope of their administrative authority and control over their budgeting and staffing. Overall, administrators of color often pay a high price in terms of personal stress and health problems for these subtle and overt barriers they face.[67]

Moreover, in other recent research Chun and Evans interviewed chief diversity officers (CDOs) in numerous private and public organizations. Most CDOs were African Americans, other Americans of color, or white women. These senior administrators often face serious workplace climate problems, including a racialization or gendering of these positions. One respondent noted how impatient top executives frequently identify a convenient manager of color or a white female manager to place into diversity positions just because they seem available, not because they wish to serve in such positions. Given often negative workplace climates, there is a high level of turnover among these CDOs—from layoffs, organizational downsizing, and internal political pressures. One respondent noted that nearly three-quarters of diversity officers in the top 50 major companies cited for their diversity in a leading journal had moved out of their positions in a recent two-year period. The researchers conclude that the "suddenness of these changes suggests a lack of value accorded to the diversity function as well as the commodification of individuals in these roles."[68] The turnover also suggests inadequate mentoring and support, especially from the typically white and male senior executives who do most hiring for diversity positions. We might note that a few other studies have demonstrated that people of color in professional and managerial positions who do get good mentoring from whites in their workplaces tend to do better in their careers than those who do not get such supportive mentoring.[69]

Profiting from Discrimination: White Benefits, Black Losses

The prominent Harvard law professor, Derrick Bell, once concluded that a major function of antiblack discrimination is "to facilitate the exploitation of black labor, to deny us access to benefits and opportunities that otherwise would be available, and to blame all the manifestations of exclusion-bred despair on the asserted inferiority of the victims."[70] Racial discrimination in employment often involves an exploitative relationship that enables white employers to take more of the value of the labor of workers of color than of comparable white workers. Today, as in the past, some employers pay black workers less because they are black. They do this directly, or they do it by segregating black workers into certain job categories and setting the pay for these categories lower than for predominantly white job classifications. The Marxist tradition has accented the way in which capitalist employers routinely take part of the value of workers' labor for their own purposes—thus not paying workers for the full value of that work. Similarly, in numerous situations white employers have the power, because of subtly or blatantly institutionalized discrimination, to take additional value from the labor of black workers and other workers of color, such as in the form of paying lower wages.

Researchers at the Urban Institute have estimated that black workers today lose more than *$120 billion* in wages each year because of the overt and subtle employment discrimination they face, dollars that substantially remain in employers' hands.[71] Employers benefit from lower wages they sometimes pay to black workers for the same work as white workers, as well as from the job divisions they have created between workers that reduce cross-racial worker organization. These divisions include job tracking and job segregation. Thus, today a majority of black men still are employed in unskilled, semi-skilled, service, or other relatively low-paid blue-collar jobs or in professional and managerial jobs disproportionately servicing black clients or consumers; or they are unemployed or in part-time employment. Bureau of Labor Statistics data indicate that substantially fewer black men than white men aged 20 and older have jobs (62 percent versus 72 percent), with a black male unemployment rate more than twice that for white men.[72] In addition, black women tend to be concentrated in service jobs, other unskilled blue-collar jobs, professional and managerial jobs substantially oriented to black clients or consumers, or moderate-wage clerical jobs. They often face serious unemployment and underemployment problems as well.

Even when politicians and media analysts describe the economy as "very good," a great many workers are unemployed or are underemployed in low-wage or part-time jobs. If the U.S. economy turns sour, as it periodically does, black workers typically face even worse conditions than white workers. When no longer needed, many less-skilled black workers are often utilized as a "reserve army" of workers—in a condition of painful poverty and unemployment, or unfairly in the prison–industrial complex—until they may be needed again. As a result of these recurring job barriers and lesser job opportunities, black workers frequently have less work experience and less stable employment careers than whites.[73]

Persisting Racial Barriers in Business

Some mainstream media and economic analysts have suggested that the solution to black employment problems is more "black enterprise," that is, the development of more small businesses in the so-called free market system. This often uninformed approach has not only ignored the fact that African Americans are already *more likely* to seek to be entrepreneurs than whites, but also typically disregarded the structural barriers faced by African Americans and many other Americans of color in creating new businesses.

Entrepreneurship efforts by black Americans and other Americans of color are often met by the stern realities of persisting systemic racism.[74]

Building a successful business requires access to the necessary economic resources. Unjust impoverishment of black Americans in the past continues as unjust impoverishment for their descendants in the present. Much research has shown how difficult it has been for African Americans to build up much in the way of family assets and resources because of centuries of far-reaching slavery, legal segregation, and informal discrimination in the present. Until the late 1960s, government-sanctioned slavery and Jim Crow segregation generally kept African Americans out of lucrative business sectors serving white consumers and communities. This extensive racial oppression has kept their descendants today from inheriting the economic resources necessary (for example, substantial home equities) to develop a significant share of business in the economy under present-day conditions of official desegregation. Until relatively recently in this country's 400-year history, African Americans were forced by blatant discrimination and overt segregation into a major economic detour away from the usually more profitable business opportunities outside their communities.[75]

Today, how well black businesspeople succeed depends substantially on certain distinctive costs of doing business, some of which are closely linked to past discrimination they or their ancestors have suffered. Not only are members of a racially subordinated group like African Americans likely to have less in the way of socioeconomic assets because of past and present discrimination, but they often lack access to important "good old boy" networks or to the business knowledge necessary to compete effectively with more privileged whites. Comparing a black and a white businessperson, Martin Katz has emphasized that "Financial advantage—and hence disadvantage—is transferable across generations" and thus that "discrimination is likely to result in racial cost disparities which can persist long after the discrimination has ceased."[76]

With a less-developed or more segregated work or business history, because of past or present racial hostility and discrimination, black businesspeople will have more trouble starting a new business venture. Even less-prejudiced white lenders will be less willing to loan to black entrepreneurs with fewer resources or a less-developed work or business history. The abolition of some blatant discrimination, which was attempted through the 1960s civil rights movement and laws, has not dramatically restructured the economic resources and business inheritances that have unjustly favored whites for centuries, and still persist today. Institutionalized racism remains a continuing business reality.

If a black entrepreneur manages to start a business, he or she is likely to face an array of racial hurdles. One review of many studies found that black contractors and other contractors of color face problems getting government contracts and that, if they get contracts, they may often face much hostility from white competitors, such as sabotage at their work sites. They may also endure hostile racist comments in carrying out business contracts, and many often face racial barriers in securing significant financing for their business. Restricted access to financing, including venture capital, clearly reduces the viability and potential of new businesses.[77]

Very important too is the problem of being excluded from pre-existing white business networks. Most business sectors have critical networks of interrelated white businesses, often termed "good old boy networks." This term signals that many white businesspeople are at least dimly aware of this non-meritocratic way in which the vested interests of whites are commonly protected and extended, to the disadvantage of businesspeople who are not white. Without fair access to these established business networks it is hard to get a viable share of local contracts in various business sectors.[78] Even those operating with mostly black customers frequently encounter serious difficulties with certain elements of systemic racism. Adia Harvey Wingfield studied black entrepreneurs who had started beauty salons and found that they faced very significant discriminatory barriers. "Because of lenders' discriminatory practices, owners' limited social networks, and white patrons' unwillingness to patronize some of these establishments, black entrepreneurs find themselves limited in the types of business ventures they are able to develop." These women have had to work very hard "to develop viable businesses in part by capitalizing on the beauty concerns that have their origins in the gendered racist ideals which abound in the larger society."[79] Wingfield suggests the concept of *systemic gendered racism* for the complexity of societal pressures and discriminatory conditions that black female entrepreneurs routinely face.

Over the last century the overwhelming dominance of whites, and especially white men, in executive and other leadership positions in most major business organizations and many other important societal organizations has created what some researchers call the "white standard" or "white prototype," that is, the deeply held framing in most people's minds of effective leaders necessarily being white (or white male).[80] This framing is very powerful and inclines a great many people to automatically attribute leadership strengths to whites or white men—another core feature of the dominant racial frame that unfairly assists the latter in creating successful business enterprises.

Racial Barriers in Education

Segregation and Resegregation in the Public Schools

Opinion polls indicate that the overwhelming majority of whites believe black Americans have as good a chance to get a good education as white

Americans. Less than half of black Americans feel the same. Social science data show that this majority-white view is quite misinformed. One reason for continuing racial inequalities and segregation in education lies in pervasive housing segregation documented earlier in this chapter. Whether in a central city, the suburbs, or rural areas, persisting housing segregation generally sets significant limits on the amount of school desegregation possible without substantial pupil transportation.

Recent research reveals that in most areas black and Latino children still experience great, and often increasing, school segregation. Three-quarters of black students and 80 percent of Latino students currently attend a school that has a majority (50–100 percent) of students of color; about 40 percent of both groups attend schools where whites are 0–10 percent of students.[81] These highly segregated schools generally have more children from low-income families and far fewer educational and economic resources, including relatively fewer dollars spent for each pupil and less-experienced teachers, than predominantly white public schools. Millions of children of color remain "locked into 'dropout factory' high schools, where huge percentages do not graduate, have little future in the American economy, and almost none are well prepared for college."[82] Note that, although they too are supported by federal government money, public charter schools are on average *more* racially segregated than other public schools, and thus do not provide a way out of the harsh contemporary reality of school segregation.

At least since the 1970s the executive and judicial branches of the federal government have often allowed, and sometimes encouraged, resegregation of public school systems that had in the 1950s and 1960s been under pressure or court orders to desegregate. By the 1970s conservative appointments to the Supreme Court presaged a long-term movement, lasting to the present, away from eradicating the burdens of "slavery still unwilling to die" in public schools. By the 1990s federal courts were allowing public school systems to abandon desegregation. In cases such as *Freeman v. Pitts* (1992), a conservative Court made it clear that they viewed large-scale resegregation of public schools to be constitutional, so long as it was not done with overtly expressed racist motivation.[83]

Public schools are resegregating across the country, substantially because of decisions of conservative, mostly white judges and other government officials. During the George W. Bush era (2001–2009), numerous federal judges and other federal officials worked with local officials to end even voluntary school desegregation, as well as other antidiscrimination programs. In 2007, as noted previously, a conservative Supreme Court majority knocked down even modest voluntary desegregation programs in Seattle and Louisville. In addition, the Bush administration's "No Child Left Behind" (NCLB) law put increased pressure for change in pupil achievements on segregated public schools and teachers in low-income communities, yet did not provide them with the necessary resources to bring such significant changes in educational achievements for low-income students. In effect, this NCLB approach represents a type of colorblind racist thinking that "names the symptoms, rather than the causes, of racial inequality."[84]

Research also shows that the lack of educational achievement for most children of color is not because their parents are not supportive of education—a view sometimes argued by whites and others to explain persisting differences in educational outcomes. One Department of Education report showed that 94 percent of black parents checked on their children having completed homework, as compared to 82 percent of white parents. In surveys and other studies the overwhelming majority of black parents and other parents of color reveal themselves to be strongly committed to better educations for their children.[85]

The continuing racial segregation of public schools is not accidental, nor is it the fault of communities of color. Over several decades a great many white parents, politicians, and school officials have worked hard to keep their public schools as white as possible. There are various mechanisms to implement such goals. For example, one research report on New York City schools found widespread racial steering and channeling of students. The system's personnel tended to channel white students disproportionately into certain schools and programs, and students of color disproportionately into other schools and programs. The report describes this as a type of institutional racism rooted in conscious racial prejudices, malign neglect by officials, and a lack of representation in decisionmaking by families of color served by the public schools.[86] In addition, a recent New York City study interviewed 39 upper-middle-class white parents about their school choices for their young children beginning public education in the city. Most indicated they did want a racially diverse education for their children, with an awareness of the more diverse and globalizing U.S. society. Yet they chose predominantly white schools and programs in their school district. The researchers suggest that

> school choice policies allowing for the creation of more diverse public schools would be welcome by many of the parents who tend to have the most choice in the educational system. Lacking such options, and faced with the choice between classrooms filled with mostly white and relatively affluent students versus those enrolling mostly black and Latino lower-income students, the parents we interviewed opted for the former, all the while lamenting the distinctions between the choices.[87]

Most clearly indicated that they did not want their children to be in a mostly white school or one with a small minority of whites among a majority of low-income children of color, yet almost all schools fit into one of these categories. The ongoing and well-institutionalized racism of the larger society shapes not only broad patterns of housing segregation, and thus much of the distribution of students in public schools, but also the great inequality of educational resources and opportunities among schools even across a particular urban school district.

Once inside public schools, many students of color face discrimination by some teachers and administrators. A Florida study by David Figlio examined records for 55,000 students from families with two or more children in a major district's schools and found that black students with supposedly black-sounding names averaged lower scores on reading and math tests, and got fewer recommendations for gifted classes, than their own brothers or sisters without such names. "The estimated relationship between names and test scores suggests that a reasonably large fraction of the Black–White test score gap can be explained by children's naming patterns."[88] According to this study, black children with exotic-to-whites names probably get less attention from white teachers who assume their names indicate they will not do well.

Even at relatively desegregated and diverse high schools, the orientation of white students can be openly racist and problematical. Recently, a group of white students at a New Jersey high school created a "White Girls Club." They posted racist commentaries and photos of racist performances in social media and wore T-shirts with "White Girls Club" on them to school. When critically questioned by other students, they took great offense and insisted they were right, as in this comment from a member of the club: "Sometimes I wonder if I crossed a line, but then I remember I'm white and I can do whatever the (expletive) I want."[89] One black high school student commented about the impact:

> This is probably one of the most hurtful things I have ever experienced in my life. I have been friends with these girls, and it makes me feel as if I've done something personally wrong as a black woman. I also see that these girls are not remorseful.[90]

Note again the arrogance and sense of privilege that is at the center of the white racial frame, including among younger whites in school settings that are racially diverse.

Racial Barriers at Colleges and Universities

In spite of the numerous obstacles that many black children and other children of color face in getting equal and first-rate K–12 educational opportunities, their educational achievements have been significant. Today, younger black Americans are only a little less likely to have completed high school than comparable whites. Among those aged 18–24 in one recent year, nearly 94 percent of whites had completed high school, compared to about 87 percent of similar African Americans (and 77 percent of Latinos).[91] By this age most African Americans have gotten at least a high school diploma, albeit often one from a high school that did not have the more substantial educational resources and college-oriented programs available to a majority of white students. Still, their personal achievements have closed much of the racial gap in educational attainment. However, this closing of the educational gap has not translated into an end of discrimination in education or in job markets.

African Americans and other Americans of color face many difficulties in getting a good college education, which is increasingly necessary for decent-paying jobs. Discrimination, whether blatant, covert, or subtle, is still commonplace at most stages of education at historically white colleges and universities. For example, subtle discrimination persists in some of the standard screening measures used for admissions at undergraduate and graduate levels. How educational merit is measured, usually by standardized tests, has largely been mostly determined by white educators. Historically, college entrance tests and related screening devices have been designed by whites from middle-class backgrounds. Indeed, leading social scientists of the 1910s and 1920s who helped to develop the forerunners or early versions of today's college entrance tests, such as Princeton University's Carl Brigham, were outspoken white supremacists. Sociologists Zuberi and Bonilla-Silva have demonstrated that some important psychometric and other statistical approaches developed by the social sciences have roots in early attempts to demonstrate white racial superiority.[92]

College entrance tests and similar diagnostic tests have often been designed, consciously or unconsciously, to measure the things that white middle-class people know or do well. For example, college entrance tests have used questions about such things as sailing, toboggans, and polo, topics more familiar to middle- and upper-class whites than to most working-class people, including many people of color. In addition, most tests are written in the variant of the English language most accessible to white middle-class people.[93] White middle-class youth often do better than those from certain other racial groups on such tests because they mostly come from families with substantial economic and cultural resources (such as numerous computers, substantial libraries, and test tutoring), resources often linked to the unjust enrichment of their white ancestors during the slavery or Jim Crow eras, as well as to racial privileges they and their parents have in society today.

Students of color are also less likely to have families that can support their college attendance, substantially because of the negative socioeconomic impacts on their families of past and present racial barriers. One Department of Education study showed that the percentage of all black students who started college coming from families with yearly incomes less than $32,000 was nearly half, which compared to about 16 percent of white beginning students.[94] Better family incomes usually mean access to better-resourced high schools, and subsequently to colleges and universities. Generally speaking, white middle-class students tend to have a better-resourced pre-college education, which gives them an edge in scoring well on entrance tests, enrolling in higher-status colleges and universities, and completing college programs. Their typically better family socioeconomic resources mean advantages in financing a college education and, later on, in competing for jobs.

Indeed, one 2011 study documented the great impact that income inequality and other aspects of systemic racism have on enrollment in elite colleges and universities, those whose degrees often count the most in current job markets. Black and Latino students

> are dramatically underrepresented in the most selective colleges.... The probability of enrolling in a highly selective college is five times greater for white students than black students. Even after controlling for income, white students are two to three times as likely as black students to gain admission to highly selective colleges.

This racial inequality in enrollment in more selective colleges has likely increased over recent decades.[95]

Negative Campus Climates

If they get past the entrance barriers, black students and many other students of color commonly confront a range of discriminatory barriers on and around historically white college campuses. For example, at Dartmouth College there have been a number of recent racist and anti-gay incidents, and college students who organized protests against them got online threats. At Providence College in Rhode Island, numerous black and Latino students reported an array of racial harassment incidents, including being called racist names by whites, racist stares or racist commentaries when they enter certain campus areas, racist graffiti in dorms, and extra surveillance and identification not required of white students. Some faculty of color there also reported racial framing and harassment from security personnel, as well as hate emails when they protested racism issues.[96]

White students at numerous universities have held parties mocking Martin Luther King, Jr. and the civil rights movement. Students at University of Connecticut law school had a Martin Luther King, Jr. "Bullets and Bubbly" party. Whites wore baggy clothes, had fake gold teeth, and held machine guns. Clemson University students mocked the King holiday with a "ghetto-fabulous" party. Researchers C. Richard King and David Leonard report that white students there dressed up "in blackface, drank 40s, wore fake teeth grills, and flashed gang signs." They report that, a few weeks later, white students at Santa Clara University had a "Latino-themed party" at which "young women feigned pregnancy, the young men played at being cholo and everyone reveled in the symbols and spectacle they associate with Latinos."[97]

Over the last decade or so, a great array of racist events—including a variety of these "ghetto" and blackface parties, bake sales, and skits—have taken place at many other colleges and universities. The list includes, among numerous others, Washington University, New College, University of Tennessee, University of Texas, Trinity College, Whitman College, Willamette College, Texas A&M University, University of Connecticut, Emory University, University of Mississippi, Stetson University, University of Chicago, Cornell University, Swarthmore College, Tufts University, Massachusetts Institute of Technology, Macalester College, Johns Hopkins University, Oberlin College, Dartmouth College, Syracuse University, Tarleton State University, University of Colorado, University of Arizona, University of Alabama, University of Illinois, University of Delaware, and several University of California campuses.[98]

One sociological study of Halloween events drew on 663 observation journals by college students in several regions. These students recorded many examples of white students engaging in racist costuming—that is, dressing in costumes mocking and stereotyping Americans of color. Halloween thus provides a convenient context in which whites can "trivialize and reproduce racial stereotypes while supporting the racial hierarchy."[99] Developing classroom exercises in connection with this research, Jennifer Mueller and Rosalind Chou, instructors at a southwestern university, asked students in two courses to recount what they saw at Halloween, including costumes and events at parties or while trick-or-treating. In both cases the number of racist costumes reported was relatively large. In Mueller's case her 32 students reported seeing 20 Indian costumes, four Middle Eastern (for example, terrorist) costumes, 19 Mexican/Latino costumes, 19 blackface costumes, and 40 other costumed portrayals of African Americans. In Chou's class the 33 students reported seeing five Indian costumes, six Middle Eastern/Asian–Indian (for example, terrorist) costumes, eight Mexican (for example, migrant worker) costumes, ten blackface costumes, and 22 other costumed portrayals of black Americans. The latter included "ghetto-fabulous" images, gangsters, pimps, prostitutes, crack babies, crack mothers, athletes, large-bottomed women, jungle tribesmen, and welfare mothers. In both classes almost all of the costumed events involved whites donning the costumes, and almost all were negative and mocking portrayals of people of color, with

African Americans getting the most such attacks. Students observed racialized costumes in many different settings, including student parties, restaurants, bars, neighborhoods, and church parties. These extensive racist performances by mostly well-educated whites at Halloween again reveal the deep realities of a society that is not remotely "post-racial."[100]

The various student parties with racist themes and racist participants provide social contexts that apparently seem to the students to be private backstage areas—that is, areas where they can openly enjoy blatantly racist performances. In this recurring process they propagate and extend society's dominant white frame and associated hierarchy. Racist partying makes it clear that today the white racial frame still has an array of anti-others subframes, out of which whites of various ages can act. In addition, hundreds of thousands of examples of these racist subframes can be observed in the many racist photos, often of white partying, and commentaries on the now extensive Internet social media. Significantly, when defending these recurring racist performances, most whites say that they are only "good fun" and therefore "not racist." That is, they insist they are "colorblind." One recent research study had white and black college students look at racist-themed party photos and evaluate them like they would on a friend's "wall" on a social media site. White students and others who exhibited strong colorblind ("I don't see racism") racial views were the *least likely* to see the racist-themed party photos as problematical. In addition, these students were "more likely to condone and even encourage the racial theme party practice by laughing at the photos and affirming the party goers."[101] In contrast, students scoring low in their level of colorblind racist views were more likely to oppose such party photos. Facebook alone now has more than a billion active users, so the huge number of racist-themed party photos and other racism-themed social media postings likely has a very significant impact on the millions of people who regularly view them—and especially on younger users of these media who are just learning the many elements of the dominant white racial frame.

The impact of whites' racist actions on students of color is often devastating. Leslie Houts Picca and I had 308 students of color at more than two dozen colleges and universities keep diaries of racial events they encountered for a few weeks during one semester. One typical example of blatant discrimination still found on and around many campuses can be observed in this diary account from an African American student attending a historically white college. He notes a recurring problem:

> This is one of those sad and angry nights for me. Tonight marks the third time since the beginning of the school year that I've been called a nigger by a bunch of white students on a … weekend.… At first I used to wonder where they actually take the time in their heads to separate

me from everyone else by the color of my skin. I used to just blame alcohol consumption for their obvious ignorance and racist attitudes, but I have since stopped trying to make excuses for them. I have to admit that at times like this ... I don't understand how such a system of hate could exist.... Sometimes it seems that if I am around all white people, then I become nothing more than a token Black "exhibit" for their amusement. I guess that even I have to be careful not to judge all based on a few bad examples, which more often than not is the fate of many in the black community today. The saddest thing however, is that these people, these college students are supposed to be the supposed crème de la crème, the future business and political leaders.[102]

This savvy student discusses racist attacks and commentaries endured in diverse campus area settings. He has faced epithets hurled by presumably well-educated whites. Note too that he is encountering the racist actions of "future business and political leaders." These are not isolated incidents affecting just this one black student, for the 308 student diarists of color recorded hundreds of racist events, most involving whites negatively targeting people of color.

One part of the problem in these many cases of racist incidents likely lies in the fact that many white high school students come to historically white colleges and universities, with their currently diversifying college populations, unprepared for this diverse reality. Their high schools are often overwhelmingly white, and their neighborhoods are often isolated from larger populations of color. A few recent studies have examined white first-year college students who were randomly paired with nonwhite roommates and found that these interracial relationships were different from those between randomly paired white first-year students. The interracial roommate pairs resulted in less extensive joint activities and more breakups than the all-white pairs. One study found that the unobtrusively measured racial attitudes of white first-year students predicted the longevity of these interracial roommate relationships. Those who expressed the most negative racial attitudes were the most likely to have difficulty in relating to roommates who were not white.[103]

Today as in the past, campus cultures at most historically white institutions are still strongly white-oriented and resistant to changes in their practices that involve a conventional white framing. At most such institutions the majority of white trustees, administrators, advisors, faculty members, and students have shown little desire to remake their campuses to fully integrate the interests and concerns of students of color into the mainstream of campus life and culture. One recent *Chronicle of Higher Education* survey of major private universities assessed the racial diversity of their administrative positions above the dean level.

The universities they secured data on reported only 1–5 administrators of color among their 8–42 top administrators. In addition, as we discussed previously, a disproportionate percentage of the relatively few senior administrators are in diversity and student-affairs positions at these private and public universities, a type of academic tracking and segregation away from more powerful administrative positions. The reasons for this often relate to top white administrators' racial framing of these professionals. A former top administrator at Harvard commented in an recent interview that in college settings professionals of color often have to signal to powerful whites there that they are "dominant-culture-friendly" and, if they are hired or promoted, that they will not make "life miserable by coming in here" and diversifying the organizational setting too much with people who are not white.[104]

Discrimination in Public Places

As we have already seen, racial discrimination often has a spatial dimension, and its character can vary as a person of color travels from their home space to public spaces. In one conversation I had with a black professor, he listed a substantial array of everyday discrimination he still faces in public places, including the unwillingness of white clerks to touch his hand, probably out of some stereotype of "dirtiness" or "danger." He reported white clerks treating him with substantial discourtesy in comparison with nearby white shoppers and the obsession white clerks have with the possibility of him being a shoplifter. He has periodically faced whites who stereotyped him as unintelligent at his gym and in his workplace, and whites who stared when he was walking with a white woman on the street. Much racist action still takes place in public places and public accommodations.[105]

Recall the survey noted in Chapter 5 in which nearly half the black respondents said they had recently experienced discrimination while dining out, shopping, in public transportation, in encounters with police, or at work. Restaurants are often reported to be a problem for black diners. A survey of 131 African Americans found three-quarters had encountered racial discrimination—ranging from rejection to verbal or physical harassment—in a hotel, motel, or fast-food restaurant.[106] Discrimination in restaurants includes poor service that seems racially motivated and often being seated at an undesirable table, such as at the back near the kitchen. A 2012 research study of 200 mostly white restaurant servers found that they were often negative in their views of black customers, including their views of black dining and tipping behavior. Nearly three-fifths admitted that they had treated black patrons or those who they suspected of not tipping well in a discriminatory way. Over half reported that they had seen coworkers discriminate against black customers. Some 63 percent also indicated that they had periodically heard racist comments and racist code words from coworkers, often about customers.[107] One of the ironies of current discriminatory behavior by white servers is that one of the triggers for the civil rights movement a half century ago was significant discrimination in the area of public accommodations, including in restaurants.

Significant discrimination also occurs in retail stores, in spite of the significant use of such stores by customers of color. One Gallup poll found that 46 percent of black shoppers felt they were not treated as well as whites in downtown or mall stores. A number of recent lawsuits have charged major retailers with discrimination against black customers needing to write checks and with discriminatory overcharging.[108] A report by the New Jersey Citizen Action group cited data for that state, and nationally, that showed a pattern of black and Latino car buyers being quoted substantially higher financing rates than comparable white buyers. Financing mark-up charges for black buyers averaged as much as 60–70 percent higher than for white buyers.[109] Moreover, a field audit study examined the treatment of black and white customers in retail establishments and found black customers were often not served as quickly as comparable whites. Additional discrimination takes the form of extra surveillance from sales clerks. There is a pervasive type of "consumer racial profiling," which includes "slow or rude service, required pre-payment, surveillance, searches of belongings, and neglect, such as refusing to serve African-American customers."[110] Indeed, a majority of African Americans report being followed around in stores by clerks. We observe in numerous retail settings the high cost of shopping for many black customers, as well as many other customers of color, especially the time lost and the less-than-equal shopping opportunities.

Interestingly, since its emergence in the 1990s, the Internet has become a type of public space. It has played an important role in the perpetuation of white-racist framing and associated discrimination. While the technologies of the Internet and of the related computer and mobile communications revolutions are thought to be nonracial, even the construction of these technologies has sometimes been shaped by an implicit or explicit white framing. For example, there is the pervasive and very insensitive use of "master" and "slave" language in regard to hard disks and other aspects of computer programming, as well as the routine use of white-hand pointer icons. Such unreflective usage signals, at the least, that the creators of the computer and Internet infrastructure are often racially insensitive whites.[111]

In addition, and contrary to much commentary that the growing Internet will be non-racist and facilitate antiracism, the Internet's chat and discussion forums and social media—including Facebook, Twitter, and MySpace—and other new media such as text-messaging have frequently been used to spread and reinforce a white-racist framing of society. This has, in turn, brought recurring episodes of discrimination. One recent study of a diverse group of 264 teenagers found that 29 percent of the black youth and 42 percent of other youth of color had directly experienced racial hostility and racialized mistreatment online—on social network sites, in chat and discussion forums, in online gaming, in other online settings, or in text-messaging. In addition, 71 percent of the black youth and 67 percent of the other youth of color reported that they had seen online hostility and racialization being experienced by others. This study also found that the individual discrimination experienced by these adolescents had a significant negative impact on them, in such areas as increasing anxiety or depression.[112]

We should note, on a more positive note, that many black, Latino, and Asian American posters and bloggers have used their websites and the social media to build up an active community among members of their groups and, often, to engage in discourse that reinforces a counter-framing response to, and set of strategies for dealing with, various types of white racism.[113]

Discrimination in Health Care

Data on infant mortality provide a dramatic indication of the severe impact of accumulating racism on African Americans. The most recent black infant mortality rate of 13.1 deaths per 1,000 live births is *very high* for Western countries and more than twice the white infant mortality rate (5.6). Much research makes clear that this serious inequality is substantially the result of the multi-dimensional impacts of systemic racism. For black mothers these immediate and cumulative impacts include having substantially fewer economic resources on average than white mothers, as well as having less adequate access to pre-natal and post-natal health care in a country that rations much health care according to racial and class characteristics. These factors affect not only health care options but also the psychosocial stress on black women. Ongoing stress has been associated with negative effects on health, including on birth weights of babies.[114]

Black women, men, and children frequently face recurring discrimination when they try to make use of numerous professional services, including health care services. Black patients being treated for physical or mental illness are, depending on the illness, less likely or far less likely than otherwise comparable white patients to get standard and adequate care for their medical conditions. For example, one review of the medical literature on pain found that patients of color were "more likely to have their pain underestimated by providers and less likely to have pain scores documented in the medical record compared to whites."[115]

One significant issue is the negative racial framing in the minds of many white (and white-oriented) medical personnel. One recent research study of racial attitudes using the online implicit association test examined the responses of 2,500 people who self-identified as physicians. Some 70 percent of these showed that they implicitly preferred whites to blacks, with men having a stronger preference than women. White physicians, the majority of the sample, had the strongest implicit white preference, while black physicians showed no implicit white or black preference.[116] Moreover, a Harvard study examined the connection between explicit and unconscious racial bias of 287 Boston and Atlanta physicians and their thrombolysis recommendations for white and black patients. These mostly white physicians showed no overt bias for white or black patients on explicit questions about racial matters, yet they did show a pro-white, antiblack bias on the implicit association tests given to them. As their pro-white bias increased, so did their likelihood of treating white and black patients differently in regard to medical procedures. Yet another recent study of mostly white and Asian inner-city physicians discovered that those who viewed black patient compliance with greater implicit racial bias and stereotyping were more likely to dominate dialogues with these patients and to receive more negative patient ratings.[117] The reasons for differential medical treatment along racial lines are yet to be fully explored, but clearly include the antiblack stereotypes of the white frame, as well as specific health-related stereotypes likely shared by numerous white and white-oriented health care practitioners about patients of color,

Health and Environmental Racism

Another area of discrimination faced by African Americans and other Americans of color today involves issues that are also linked closely to health concerns. Research by the pathbreaking researcher Robert Bullard and his associates continues to demonstrate widespread problems with toxic wastes for communities of color, from San Francisco to Houston to New York City. Toxic waste dumps and other garbage dumps have often been disproportionately located, usually by white officials, in or near communities of color. Citizens of color thus disproportionately bear the social and health costs of these facilities. For example, one family in Tennessee filed a personal injury lawsuit against local city and country officials after discovering that the white officials and other white residents had known for a decade that well water in their area was seriously contaminated, but had not fully informed them of the dangers. Although the lead plaintiff is very physically fit, she got breast cancer, as did her mother. Her father died of cancer, and three other relatives have also had cancers. Research into county records revealed that the nearby landfill had allowed dumping of toxic wastes for years, with toxins getting into nearby water sources for a community of color. Bullard has noted that this is another example of institutionalized environmental racism.

Their nine-year lawsuit was finally settled in 2011, and the family belatedly received some compensation for the harm the toxic waste had caused them.[118]

Research using geographical information system (GIS) techniques has shown that the distribution of hazardous waste treatment and storage facilities in towns and cities across the country often is likely to reflect extensive discrimination. Using GIS techniques, one study examined racial differences in the location of this country's hazardous waste facilities, comparing what they found with findings in previous studies that did not use these advanced techniques. They found that the extent of these "racial disparities around hazardous waste facilities is much greater than what previous national studies have reported." This was true even when they controlled for various economic and political variables that might have affected the location of waste facilities. Their data strongly suggested that "racial targeting, housing discrimination, or other race-related factors are associated with the location of the nation's hazardous waste facilities."[119]

In 2012 Bullard and his associate Beverly Wright analyzed progress in regard to environmental protection for the U.S. citizenry. They note that today the main government environmental protection approach is racially inegalitarian, for it

> institutionalizes unequal enforcement; trades human health for profit; places the burden of proof on the "victims" and not on the polluting industry; legitimates human exposure to harmful chemicals, pesticides, and hazardous substances; promotes "risky" technologies; exploits the vulnerability of economically and politically disenfranchised communities; ... delays cleanup actions; and fails to develop pollution prevention as the overarching and dominant strategy. The dominant paradigm seldom challenges environmental racism and other forms of environmental injustice.[120]

Conclusion

In the last two chapters we have only begun to delineate the extensive patterns of everyday discrimination faced by black Americans and other Americans of color. Study after study uncovers more evidence that this society is very far from the post-racial society that many people claim for it.

In the 1960s, in a national address, President John F. Kennedy explained why he had called out the National Guard—against the wishes of the governor of Alabama, George Wallace—in order to enforce a court order allowing two African American students to enroll at the then all-white University of Alabama. He said:

> This nation was ... founded on the principle that all men are created equal, and that the rights of every man are diminished when the

rights of one man are threatened.... One hundred years of delay have passed since President Lincoln freed the slaves, yet their heirs, their grandsons, are not fully free. They are not yet freed ... from social and economic oppression.[121]

After accenting this theme of slavery unwilling to die, Kennedy continued by positioning racial equality as a serious moral question for the country. Kennedy then sent to the U.S. Congress proposals that would become the 1964 Civil Rights Act. This important law officially prohibited much overt racial discrimination and officially abolished legal segregation in employment, schools, federally assisted programs, and public accommodations. Over the next few years, the 1965 Voting Rights Act and the 1968 Civil Rights Act would officially prohibit racial discrimination in voting practices and in housing. However, as we have already seen, these important laws banning discrimination are often weakly enforced or unenforced. Indeed, in a major 2013 Supreme Court decision the conservative Republican majority on that court essentially blocked much enforcement of the Voting Rights Act by the federal government. In numerous states white officials immediately took advantage of this decision to make voting more difficult for voters of color. As a result of official backtracking like this in many civil rights areas, African Americans and other Americans of color today still do not have the full and equal opportunities in major institutions that have been promised in the official liberty-and-justice rhetoric since at least the 1960s.

7
White Privileges and Black Burdens
Still Systemic Racism

In an interview project that I conducted, a distinguished black professor who taught for many years at a historically white university explained well the cost of dealing with racism:

> If you can think of the mind as having one hundred ergs of energy, and the average man uses 50 percent of his energy dealing with the everyday problems of the world … then he has 50 percent more to do creative kinds of things that he wants to do. Now that's a white person. Now a black person also has one hundred ergs; he uses 50 percent the same way a white man does, dealing with what the white man has [to deal with], so he has 50 percent left. But he uses 25 percent fighting being black, [with] all the problems being black and what it means.[1]

By virtue of an accident of birth, African Americans must typically expend an enormous amount of energy defending themselves and their families from the recurring assaults of white racism. In contrast, over lifetimes, white Americans on average have a major life-energy advantage, for they do not waste large amounts of time dealing with the impositions of anti-white discrimination.

More generally, *white privilege* includes the large set of advantages and benefits inherited by each generation of those routinely defined as "white" in the social structure and processes of U.S. society. White privileges, and the sense that one is entitled to them, are inseparable parts of a greater whole. These advantages are material, symbolic, and psychological. Let us briefly review some of these advantages and privileges.

Privileging White Experiences and Interpretations

Much research indicates that a majority of whites still have an uncritical habit of mind that accepts the existing racial order with little questioning. In this research most whites, including white youth, tend to explain persisting racial inequalities without connecting them to the larger system of white power and privilege. A majority even deny that they as a group

207

have benefited significantly from past or present racial discrimination (see Chapter 4, pp. 126–129).[2]

Karyn McKinney collected the racial autobiographies of white college students. These autobiographies reveal that most of these whites do not understand their white privilege, largely because they do not face discrimination and do not have significant equal-status contacts with people of color. Still, this and similar research has revealed that some whites, albeit a modest number, have come to better understand racial privilege. At a certain turning point, whites who have had significant and sustained contacts with people of color often come to understand more about how everyday racism operates and about their privileged racial place. Today, as in the past, a central difficulty in bringing more racial change lies in the fact that a majority of whites do *not* have close and equal-status relationships with black Americans or most other Americans of color. Indeed, most have the option to stay relatively isolated in socio-racial terms and to avoid encountering the critical views and painful experiences of Americans of color.[3]

White privilege also includes an entitlement to decipher a person of color's everyday reality. For example, the mother of one newborn reported a white nurse's comment on seeing her infant: "Oh, this one's a militant, a little Black Panther!"[4] The newborn was immediately constructed as "black" (in this case, the mother was white, the father black), and downgraded, humorously, in white eyes as an alien racial other. Whites often take it for granted that they are entitled to their interpretation of conditions of people of color without consulting them.

In addition, a majority of whites are defensive when reminded of their white privilege and position in society's racial hierarchy. In one study researchers asked groups of white college students to write an essay about the ways in which they had been privileged or had been disadvantaged because they were white. Those who were asked to write about their racial privileges later scored higher on a modern racism scale with antiblack items (for example, "Blacks are getting too demanding in their push for equal rights") than did those students who had been asked to write about the disadvantages of being white or about a race-irrelevant topic. When these educated whites had to consider racial privilege and inequality, most "justified their privileged status by denying the existence of discrimination" and accenting the white frame's antiblack stereotypes. Like other research, this study suggests whites' racial understandings typically involve a strong sense of their position on the racial ladder and a need to defend that unjustly derived position.[5]

Social Transmission of White Privilege

From the beginning, the North American system of racial oppression was designed to bring many benefits for whites. Slavery, Jim Crow segregation, and contemporary discrimination have all provided whites with many social, economic, and political advantages. For that reason whites, as individuals and as a group, have a vested interest in actively maintaining this system. Systemic racism ensures whites "greater resources, a wider range of personal choice, more power, and more self-esteem than they would have if they were … forced to share the above with people of color."[6]

Today, most whites underestimate not only the level of their privileges but the degree to which these privileges exist because they have, to a substantial degree, been passed down from white ancestors. Consider the principle of unjust enrichment. The coercive taking of one's personal possessions by an individual criminal has some similarities to the coercive taking of one's labor or earned assets by a white slaveholder or, later on, by an array of white discriminators.[7] Such unjustly gained advantages often have a strong societal inertia. When large groups of whites gained jobs, income, property, status, or wealth unjustly under slavery and Jim Crow segregation, and then passed these advantages and wealth to later generations, that did *not* make the advantages and wealth inherited (and enhanced today) by their white descendants to be justly held.

Each white generation's discriminatory actions not only create new opportunities for unjust enrichment but also provide social processes of transmission that pass earlier unjustly gained economic and cultural capital to later white generations. For centuries, the system of oppression has created extensive inequalities in life chances between whites and blacks (as well as between whites and other Americans of color), and the cross-generational transmission of these great inequalities remains critical to the continuing reproduction of that racial oppression.

Racial Consciousness: Elites and Ordinary Whites

Over the course of our history, white elites have intentionally tried to divide ordinary white and black Americans in order to reduce or eliminate the possibility of joint protests over difficult working conditions and other inegalitarian economic or political conditions. However, while there have been historical periods when some white farmers and workers have joined with their black counterparts, for most of our history the overwhelming majority of white farmers and workers have been active players in maintaining systemic racism.[8] Over the last century, a majority of white workers have usually rejected social-class solidarity with black workers, accepting the "public and psychological wage of whiteness" we have previously discussed. By doing that, they have regularly weakened their own consciousness of social class and of themselves as exploited workers under an inegalitarian capitalistic system.

Today, as in the past, white workers living in modest circumstances may not feel privileged, especially relative to elite whites. They certainly sense the need for significant economic improvements in their lives. However, because most accept the white racial frame and its racial myths and misconceptions, they seem unable to see deeply into the real sources of their class oppression under modern capitalism. Their racial framing likely makes it hard for most to understand not only the situation of the racially oppressed, but also their own situation of class oppression. Nonetheless, this lack of understanding does not mean that class oppression is not still a major part of this country's social fabric. In the U.S. today, as in the past, racial structure and class structure constantly co-exist, overlap, and interrelate. Being white includes not only a higher racial status in society no matter what one's social class is, but also *on average* having a higher social-class position and greater income and resources than if one were black. More often than not, a somewhat higher or much higher position in the class system comes with birth into the top rank in the system of racial categorization. Unmistakably, the U.S. systems of racial oppression and of class oppression routinely co-reproduce each other.

Benefits of Whiteness: A Brief Overview

Privileged Access to Societal Resources

From the mid-1600s to the 1960s this country's economy was openly run as a racist system often using black labor and Native American lands to create resources and prosperity for whites. Historically, whites have also been the direct beneficiaries of much government assistance intended to create more white prosperity and upward mobility. These "affirmative action" programs for whites have long provided a substantial basis for that prosperity and mobility. For example, in the 1600s several colonies provided significant land grants to white colonists, land unavailable to those enslaved. As we noted in Chapter 2, from 1860s to the 1930s the federal government, operating under the homestead acts, gave away millions of acres of government land for little or no cost to white families homesteading midwestern and western areas. African Americans were generally excluded from access to this land because they were then enslaved (in the 1860s) or, later during the Jim Crow era, because they were locked into the near-slavery of debt peonage in southern agriculture. Overt violence was used by Klan-type groups to drive out many black families that did manage to gain a little land on their own. The federal homestead program created many billions of dollars of wealth for white homesteaders and their descendants, with the latter often benefiting *to the present day.*[9]

Numerous large-scale preferential programs for whites have been implemented for centuries. Later white entrants into the U.S., such as millions of immigrants from southern and eastern Europe, benefited greatly from antiblack discrimination during the late nineteenth and early twentieth centuries. Some conservative scholars have tried to argue that the societal situation of African Americans since desegregation in the 1960s is essentially similar to the harsh societal conditions faced by the hardworking white European immigrants in the decades just before and after 1900.[10] However, this historically naive view ignores the huge advantages that white immigrant groups generally had over the black Americans who were already in the cities into which these immigrants settled. The European newcomers were able to move up the economic ladder because most arrived when the economy was expanding greatly and jobs were relatively abundant; because many had some skills or money resources; because most faced much less discrimination than black urbanites; because they were not excluded from residential areas near workplaces as black urbanites often were; and because cities were then increasingly under control of political machines oriented to the immigrant voters. As a result, these immigrants and their descendants were generally able to do much better economically, politically, and residentially than the black Americans who had already resided in the country for centuries before these immigrants arrived.[11]

Moreover, until the 1960s most unions discriminated openly against black workers, reinforcing racial segregation in the labor market and increasing white workers' incomes relative to those of black workers.[12] Not surprisingly, this long history of white workers' racial privilege is the backdrop for present-day privilege. In recent years many black workers have still confronted informal job tracking favoring white workers, as well as informal discrimination in unionized and other blue-collar workplaces created or collaborated in by white workers. In examining such workplaces, numerous researchers have found that these discriminatory practices range from subtle to blatant harassment—such as putting hangman's nooses or racist effigies at black workers' job positions—and that white managers often ignore these actions. By means of everyday discrimination, white workers maintain their dominance of certain desirable jobs in many settings. As a result, black workers and other workers of color are frequently kept in a state of stress that may keep them from performing as well as they might otherwise, or that forces them to quit—responses that mean more job opportunities, promotions, or other benefits for white workers.[13]

More Government "Handouts" for Whites

In the first decades of the twentieth century yet other major government-controlled resources were given away, or made available on reasonable terms, almost exclusively to white Americans. The Air Commerce Act gave U.S. air routes to new companies, mainly those started by aviators who

212 · White Privileges and Black Burdens

had been trained during World War I. African Americans were not allowed into the Army Air Corps and had no opportunity to participate in this giveaway of major resources that over time generated significant wealth. Numerous other economic resources and opportunities, such as access to government-controlled mineral resources and the radio and television airwaves, were similarly kept from African Americans, especially in the early twentieth century, by means of overt racial discrimination.[14]

Similarly, during the 1930s and 1940s, numerous federal New Deal programs provided very discriminatory access to yet more important resources. As noted in Chapter 2, key government programs heavily favored whites. One of the most important subsidy programs was the Federal Housing Administration's (FHA's) loan insurance and related programs, later buttressed by veterans' housing programs. These enabled millions of whites to buy their first homes. Many whites accumulated enough home equity to use later on for start-up capital for businesses or funding education for children and grandchildren. Other 1930s New Deal programs provided much important aid to white farmers, bankers, and business executives, enabling them to survive the Great Depression and to thrive during World War II and the post-war years. Their white descendants have greatly benefited, to the present, from these discriminatory federal programs.[15]

While many relief programs of the Great Depression and most post-war housing and veterans' programs looked nondiscriminatory on their face, and sometimes African Americans did benefit from them, their routine administration was usually left in the hands of local white officials. These officials generally privileged white individuals and families in need, and black individuals and families got *far less* government assistance than they deserved. Some major programs such as Social Security intentionally excluded lower-paid categories of workers, such as household workers and farm workers, categories where many black Americans and other Americans of color worked. As Katznelson has put it, the era of aggressive public assistance programs from the 1930s to the 1960s was one when government "affirmative action was white."[16]

The growing number of federal government contracting programs after 1940 made contracts available more or less exclusively to white businesses. Firms owned by Americans of color were not allowed significant access to these contracts until the 1970s. In the decades just before and after World War II many government programs helped white builders, contractors, and other businesspeople to get a start and often to thrive. Over the decades since, these and other multibillion-dollar federal aid programs have helped to build up prosperity for many white businesses.[17] Recall again the recent research by Mueller cited in Chapter 1, which showed that the histories of contemporary white families reveal five times more access to an array of these government-derived assets as the histories of contemporary families of color.

Cultural, Legal, and Political Advantages for Whites

Whites have profited not only economically but also educationally, politically, legally, and aesthetically from centuries of systemic racism. Whites have, on the whole, had much greater access to good educational programs than have black Americans. Until the 1960s, most colleges and universities—except historically black colleges—were all white or nearly so. Today, white students' access to first-rate college programs is significantly greater than for black students—and unencumbered by the racist barriers black students currently face. For most of the years since public elementary and secondary schools were first created on a significant scale in the nineteenth century, they have been overtly segregated along racial lines. The period of active school desegregation was brief, and resegregation is increasingly the trend (see Chapter 6, pp. 191–194). Typically, all-white or mostly white public schools have better educational resources and facilities than schools composed predominantly of students of color. Once a family's children have access to good educational capital, they are more likely to be successful in securing good jobs and housing, and thus to pass along substantial economic and cultural benefits to their descendants.

Generally speaking, much contemporary U.S. culture is still substantially shaped by the white population's European heritage. White views and values, especially those of Anglo-Protestant groups, have been determinative in U.S. political–economic and legal development. From the 1600s forward, European-origin whiteness has been the normative standard for much of what is valued in society. The dominant language has long been English, with the most privileged variant and accent being that of middle-class whites. (All people speak English with an accent.) Those not from Europe have had to adopt the language of the dominant white group. In addition, the core legal system is rooted substantially in the English legal system, and the capitalistic economy is heavily European in its values. The U.S. political system was also crafted using European political ideas. Today this political system often does little to implement real democracy in its operations at state, local, and federal levels. Indeed, from the beginning the U.S. political system has allowed those with substantial money, usually well-off whites, to generally control the major political institutions.[18]

In recent analyses of U.S. society, there is a tendency to play down this white-European dominance in favor of a "melting pot" perspective that sees the central U.S. culture as a grand mixture with substantial input from many and diverse immigrant groups over several centuries, including

Africans and other immigrants of color. However, apart from a few matters such as popular entertainment, music, certain sports, and, to some degree, religion, most of the U.S. culture and political economy is still heavily shaped by white Anglo-European values, practices, and arrangements.

Controlling Institutions: The Dominant Role of White Men

Not only have whites dominated the economic, political, legal, and educational values of this society, they have also been in firm control of most of the key roles and top positions in all the powerful institutions for centuries. In earlier chapters we have seen how this dominance was established, and then transmitted over generations. Today, all major large-scale institutions remain white-normed and white-framed in their internal sociocultural structures, and white individuals are mostly in command at and near the top.

Even after decades of affirmative action efforts for Americans of color and white women, the overwhelming majority of those who run most of the more powerful political, economic, and legal organizations in society are still white men. *One* exception is the current U.S. president, the first American of color there. Research shows that there is a concrete ceiling that generally blocks black Americans, many other Americans of color, and white women from many higher-level institutional positions. White men disproportionately control most powerful U.S. institutions. For example, most higher-level executives in various business sectors are white men. Clear evidence of the corporate world's failure to promote meritorious black employees is the fact that so few Fortune 500 companies have ever had a black executive as the very top. In the most recent count there are only four black CEOs (0.8 percent). There are also only six Latino and nine Asian CEOs. Whites thus make up 96 percent of CEOs, and 93 percent are white men. In contrast, the U.S. workforce is about 64 percent white, and just 33 percent white male.[19]

In recent years numerous white commentators have made increasing use of the idea that whites have labeled "reverse discrimination." Surveys indicate that many whites believe that discrimination against people of color has disappeared or declined dramatically and that whites, especially white men, are now major victims of discrimination. However, recent research shows that this is a convenient fiction. Drawing on interviews with many whites, Nancy DiTomaso has found that the persisting opposition by most of them to affirmative action is not so much about fear of "reverse discrimination," but much more about the way in which effective affirmative action programs have sought to weaken old patterns of institutionalized *favoritism* for whites—for example, the often institutionalized bias favoring whites in competition for most of society's better-paying jobs. In the nearly 1,500 job situations that her respondents talked about in detailed interviews, she found only *two* situations where a white person might have lost a job because of an affirmative action effort on behalf of black Americans.[20]

While an isolated few white men in historically white institutions have occasionally lost one opportunity for hiring or advancement because of a modest affirmative action program—usually to well-qualified white women or people of color—societal statistics also contradict the notion of widespread reverse discrimination affecting white men. We have examined numerous data on white male dominance previously, such as their overwhelming dominance at the top of hundreds of major corporations. Indeed, the most successful "quota" program in U.S. history appears to be the one that sees to it that well-off white men dominate exclusively or very disproportionately most of our powerful institutions.

Note too that white men still dominate among those Americans with the greatest amounts of wealth. A recent *Forbes* study of the wealthiest 400 Americans found that almost all (96 percent) are white. Only one (Oprah Winfrey) is black, and women of all backgrounds make up just 10 percent. The overwhelming majority again are white men. Most have inherited substantial money capital and/or significant cultural capital—such as access to a very good education and important networks—that has enabled them to move up economically over their lifetimes. Contrary to much public discussion, the majority of these are not "self-made men."[21]

White Women: Second-Class Citizens in White America

What scholars call *intersectionality* is again important here—the reality of being white and female. White women are also significantly underrepresented at the top of major corporations and other powerful organizations, as we see in the 2012 figure of just 14 white women serving as Fortune 500 CEOs. Although they are a majority of all U.S. workers, these 14 women, plus four women of color, make up less than 4 percent of the top CEOs. These modest numbers of white women at the top in business and numerous other organizational sectors make it clear that white women have not penetrated these decisionmaking heights in anything akin to proportionate numbers. Gender discrimination remains central, and changes have come slowly. As we have seen in previous chapters, white women have historically played a much less central role than white men in creating and maintaining our ongoing system of racial oppression. No women were among the prominent founders. While white women were not explicitly singled out for gender oppression in the new U.S. Constitution, they were seen by most male founders as unequal by nature and in need of male control. State and federal laws made sure that they were second-class citizens under a father's or other male's control. In the early United States white women had certain important legal rights, in contrast to the situations of black women and men. Constitutionally, they were "free persons" and thus had limited rights, albeit those allowed by white men who made the laws. In contrast, as the *Dred Scott* case (1857) made clear, black Americans "had *no rights* that the white man were bound to respect."[22]

Moreover, from the late 1600s to the 1860s white women in the middle-income and upper-income groups sometimes inherited significant socioeconomic resources, including on occasion enslaved African Americans gained under inheritance laws. In subsequent decades, many white women at these class levels have benefited from the labor of exploited black servants (usually women) working in their homes. Over several generations, many white women have also benefited to a significant degree from the undeserved enrichment of their families through the discriminatory arrangements of slavery, legal segregation, and contemporary racial discrimination. For centuries white women's access to economic and cultural resources, privileges, and opportunities—though significantly restricted by patriarchy and sexism—has on the average been significantly greater than that of black women or men. Still, we should keep in mind that it is white men (especially elite men) who have played the most central role, to the present day, in creating, shaping, and maintaining the ongoing system of racial oppression.[23]

The Many Costs of Racial Oppression

Unjust impoverishment and the struggle against racism for Americans of color are the other side of the unjust enrichment and enhanced opportunities for whites. In earlier discussions we examined many burdens and barriers that constitute racial oppression, including discriminatory barriers in employment, housing, education, law, politics, and public accommodations. For African Americans and other Americans of color this recurring and widespread discrimination has many costs and consequences—not only economic costs but also psychological, physical, family, and community costs.

Substantial Economic Costs

In recent decades census data have shown the median family income of black families to be consistently in the range of 55 to 62 percent of the median family income of white families. During the late 1980s and into the 1990s this percentage declined. In the late 1990s black median income was still about 60 percent of white median income, and today it is just under 60 percent. Current data indicate that black households still have a much lower median household income ($32,229) than white households ($55,412). Consider too the cumulative impact of such family inequality. Examining data for the generation of Americans now entering retirement years, researchers have estimated that the average white baby-boom family will earn $450,000 *more* than the average black baby-boom family over their respective lifetimes of work, assuming about 45-year work lives. This is one major economic cost of being black.[24]

In addition, the percentage of Americans in poverty remains high, about 15 percent in the most recent (2011) data. Additionally, black Americans face poverty at a much greater rate (27.6 percent) than white Americans (9.8 percent), and also an unemployment rate much higher than for whites. Black workers are often among the first laid off during economic downturns and among the last to be recalled. Coupled with a high unemployment rate is a depression-like underemployment rate. In recent decades this rate has been one-third or more of black workers in many areas, much greater than for whites. Underemployment includes workers without jobs and those who can only find part-time work or who make very low wages.[25]

One dramatic indicator of generations of accumulating and privileged white access to material and educational resources is seen in measures of family wealth. Recent government data indicate that the median wealth (total assets minus total liabilities) of white families is far greater than that of black and Latino families. In the 2010 Survey of Consumer Finances the median wealth of white families was $124,000, nearly eight times that of black families ($16,000) and Latino families ($15,000). (Earlier 2007 and 2009 surveys showed even greater wealth gaps.) This wealth inequality has stayed very high for many decades. In addition, over the life cycle—that is, as the adults in families age—these racial inequalities in family wealth tend to increase. The wealth of white families is much higher than that of black (and Latino) families substantially because of the housing equities built up over generations of discrimination limiting black access to housing and other socioeconomic resources.[26] White families tend to have higher average income and less unemployment, and they are far more likely than black (and Latino) families to have significant wealth in such important things as interest-bearing bank accounts and stock in companies. Even white families in the lowest income fifth of white families have greater net worth than black families with substantially higher incomes. Wealth is more than just money, for "it's insurance against tough times, tuition to get a better education and a better job, savings to retire on, and a springboard into the middle class. In short, wealth translates into opportunity."[27]

A recent National Urban League *State of Black America* report has summarized the current state of the socioeconomic and criminal justice conditions faced by black Americans. Today black Americans are much more likely than whites to be unemployed, to live in poverty, and to be imprisoned. This report uses an Equality Index, a statistical summary measure of white–black inequalities in the economy, education, health, community engagement, and the criminal justice system. Their 2013 summary Equality Index shows a little decline in the overall societal position of African Americans relative to whites—72.6 percent in 2007 to 71.7 percent in 2013. (Equality with whites would be 100 percent.) The economic area shows the most relative inequality, and the data reveal a little increase in economic inequality from 2007 to 2013. Their data also show much relative inequality and some decline over this period on a composite social-criminal justice measure (from 65.4 percent to 57.1 percent). Their calculations also indicate significant inequality on a composite health measure (from 75.3 percent to 76.9 percent) and a composite education measure (from 78.8 percent to 79.6 percent) relative to whites, although on both of these there was a little improvement over this period.[28]

Recent research reports have made clear that wealth inequality is true for black Americans in all income classes, including the middle class. They reveal the serious to devastating economic losses many black middle-class families took as a result of the great recession of the 2000s. The black (mostly lower) middle class was hit hard by rising unemployment, declining home values, and less money in retirement plans. A substantial majority of black Americans who grew up in the middle-income group will likely not be as economically advantaged as their parents' generation.[29]

Some of these income and wealth-inequality data do briefly appear in the mainstream media, but there is usually no attempt to understand the role of centuries of systemic racism in creating much of this inequality. Instead, many public commentators repeatedly suggest that black workers and their families are mostly to blame.

The Value of Stolen Black Labor

Gaining an adequate explanation for such large racial inequalities requires much deeper probing. Undeserved impoverishment for blacks and undeserved advantages for whites began at a very early point in this country's history. Much of the economic advantage and prosperity of whites in earlier centuries came directly or indirectly from the labor of enslaved Africans and African Americans, or from the country's economic development spurred by profits from slave farms, slave plantations, and the slave trade.

James Marketti once estimated the dollar value of the labor taken from enslaved African Americans from 1790 to 1860 at, depending on historical assumptions, from at least $0.7 billion to as much as $40 billion (in 1983 dollars). This is what black individuals and families lost in income because they did not have control of their own labor. Taking into account lost interest on this stolen wealth from then to the present, the economic loss for black Americans is put at from $2.1 to $4.7 trillion (in 1983 dollars).

Extending this calculation for the entire period from the beginning of enslavement in the 1600s, and calculating it in terms of current-year dollars, would increase the dollar value of this lost wealth to a much higher figure.[30]

After the Civil War, newly freed black Americans faced continuing economic oppression. There were proposals in Congress to give those recently freed some land—the famous "forty acres and a mule"—to begin new lives. Yet relatively few black families got access to the land promised, and inequality in agricultural land was a major cause of persisting racial inequalities after the war. Using antiblack violence, as well as Jim Crow laws, whites in southern and border states denied blacks access to good land, fair credit arrangements, political power, and educational capital. The costs of Jim Crow for black workers included little access to economic capital over the next several generations—even in the form of small businesses or farms—and lower wages stemming from widespread white discrimination. Economic losses were again high. Researchers have estimated the costs of the labor market discrimination against black Americans for the years 1929 to 1969 (in 1983 dollars) at $1.6 trillion.[31] Calculating the cost of discrimination for a longer period, from the end of slavery in 1865 to 1968, the end of legal segregation, and putting it into current-year dollars would increase the cost estimate to far more. Moreover, since the end of official segregation black Americans have suffered additional economic losses from discrimination. For the year 1979 alone, one estimate of the cost of discrimination in employment was $123 billion for black workers. In addition, recall the Urban Institute estimate that today black workers lose more than $120 billion annually because of employment discrimination.[32]

A simple total of the current economic worth of all black labor stolen by whites through the means of slavery, segregation, and contemporary discrimination is huge—perhaps six to ten trillion dollars. This latter figure is exceedingly high, indeed nearly two-thirds of the gross domestic product (GDP) generated in the United States in 2012. In addition, these monetary figures do not include other major costs—the great pain and suffering inflicted, the physical abuse, or the many untimely deaths. Consideration of this massive non-economic damage needs to be figured into the ultimate social cost accounting for this country's white oppression targeting African Americans. Adding in the economic and non-economic costs inflicted on other Americans of color would raise the total social cost of systemic racism to a staggeringly high figure.

Economic Consequences of Racial Barriers

In order to build up successful families and provide for children, parents need access to significant economic, educational, and other social resources. Exclusion from even one major opportunity to secure resources can have immediate and long-term consequences for families. Stephen DeCanio has developed an economic model that suggests that African Americans who had no significant material property because of slavery and who were emancipated without the promised arable land were as a group fated to endure major long-term economic inequality compared to whites even if they had experienced favorable employment conditions, which they did not. The initial gap in land access "would have produced by itself most of the gap in income between blacks and white Americans throughout the late nineteenth and early twentieth centuries."[33] This huge racial disparity has passed along to subsequent generations, to the present. The long-term impact of initial inequality in agricultural resources would "prevent attainment of racial equality even if current discrimination ended and blacks and whites had identical tastes and preferences."[34] Not only were black families substantially excluded from homestead lands by law or violence, they were forced into racially segregated schools, workplaces, and residential areas. Legal segregation in the South and de facto segregation in the North generally kept black families from generating the socioeconomic resources necessary to compete effectively with whites over many generations.

The impact continues into the present. Consider a black person and a white person trying to set up a new business. Often such entrepreneurs must draw on family savings, such as a house equity, or borrow from relatives and banks. The black entrepreneur is much less likely than a white entrepreneur to have significant personal or family resources to draw on because his or her family has been unable to build up economic resources over generations of systemic racism. A black entrepreneur is more likely to face discrimination today in getting bank loans. Once white families garner economic resources, they may invest those assets and profit from what might be called the "money value of time." Having significant economic and other family resources, often unjustly gained because of systemic racism, over some period of time allows for the further enhancement of family resources. In the past, however, the black businessperson's parents and grandparents likely faced extreme racial segregation, which cut down sharply on what they could earn, save, and pass on to later generations.

Even if the black entrepreneur's predecessors had been able to start a small business, they would very likely have been limited to black customers and a black community. Such a business would have had no name recognition outside that community. Jim Crow segregation reduced business visibility and the effects would persist into later generations of business operation. This has not been a problem confronting most white businesses. Lack of capital or name recognition stemming from past discrimination means that today the black business may well have much more trouble than an otherwise comparable white firm in getting new customers and employees. The removal of legal segregation in the 1960s did not get rid of its substantial and lasting impact in the current economy.[35]

Today, as we have seen previously, there is relatively little monetary inheritance across the generations for most black families. The majority of those securely in the middle class today are first generation, so they have not had the time to accumulate substantial assets for several generations like the majority of white middle-class families. Historically, a great many whites have gotten some advantages in terms of the transmission of material assets in the form of homes, savings, land, securities, or small businesses. Many have gotten other significant advantages, such as access to quality education, that translate into material advantages. Centuries of discrimination in employment and housing mean that today black families are significantly less likely to own their homes than whites. Discriminatory practices in home sales, loans, and insurance have long limited the ability of black Americans to build up housing equities that whites have often used to start a business or help the next generation to get a better education.[36]

Recent research has also shown that the current white–black differential in wealth is *not* the result of differences in savings rates, but exists because black individuals generally inherit little from their families. Whites are much more likely to inherit significant wealth. Oliver and Shapiro summarize the impact of various affirmative-action programs for whites:

> There is a long and rich history that includes the homestead act of 1862 and the land-grant colleges of the 19th century, Federal Housing Administration loans, Social Security, and the GI Bill, as well as the continuous benefits of tax codes that subsidize homeownership, property, and wealth. America's broad middle class accumulates two thirds of its wealth through homeownership enabled more by federal actions than private thrift, savings, and investments. The reach of these social-investment actions, however, by both intent and omission, has not been extended to low and moderate-income families, and only barely to Hispanics and African Americans.[37]

Interestingly, in recent opinion polls whites often say that black Americans are now roughly equal with them, responding as though they do not see the many barriers and costs of racism faced today by black Americans (see Chapter 4). However, at some level or in some settings, most whites seem aware that being black in America does involve major personal, family, and economic costs. Political scientist Andrew Hacker has reported on asking white college students how much they would seek in compensation if they were suddenly changed from white to black. Most white students indicated that "it would not be out of place to ask for $50 million, or $1 million for each coming black year."[38]

Additional Cultural Costs

From the colonial period to the present, African Americans have taken much strength from their social and cultural heritage, one rooted in extended families and friendship networks. The knowledge carried in these networks includes positive values and perspectives on life, as well as portraits of role models that buttress identity and self-respect. Black Americans have had to be like experienced anthropologists and know white society well in order to survive or thrive; they have had to be experts on how to respond to hostile white actions. Black American culture has not arisen freely but under conditions of oppressive slavery, segregation, and contemporary discrimination. It thus has important elements of cultural resistance and counter-framing to white racism. While this black culture has many strengths, and draws on its African heritage, it also reflects the past and present exclusion of black Americans from the many privileges and resources available to whites, as well as the **forced assimilation** into Anglo-American ways pressed on black Americans. Reflecting on earlier centuries, legal scholar Patricia Williams has concluded that black enslavement "was that of lost languages, cultures, tribal ties, kinship bonds, and even of the power to procreate in the image of oneself and not that of an alien master."[39]

In recent years some analysts have tried to counter arguments that racism is still systemic with the contention that the U.S. now has very much of a "rainbow culture." The suggestion is that many whites accept much of the music (for example, jazz and rap) and some other entertainment that has emerged from black communities. However, whites in decisionmaking positions, such as at the head of powerful media corporations, generally control the way in which even black music and entertainment elements move into the white-dominated culture. In its early stages after the 1960s civil rights movement rap (hip-hop) emerged as protest music and commentary, as a type of resistance against a white-racist society. However, as it came under the control of these media corporations, much of this black cultural assertiveness against racism has been significantly channeled or watered down. As Ellis Cashmore has put it, whites have converted much of this black culture "into a commodity, usually in the interests of white-owned corporations" and "blacks have been permitted to excel in entertainment only on the condition that they conform to whites' images of blacks."[40]

This apparently respectful acknowledgment of black cultural achievements conceals, just below the surface, old white-framed stereotypes of black Americans as entertaining, hypersexualized, thug-like, or marginal to the mainstream. In addition, much of what was once a protest music form, rap and hip-hop, is substantially altered, and no longer has the power of antiracist resistance that it once had. The absorption of a few elements of a subordinated culture into the dominant culture does not mean much if there is little change in the fundamental aspects of the dominant culture and society, such as in its prevailing legal practices, discriminatory ways of employment, and discriminatory political and business practices.[41]

The Broad Psychological Impact

Writing at a time when efforts at racial desegregation were starting to be reduced in the 1960s, Dr. Martin Luther King, Jr. contended that, if racism is to be eradicated, then whites "must begin to walk in the pathways of [their] black brothers and feel some of the pain and hurt that throb without letup in their daily lives."[42] In much recent research many black Americans have indicated that they still feel like "outsiders" in the United States. The omnipresent reality of white hostility and discrimination generates this distressed feeling. Racism is constructed not just in racist framing in white minds, but also in the ways that whites interact with black men, women, and children. Thus, when a black person enters an organization that is predominantly white or walks down a street where whites are numerous, "race" is seen and created in those specific places by recurring white framing, animosities, and actions. In important interactions with whites, blacks are often excluded from full human recognition, important social positions, and significant societal rewards.[43]

Recurring discrimination can bring a significant psychological toll. Frequently when a black man is near, white women will tightly clutch their purses and white women and men will take such defensive actions as getting out of elevators, crossing the street, or locking car doors. If such actions come to whites' attention, they tend to view them as "minimal slights." Yet these actions can have a negative and lasting impact, for the targeted black man will probably feel like an outcast or alien. At a minimum, every black person has to develop some strategies to counter this psychological warfare by whites. Contemporary social science has documented the severe negative effects that such dehumanization has on physical and emotional health.[44]

Recurring Challenges to Self-Confidence and Identity

The impact of everyday racism includes a range of psychological reactions—from anxiety and worry to depression, anger, and rage. In interviews with many African Americans, my colleagues and I have found that they speak poignantly about the recurring impact of blatant and subtle discrimination on the self-esteem and self-confidence of themselves and of friends and relatives. In recent research we have found that a great many African Americans, especially older women and men who had significant experience with Jim Crow, today suffer from something like the post-traumatic stress syndrome—with its pain, depression, and anxiety—that has been documented for military veterans of some U.S. wars.[45]

Many African Americans are especially concerned about the negative impact of white racism on the youth. Psychologists have extensively examined the impact of racist stereotypes on student performance. In numerous studies by Claude Steele and his colleagues, black and white students have been given skills tests similar to the Graduate Record Examination (GRE). When this examination was presented to black students as a test of their "intellectual ability," they did less well on the tests than white students of comparable ability. In contrast, when the test was presented to the black students without the suggestion that it was a type of intelligence testing, they performed at a level similar to that of the white students. This is a situation of "stereotype threat," one where commonplace stereotypes are brought to the front of black students' minds. Stereotype threat can distract and create anxiety and self-consciousness that hurt test performance. The stereotype threat in research settings has a short-run impact on performance, yet in the longer term, recurring stereotype threats in society can seriously "undermine the identity" of those greatly affected.[46]

Indeed, ours is still a society where the lack-of-intelligence stereotype is regularly pressed on black Americans and some other Americans of color in schools and through the mainstream media. Discussion of white–black "IQ" differentials reappears every few years, usually resurrected by conservative or uninformed whites. Spoken or written stereotypes, when repeated, can have a negative impact, perhaps reducing a person's effort to achieve important personal or family goals. From cradle to grave, whites force black Americans to live out their lives under a constant bombardment of racist-stereotype threats and, as a result, to create an important repertoire of psyche-saving measures to counter them.

Rage and Energy Loss

Some time ago, psychiatrists William Grier and Price Cobbs examined the extent to which anger and rage among black Americans are created by the pervasiveness and complexities of everyday discrimination. Drawing on clinical interviews, they concluded that successful psychological counseling with black Americans must deal directly with this omnipresent discrimination. They concluded that black Americans "have been asked to shoulder too much. They have had all they can stand. They will be harried no more. Turning from their tormentors, they are filled with rage."[47] Today, anger and rage over white racism are still commonplace. Overtly expressed or silent, this rage can lead to inner turmoil, emotional withdrawal, and physical problems.

The seriousness of black anger over discrimination is made clear in the following comments from an interview with the distinguished black professor whose quote opened this chapter. Replying to a question about the level of his anger (on a scale from one to ten) toward white racism, he answered:

> Ten! I think that there are many blacks whose anger is at that level. Mine has had time to grow over the years more and more and more until now I feel that my grasp on handling myself is tenuous. I think that now I would strike out to the point of killing, and not think anything about it. I really wouldn't care. Like many blacks you get tired, and you don't know which straw would break the camel's back.[48]

In his interview he made it clear that he gets most angry from observing the discrimination that white Americans constantly inflict on black youth.

Dealing with racism regularly entails an array of other psychological costs as well. For example, a rather vigilant, cautious, and/or defensive approach to life is usually necessary. Some psychologists have pointed out that to survive everyday racism a black person has to view every white person as "a potential enemy unless he personally finds out differently."[49] Recall too the opening chapter quote from the distinguished black professor that noted the energy loss imposed on African Americans. The latter must expend an enormous amount of energy defending themselves and their families from the assaults of racism on a recurring basis and over lifetimes. As a consequence, black men, women, and children may not be able to achieve what they might otherwise have achieved. This energy drain may also mean they do not have as much energy to put into their families, organizations, and communities as they might otherwise have had. In contrast, over lifetimes white Americans on average have a major life-energy advantage, for they do not waste large amounts of energy dealing with antiwhite discrimination.

The Negative Impact on Physical Health

The stress, anger, and rage created by everyday racism can generate serious physical health consequences. When asked in interview studies about the costs of the discrimination they face, African American respondents frequently cite a broad range of health problems—from hypertension and stress diabetes to stress-related heart and stomach conditions. Several studies have examined the relationship between experiences with discrimination and various diseases, especially stress-related diseases.

For example, one study of a large sample of black women found modest statistical associations between breast cancer incidence and level of reported experience with discrimination. This relationship between cancer incidence and discrimination experience held true when other factors affecting cancer risk were controlled for.[50]

One qualitative field study that my colleagues and I conducted involved focus group interviews with middle-class African Americans. Several participants gave details on how high blood pressure and other health problems were linked, at least in part, to everyday discrimination. One nurse in the Midwest commented on her body's reactions to a workplace with a hostile racial climate:

> That's when I got high blood pressure. And my doctor … I told him what my reaction, my body's reaction would be when I would go to this place of employment … which was a nursing home. When I turned into the drive-way I got a major headache. I had this headache eight hours until I walked out that door leaving there. I went to the doctor because the headaches had been so continuously. And he said … "You need to find a job because you do not like where you work." And within myself I knew that was true. But also within myself I knew I had to have a job because I had children to take care of. But going through what I was going through wasn't really worth it because I was breaking my own self down … it was constant intimidation. Constant racism, but in a subtle way. You know, but enough whereas you were never comfortable…. And then I finally ended up on high blood pressure pills because for the longest, I tried to keep low. I tried not to make waves. It didn't work. I hurt me.[51]

Contemporary racism literally makes people sick. Like other research studies using in-depth interviews with black Americans, we found that they often associate the discrimination they encounter over a lifetime with such physical problems as chronic fatigue, back pain, insomnia, and recurring stomach problems and headaches. Discrimination has physical and psychological impacts.

Much health research has focused on high blood pressure. In these studies most black respondents report significant problems with discrimination. However, the statistical relationship between reported discrimination and high blood pressure has varied, with some studies reporting a clear relationship between reported level of discrimination and high blood pressure, while others have not. One reason for the variability may be the way in which African Americans deal personally with and recall everyday discrimination. For example, one study found the highest blood pressure levels in older black adults who verbally reported the least discrimination. These researchers suggested that in this reporting of less discrimination there may be some internalized oppression going on—that is, some older respondents blame themselves and view unfair treatment by whites as deserved or may use denial of the discrimination they have faced as a coping strategy.[52]

Numerous studies document the often severe impact of everyday racism on various other diseases for African Americans and other Americans of color. One review article examined various links between discrimination and the disparity in rates of heart disease for black and white Americans, with the former having substantially more heart problems than the latter. The researchers conclude that institutional racism "can lead to limited opportunities for socioeconomic mobility, differential access to goods and resources, and poor living conditions," all of which have negative impacts on cardiovascular health. Another impact on health comes from stress that racism causes, which "can induce psycho-physiological reactions that negatively affect cardiovascular health." A third impact lies in the "negative self-evaluations of accepting negative cultural stereotypes as true (internalized racism)."[53] This study might also have added a note on the impact of the frequent discrimination that African Americans and other Americans of color face in dealing with white medical personnel (see Chapter 6, pp. 202–203).

Demographic data on longevity indicate the physical harshness of racism in cold statistical terms. African Americans average significantly shorter lives than white Americans, which has been true for centuries. Historical studies indicate that most enslaved black Americans died by the age of 40, while on average white slaveholders lived more than 40 years. By 1900 the life expectancy for an average black person was only 32–35 years, about 16 years less than that for the average white person. Today, this black/white gap has closed significantly but is still large. As I noted in Chapter 1, today the average black person has a life expectancy three to five years (female/male) less than the average white person. Among major racial groups, African Americans have the lowest life expectancy and highest death rates in numerous death categories. For many deceased African Americans, everyday racism could indeed be listed on their death certificates as a major cause of death.[54]

A Complex and Accumulating Burden

Thinking in terms of the complex and cumulative impacts, Rodney Coates describes everyday racism as a cage:

> To the casual observer, each wire does not appear to be sufficient in and of itself to retain the bird. But when viewed from either within or as a whole we see a finely constructed cage. The problem, from a pedagogical, policy, research, or activist perspective, is that we tend

to concentrate on only one wire or phenomenon, removal of which leads to great anticipation that the war has been won. Unfortunately, while even more insidious wires are being constructed, the others are left intact.[55]

Repeated encounters with white-racist framing and racial mistreatment accumulate across many institutional arenas and over long periods of time. The lifetime number of such encounters for the average black adult is undoubtedly in the thousands. Moreover, the impact on an individual is usually much greater than what a simple summing of her or his experiences might suggest. The cumulative impact of psychological and physical problems directly or indirectly linked to everyday racism can likely be seen in the significant differentials in health and in life expectancy noted previously.

For many white commentators, what they view as the little discrimination remaining in society is only a problem of individual bigots and localized impacts. This view is way off the mark. Today, as in the past, the recurring assaults of blatant, covert, and subtle racism have strong effects not only on individual African Americans and other Americans of color, but also on their larger social circles, for the reality and pain of repeated discriminatory acts are usually shared with relatives and friends as a way of coping with such inhumanity. Over time the long-term pain and memory of one individual becomes part of the pain and collective memories of larger networks, extended families, and communities. This negative impact requires the expenditure of much individual, family, and community energy to endure the oppression and to develop important counter-framing and active strategies for fighting back.[56]

The Price Whites Pay for Racism

Recall the 1960s Supreme Court decision where Justice William O. Douglas argued that the "true curse of slavery is not what it did to the black man, but what it has done to the white man. For the existence of the institution produced the notion that the white man was of superior character, intelligence, and morality."[57] Such white-racist thinking entails living a lie, for whites are not in fact superior in character, intelligence, or morality.

According to surveys cited previously, a majority of whites do not have much empathy for the suffering of those who face racial discrimination. For a great many, participation in racial discrimination, or winking at its practice by other whites, feeds a distancing of the racialized others. This distancing feeds further discrimination, social alexithymia, or insensitivity. Not surprisingly, analyses of corporate workplaces have concluded that discrimination by many white male executives and managers often lies in their inability to deal well with any group—be it black or female—that is quite different socially from themselves. As a result of this difference, there is an often unconscious failure to extend to the racialized others the same recognition of humanity they enjoy themselves.[58]

Living a Rhetorical and Hypocritical Ethic

Traditionally optimistic approaches to U.S. racial matters have accented the egalitarian values supposedly held by the majority of white Americans. Some decades back, Gunnar Myrdal, a Swedish social scientist, and his U.S. colleagues conducted a major study of Jim Crow segregation, reported in the influential 1944 book, *An American Dilemma*. Representing the small liberal wing of the U.S. elite, these researchers argued that whites were under the spell of the American creed. This creed encompassed the "ideals of the essential dignity of the individual human being, of the fundamental equality of all men, and of certain inalienable rights to freedom, justice, and a fair opportunity."[59] As they saw it, this abstract equality ethic, as stated prominently in U.S. law and public rhetoric, was in great tension with the society's legal segregation—thus the phrase "an American dilemma."

However, as sociologist Oliver C. Cox pointed out in a review at the time, they failed to fully understand that the problem of U.S. racism is not at base a problem of failed ideals, but rather of the social, economic, and political interests of whites as a racially privileged group. The vested interests of whites orient them to keeping in place an extensive system of racial privilege and hierarchy that works to their advantage; for most, this outweighs their mostly *rhetorical* commitments to equality and justice values. Today, the majority of whites still have at best a limited commitment to equality and justice ideals in their everyday practices. The evidence in this book strongly suggests that most do not yet wish to see such principles actively incorporated into a thoroughly reconstructed, fully egalitarian U.S. society.[60]

Suffering for the Racist System

Some of the price that systemic racism has demanded from whites can be calculated in lives. For example, the slavery system not only cost millions of African and African American lives over the course of its bloody existence, but it also took some white lives. Being a white sailor on slave ships or a white slaveholder or overseer on slave plantations was often a dangerous job, as those enslaved sometimes lashed out at or killed their immediate oppressors. The 1860s Civil War took 620,000 lives on both sides. African American soldiers died in significant numbers fighting against slavery and for the Union, but most of those soldiers killed and maimed were ordinary white farmers and workers.[61]

In the past and the present, ordinary white farmers and workers who accepted the psychological wage of white superiority have been much less likely to organize effectively with farmers and workers of color. For centuries, this lack of united organization has meant less desirable working and living conditions for ordinary Americans, including white Americans. Today, the impact of historical Jim Crow segregation can still be seen in continuing divisions between many white workers and workers of color. When white workers have refused to organize effectively with workers of color against exploitative employers, they have often received less in the way of wage and workplace improvements than they might have secured.

Before and after the Civil War, ordinary whites paid a heavy political price for systemic racism. In creating an undemocratic society where barbaric violence against African Americans was enshrined in many laws, such as fugitive slave laws, or legitimated by informal practice, such as thousands of brutal lynchings, whites lost some liberty as well. This was especially true for southern and border states with large numbers of enslaved black Americans where the system of social control for enslaved blacks spilled over into greater political inequality for less-powerful whites than in the North. The dominant political arrangements, for whites as well as blacks, were authoritarian—with elite-dominated, one-party political systems the general rule. Autocratic white elites dominating local and state governments were typically uninterested in providing adequate public health programs, schools, and colleges, for ordinary whites or for blacks.[62]

Today, southern states still reflect this heritage. As a group, these states have larger proportions of poverty-stricken citizens and generally weaker public schools and universities, public health programs, and other programs providing for the general welfare of citizens than do the northern states as a group. Inferiority in public services affects the white, black, and other citizens of these states in very significant ways. In addition, the intense political conservatism of the substantial majority of southern white voters today is in significant part a lingering consequence of the South's extraordinarily racist past.[63]

Some Costs of Social Isolation

Today white and black Americans are substantially segregated in terms of residence and neighborhood. As we have seen, such segregation has had severe consequences for black Americans, limiting access to jobs and services. It has also had some negative consequences for whites who have fled the central cities and moved to distant suburbs, directly or indirectly for racist reasons. In the process white families have generally paid a price in terms of higher housing costs, long-distance commuting, pollution from automobiles, and problems associated with central city decline. This suburban expansion is costly in terms of infrastructural costs—for transportation, water, and sewage systems—that increase greatly with sprawling suburban and exurban development. Residential segregation and residence/job mismatch have also been shown to affect overall metropolitan economic growth.[64]

Whites pay for continuing racism in elevated levels of racialized fear and ignorance. Recall the Chicago study of two adjacent suburbs, one white and one black (Chapter 4, p. 137). Whites there were found to reside in an isolated bubble where they were generally able to live out their lives with few experiences that enabled them to get to know black Chicagoans. They were often fearful of their black counterparts because they had few contacts. Such isolation is serious because it means that whites with greater privileges and power do not have the experience necessary to view other Americans with accuracy and sensitivity. Most do not understand the oppressive reality faced by African Americans and other Americans of color. Thus, social scientist Gary Orfield suggests that whites growing up in heavily white suburban enclaves typically have "no skills in relating to or communicating with minorities."[65] In the future, as the country becomes more diverse, this white orientation will become a major disadvantage. In addition, such white isolation will be more of a handicap as the United States becomes yet more involved in international trade and diplomacy in a world where the political and economic leadership is becoming diverse and where non-European countries are becoming ever-more powerful politically and economically.

Conclusion

Systemic racism has had, and currently has, profound human consequences. This is regularly recognized by international agencies. United Nations reports calculate a Human Development Index (HDI). The HDI is an evaluation of quality of life and incorporates data on income, health, and education indicators for various countries and for subgroups within these countries. For 186 countries examined in the most recent (2012) index, the United States ranked just fourth in terms of its overall quality of life. A similar index, the American Human Development Index, rated quality-of-life statistics for black Americans, Latinos, Native Americans, Asian Americans, and whites. White Americans and Asian Americans ranked at the top on this quality-of-life index, while African Americans, Native Americans, and Latinos ranked significantly lower. The quality of life for African Americans as a group remains relatively low, and that of white Americans relatively high, by national and international standards.[66] These figures for African, Native, and Latino Americans underscore some of the long-term costs of systemic racism.

To these statistics should be added centuries of uncounted suffering, health damage, and rage over injustice. Only by adding all these important factors together can one assess accurately the long-term impact of slavery, segregation, and continuing racism. The total cost of four centuries of systemic racism has been extraordinarily high. While whites as a group do pay some price for the centuries-old system of U.S. racism, that price pales when put up against that paid by African Americans and numerous other groups of color.

8
Systemic Racism
Other Americans of Color

Southern Poverty Law Center (SPLC) researchers interviewed 500 working-class Latino Americans in towns and cities in Tennessee, North Carolina, Louisiana, Georgia, and Alabama. More than two-thirds reported that they had regularly been the victims of racism. Anti-Latino hostility and discrimination ranged across an array of incidents mostly perpetrated by whites:

> [Latinos] are routinely cheated out of their earnings and denied basic health and safety protections. They are regularly subjected to racial profiling and harassment by law enforcement.... And they are frequently forced to prove themselves innocent of immigration violations, regardless of their legal status. This treatment—which many Latinos liken to the oppressive climate of racial subordination that blacks endured during the Jim Crow era—is encouraged by politicians and media figures who scapegoat immigrants and spread false propaganda.[1]

While the West and Southwest have traditionally been the home for most Latinos, the Latino population in the South has grown rapidly in recent years.

In the twenty-first century Latino Americans in various regions still face much racial hostility and discrimination, mostly from whites acting out of an anti-Latino subframe of the white racial frame. That centuries-old white frame, central to antiblack thinking from the days of slavery to the present, has been expanded by whites since the mid-nineteenth century to cover Latino, Asian, and other immigrants of color, as well as their many descendants.

Foundational and Systemic Racism: A Brief Review

In recent years some scholars and other analysts have argued that social science researchers, government agencies, and the media give (1) too little attention to the racial histories and discriminatory situations of groups such as Latino, Asian, and Native Americans and (2) too much attention to the racial history and current situation of African Americans.[2] On the first point, they are quite correct, for a review of current research and policy literatures reveals that these Americans of color have not received nearly the research or public policy analysis and attention that they deserve, especially given their long struggles with white racism in this society.

However, on the second point, they are generally incorrect. Much more in-depth attention needs to be given by researchers and policymakers to the history and contemporary situation of African Americans. A comprehensive understanding of the racial situations of all Americans of color, those who are black and those who are not, requires digging deeply into U.S. history to uncover the system of racial oppression in the foundation of the nation created by Europeans and European Americans in the seventeenth and eighteenth centuries. White elites and the white rank-and-file were central to an extensive land theft and enslavement process from the first decades of European colonization. By the mid-seventeenth century those enslaved, mostly African Americans, were positioned and viewed by European Americans and their new legal system as chattel property. This white-on-black enslavement, coupled with the genocidal seizure of Native American lands, was well institutionalized and rationalized in an evolving white racial framing of society. Thus, white-on-black oppression has been a central reality of this society from its first century. Antiblack oppression, for centuries, has penetrated every major area of this society, and thus has shaped the lives of Americans of all racial backgrounds.

African Americans have played no role in creating the dominant system of oppression, except to be its targets and resisters. They have had no role in creating the dominant racial frame rationalizing this oppression, although they had actively resisted that framing and the systemic racism of which it is part. Today, as in the past, how most of these racial patterns are implemented and discussed is largely controlled by white elites, including those in the U.S. media and higher education.

Viewed historically, African Americans have been oppressed much longer by white Americans than any other group except Native Americans. Over nearly four centuries whites have stolen much of the value of black labor under slavery, segregation, and contemporary discrimination. The extremely large number of black Americans who were, and are, oppressed underscores the central significance of white-on-black oppression. Between 1619 and 1865 approximately six to seven million black Americans lived under conditions of slavery in North America.[3] Moreover, between 1619 and today tens of millions of black Americans have lived in this country—and thus have had their labor taken and their lives burdened and truncated by slavery, segregation, and contemporary discrimination. The total number historically is larger than for any of the other groups that have suffered racialized oppression in this country.[4]

Over the centuries white Americans have devoted enormous amounts of energy to oppressing black Americans—initially for labor reasons and later for a range of economic, social, and ideological reasons. To this point in U.S. history, whites as a group have put less time and physical and mental energy into exploiting and oppressing groups such as Asian and Latino Americans, if only because the latter have been in this country in very large numbers for shorter periods of time.[5] Once systemic racism was established in the seventeenth century, substantial individual and collective resistance by black Americans forced whites to put even more effort into maintaining white-on-black oppression. For the first 200 years of colonial development, the only other non-European groups of great concern to European Americans were Native American societies, which were often seen as enemies to be destroyed or driven far from white borders. Until the 1870s these indigenous societies usually rimmed the boundaries of white American expansion on the continent. Over several centuries Indian societies were generally able to confront whites on their turf and draw on strong indigenous resources. Whites were intent on the destruction or displacement of the indigenous societies by whatever means were necessary. However, by the 1870s Native Americans had lost the ability to make treaties as separate nations, and those surviving white expansion were usually forced into isolated reservations, where they have periodically been targets of private and government intervention intending to steal more land or other resources, destroy community solidarity, or force acculturation to white culture.[6]

While they have been the recurring targets of extreme white brutality and recurring genocide, Native Americans have not played as central a role in the *internal* socio-racial reality of the colonies or the United States as have African Americans. Native American labor never became integral to the booming eighteenth- and nineteenth-century economy of the new white-controlled country, nor were Native Americans integrated as a group into the new country's core socioeconomic institutions. Still, the ideological notions of white supremacy and superiority over those viewed as "inferior" peoples were early honed by white colonizers in regard to both Native Americans and African Americans. Whites mostly viewed Native Americans as uncivilized "savages" to be driven away or killed off in genocidal invasions. Early on, anti-Indian ideas and imagery became part of the developing white racial frame.

During the first century of development a sense of white identity was brought about both in regard to the Native Americans on the borders of white territory and in regard to African Americans within the midst of the white colonists. By the late 1700s, however, this sense of whiteness was increasingly asserted mostly in terms of white views of a contrasting and undesirable blackness. This orientation has persisted. For centuries now, a majority of whites have viewed the country in substantially white–black terms. Numerous research studies of whites strongly suggest that the racist socialization of whites in regard to Americans of color other than black Americans is usually less systematic and basic to white identity, emotions, and practices.[7]

Implementing the Racial Status Continuum: Immigrants of Color and Their Descendants

The longstanding structure of white-on-black oppression has regularly been extended by whites for each new non-European group, including those who have mostly come into the U.S. sphere of direct domination since the nineteenth century. U.S. society is not a multiplicity of disconnected racisms directed at various peoples of color. The structure of racial domination developed for enslaving African Americans and killing off or driving away Native Americans was extended by descendants of the early white colonists and founders for the oppression of other non-European groups. From the mid-nineteenth century to the present, numerous groups of non-Europeans—such as Chinese, Japanese, Mexican, and Puerto Rican Americans—have been brought into this highly racialized U.S. system, often to be exploited for their labor. White elites and the white public have long dominated and evaluated later non-European entrants coming into the United States from within the previously established and highly imbedded system of antiblack oppression and its centuries-old white racial framing.[8]

Each new immigrant group is placed, principally by dominant whites, somewhere on a *white-to-black status continuum*, the still commonplace measuring stick of social acceptability. This socio-racial continuum has long been imbedded in white framing and practices, as well as in the developing consciousness of Americans of color. Generally, the white-imposed **racial continuum** runs from white to black, from "civilized" whites to "uncivilized" blacks, from high intelligence to low intelligence, from privilege and desirability to lack of privilege and undesirability. Since the seventeenth century, blackness has been conceptualized as the opposite of whiteness and European-ness.[9] Central to U.S. society is a comprehensive white-superiority framing imbedded in an underlying social-structural reality. "White" and "black" are socially constructed categories riveted to a white-dominated structure of racial oppression, and it is those with the greatest power, white Americans, who substantially control who gets placed where in the continuum's racial categories. This longstanding continuum accents physical characteristics, color coding, and other elements in which European American features and cultural norms are highly privileged.

On occasion, some Americans of color are placed by whites toward the privileged white end of the racial spectrum. Thus, some Latinos and Asian Americans have from time to time been classified as "honorary whites" or "near whites," such as in white-led, anti-affirmative-action efforts where Asian Americans are praised as being the equals of whites who supposedly need no antidiscrimination protection or affirmative action. In addition, legal scholar Frank Wu has accented the opposite phenomenon in which some people of color are defined as "constructive blacks," as being near or at the black end of the racist continuum.[10]

The treatment of Americans of color has varied according to their time of entry, size, culture, physical characteristics, and economic resources. In the case of Asian and Latino groups, for instance, whites have often emphasized a key dimension to the placement equation, that of "foreignness." In every case it is the dominant group that has set the major terms for a new group's incorporation, framing, and continuing mistreatment. One study of early California history shows that Mexican, Asian, Native, and African American groups did not develop there in the same way, yet each was shaped by the pre-existing framework of white supremacy, the central organizing principle of society brought by white migrants from eastern U.S. states. These whites brought a well-developed white-racist frame rationalizing black subordination and applied their racist ideas, with embellishments, to other groups also seen as biologically, intellectually, and culturally inferior.[11]

For later groups of non-European immigrants, whites' racist framing and practices targeting them have been tailored to the particular entry or mobility conditions of these immigrants. When, for instance, Asian or Latino groups have become important for white employers seeking their labor or brought into the country for other reasons, whites have ranked and categorized them along the light-to-dark (and close/not close to European American culture) continuum used for previous groups. Often the lighter-skinned a group is, and/or the more Anglicized it seems to whites, the better it will be treated and viewed.

Some Later Entrants into the Racist System: Chinese and Mexican Immigrants

Over the nineteenth century yet more non-European groups were brought into the ever-expanding, white-controlled land area of the United States. The racist system developed for African Americans in relation to white communities was extended to Asian, Native American, and Mexican groups. Historical circumstances, particularly timing and mode of entry into the sphere of white domination and the group's size and prior resources, have usually meant a significant difference in experiences with whites. Let us examine briefly the experiences of important immigrant groups from China and Mexico.

Chinese Immigrants

By the late nineteenth century the United States was involved in major imperialistic pursuits in Asia and elsewhere around the globe. U.S. and European missionaries and businesspeople moved across the world. Western incursions disrupted numerous Asian economies and sometimes stimulated out-migration. For example, in the mid-nineteenth century various white-run enterprises in Hawaii and on the Pacific Coast were seeking low-wage workers. U.S. labor recruiters secured 200,000 Chinese workers between 1848 and 1882 to work on railroads, in mines, and in personal service jobs. Chinese immigrants were sought as low-wage workers who would set a model of hard work for other workers. When Chinese labor was imported in the 1850s, whites already had in place a well-developed system of black oppression and racist framing. This white-supremacist system was adapted and expanded to encompass these Asian immigrants. Anti-Chinese images and stereotypes took root not only in the views of the white elites seeking to justify exploitation of Chinese laborers, but also in the views of ordinary white workers facing competition from these immigrants.[12]

As historian Ronald Takaki has pointed out, at an early point Chinese immigrants were often associated "with blacks in the racial imagination of white society."[13] They were grouped with African Americans, with both groups being seen as dangerous to the health of U.S. politics and society by many whites who framed the society in aggressively white-supremacist terms. Even into the late 1920s, the U.S. Supreme Court upheld state laws placing Chinese Americans in racially segregated black (not white) schools. Early on, the *San Francisco Chronicle* compared Chinese workers to African slaves: "When the coolie arrives here he is as rigidly under the control of the contractor who brought him as an African slave was under his master in South Carolina or Louisiana."[14] These Asian immigrants were racially subordinated as workers with very few rights. Racial slurs like "coolie" became part of the expanding white racial frame.

Over several decades many whites came to frame these immigrants as another threat to whites' racial purity. In 1880 the California legislature passed a law prohibiting whites from marrying a "negro, mulatto, or Mongolian." The racial slur "mulatto" referred to someone with black and white ancestors, while the racial slur "Mongolian" meant Asian. Earlier, in 1854, the California Supreme Court overturned a lower court's ruling convicting a white man of murder on the basis of testimony by Chinese Americans. A California law declaring that "no black or mulatto person, or Indian, shall be permitted to give evidence" against a white person was said by this court to include the Chinese because they fell under the term "black person." The court explicitly said that the term "black" includes "all races other than Caucasian."[15]

In the 1840s, thousands of whites began to migrate to California. Chinese and other Asian workers were intentionally used by white employers to displace better-paid white workers. With increasing competition between white and Chinese laborers came the adaptation and application by these white workers and their allies of negative racist stereotypes, images, and epithets already used to defame black Americans. Chinese immigrants were called "niggers" or similar epithets and characterized in racist imagery as savage, deviant, criminal, or child-like. In cartoons Chinese Americans were often portrayed as having what were thought of as African features such as darker skin and big lips. Once again, whites portrayed themselves as the physically superior, aesthetically incomparable, and highly civilized group. Instead of working to build alliances with Asian American workers against exploitative employers, white workers persisted in their commitment to a white racial consciousness, and whites-only unions frequently led the growing anti-Asian agitation.[16]

Together with other leading newspapers, the *New York Times* compared "millions of degraded negroes in the South" with a "flood-tide of Chinese ... with all the social vices."[17] The country's media spread the racist imagery of an inassimilable and dangerous foreign "flood" of immigrants—a theme still common in some anti-Asian and anti-Latino framing today. This white fear of being overwhelmed by those who are not white and do not fit well into established white culture is an old theme that began in eighteenth-century antiblack racism—in, for example, the intellectualized racism of Thomas Jefferson (see Chapter 3).

Over time whites did distinguish the Chinese immigrants from African Americans. While both groups were often framed as lazy, devious, or criminal, Chinese Americans were additionally stereotyped as culturally alien and undesirable immigrants. A racist law *excluding* "undesirable" Chinese immigrants was passed in 1882 by the Congress. Only in World War II, when China was a U.S. military ally, were Chinese immigrants—and then only 105 a year—again allowed to legally enter the United States. In the intervening decades, the overwhelming majority of whites viewed these Chinese Americans not as "real" Americans but rather as an alien and excludable "race." For example, in 1896, even as he defended some rights for blacks as the lone dissenter in the *Plessy v. Ferguson* antiblack segregation case, Supreme Court Justice John Marshall Harlan added this negative comment: "There is a race so different from our own that we do not permit those belonging to it to become citizens of the United States. Persons belonging to it are, with few exceptions, absolutely excluded from our country. I allude to the Chinese race."[18]

Researcher Claire Jean Kim has argued that Asian immigrants have long been triangulated between whites and blacks, with a negative evaluation on the two axes of superior/inferior and of insider/foreigner. Initially, the white view of Chinese immigrants stressed their similarity to African Americans in inferior racial status, but over time the dimension of foreignness was given ever-greater emphasis.[19] The established U.S. system of white supremacy, with its ingrained racist framing and discriminatory practices in all major institutions, was again extended and adapted, this time for Chinese Americans. As Gary Okihiro has put it, "insofar as Asians and Africans share a subordinate position to the master class, yellow is a shade of black, and black, a shade of yellow." The two groups are kindred peoples "forged in the fire of white supremacy."[20]

Other Asian Immigrants

After the Chinese were excluded in the 1882 law, there was a division among whites regarding more Asian immigration. Needing labor, some West Coast employers pressed hard for new workers from Asia. Soon, modest numbers of Japanese and Filipino workers were imported to fill low-wage jobs in Hawaii and on the West Coast. However, many whites—including some powerful members of the elite—were still opposed to the presence of more Asian immigrants, typically on blatantly racist grounds.

Initially, Japanese and Filipino immigrants had to endure white-supremacist attacks that characterized them, like African and Chinese Americans, as unintelligent, physically ugly, lazy, or unmanageable. In chorus with other white supremacists, James Phelan, a U.S. senator from California, claimed that Japanese immigrants were a threat to the "future of the white race, American institutions, and Western civilization."[21] Aspects of antiblack imagery were applied to these Asian immigrants, but whites especially emphasized their "foreign" character. Like the Chinese, the Japanese faced anti-foreign stereotypes portraying them as unassimilable and threatening to the dominance of the "white race." Opposition to Japanese immigration led to the infamous "Gentleman's Agreement" between the United States and Japan, whereby under U.S. government pressure the Japanese government cut off most immigration. Similarly, the modest numbers of Filipino immigrants permitted in the 1900 to 1930 period were cut sharply to just 50 a year by the 1930s.

Interestingly, in the late nineteenth and early twentieth centuries, some whites were opposed to overseas imperialism in Asia and Latin America because they feared such involvement would bring immigrants of "inferior" blood into the U.S. mix. However, other white supremacists lauded U.S. and European imperialism because it meant that whites brought "civilization" to their "little brown brothers" overseas. Many whites shared the sentiments in British poet Rudyard Kipling's poem of the time: "Take up the White Man's burden / Send forth the best ye breed." In this view superior whites had a missionary obligation to civilize the world's peoples of color. This latter view won out in the United States. When the U.S. military defeated Spain in the 1890s Spanish–American War, the Philippines and Cuba became colonies in the U.S. empire.[22]

Realizing that classification as near-black on the white-to-black status continuum means consignment to extreme oppression, Asian immigrants and their descendants have often tried to break out of this white-determined racial classification. The Naturalization Act of 1790 explicitly limited the privilege of naturalized citizenship to "white" immigrants. This designation of white was created in opposition to black, and for decades being non-European meant being classified politically and legally as more or less black in the minds and practices of whites in power. Between 1878 and the 1920s numerous U.S. courts examined applications for naturalization from members of Asian groups. In an 1878 case, *In re Ah Yup*, a federal judge decided that a Chinese immigrant could not become a naturalized citizen because he was not white. This decision explicitly cited the classification of races by the European racist thinker Johann Blumenbach in arguing that the meaning of "white person" was generally viewed as not including Asians. These court cases decided that those who were partially or totally Asian were not white and were thus ineligible for citizenship. This explicitly racist criterion for U.S. citizenship was not eliminated until the 1952 Immigration and Nationality Act.[23]

The Incorporation of Mexican Immigrants

The first Mexican residents of the United States did not immigrate, but were brought into the United States as a result of the Mexican–American War of the 1840s. Mexicans were incorporated into the expanding U.S. empire by the conquering whites. Whites who invaded northern Mexico in the early nineteenth century were often from the slaveholding South, and some brought in enslaved African Americans.

Whites who migrated to these southwestern areas usually carried the system of white racism in their minds, propensities, and practices. They applied their white-supremacist, antiblack framing to Mexicans, who were viewed as intellectually, physically, and culturally inferior. At the time of the Anglo-American invasion of Texas and California numerous Mexicans, including in leading families, had some African ancestry. This multiracial heritage fueled racist reactions to Mexicans by whites immigrating there. They called Mexicans "niggers" or other racist epithets and treated them in the discriminatory ways they did African and Native Americans. Stephen F. Austin, a white adventurer who founded new Texas communities, viewed Mexicans as a "mongrel Spanish-Indian and negro race."[24] In the congressional debate over annexing northern Mexico, a leading U.S. senator, John C. Calhoun, opposed such annexation. The United States had never incorporated into the Union any but the Caucasian race.... Ours is a government of the white man.... [T]here is no instance whatever of any civilized colored race, of any shade, being found equal to the establishment and maintenance of free government.[25]

Nonetheless, annexation took place. Whites had no trouble moving from malevolent conceptualizations of the "black race" to similarly venomous views of other "colored races." Such views became part of an expanding white-racist framing of society.

By the early 1900s, agricultural and industrial expansion created an increased demand for low-wage labor in the Southwest. White employers recruited large numbers of Mexican laborers for farms and factories, with federal assistance. After a decline in Mexican labor importation during the 1930s Great Depression, throughout World War II white employers again sought Mexican workers for low-wage jobs. Periodically since then, employers and their allies in government have sought Mexican workers to do low-wage agricultural and manufacturing jobs, even as growing numbers of political groups have agitated against such immigration. By bringing in large numbers of Mexican workers, employers have helped to change the U.S. demographic and political landscape in often dramatic ways.

Like black Americans, Mexican Americans have been recurring targets of white-supremacist actions. In fact, the first extensive discrimination targeting U.S. Latinos was aimed at Mexican Americans in the mid-nineteenth century. After the Mexican–American War, many Mexican families lost their lands by force or chicanery to white newcomers. Those who lost lands often became landless laborers or sharecroppers on land formerly owned by Mexicans or Mexican Americans.[26]

In the century after the war with Mexico, Mexican Americans in numerous areas faced blatant discrimination and overt segregation in employment, housing, schools, and public accommodations. Blatant discrimination was often backed by white violence and lasted into the 1960s—with some continuing to the present. In the Sunbelt states this usually informal discrimination was a logical extension of, and often patterned on, that developed for black Americans, but whites added embellishments—such as hostility to many uses of the Spanish language—to their racist framing and discriminatory practices. For decades Mexican American children, to take just one example, were punished for speaking Spanish in schools and their names were Anglicized.[27]

In 1897 a white federal judge ruled that a Mexican American petitioner could become a naturalized U.S. citizen only because of treaty agreements associated with the 1840s war with Mexico. The racist judge declared that if a "strict scientific classification of the anthropologist should be adopted, he would probably not be classed as white."[28] Racial classification is often a matter of government action. Well into the middle of the twentieth century prominent whites, in state legislatures and the Congress, publicly described Mexican Americans as mixed-race "mongrels" or "inferior coloreds"—often with reference to their "inferior" Indian or African "blood." In contrast to white framing of Asian immigrants, in the case of Mexican Americans many whites have given much more attention to this "mixed blood," indeed to the present day. Again we observe the U.S. racial hierarchy and its rationalizing frame in operation.[29]

Anti-Mexican framing and discrimination developed among white workers as well as in the elites. Because of competition with Mexican workers—especially after the large-scale immigration beginning in the 1910s—white workers and union organizations frequently participated in hostile verbal and physical attacks on Mexican immigrants, including many lynchings.

In some settings, in the past and the present, Mexican Americans have been able to fight discrimination better than African Americans. One reason is that the white discrimination faced by Mexican Americans has often been more informal. Another is that as a group Mexican Americans have historically had somewhat greater resources to draw on. Mexican, other Latino, and Asian immigrants to the United States in the last century have usually had the ability to maintain strong links to their home country. These ties have provided family and moral support, and sometimes monetary aid, in the face of racist barriers. For these immigrants and their descendants, home country ties have generally not been destroyed by centuries of oppression, as they have been for most African Americans. In addition, from the 1850s to the 1920s people of Mexican descent on both sides of the U.S.–Mexico border had a history of armed struggles against oppressive whites, struggles that inspired later generations to openly fight anti-Mexican discrimination.[30]

When Chinese, other Asian, and Mexican immigrants were brought into the United States by employers seeking to exploit their labor, most whites automatically placed them in a racialized status much inferior to that of native-born whites. They were initially categorized at or near the "black end" of the white-to-black racial continuum. This placement has not meant that Mexican Americans or other Americans of color have shared exactly the same treatment from whites as African Americans, but history shows that whites, especially elites, substantially shaped the conditions for each group's incorporation into society, for their level of economic and political development, and for the character of the racial oppression they face.

Intermediate Placement and Status

From the first stages of the development of systemic racism in the seventeenth century, African Americans were placed at the bottom of the racial hierarchy, with the only other non-European groups—the Indian societies—usually being destroyed or forced beyond white-controlled territory. As new non-European groups entered the country from the 1840s to the early 1900s, they were initially placed near the black end of the racist continuum in terms of the white racial framing and oppressive practices. Over time, as noted previously, the more powerful whites have allowed the movement of some people of color to an intermediate position on the white-to-black racial continuum.

Some Americans with ancestral roots in Asia or Latin America have been able to alter their racialized status within the white-dominated society, but only because whites have come to see them as "better" in racial, physical, and/or cultural terms than African Americans. Writing in the 1940s, sociologist Oliver Cox emphasized the determinative importance of this white-controlled ranking:

> Whenever there are two or more races in the same racial situation with whites, the whites will implicitly or explicitly influence the relationship between these subordinate races.... The race against whom the whites are least prejudiced tends to become second in rank, while the race that they despise most will ordinarily be at the bottom.[31]

Certain lighter-skinned, more white-looking, more acculturated—as defined by whites—subgroups among Asian and Latino Americans have sometimes been viewed and framed by whites as more acceptable than the darker-skinned, less white-looking, less acculturated members of these same groups. At various times in history, some Asian and Latino Americans have been accepted by whites in an intermediate racial status, especially if they are a small part of a local population or intermediate placement is of benefit to whites. In the early decades of Anglo-American settlement in the Southwest, a few lighter-skinned Mexican Americans in Texas, New Mexico, and California, especially those with land and money, were treated as "honorary whites." After World War II, to take another example, Japanese Americans, including some who had been in U.S. concentration ("detention") camps, were more likely to be hired than African Americans in better-paying job categories in California. Their educational attainments were one reason, but so was their placement by whites in a more **intermediate status** on the societal racial continuum.[32]

More recently, a few groups among Latinos, such as lighter-skinned, middle-class Cuban Americans and South Americans, and certain groups among Asian Americans, such as middle-class Japanese, Chinese, and Asian-Indian Americans, have periodically been accepted by whites as closer to the white than the black end of the old racial continuum. Nonetheless, this near-white placement can be unstable and fluctuating. And it is not ordinarily extended by whites to the majorities of certain racialized groups, such as Mexican Americans and Puerto Ricans.

Whites make much use of placement in the intermediate status to keep the racist system flexible but intact. For example, when mainstream media or other analysts say positive things about the success of certain Asian or Latino American groups, they tend to single out those who are lighter skinned or especially "assimilated" and "white-acting." They point to achievements of selected middle-class Japanese Americans, Asian-Indian Americans, or Cuban Americans to suggest that these Americans are working harder and conforming better to the white-determined core culture than African Americans. Whites and others operating out of the dominant racial frame often cite some in these groups as examples of achievement "who do not need affirmative action." In this way the dominant racial frame and hierarchy are protected, as one group of color is played off against another, to white advantage.[33]

Since the 1960s certain Asian American groups, such as Japanese or Asian-Indian Americans, have been cited by white opinion makers as "**model minorities**." Whites, especially elites, again have determined how these groups are to be viewed. At earlier points in history, these and other Asian Americans were typed negatively as "black" or "near-black" on the racial continuum, but now certain people within that Asian umbrella category are publicly constructed by whites as nearer to white. Somehow, their "nonwhiteness" and their foreignness are not as much of a problem in the white mind as they once were. Not surprisingly, the stereotyped "model minority" term and framing were originally created in the 1960s by white social scientists, media commentators, and politicians who sought to condemn African Americans for their protests against discrimination. Certain Asian Americans were said by many whites to be moving up the socioeconomic ladder unhindered by discrimination and without such protests. Today, these Asian Americans are still often said to be models of success because of their commitment to the "work ethic" and other values of importance to such white analysts.[34]

This model-minority stereotyping remains very much a part of the contemporary white racial frame. It not only misrepresents the condition of Asian Americans, many of whom are relatively poor and most of whom still suffer significant discrimination of various types at the hands of whites, but also creates resentment among non-Asian Americans of color because it is widely used to assert that the U.S. is now a just society. The ability of whites, especially the powerful, to control much of the placement of peoples of color on the white-to-black continuum and to define their societal position is a valuable tool used for the continuing reproduction of systemic racism.

The Position of Immigrants and Their Children

Until the increased immigration that began in the 1960s, there were modest numbers of Asian and Latino Americans. Today, their numbers are growing significantly. Majorities of the larger Asian American groups, except for Japanese Americans, and majorities of the larger Latino groups are currently immigrants or their children. These important groups tend to be concentrated in metropolitan areas in western and southwestern states and in a few other large metropolitan areas like New York, Chicago, and Miami. In the last few decades we have seen an increase in numerous areas in anti-immigrant groups and in hostile agitation targeting immigrant groups. Nonetheless, and in contrast to previous eras, national opinion polls show today that only a small percentage (about 16 percent) of Americans view immigration, including Asian and Latino immigration, as a national problem that should be a top priority for legislative action.[35]

However, in certain geographical areas with substantial numbers of Latino and Asian immigrants, such as Texas and California, Latino and Asian American communities are much larger and play a more significant role in interracial relations than elsewhere. There immigrants of color, especially Latinos, have periodically been targeted in openly racist terms by white-run nativistic groups. For them the foreignness imagery is very strong. In these areas a great many whites have shown greater antagonism than people in other areas toward bilingual programs and assisting immigrants with public services. For example, a Proposition 187 campaign in California in the 1990s tried to restrict hospital and other services for undocumented immigrants, but the proposition that passed was voided by the courts. Other state legislatures have attempted to pass similar measures. A Proposition 209 campaign in California successfully eliminated affirmative action programs for college students of color, which especially hurt Latino and black students. In addition, a late-1990s Proposition 227 campaign successfully put limits on bilingual education in California, thereby destroying some of the most effective learning programs for immigrant children.

Interestingly, some social science research suggests that a pre-existing conservative political and social framing is more important in shaping increases in certain states' anti-immigrant legislation than actual numbers of Latino immigrants. After studying anti-immigrant legislation passed by state legislatures, two researchers concluded that

> ideological framing is the most consistently important factor determining legislative responses to newcomers.... The current rush

to legislation is a made-up crisis.... These immigrants have become part of a larger political dynamic and positioning based on racialized fears and misperceptions about the impact of immigration.[36]

Gradually Blending In?

Some social commentators and analysts today actually see the children and grandchildren of recent Asian and Latino immigrants, as well as the descendants of earlier immigrants in these groups, as progressively blending into the dominant white group and becoming "white." Nathan Glazer has described Asian and Latino Americans as becoming significantly less different from whites in residence, income, and attitudes. Eventually the "two nations" making up the United States will "become the black and the others."[37] Political scientist Andrew Hacker has argued in the case of Asian and Latino American groups "none of the presumptions of inferiority associated with Africa and slavery are imposed on these other ethnicities."[38] As he sees it, later generations are gradually merging into the white category through conformity to white ways and movement into the middle class.

However, arguments that Latino or Asian Americans are gradually or rapidly blending into the dominant white group are problematical. Some commentators seem to accent such a blending into whiteness because it enables them to distance themselves, and white society, farther from African Americans, whom they view as the most troubling racial group.[39] Perhaps most problematical for the progressive blending arguments is the reality of continuing and substantial discrimination by whites against Latinos and Asian Americans, including those who are middle class (see below).

Some surveys do indicate that whites are more willing to accept Asian Americans and Latinos into their neighborhoods and certain other social arenas than African Americans. One sign of partial acceptance of Asian and Latino Americans as intermediate groups on the racial continuum can be seen in public white attitudes toward intermarriage. In one survey 37 percent of whites said they would be opposed to a close relative marrying a black person, and only 23 percent said they would approve of such an intermarriage. This contrasted with somewhat greater approval among these white respondents for white–Asian intermarriages and white–Latino intermarriages in their families.[40] (In addition, a few other surveys asking how whites feel about white–black intermarriage in general reveal smaller percentages opposed.)

Interracial marriages are increasing in number, but are still a modest proportion of marriages. A 2012 Census report showed that just 9.5 percent of all opposite-sex married couples had spouses with different racial backgrounds (including Hispanic). The overwhelming majority of all marriages are still within racial groups. In addition, a substantial majority of intermarriages involving whites are between whites and groups other than blacks. A recent Pew Center analysis of newlyweds found that 15 percent were in interracial marriages. About 57 percent of these new interracial marriages were between whites and either Latinos or Asian Americans—with just 12 percent between whites and black Americans. Even so, many contemporary analysts view this modestly growing percentage of interracial marriages involving whites and Latinos or Asian Americans as an important indicator that these nonblack groups are progressively blending into the dominant white society and are a signal of an end to the U.S. as a racist society.[41]

In several ways, however, intermarriage figures are ambiguous or problematical measures of the pace and character of such assumed societal change. Many intermarriages may represent two people relating to one other for distinctive reasons that may not indicate broad societal changes. For example, historically many white–Asian marriages have been between white men and Asian war brides from areas where the U.S. government has been involved militarily. These relationships account for a significant number of current intermarriages. There is also a growing international trade in Asian and Latino brides for white men. In these cases the patterns of intermarriage disproportionately reflect certain distinctive choices of individuals, including white men who are seeking "traditionally submissive" mates, rather than a broad and mutual adaptation between members of two different racial groups.[42]

Moreover, the idea of some assimilation-oriented analysts that slowly increasing numbers of intermarriages signal an end to white racism is highly problematical. On the one hand, there is still much publicly expressed opposition or discomfort with racial intermarriage, as noted previously. Indeed, the low rate of white–black marriages today, as compared to other intermarriage rates, likely signals the continuing reality of antiblack framing among many whites. In addition, we know from research previously cited that many whites will say one thing in public or to strangers like pollsters—for example, adopt an "I am colorblind" approach—and do yet another when it comes to comments among relatives or friends, as well as in their discriminatory actions in various settings. Several studies of white–black and other interracial dating and marriages indicate that the couples in these relationships are often not treated well by some white relatives, friends, and other community residents. While whites in the communities where these couples reside may say publicly in surveys that they generally have no opposition to white–black relationships, they will also emphasize that they view such relationships as likely being troubled, internally or externally, and somehow problematical. Thus, as Erica Childs explains from her data on white–black couples, the problems "identified by the community groups were addressed differently by the couples. For example. whites described interracial relationships as unnatural, non-traditional, or plagued by cultural differences, while the couples discussed their relationships as the same as intraracial couples."[43] Such recurring white questioning of, or opposition to, these relationships—as well as the pain that white reaction causes for couples—are significant evidence that increases in interracial relationships do not signal an end to racism.

Is Becoming White a Real Possibility?

Today, many analysts who are especially hostile toward or critical of the large numbers of Latino and Asian immigrants in the United States tend to accent certain groups within these broad umbrella categories, such as Mexican Americans or Southeast Asians (for example, the Vietnamese), respectively. The latter groups, it seems, look and act less like middle-class whites, at least as seen by many whites. Anti-immigration analysts pick among groups in the umbrella Latino and Asian categories to suit their ideological purposes. As these groups have grown, intense opposition has emerged from some sectors of white America. We noted previously the former *Forbes* editor Peter Brimelow's assertion that the American nation "has always had a specific ethnic core. And that core has been white."[44] Analysts like Brimelow and media commentator Patrick Buchanan seem worried about large numbers of immigrants of color threatening "Western culture" by watering it down. Less-strident views making the same point about the supposedly deteriorating "white core" of society can be found in prestigious journals such as *Foreign Affairs*. These nativistic analysts certainly do not view Latino and Asian immigrants and their children as white or as blending easily into a white-dominated society.[45]

Moreover, being categorized as nearer the white than the black end of the old racist continuum does not mean that a group, or member of a group, is viewed as being truly "white" by whites. According to some research, most whites do *not* see the larger groups of Latino and Asian Americans as white. We gave a questionnaire to 151 self-defined white college students asking them to place a long list of U.S. racial–ethnic groups into "white" or "not white" categories. Very large majorities indicated groups like the following were clearly "white": Irish Americans, English Americans, German Americans, and Italian Americans. In contrast, not one listed African Americans as white, and substantial majorities classified all listed Asian American groups (such as Japanese Americans and Chinese Americans) as not white and all listed Latino groups (such as Mexican Americans and Puerto Ricans) as not white. This group of relatively well-educated whites had no trouble placing these groups on the racial–color continuum that is still central to in their everyday framing of

U.S. groups. These data strongly suggest that very substantial majorities of white Americans are not yet incorporating groups of color into a white, or even near-white, category in their minds.[46]

Moreover, surveys have found that the majority of Latino Americans typically do not see themselves as white when they are allowed an array of options. In one major 2002 Pew Hispanic Center/Kaiser Foundation survey of nearly 3,000 Latinos, modest percentages of numerous Latino groups identified their group as "white" when given the standard (and limited) U.S. Census Bureau's categories of white, black, Asian, American Indian, and Pacific Islander, with just one exception. Just 17 percent of the Mexican American respondents identified as white, compared to 19 percent of Puerto Ricans, 14 percent of Central Americans, and 29 percent of South Americans. (The exception was Cuban Americans, 55 percent of whom chose white.) Majorities of the Mexican American and Puerto Rican respondents, from the largest Latino groups, chose Latino/ Hispanic as their racial identity, as did the sample as a whole.[47] In a 2011 Pew survey most of the Latino respondents again did not see themselves as fitting neatly into the Census Bureau's standard categories. Asked to state their racial group in the somewhat changed census terms, 51 percent chose "some other race" or "Hispanic/Latino." This time, 36 percent of the total group identified as white, with 10 percent identifying as black, Asian, or multiracial. Interestingly, on another question 47 percent said they were very different from the "typical American." Being Latino in a white-dominated United States is clearly a difficult and complicated experience.

In addition, some field interview research on Asian Americans suggests that most of them do not see themselves as white, although many try to conform aggressively to the ways of whiteness in order to adapt in this racist society. Clearly, having an intermediate status on the white-imposed racial spectrum does not mean that one is seen, or easily sees oneself, as fully white.[48]

Some scholarly and media analysts have argued that the growing population of "multiracials"–Americans who openly identify as belonging to more than one racial group—will eventually weaken or force a replacement of the conventional racial categories, and thus the dominant racial ladder. In the 2010 census about 97 percent of the population identified as being from one racial group, while 2.9 percent identified as being from two or more racial groups. Frequent media articles have argued that these multiracial Americans are the "wave" of the future and signal an end to a racist America.[49] Researcher Sharon Chang has noted an important article in *Psychology Today* titled "Mixed Race, Pretty Face?" that accents the supposed greater beauty and health of European-Asian multiracial people, as well as their positioning as part of a "new white" group. Such "multiracial chic" articles are often used, especially by white analysts, to celebrate a post-racial America where whites are just one racial group among many.[50]

Clearly, the small population of Americans who identify as multiracial is growing, but knowing its actual size is complicated because of pressures in some areas for a person not to identify as multiracial. One recent study examined whether Californians with white–black or other mixed-racial heritage could successfully assert a multiracial or white identity. Interviewing 46 Californians with multiracial ancestry, the researchers found that those who were Asian–white or Latino–white in parentage were usually able to self-identify successfully as either multiracial or white. However, those who had black–white parentage mostly identified as black because that is how others usually viewed them. The researchers speculated as to whether the multiracials who did *not* have black parentage might eventually become part of an expanded "white" category.[51] Interestingly, one of very few contemporary books on raising multiracial children is by a white author with multiracial children, Donna Jackson Nakazawa. Among her often savvy comments for parents of multiracial children she makes incomplete comments about the age at which children learn about racial matters (much younger than she suggests[52]) and too optimistically accepts into the white-promoted theme that multiracial children signify a post-racial America.[53]

There is no research evidence that the increasing number of Americans accenting their multiracial ancestry, or the increasing number of interracial couples with multiracial children, has had any major impacts on the persisting and well-institutionalized power and privilege of whites, who still remain firmly as the top group in the racial hierarchy.

Continuing Racial Framing and Discrimination: Asian Americans

As noted previously, an intermediate status on the established white-to-black racial continuum does not bring mean equality in rights or privileges with whites. There is still much racial framing and discrimination directed at intermediate groups. We only have space here to briefly sketch the contours of this negative framing and discrimination (see notes for more research).[54] For example, one large survey of Asian, Latino, and African Americans found substantial majorities of these groups felt that there is much racial discrimination targeting their group, that all three groups face similar racial problems and should develop coalitions, and that the country would be in better shape if more Asian, Latino, and African Americans were in positions of authority in major institutions.[55]

Numerous recent studies show that, even though many Asian Americans are moving into the economic mainstream and suburban neighborhoods, they still face racial discrimination in numerous areas, including employment, housing, public accommodations, policing, and government service and politics. We have noted some examples of this discrimination in previous chapters. Recall that in Chapter 6, I described a recent field study using white testers and testers of color that found significant housing discrimination targeting Asian Americans. In addition, a study of New York restaurants used white and Asian American testers and found anti-Asian discrimination there.

In national surveys Asian Americans also report much discrimination. In a recent Pew survey one in five Asian American respondents reported facing racial discrimination in the last year. One in ten had faced racist name calling, and one-eighth or more indicated that being Asian hurt them in looking for a job, getting promoted, or seeking admission to college.[56] We should note too that since Asian Americans are often reluctant to talk about discrimination, such survey and interview results likely provide significant underestimates of the discrimination that these Asian Americans regularly encounter. Additionally, in an in-depth interview study involving 43 middle-class Asian Americans, researchers Chou and Feagin found that they frequently described facing discrimination from whites in schooling, policing, business, and employment settings. In this interview study and others like it, Asian Americans have recounted discrimination ranging from blatant and obvious, to rather subtle, to quite covert.[57]

The workplace is one of the more common areas where they face such discrimination. In a recent survey of professionals of color in government and non-profit workplaces a majority of Asian American male professionals and a near-majority of Asian American female professionals reported racial, gender, and other discrimination.[58] Commonly cited examples of employment discrimination in several studies include omnipresent "glass ceilings" in historically white workplaces that keep most Asian American employees from moving up to higher-level white-collar positions. Researcher Lei Lai makes a strong case for more public questioning of the model minority stereotype, especially in regard to such employment discrimination. She reviews research showing that Asian American employees face glass ceilings severely limiting their promotion opportunities. She also cites the way in which the model imagery deflects attention from more negative stereotypes that Asian Americans face, keeps them from being seen as "real" Americans, and frustrates attempts of less advantaged Asian Americans to secure the support they need from government programs.[59]

Violence against Asian Americans has been a serious problem for decades. For example, in one incident several Asian American students were excluded from service at a Syracuse restaurant, then were beaten by hostile whites as they left. The 2012 FBI hate crime report listed 175 hate-based crimes in which the victims were targeted because of a bias against Asian or Pacific Islander Americans, a figure probably much lower than the actual number because most police jurisdictions do not report hate-based crimes. Indeed, a few U.S. Civil Rights Commission reports have indicated that in numerous communities the typically white-controlled police agencies are slow to offer adequate protection to Asian Americans from hate-based crimes, crimes that seem to be on the increase.[60]

Political discrimination remains a problem. One California study of the redevelopment of a shopping center showed how the white minority in a substantially Asian American urban area forced a redevelopment project to be done their way. "Rather than reflecting the city's current and future position as a major node for Asian-themed businesses, the shopping center was remodeled to provide a place where whites could shop and 'feel at home.'"[61] In other urban political decisions in California white leaders, revealing negative Asian framing (such as "Chinese invasion"), have favored white businesses and development ideas over Asian American businesses and development ideas. In recent research on San Diego, Leland Saito has shown how urban development and historic preservation efforts favor white structures and interests over those of Chinese American and African American communities.[62]

The model-minority imagery circulated in the media deflects public attention not only from discrimination that Asian Americans face, but also from other community problems. For example, a larger percentage of Korean, Vietnamese, and Chinese Americans fall below the poverty line than does the U.S. population as a whole.[63] Research on Asian Americans has also found significant health impacts stemming from recurring discrimination—as well as from related factors such as the intense pressures to conform to white ways to avoid discrimination. (One Pew survey found that 39 percent of Asian American respondents felt that Asian immigrant parents "put too much pressure on their children to do well in school," a much higher percentage than felt that way about all U.S. parents.[64]) A study of Korean immigrants found negative effects on their mental health in their first years in the U.S., and significant mental problems later too. Moreover, Asian American teenagers have the highest levels of depression for any racial group. Studies of young and old Asian Americans have found relatively high levels of suicide, often the highest among U.S. groups. Such mental health problems, as well as certain physical health problems, can often be reasonably linked, at least in part, to the great stress that comes from dealing with anti-Asian racism and attempting to conform to white-imposed sociocultural pressures in educational, employment, and other historically white environments.[65]

Continuing Racial Framing and Discrimination: Latino Americans

A 2011 Associated Press survey found that just over half of whites explicitly admitted to holding anti-Latino views, and even more signaled such a negative perspective on the Implicit Association Test that measures much unrecognized bias.[66] Not surprisingly, thus, research studies reveal that Latinos regularly face significant discrimination from whites. Employment discrimination is one major problem area. A 2013 national survey of Latinos in various classes by the Pew Center found that 22 percent of first-generation Latinos and 25 percent of second-generation Latinos reported that being Latino hurt job-finding chances. About a fifth of both generations reported that being Latino hurt job promotion chances.[67]

The SPLC study cited in the chapter opening reveals that Latino immigrants and other working-class Latinos are frequently discriminated against by employers, who often do not pay them what they are owed or do not provide safe working conditions.[68] In a recent southwestern study, Hilario Molina interviewed immigrant day-laborers. They reported encountering much racist framing from whites, including employers. These whites were often concerned that immigrant workers will not assimilate well to the Anglo-American culture and will force major changes in it. The undocumented workers also reported that they encountered significant stereotyping out of the white frame from Mexican American subcontractors they worked with. In this use of conventional white stereotyping by other Mexican Americans, the "elite white male remains unseen but active in racializing the social and structural activities."[69]

Both in the South and in the North, government agencies, usually directed by whites, have implemented discriminatory legislation targeting Latino immigrants. Local government agencies in the Northeast have developed laws limiting the number of people in a house, or have selectively enforced pre-existing but little used occupancy restrictions, just to make Latino immigrants' lives so difficult they will leave these communities. These white-dominated communities often seek out the low-wage labor that immigrants provide, yet do not welcome them after the workday is over.[70]

Middle-class Latinos also face significant workplace and other discrimination from whites. In the previously mentioned study of professionals of color in government and non-profit workplaces, 66 percent of the Hispanic male professionals and 71 percent of the Hispanic female professionals reported racial, gender, or other discrimination.[71] Moreover, in interviews with 72 mostly middle-class Latinos across the country, José Cobas and I recently got numerous accounts of anti-Latino discrimination. This reported discrimination ranged from blatant to subtle and covert and was reported not only for workplaces but also for shopping sites and encounters with police officers. Similarly, drawing on interviews with Latino lawyers, political scientist Maria Chávez has demonstrated the broad range of racist framing and discrimination that they regularly face.[72]

A recent Pew Hispanic Center survey found that among Latinos a majority viewed anti-Latino discrimination as a major problem in public schools as well as workplaces. Sixty-four percent viewed public schools as riddled with anti-Latino discrimination, which contrasted with 58 percent reporting the same for employment settings. Other studies have shown that racial climates in historically white college settings are also often hostile for students of color. While Latino students who are first-generation immigrants tend to be optimistic about educational settings, native-born Latino students indicate that they are well aware of the discrimination they encounter on and around college campuses.[73]

Anti-Spanish hostility and discrimination are common problems faced by Mexican Americans and other Latinos in all classes and nationality groups. Recall that in the 1990s a majority of white voters in California, many apparently fearful of Latino immigrants, voted for ballot propositions to abolish government services for immigrants, eradicate affirmative action for Latinos, and reduce bilingual programs. White politicians and voters in other regions have pressed for similar restrictions. White hostility to the Spanish language faced by early Mexican American residents of the Southwest persists—in the "English only" movement, in white opposition to bilingual education, and in the commonplace mocking of the Spanish language and Latino cultures. Consider too Jane Hill's research (Chapter 4, p. 122) on the mock Spanish used by whites in the media and other settings. Many whites use an array of made-up Spanish phrases such as "el cheapo" and "hasta la vista, baby," mocking that often reveals an underlying racist framing of Latinos.

Racial profiling by the police and other authorities is yet another problem for Latinos. One recent national survey found that not even half of the Latino respondents were at least fairly confident that local police officers usually treated community residents fairly. Numerous local and federal police agencies across the country have enforced U.S. immigration laws in a way that signals "systematic racial profiling and has made Latino crime victims and witnesses more reluctant to cooperate with police. Such policies have the effect of creating a subclass of people who exist in a shadow economy, beyond the protection of the law."[74] This common racial profiling, often based on stereotypes from the dominant racial frame, has had an impact well beyond the immigrants who are officially its targets: "Even legal residents and U.S. citizens of Latino descent say that racial profiling, bigotry and myriad other forms of discrimination and injustice are staples of their daily lives."[75]

Additionally, across the U.S. hundreds of racially linked crimes targeting Latinos are reported annually. The most recent FBI report on hate crimes indicated that there were 534 victims of anti-Latino crimes in the previous year, again likely lower than the actual figure because of under-reporting by police agencies. Attacks have ranged from racist graffiti making threats of violence—often painted on homes or businesses or circulated on the Internet—to violent attacks on individuals, such as the racially motivated killing of Latinos recently in southern and eastern cities.[76] One example took place in Houston, when a middle-class Mexican American teenager was sodomized by whites yelling anti-Latino and "white power" insults at a suburban party. The assault victim was hospitalized for months and later committed suicide. Another attack took place in Shenandoah, Pennsylvania, when white youth beat a Mexican American to death while yelling racist epithets and commentary like "This is America. Go back to Mexico." The attackers were sentenced to just nine years in prison.[77] Not surprisingly, researchers have found that many Latinos in various areas live in great fear of white youth and police officers.

As with other Americans of color, this anti-Latino discrimination and the stress stemming from it have had significant impacts on individual and community health. Numerous health research studies have demonstrated negative effects on psychological and physical health resulting from Latinos' everyday struggles with racial discrimination.[78]

Some Costs of Intermediate Status

Consider too that Latino and Asian Americans who are placed into an intermediate or near-white status, or seek that status for themselves, endure various costs from such placement. One cost may be self-deception. The white-crafted "model-minority" stereotype has been accepted by some Asian Americans, such as some youth growing up in predominantly white suburbs. According to a few researchers, some youth have come to think of themselves and their group in terms of the model-minority imagery, probably because it superficially appears to be positive. They do not yet understand the racist purpose for which this imagery was created. As they move beyond their friendship groups and school settings into the larger society, such as into white-dominated employment settings, they will probably learn that some whites target Asian Americans with racist framing and discrimination, which will prevent them from achieving the status suggested by the deceptive model-minority stereotype.[79]

Research studies indicate that many Latinos and Asian Americans have felt pressured to adjust or abandon their national identities and cultural backgrounds in order to be as white-conforming as they can. In an important documentary, communications researcher Janice Tanaka has shown the negative impact on Asian Americans of intense pressures for adaptation to white ways. In interviews with third-generation Japanese Americans she found that their second-generation parents—most of whom had been interned as youth (and as U.S. citizens) in barbed-wire "internment" camps by racist white officials during World War II—were greatly affected by that forcible incarceration. After the war the second generation put great pressure on themselves and their children to conform to white norms and perspectives, probably in the hope of preventing a future such outrage. Yet Tanaka found that the effects of this hyperconformity to whiteness have often been very negative, with significant numbers facing great personal distress, painful self-blame, physical or mental illness, or alcoholism and drug addiction. Some have committed suicide as a result of stress ultimately grounded in the realities of anti-Asian racism.[80]

Today, there is often much pressure on Asian Americans to adapt to whiteness that comes from the media and white peer groups, especially in white-majority suburbs, as well as from parents or other relatives. In one interview that I conducted, an Asian American college senior, a second-generation Filipino American, explained the impact of racism on her family thus:

> Honestly, I think the way a lot of us [Asian Americans] think about racism is that we don't. I mean, even though it's … something I've thought about a lot, it's still even for me a hard topic to think about. Because it's hard to see, when you don't discuss it often…. To me, racial oppression's like a silent killer.

As this young woman sees it, many Asian Americans try to suppress their consciousness of the silent killer. She also commented on how the pressures work in her networks:

> And for me, for Filipinos…. When the kids are born, they check out the nose—it's good if it's pointy, narrow, not too wide—the skin tone—my mom worried that people would say stuff about my sister because she was slightly darker-complected when she was born. I was brought up to think that being called mestizo was this huge compliment. Being called mestizo was like being told "you look more Spanish, that's good, that's beautiful." The idea of "pure" Filipino had negative connotations. "Pure" Filipino means having a non-Spanish, non-Chinese last name, wider nose, darker skin, mountain, backwards…. We grew up thinking white—white is good, not oppressive—if anything, civilizing, educating. Learning about racism is hard to internalize; it's hard to think about, hard to be really convinced that it's going on…. Without the kind of collective memory that blacks have that informs them of their past, their cultural pride—it's easy to get sucked into a white mentality.[81]

This perceptive student draws on her research and experience to describe the ways in which many Asian Americans have been significantly affected by the white-to-black racial continuum. Similarly, research by Chou and Feagin examining interviews with middle-class Americans from numerous

Asian nationality groups found that many dealt with contemporary anti-Asian discrimination by prizing whiteness and trying to conform to what they saw as white ways of doing and acting.[82]

Sociologist Nestor Rodriguez has noted a parallel phenomenon of whiteness pressures among Latinos. Most Latinos, including those up the income ladder, experience recurring racism, but "some do it in a state of denial, that is, they deny the reality of anti-Latino bias, discrimination and prejudices around them. And they push their children into an Anglo-like existence." Some social science research documents that such denial of racial bias and attempted conformity to Anglo-whiteness are common responses to anti-Latino racism for many Latinos, especially those who are lighter skinned and in the middle or upper classes. Such conforming responses likely do reduce some white discrimination, yet they increase personal or family stress and likely interfere with a clear recognition of how racism operates.[83]

Racially Framing Native Americans

While we do not have the space here to cover the array of contemporary white racism that affects Native Americans, let us briefly consider a few examples that illustrate the continuing racist framing and related oppression that face indigenous North Americans. For example, contemporary social media and other website commentaries often reveal much about whites' racially framed views of Native Americans. One recent research study examined more than one thousand comments posted at online newspaper forum sites about the controversy over getting rid of the Native American "mascot" of the University of North Dakota's "Fighting Sioux" sports teams. Many people, most clearly or likely white, posted comments strongly supporting the stereotyped nickname and logo and revealing significant "ignorance about American Indian culture and even disdain toward American Indians."[84] Numerous hostile comments went well beyond the mascot controversy to racially frame and attack Native Americans nationwide.

One category of comments involved whites' framing Native Americans as greatly inferior and highly unvirtuous, in racial or cultural terms, especially as compared to whites. Some commenters threatened to retaliate against Native Americans if the mascot was eliminated. Such hostile reactions again reveal how the anti-others aspect of the white frame insists on the lack of virtue of those subordinated and is linked to an often arrogant sense of white virtuousness. Another category of online commentaries involved whites' surprise at, or trivialization, of the mascot issues. Some asked why the Indian mascot should even be viewed as a problem, or why now, or why in North Dakota. Other remarks downplayed the mascot as an issue or insisted that it would be too costly to change it. Yet other comments, grouped by researchers into a "white power and privilege" category, insisted that whites were the real victims, called for gratitude from Native Americans for this Indian mascot recognition, or made paternalistic comments such as "just get over it."[85]

Most of these online commentaries reveal a white-centered racial framing that insists on whites having the sole right and power to define the situation, and in a way favorable to white group interests. Dissenting Native American perspectives, and opposition to racially stereotyped mascot imagery, are not considered to be worth taking seriously. Significantly, too, these researchers conclude that their research supports the findings of psychologists that the "presence of a Native-themed nickname or logo ... can negatively affect the psychological well-being of American Indians on campus at UND, in the North Dakota community, and beyond."[86]

The North Dakota situation is not unique. The very negative racist epithet, "redskins," is part of the name and the imaged mascot for a professional football team in Washington, DC. Periodically, that name has been challenged by Native Americans in demonstrations and in court as racist and highly offensive. Yet, the white team owner has made clear his view, which is out of the center of the dominant white frame: "As a lifelong Redskins fan, and I think that the Redskins fans understand the great tradition and what it's all about and what it means.... We'll never change the name. It's that simple. Never—you can use caps."[87]

Most media commentators have supported his view, if less vigorously, as did a majority of Americans polled in a 2013 Associated Press–GfK survey. Such strong media and public support suggests how pervasive the conventional racist framing of Native Americans is in this country—and, in particular, how uninformed most Americans of non-Indian backgrounds are about the extraordinarily racist meaning of that team name since the nineteenth century. While "redskins" was initially used by whites and Native Americans to distinguish groups on the basis of skin color, it later came to refer to the scalps, skins, and bodies of Native Americans presented by white hunters to officials for their bounty rewards. Over the last century or so, moreover, many Native Americans have had to endure recurring white-racist taunts like "dirty redskin" or "lazy redskin." As one Native American leader and plaintiff in a court case involving the National Football League and racist terminology, Susan Shown Harjo, has put it, "This is a really good example of why you never put racism up to a popular vote, because racism will win every time. It's not up to the offending class to say what offends the offended."[88] From this viewpoint, informed by much well-documented indigenous American experience, the view on racist language that counts most in a just world is that of the targets of racial oppression.

Similarly arrogant white reactions to questioning of white-racist language and framing of Native Americans can be seen in anthropologist Jane Hill's report on whites' online reactions to organized Native American objections to an old racist name for one Arizona mountain—"Squaw Peak." White commenters used mocking and racist language, including an insistence on preserving the name of that mountain as "Squaw Peak," even though Native Americans and others pointed out that "squaw" has long been a derogatory term used by whites for Native American women.[89] Most white commentators reacted to this attempt to eliminate racist naming in ways similar to those many used in regard to Native American mascots. Indeed, today there are still numerous recreational and public accommodations facilities in the Southwest that make prominent use of racist naming or other racist framing of Native Americans.

Resistance to Racial Oppression

In spite of intense pressures to conform to white folkways, many Latino and Asian Americans actively resist the racial hostility and discrimination that oppresses them. For example, during the periodic anti-affirmative action drives by whites in California and other western areas, many Asian and Latino American students have worked aggressively with African American students and others against these conservative and regressive efforts designed to maintain the racial status quo. These activists have certainly been willing to be viewed as activist students of color, and they have been joined in such efforts by older Asian and Latino Americans. In spite of pervasive assimilationist and conformity pressures, many Asian and Latino Americans do not deny the reality of continuing racism and openly organize against it in important community and national organizations.

Since the 1960s, like many African Americans, many Asian and Latino Americans have joined in activist organizations as a collective countering response to racism. Among Mexican Americans, for example, movements like the La Raza Unida Party and the Brown Berets have pressed for an end to racial discrimination and accented a perspective sometimes called "Chicanismo." Periodically, groups like the National Council of La Raza have brought together a diverse group of Latinos to work on issues such as increasing positive representations of Latinos in the media and developing political coalitions. Similarly, pan-Asian civil rights groups have forcefully asserted Asian American interests and concerns about racial discrimination and marginalization. They have pressed for an end to anti-Asian hate crimes, better police protection for Asian communities, a rejection of racist terms like "Oriental" in the press, and effective political organization. In New York and several West Coast cities activists have created important pan-Asian political and university organizations.[90] We will return to these issues of individual and collective resistance to racism by Americans of color in the next chapter.

Hostility among Subordinated Groups: Using the White Racial Frame

Systemic racism affects everyone caught in its web. It provides the broad and influential social context for relations between all Americans, those defined as white and those defined as not white. Intermediate groups on the society's racial continuum often come to stereotype, frame, and oppress those below them on the ladder, who may in turn retaliate, and these intergroup conflicts generally reinforce the racist system set in place by and for whites. Historically, whites have encouraged groups below them on the racial status ladder to negatively assess and disparage each other. Racial stereotypes, images, and other framing held by people in one racially subordinated group that target people in other subordinated groups are not independent of the larger context of white racism. Many racial stereotypes and prejudices carried in subordinated communities exist because of the dominant racial frame that was originally created by whites to rationalize white-on-black oppression. As African American scholar Charles Lawrence has put it, "we use the white man's words to demean ourselves and to disassociate ourselves from our sisters and brothers. And then we turn this self-hate on other racial groups who share with us the ignominy of not being white."[91]

The white-racist system intentionally fosters racial stereotyping and hostility between groups of color. When those higher on the racial ladder express racist views about those lower, this helps preserve the systemic racism that benefits whites the most. By asserting that one's own group, though subordinated, is still better than those considered lower, members of an in-between group underwrite the racist ladder of privilege. Intergroup stereotyping and hostility among communities of color are useful for whites who can thus assert that "everyone is prejudiced."

What most Americans know about an array of racial matters beyond their experiences and collective memories is mostly what they are taught by mainstream avenues of socialization, such as the movies, television, radio, music videos, Internet websites, and the print media, all of which circulate the white racial frame across the country and, indeed, across the globe. Racist framing and practices are not just generated within the United States, but are often generated or perpetuated by an international white-racist order. Much negativity *between* groups of color thus reflects the impact of white-generated racial framing and other aspects of systemic racism. As Lawrence has expressed it:

> When a Vietnamese family is driven out of its home in a project by African-American youth, that is white supremacy. When a Korean

store owner shoots an African-American teenager in the back of the head, that is white supremacy. When 33 percent of Latinos agree with the statement, "Even if given a chance, [African Americans] aren't capable of getting ahead," that is white supremacy.[92]

Positioning one's own group closer to whites frequently involves the articulation of strongly antiblack views and some participation in antiblack discrimination. We have seen this historically in the actions of European immigrants like the Irish as they were seeking to be defined as white. Similarly, in recent years some Latino leaders and other Latinos have actively tried to reposition their group "on the racial spectrum so that they ended up closer to the side of privilege and whiteness than to the side of color and minority-group status."[93] These leaders and those persuaded by them often attempt to reposition themselves by parroting antiblack stereotypes and creating positive stereotypes for their group, such as an accent on a strong work ethic.

Recently, one large survey of Latino and Asian Americans, a majority of whom were immigrants or their children, found large percentages agreeing with a strong racial stereotype of African Americans—that is, with the statement that "I am generally afraid of African Americans because they are responsible for most crime." In this survey the Latino and Asian Americans were also asked how comfortable they were in doing business with other racial groups, and a majority of both chose whites as the group they were most comfortable with.[94] In various studies we observe that pressure on Americans of color, and especially immigrants and their children, to orient themselves to whites and whiteness is strong, and probably exists even before arrival in the United States. Many immigrants bring negative views of black Americans from their home countries. Racist movies and other racist media productions created by U.S. corporations are shown regularly across the globe, including in Asia and Latin America.

Significantly, a survey in a North Carolina city found that the level of racial stereotyping of black Americans by Latinos was not reciprocated. While the black respondents there did report some anti-Latino views, on the whole they had far more favorable views of Latinos than the Latinos there had of black Americans. In addition, a Los Angeles study found that in areas where black neighborhoods had seen significant Latino immigration, the scale of the Latino immigration was not correlated with the level of anti-Latino prejudice among black residents, except where there was a huge socioeconomic gap between the two groups.[95] We should note, too, that recent research demonstrates that Latino immigration has mostly had beneficial impacts on the U.S. economy. Few native-born workers lose jobs to undocumented Latino immigrants, and the latter pay more taxes than they as a group receive back in government benefits.

However, the relatively few native-born workers who do directly compete with immigrant workers are disproportionately low-wage black and Mexican American workers, yet they too benefit from the economic growth spurred by immigrant workers. Indeed, economist Jack Strauss concludes from extensive analysis that even the African Americans in metropolitan areas "with more Latino immigration experience significantly higher wages, lower unemployment, and higher job creation."[96]

In addition, given their many generations of experience with white racism, African Americans seem to be generally more realistic about the racialized character of the proverbial "American dream," and less likely than other Americans of color to accept the conventional rhetoric of the white racial frame in this regard. One survey of African, Asian, and Latino Americans found significant differences in views on societal opportunities. While over half the African American respondents did not think that the American dream ("If you work hard … you will succeed in the United States") was actually available to their group, substantial majorities of the Asian American and Latino respondents thought that the American dream was indeed available for their groups.[97]

We should note too the related issue of the internalization of the white racial frame. Numerous researchers have noted the ways in which oppression becomes *internalized* when Americans of color adopt negative racially or ethnically framed views about their own group. For example, one study of recent Korean and Vietnamese immigrants found a process of intra-ethnic othering in which some in each group viewed others in stereotyped terms. Thus, those who were "too ethnic" were called and stereotyped by yet other members of their Asian groups by the derogatory term, FOB ("Fresh Off the Boat"). Those who were considered "too assimilated" by other members of these Asian groups were stereotyped and called out as "whitewashed." Those labeled FOBs were given that label because they engaged heavily in behavior linked to their home cultures, including traditional ways of dressing and socializing with people like themselves—actions negatively characterized by many whites as well. Those considered whitewashed were those who were viewed as too eagerly adapting to white ways and as giving up the important traditional customs. While some intra-ethnic othering attempts to resist the inferior racial status imposed by whites, "it does so by reproducing racial stereotypes and a belief in the essential racial and ethnic differences between whites and Asians."[98] Yet again we observe the extensive reach and power of the dominant white racial frame.

Conclusion

After much land was stolen, often violently, from North America's indigenous peoples, European Americans stole the labor of African

Americans. For nearly four centuries those whose stolen labor has been so central to the development of prosperity for white Americans—African Americans—are those who have most extensively endured whites' racialized control, segregation, and discrimination. As a group, African Americans may also be the most American in their highly blended ancestry. They are among the most American in the amount of time (nearly four centuries) spent working to build the prosperity of the new nation, yet they are also among the *least* American historically in terms of their rights, privileges, and opportunities. The age-old oppression endured by African Americans is much more than a mental construction in white heads. Their oppressive reality is one that has been economically, physically, socially, and ideologically constructed in extraordinarily thorough ways.

Social science research on torture has found that people can endure much if there appears to be some hope of escape from such severe conditions, but torture is much harder to endure when it has gone on for a long time and those tortured feel there is no hope of escaping. Drawing on this insight, one can perhaps understand why African Americans often have a different sense of how burdensome, omnipresent, and imbedded is the system of racist oppression than do other Americans, including some other Americans of color. Today as in the past, black Americans must operate with collective memories of 9 to 15 generations of white oppression and with its persisting antiblack framing and patterns of everyday discrimination. As a group they have an amplified culture of resistance and counter-framing (directed at the white racial frame) that has enabled them to endure and counter racialized oppression for centuries. Many generations of oppression create a deep, critical, and nuanced perspective that may be somewhat different from that developed over one to three generations of discrimination. Majorities in most Asian American and Latino groups are immigrants and the children of immigrants. Some research indicates that, compared with native-born African Americans, many immigrants of color seem less aware of, or downplay, the discrimination they face at the hands of whites—in part because they are trying to establish an economic toehold and in part because they compare their current situation with that of the home country, and by this latter standard the U.S. often looks good. As we noted above, they tend to be more optimistic about securing the "American dream."

Nonetheless, it seems likely that as current and future U.S.-born generations of Latinos and Asian Americans come of political age, the barriers and pain of systemic racism will be attacked much more openly, and many more will likely come to share the views of African Americans about openly and assertively organizing to bring major changes in the racist system. Historically, in organized pursuit of civil rights and equality in the United States, African Americans have often led the way. Since the early 1900s they have forced the passage of all major U.S. civil rights laws and the majority of the pivotal executive orders and court decisions protecting or extending antidiscrimination efforts. Latinos, Native Americans, Asian Americans, and others have often utilized these civil rights mechanisms to fight discrimination against their groups, and such efforts will likely continue well into the future.

African, Asian, Latino, Native Americans, and other Americans of color all have histories of white oppression and of attempts to liberate themselves from that. They have all had to struggle hard for human dignity and equality in this society. Since the various forms of racial oppression have drawn heavily on the white-racist framework long created for black Americans, most forms of white-racist attitudes and practices directed against the numerous U.S. groups of color reproduce and reinforce each another. Moreover, the character of the white racism faced by a group can vary depending on its time of entry into the country, region of entry, size, cultural characteristics, or physical characteristics as perceived by the dominant group. As we have seen, in earlier periods whites placed new Asian or Latino groups near the "black end" of this society's racist continuum and targeted them for racial oppression. Later in the process of group interaction, some in groups within these broad umbrella categories have been moved, again by powerful whites, to an intermediate position or one closer to the "white end" of the racist white-to-black continuum. The purpose of this placement is often to destroy coalitions among peoples of color, and to protect the system of white power and privilege.

In the last few decades, this racial process of intermediation has increased in importance, likely because the United States is becoming less white in demographic composition. Taking a panoramic view, one might speak of the "Brazilianization" or "Latinamericanization" of the United States. Like other Latin American countries, Brazil's racialization process has called out and distinguished certain mixed-racial groups and placed them in a middle status between those Brazilians mostly of African ancestry and those of mostly European ancestry. The middle groups are socially more acceptable to whites than Afro-Brazilians.

Possibly, a more fully developed tripartite Brazilian pattern—with clearly recognized and named intermediate groups providing a social buffer between whites and blacks—may be the future for the United States. Because of the apparently privileged position of intermediate groups, white Brazilians have long proclaimed their country to be one not seriously infected by white racism. Not surprisingly, many North American whites have taken a similar position, citing the advancements of certain groups in the Asian American and Latino communities, and their economically enhanced status, as evidence that the U.S. has become a "democracy" no longer infected by white racism. Many whites in Brazil and the United States have adopted a similar colorblind racial framing in which they claim, falsely as we have seen, that there is no longer a serious problem of white racism in either country.[99]

9

Antiracist Strategies and Solutions
Past, Present, and Future

In the summer of 2009 the U.S. Senate belatedly passed a brief resolution apologizing for some racial injustice:

> The Congress (A) acknowledges the fundamental injustice, cruelty, brutality, and inhumanity of slavery and Jim Crow laws; (B) apologizes to African-Americans on behalf of the people of the United States, for the wrongs committed against them and their ancestors who suffered under slavery and Jim Crow laws.[1]

Although this non-binding apology accented the injustice of slavery and Jim Crow, numerous white senators insisted on a disclaimer to explicitly bar African Americans from seeking *any* reparations for the role of the government in this officially recognized oppression. In effect, such an apology operates to salve white consciences, yet provides no commitment to deal with the long-term impacts of racial oppression. Indeed, there is no mention in this resolution of the need for forceful congressional action to sharply reduce contemporary racial discrimination.

In the United States the liberal and moderate sectors of the white elite have an inordinate fondness for symbolic resolutions like this toothless apology and for setting up commissions to study U.S. problems. Over the last century, at least a dozen major government commissions and committees have looked into problems of antiblack and other racism. For instance, in 1997 President Bill Clinton set up a seven-member advisory board to start a "national conversation on race." The board's final report, *One America in the 21st Century*, presented substantial findings on widespread racist framing and discrimination, but concluded with mostly modest solutions.[2] Most importantly, no serious congressional action has been taken to implement this report's most important recommendations, such as significantly increasing the scope and enforcement of current civil rights laws.

Today, U.S. society remains imbedded in a racist system. It was founded as such, and no large-scale action has ever been taken to rebuild this system of racism from that foundation up. European colonists incorporated land theft and slavery into the political–economic process and structure of the country that became the United States. After the Civil War large-scale African American enslavement was replaced by the near-slavery of legal segregation in southern states, border states, and some northern areas, while much de facto segregation continued in the rest of the North. These institutional arrangements were designed to keep antiblack oppression in place. Periodically, the racist structure has been altered, in the 1860s when slavery was abolished and in the 1960s when legal segregation was replaced by the current system of more informal racial oppression. Other Americans of color have periodically been incorporated into U.S. society by whites operating from within this well-established white-racist framework. The U.S. house of racism has been remodeled somewhat over time—usually in response to protests from those racially oppressed—but its formidable societal foundation remains firmly in place.

What is the likelihood of future societal change on the scale required to replace this persisting racial foundation? On this point, there is some pessimism among leading U.S. intellectuals. For some time, African American analysts have pointed to the great difficulty of bringing large-scale changes in systemic racism. In the 1940s sociologist Oliver Cox noted that "because the racial system in the United States is determined largely by the interests of a powerful political class, no spectacular advance in the status of Negroes could be expected."[3] More recently, leading constitutional scholar Derrick Bell contended that

> black people will never gain full equality in this country. Even those herculean efforts we hail as successful will produce no more than temporary "peaks of progress," short-lived victories that slide into irrelevance as racial patterns adapt in ways that maintain white dominance.[4]

Developing the concept of "racial realism," Bell has no illusions about how hard it is to change the foundational realities of this racist society.

Nonetheless, the racist patterns and arrangements regularly generate open resistance and organized opposition. These oppressive patterns have occasionally been altered to some degree by antiracist movements in the past, and they can conceivably be changed again if the effort is great enough. Future domination of U.S. society by whites is not automatic. Viewed over the very long term, no hierarchical system is permanent, and it must be constantly reinforced by its main beneficiaries. If we think dialectically and discern the social contradictions lying deeply beneath the surface of this society, we see that the racist system has created some seeds of its eventual destruction. Thus, this racist system is legitimated by widely proclaimed ideals of equality and democratic participation, ideals that have provided it with some respect internally and internationally. While the equality ideals have been used by whites, in the past and present, to gloss over its persisting racial oppression and inequalities, they have also been vigorously adopted as major bywords for all movements of the oppressed. Ideals of equality and democracy are taken seriously by African Americans and other Americans of color and have regularly spurred them to protest oppression. The honed-by-struggle ideals of equality, justice, and civil rights are critical tenets of the antiracist counter-framing that has emerged over centuries of protest, and they are periodically implemented in contemporary antiracist actions. They have served as important rallying points and sometimes increased group solidarity. The situation of long-term racial oppression has pressed African Americans—and, sometimes, other Americans of color—to unite for their own survival and, periodically, for large-scale protest.

Demographic Changes and Challenges

Until major crises in this society occur, most whites seem unlikely to see the need for large-scale social justice and egalitarian reforms. They are too constrained by their own social privileges and racial framing, by their personal and group interests, to see the need for radical structural change in society's racial patterns. Still, at certain times in history new social options appear, especially if major societal contradictions increase.[5]

The Coming White Minority

Current population trends are creating societal contradictions that will probably lead to a major societal transformation, including the likely reduction in some or much white domination over Americans of color. Today, people of European descent are a modest minority (less than one-fifth) of the world's population and are still decreasing in proportion. Americans of European descent are also decreasing in their proportion of the U.S. population. Since the 1970s a substantial immigration of people of color from Latin America, Asia, and the Caribbean has helped to change the demographic makeup of this society in a more populous and racially and ethnically diverse direction. Today white Americans are about 62 percent of the U.S. population, down from 69 percent in 2000. According to the most recent (2010) census whites are a minority of the population in California, Texas, New Mexico, and Hawaii—and soon will be in a dozen other states. If future birth and immigration rates stay similar to those of today, about half the population will be Americans of color no later than about 2042. Half the U.S. population under the age of 18 will be children of color no later than about 2023. By about 2050, the Census Bureau estimates, a substantial majority of a U.S. population of an estimated 429 million will be Americans of color.[6]

In future decades this significant and ongoing demographic shift will likely bring more pressure for social, economic, and political changes. By the mid-2020s a majority of all U.S. elementary school students will be African, Latino, Asian, and Native American. They and their parents will doubtless strive for greater input and fairer representation in the operation, staffing, and curricula of many currently white-dominated school systems. By the 2030s more than half the working-age population will be workers of color. One has to wonder whether these majority workers will raise questions about having to support many elderly whites (e.g., by paying substantially into Social Security) who have long maintained patterns of racial discrimination targeting them. The composition of the voting population will continue to change dramatically. In the 2008 presidential election one-quarter of voters were voters of color, and they gave a substantial majority of their votes to the first president of color, Barack Obama. This pattern was repeated in Obama's reelection in 2012. By the late 2020s, moreover, a majority of young adults, and probably of young voters, will be people of color. As voting majorities change from majority white, there will very likely be significant changes in jury composition, the operation of the criminal justice system, the makeup of many government agencies, legislatures' composition, and thus some priorities for legislation in numerous legislative bodies. Where voting majorities change, we will likely observe far fewer white politicians opposing antidiscrimination laws or pressing for new laws restricting Latin American and Asian immigration and government support for new immigrants.[7]

Negative White Responses and Reactions

Most Americans are becoming aware of these significant changes. Indeed, a substantial number of whites seem to fear a more multiracial future where they will be the statistical minority of the population—and likely, at least eventually, of entrepreneurs, employees, voters, and political officials in many places. In the 1990s Dale Maharidge wrote a provocative book, *The Coming White Minority*, focused on demographic changes already evident in California. In his view the fears of whites were being underestimated: "Whites dread the unknown and not-so-distant tomorrow.... They fear losing not only their jobs but also their culture."[8] More recently, an experimental psychological study presented white college students with demographic projections showing white Americans becoming a statistical minority of the population. These whites became more angry and fearful of Americans of color than the white students who were not shown the demographic projections. "Whites who viewed the future projections also felt more sympathy for their ingroup than whites in the control condition."[9] Just thinking about the coming white minority triggered white anger and fear of the future among these well-educated, mostly younger whites. Recall too the study cited in Chapter 4 in which many whites surveyed indicated that they felt whites were now losing out in society; they viewed antiwhite bias as higher now than antiblack bias. Nationally, a great many whites seem to look at the contemporary demographic and other societal changes from within the old white racial frame and cannot visualize a United States highly diverse in racial terms, minority white, and more democratic and egalitarian.

Moreover, whether Americans of color become substantially more powerful economically and politically in future decades depends on several important factors, including the strength of their political coalitions and the potency of countering measures taken by the white elites and public to maintain whites' great power and privilege in society. Indeed, many whites may respond to their new statistical-minority status with various strategies of social resistance. Some may try to enhance racial separation and segregation in residential and other spatial terms. Today we see some evidence of this in the continuing balkanization of residential patterns. Since the 1970s many whites have moved from large cities with growing populations of color to whiter suburban areas, exurban and rural areas, or guarded-gated communities within central cities. Over the decade prior to the last (2010) census, 42 of the 100 largest metropolitan areas saw a decline in their white populations, and 86 saw a decline in the number of white children under 18. Today, in 22 of the metropolitan areas whites are a statistical minority, and in 35 of them white children under 18 are a minority. In these largest metropolitan areas Americans of color made up 98 percent of population growth over this decade. Demographic studies also show that the largest metropolitan centers—especially immigrant "magnets" like New York, Los Angeles, San Francisco, Chicago, Washington, and Miami—have gained many new residents from other countries, but have lost millions of native-born residents to yet other cities, large and small. Many U.S. counties with substantial population growth from internal domestic migration have had little or modest growth in the external immigrant population; these counties are becoming whiter and older. Whites are dispersing to a significant degree to smaller metropolitan areas, exurban areas, and towns; for the most part these areas are overwhelmingly white. These demographic trends are creating new spatial patterns of racial segregation.[10]

In addition, within counties, towns, and cities, this society is still substantially segregated along racial lines. This is especially true for younger Americans. As demographer William Frey has summed it up: "Segregation levels for black and Hispanic children are higher than for their adult counterparts, despite a general reduction in segregation over the last 10 years."[11] Most white Americans and most Americans of color of all ages live substantially separate lives in their schools and neighborhoods.

The workforce continues to be substantially divided, with disproportionate numbers of workers of color in lower-paying job categories or facing chronic unemployment, and disproportionate numbers of whites dominating the better-paying, relatively more secure jobs.

There is significant political separation along racial lines, which the changing demography may be accentuating. Over the last few decades the Democratic Party has become ever-more diverse, with large percentages of black, Latino, and Asian American voters voting for the Democratic Party in recent elections, including the pathbreaking 2008 and 2012 presidential elections. In 2012, for example, 93 percent of African American voters opted for Barack Obama, as did 90 percent of Native Americans, 71 percent of Latinos, and 73 percent of Asian Americans.[12] In contrast, in 2008 and 2012 the Republican Party won a substantial majority of white voters, even as they lost. This voting pattern was substantially the result of different party strategies. In the 1990s Ralph Reed, an important Republican leader, reviewed the past and future strategies of his party and openly asserted that in the future strategy "you're going to see a new Republican Party that is still primarily white and that is fiscally and morally conservative, but that also is attempting to project an image of racial tolerance and moderation."[13] This pro-white strategy was used successfully in the Ronald Reagan and George H. W. Bush campaigns of the 1980s and in the George W. Bush campaigns in the 2000s. Between the 1960s and the 2000s, thus, a great many working-class and middle-class whites, particularly in southern and border states, moved into the Republican Party, many substantially because of racial issues.[14]

In the last several presidential election years, the Republican Party's presidential convention has been overwhelmingly white in its delegates. At the 2012 convention, which nominated whites for president and vice-president, no more than 9 percent of Republican delegates were estimated to be people of color. Only 2.1 percent were African American. In contrast, just over 26 percent of the 2012 Democratic convention delegates were black, up significantly since 2008. (Some 14.4 percent were Latino.) This Democratic Party convention was the first party convention to nominate an African American for a second term.[15] In addition, in 2012 the Republican National Committee had only two blacks among its 165 members. The Democratic National Committee had 101 black members, nearly 23 percent of its about 446 members. At the time there were also 41 black Democrats in the Congress, compared to just two black Republicans. In addition, black Democrats made up nearly 99 percent of all black members of the country's many state legislatures. Well into the twenty-first century the Republican Party remains antagonistic to many civil rights, immigration, unemployment, and other issues of concern to a majority of voters of color, and thus currently secures a minority of their votes in major elections.[16]

The Importance of Black Resistance to Oppression

Systemic racism has developed within a framework of constant protests from its racialized targets. Many whites have traditionally viewed African Americans and many other Americans of color as unwilling to help themselves, but this is a rationalizing myth from the white racial frame. For centuries the religious, civic, and civil rights organizations of Americans of color have not only engaged in self-help community projects but also striven to improve the country's general welfare by regularly pressing forward on goals of equality and justice. Black Americans, in particular, have not quietly accepted oppression as hapless victims. They have regularly fought back, like other oppressed peoples historically. They protest, survive, and even thrive in spite of racist subjugation. Since the seventeenth century, African Americans have taken much strength from the collective heritage transmitted through extended families and community networks. The important knowledge carried there includes numerous positive values, perspectives on life, and assertive counter-framing. Living in a society with a dominant white-European-oriented culture has forced black Americans, as well as other Americans of color, to become bicultural. They must know white society well and become experts on how to respond to discriminatory actions. This expertise includes antiracist counter-framing aimed at the white racial frame and learned strategies of protest against oppression passed across many generations.[17]

A comprehensive theory of systemic racism recognizes the impact of resistance strategies developed by African Americans and other Americans of color on the type and character of the continuing arrangements of oppression. Out of their recurring experience with white racism has often come a strong counter-framing and consciousness that regularly leads to significant protests and occasional large-scale revolts. To this stage in U.S. history, the most significant alterations in systemic racism have come when black Americans and their allies, including other Americans of color, have organized and battled for societal change.

Past and Present Patterns of Black Resistance

African American resistance began in the earliest days of slavery. Those enslaved responded in many ways—ranging from passive acquiescence, to flight on a large scale, to attacks on slaveholders and their property, to insurrections. In the early decades of the nineteenth century black and white abolitionists held many protest demonstrations against slavery and created antislavery organizations—thereby helping to end slavery.[18] After the Civil War, black Americans engaged in extensive political and community organizing. In the late 1860s and 1870s the Reconstruction South developed significant multiracial democracy—with many black men (but no women) participating in local politics. State constitutional conventions and legislatures included black delegates, and 22 black men served in the U.S. House and Senate. Non-elite whites and blacks worked together to bring much progressive change, such as public schools and prison reforms, to the formerly oligarchical South. This experiment in expanded democracy was soon repressed by the killings and terrorist actions of many whites led by the old southern gentry and working through new white terrorist organizations like the Ku Klux Klan.

Not long thereafter, in the early 1900s, a new civil rights movement was born, soon taking the form of the National Association for the Advancement of Colored People (NAACP). After decades of legal efforts and organizing by the NAACP and other black organizations laid much of the groundwork, there was an important spurt in civil rights protests from the 1940s to the 1970s, with many black men, women, and children participating in local and national protests for freedom and justice. One strategy was the boycott, such as the one that targeted segregated buses in Montgomery, Alabama, and brought Rosa Parks, the seamstress and NAACP activist who refused to be racially mistreated on a bus, and Dr. Martin Luther King, Jr., who was asked by local activists to lead the movement, to national attention as important leaders in the reinvigorated civil rights movement.[19]

Soon thereafter came many sit-ins, freedom rides, and other demonstrations by African Americans challenging legal segregation in the South and informal segregation in the North. New organizations oriented toward greater political and economic power for black Americans included the Student Nonviolent Coordinating Committee (SNCC), the Congress of Racial Equality (CORE), and the Black Panthers. Often rooted in a strong base of black churches and civic organizations, this activism provided money and mobilized people, which enabled civil rights organizations to achieve successes in forcing a dismantling of official segregation. One lesson added to the book of resistance strategies by this rights movement was that destruction of systemic racism would require more than speeches and traditional politics. **Nonviolent civil disobedience** was an important strategy that African Americans developed for dealing with both official and informal racism. Dr. King and other black leaders became the critical U.S. theorists of the counter-frame idea that significant change only comes from creative social disruptions, especially those carried out by strong grassroots organizations. Note too that black and other civil rights movements of the 1950s–1960s era often started with a small group of dedicated protesters. Once underway, because of creative organizing and community links of the protesters, a large number of people in black communities would join in—as happened in the famous Greensboro, North Carolina, sit-ins and the 1963 confrontation in Birmingham.[20]

Successes and Limitations of Protest

Many victories came out of the 1950s–1960s civil rights movement, including the passage of major laws prohibiting discrimination in employment, voting, and housing. The 1964 Civil Rights Act, perhaps the most important, prohibited discrimination in many areas. Title I set down protections for voting in elections. Title II asserted:

> All persons shall be entitled to the full and equal enjoyment of the goods, services, facilities, privileges, advantages, and accommodations of any place of public accommodation ... without discrimination or segregation on the ground of race, color, religion, or national origin.

Title III required desegregation of public facilities operated by governments. Title IV authorized federal action to encourage desegregation of schools, and Title VI prohibited discrimination in programs receiving federal assistance. Title VII prohibited discrimination in employment. It became illegal for an employer (1) to "refuse to hire or to discharge any individual or otherwise discriminate against any individual with respect to his compensation, terms, conditions, or privileges of employment, because of such individual's race, color, religion, sex, or national origin"; or (2) to "limit, segregate or classify his employees in any way which would deprive or tend to deprive any individual of employment opportunities or otherwise adversely affect his status as an employee."[21] Title VIII required the collection of voting statistics.

The many black Americans and other Americans actively protesting during the 1940s–1960s civil rights era had pressured the mostly white legislators to pass one of the most strongly worded antidiscrimination laws in any country. However, in the years since the civil rights movement, these civil rights laws and court desegregation decisions have frequently been overwhelmed by the scale of the discrimination they deal with and by white backtracking. These laws were mostly crafted by the white political elite under pressure from grassroots protest movements. The laws were never intended to fully uproot systemic racism. While they eliminated Jim Crow segregation, they have often been unenforced or weakly enforced, and thus have been ineffective in ending much informal discrimination. Each year, researchers and civil rights enforcers estimate, *millions* of acts of racial discrimination are perpetrated by whites against Americans of color. Most are not countered and substantially remedied by the enforcement of civil rights laws. Local, state, and federal agencies with civil rights responsibilities usually have neither the resources nor, all too often, the will to vigorously enforce antidiscrimination laws. State agencies like the New York Division of Human Rights and federal agencies such as the

Equal Employment Opportunity Commission typically have such a large backlog of cases that most victims of discrimination cannot achieve timely and appropriate remedies. Local, state, and federal agencies dealing with discrimination complaints process fewer than 100,000 or so each year, and most of these are resolved with no serious penalties for discriminators.[22]

As they have been enforced—or, more often, weakly enforced—over several decades, civil rights laws can contribute to the persistence of discrimination by making it difficult to file a successful complaint against a discriminator. Procedures are often lengthy and bureaucratic. In spite of common beliefs to the contrary, we have never had a determined and unrelenting enforcement of major civil rights laws in all significant institutional areas, such as housing and employment. Moreover, by providing a rhetoric of equal opportunity, these laws allow whites to assume that the problem of serious discrimination has largely been solved. While significant improvements in enforcing civil rights laws have been made during the Barack Obama administrations, a major step in a renewed antiracist strategy for dismantling systemic racism would be a yet more extensive program of aggressively enforcing current civil rights laws.[23] To get such accelerated civil rights enforcement we need, among other things, to replace the current, mostly white, leaders in most major institutional sectors with a much more representative and democratic group of leaders who support serious enforcement and other efforts at racial change. We also need to put much more in the way of socioeconomic resources into these efforts.

Community Control as a Strategy

Between the 1960s and today the civil rights movement has generally declined in number of public protests and in public visibility. One reason is that, at least for a time, civil rights laws, progressive court decisions, and affirmative-action efforts suggested a societal commitment to real racial change. Another reason was the hiring or co-optation of many middle-class African Americans, who had formerly been a major source of civil rights activists, in corporations and government agencies where they had largely been absent. Yet another was government repression of more radical change-oriented groups such as the organized police campaign against the Black Panthers, a militant group calling for an end to police brutality and an increase in black control over black communities.

Government-sponsored civil rights progress came to a standstill, even backtracked, in the 1980s and early 1990s, and again in the first eight years of the 2000s, when enforcement of civil rights laws and the implementation of remedial programs for discrimination were cut back or eliminated under the administrations of Ronald Reagan, George H. W. Bush, and George W. Bush. For example, a draft report of the U.S.

Commission on Civil Rights summarized George W. Bush's civil rights record in the 2000s: "President Bush has implemented policies that have retreated from long-established civil rights promises in each of these areas."[24]

Yet, even in the difficult period since the 1980s, black civil rights and other organizations have periodically responded with public demonstrations for expanded civil rights and social support programs in Washington, DC, and other cities. There have been numerous local protests against racism and for community solidarity, as well as a few national demonstrations, such as the 1995 Million Man March in Washington, DC, accenting the need for black solidarity. Local protests periodically focus on incidents of antiblack violence, such as in the 2009 protests in Oakland, California, over the killing of an unarmed black man by a police officer. There have been numerous efforts to organize black workers against exploitative employers and black communities against waste dumps and other environmental hazards. Recently, black civil rights organizations have assertively and regularly protested state government cutbacks in educational and other social support programs in states from North Carolina to Texas. Like numerous Latino organizations, they have also organized substantial protests against white conservative legislative and judicial attempts to increase government barriers (for example, requiring photo-IDs) to voting, which have expanded in southern states, often in response to a facilitating 2013 Supreme Court decision. In addition, since the early 2000s numerous Latino organizations have organized extensive protests—from Rhode Island to California—on behalf of the rights of immigrants of color.[25]

Dissatisfaction with stalled progress or backtracking on official commitments to racial desegregation has periodically led black activists, organizers, and intellectuals to press for separatist and cultural–nationalist strategies. During the 1920s and 1930s there was an outpouring of novels, music, and other arts celebrating African American traditions and interests—the Harlem Renaissance. Coupled with this cultural renaissance was an accent on expanding black businesses and civic institutions. In organizations like the Nation of Islam since the 1940s, numerous African Americans have rejected racial integration as the central goal and accented a black community control or separatist strategy. Sometimes, this strategy has been coupled with a call for reparations for centuries of racial oppression.[26]

Periodically since the 1960s many African Americans have shown a renewed interest in community control strategies. Isabel Wilkerson interviewed middle-class black Americans in Los Angeles after a major 1990s riot. They were angry over police brutality and other racism issues. As a group, they were increasingly interested in buying from black businesses and greater black solidarity. In addition, in a major policy-oriented book *Integration or Separation?* Roy Brooks documented the drawbacks of the racial-integration strategy as actually practiced. In his view African Americans should continue the traditional integration strategy, but couple it with strong community-focused strategies that have long been necessary for their economic and psychological well-being.[27]

Working in the tradition of Malcolm X and W. E. B. Du Bois, numerous black scholars and community leaders have periodically reiterated the importance of African values and traditional perspectives for African Americans. They reject myths of European cultural superiority and call for African Americans, as anthropologist Marimba Ani puts it, to refocus their "energies toward the recreation of cultural alternatives informed by ancestral visions of a future that celebrates Africanness."[28] In this Afrocentric perspective societal revolution begins not with open warfare but with an assertive counter-framing against the white racial frame and white practice arising out of it. African Americans have not been alone in developing this resistance perspective. For example, a major antiracist counter-framing that rejects European myths and assertions of cultural superiority has been asserted by some Latino (especially Chicano) groups and many Native American groups over centuries of European intrusion and dominance in North America. Periodically, numerous groups of color have forcefully resisted white colonization of both lands and minds.

Some Individual Strategies of Resistance

As the 1960s civil rights movement demonstrated, successful antioppression movements require a shattering of negative racial images in the minds of the oppressed themselves. How to increase this self-consciousness remains an ongoing task for antiracist struggles. Consciousness-raising among Americans of color includes self-inquiry into one's attitudes as well as a parallel dialogue with others. The African revolutionary Frantz Fanon cogently stressed that an "authentic national liberation exists only to the precise degree to which the individual has irreversibly begun his own liberation."[29]

African Americans have pioneered in this process of individual liberation. Since several researchers have documented these individual strategies for dealing with discrimination in detail elsewhere, let us note just one major example here. In a national study of middle-class respondents, a black professional explained her approach to whites:

> I know I have very little tolerance for white people who expect me to change my behavior to make them comfortable. They don't change their behavior to make me comfortable. I am who I am. Either they sit with me and work with me respecting that, or you can't sit and work together.

After indicating that she does not generally tolerate racist attitudes or remarks, she then adds:

> Then there are other people, who are personal friends, who may make a racist statement, and it's really based on their ignorance and their lack of understanding, and I'll take the time to deal with it. There's a young white woman that I work with now, and she's really not worked with a lot of different people of color, and she uses the term, "you people," and I bring it to her attention, And she's like, "oh, oh," and so it's an education, we're working together. But I don't generally accommodate white people's conflicts.

Like most African Americans, she tailors her response to expressed racist attitudes to fit the situation and the person.[30]

Over a lifetime of much experience with whites, African Americans often develop a counter-framing to the dominant white frame and an array of countering strategies to fight whites' racist attitudes and practices. In interview studies they frequently speak of withdrawing to fight another day. At other times, they describe open confrontations with white discriminators, with all the costs that can entail. As in the above account, they often distinguish among whites, taking time to educate those who seem to be open to change. Many black Americans and other Americans of color, like this woman, have actively worked for their own liberation from racial oppression.[31]

The Equality Ideal: Black Support, White Resistance

From the 1600s to the present, the racial subordination of Americans of color has contradicted the ideals in the Declaration of Independence—the emphasis on "all men are created equal" and the inalienable rights of "life, liberty, and the pursuit of happiness." However, as white men with property, the U.S. founders had in mind their own freedom and equality in regard to British political control. Still, once the genie of freedom was let out of the bottle, many other Americans have pressed for full inclusion under these great human ideals of liberty, justice, and equality.

For centuries African Americans and other Americans of color have regularly forced white Americans to confront or implement these grand ideals. Perhaps the first great manifesto for full human equality in U.S. history was the 1829 *Appeal to the Coloured Citizens of the World* by the brave black abolitionist David Walker. In his widely circulated manifesto, Walker quoted the words "all men are created equal" from the Declaration of Independence and then added for his white readers this critique:

> Compare your own language above, extracted from your Declaration of Independence, with your cruelties and murders inflicted by your cruel and unmerciful fathers and yourselves on our fathers and

on us—men who have never given your fathers or you the least provocation!... I ask you candidly, was your sufferings under Great Britain, one hundredth part as cruel and tyrannical as you have rendered ours under you? Some of you, no doubt, believe that we will never throw off your murderous government and "provide new guards for our future security."[32]

He then assured his white readers that black Americans *would* take strong action to achieve freedom and justice. Walker's manifesto created fear among slaveholders, who realistically saw it as an incitement to revolution. A bounty was placed on Walker's head by slaveholding interests, and he may have been poisoned in June 1830 for his advocacy of liberty and justice for all.

After the Civil War African Americans again pressed hard to secure meaningful freedom and equality, including the right to vote and hold office, equal treatment in public accommodations, fair economic opportunities, and just treatment in the judicial system. Leaders like Frederick Douglass and Sojourner Truth forcefully enunciated ideals of liberty and justice for all. Moreover, in the early 1900s, new civil rights movements emerged, and yet more black leaders spoke out for implementation of these ideals. For instance, in a 1902 lecture, Anna Julia Cooper, a leading activist for the poor and early African American feminist, noted how

> dragged against his will over thousands of miles of unknown waters to a strange land among strange peoples, the Negro was transplanted to this continent in order to produce chattels and beasts of burden for a nation "conceived in liberty and dedicated to the proposition that all men are created equal."

Elsewhere, she added that black men and women are endowed with the inalienable rights of "Life, Liberty, and the pursuit of Happiness" and have a "right to grow up, to develop, to reason and to live" just like whites.[33]

During the 1950s and 1960s a reinvigorated civil rights movement again accented these ideals. Hundreds of thousands of participants in these antiracist movements were greatly influenced by national and international ideals of social justice and equal rights. Just before his 1968 assassination, Dr. Martin Luther King, Jr. passionately argued for racial equality. He noted that a major problem was getting whites to understand the meaning of the civil rights movement, for there is "not even a common language when the term 'equality' is used. Negro and white have a fundamentally different definition." Dr. King added that black Americans

> have proceeded from a premise that equality means what it says, and they have taken white Americans at their word when they talked of

it as an objective. But most whites in America in 1967, including many persons of goodwill, proceed from a premise that equality is a loose expression for improvement. White America is not even psychologically organized to close the gap—essentially it seeks only to make it less painful and less obvious but in most respects to retain it.[34]

Dr. King's commentary is as accurate now as then. Because of centuries of civil rights movements by Americans of color, the white public's understanding of equality and the color line has slowly been transformed from the idea of the founders that only white men had a right to liberty, justice, and political representation to a much broader view. Recent surveys suggest that the white majority now holds this view: In principle, all men and women have a right to legal and political equality, as well as to equal opportunities in employment, housing, and education. However, for the white majority even this extension and understanding of equality dates only from the 1970s and today does not mean that most whites wish to see a truly egalitarian societal reality, or even thorough racial integration. For example, in a recent Gallup poll a significant majority of black respondents (59 percent) felt there was still a major role for government in taking action to improve the socioeconomic conditions faced by black Americans, yet a quite small percentage (19 percent) of white respondents felt the same way. In addition, a majority of black respondents thought the country needed more civil rights laws, but again few whites felt such action was necessary.[35] Similarly, when younger (18–25) Americans were asked in another recent survey about affirmative action to redress past discrimination, only 19 percent of white youth supported such remedial programs, as compared with 75 percent of black youth and 63 percent of Latino youth. Today, as we have seen throughout this book, the overwhelming majority of whites do *not* accept the goal of aggressively reducing substantial group inequality in historically white institutional areas and, thus, do not support major government actions in that regard.[36]

A majority of whites believe that in many areas Americans of color already have racial equality. One national survey found that 61 percent of white respondents felt the average black person had health care access equal to or better than that of the average white person. Half felt that black Americans had a level of education similar to or better than that of whites and that, on average, whites and blacks were about as well off in the jobs they held. As we have seen in previous chapters, such white views are quite incorrect. Altogether, 70 percent of the whites in this survey held one or more *erroneous* beliefs about white–black differentials in contemporary life conditions. Moreover, another recent national survey found that most whites thought the United States was now living up to the liberty-and-justice ideals of the Pledge of Allegiance. In contrast, more than half the black respondents felt the country was not living up to them.[37] In yet another national survey more than 80 percent of the black respondents reported widespread racial discrimination. Only one-fifth felt things were better today for black Americans than a few years ago; just 44 percent felt that life would be better in the future.[38] As Ralph Ellison long ago expressed it, the ultimate goal for African Americans is the creation of real democracy in which a black person will be "free to define himself for what he is and, within the large framework of that democracy, for what he desires to be."[39]

White Responses to Pressure for Change

Since the 1960s civil rights revolution white Americans, including the elite, have faced a recurring ideological and moral crisis. They have experienced a growth in strong liberty-and-justice and other antiracist ideas among Americans of color who are fighting and organizing against persisting racism. Protest against white dominance includes not only overt confrontation but also the development of a strong counter-frame—in the case of black Americans, an antiracist counter-frame generated over a long period of fighting oppression. Periodically, this antiracist counter-framing has helped to generate an ideological or moral crisis for many white Americans.

Remedial Strategies: Moderates and Liberals

From the 1940s to the 1960s an accent on modest racial integration and anti-segregation action was the orientation of the elite's more liberal wing, although not of the elite as a whole nor of the white public. Reflecting the views of some of these elite men and of increasing numbers of social scientists in the 1940s, Gunnar Myrdal argued in *An American Dilemma* that biological racism was discredited and antiblack discrimination should be remedied. Myrdal's solution accented the need for ethical changes by many individual whites, who would take action to change institutions. Myrdal and his associates pressed for gradual, one-way integration of black Americans into exclusionary white-controlled institutions.[40] Such one-way assimilation, however, does not aim at fully remaking these racist institutions.

By the 1950s the white elite and public were confronted by black and other protesters risking their livelihoods and lives in the new civil rights strategy of non-violent confrontation and civil disobedience. By making moderate desegregation and other policy concessions to these pressures in the 1950s and 1960s, white decisionmakers probably averted more serious protests and more extensive societal changes. New civil rights laws eliminated official segregation, and remedial programs for discrimination began a gradual process of placing some, often modest, numbers of African Americans, other Americans of color, and white women in historically white male workplaces and other institutional settings. However, for the most part white moderates and liberals have only sought to eliminate the most blatant forms of discrimination and to provide some increased societal opportunities for Americans of color.

The much-criticized affirmative action (a term originally meaning just "positive action") programs of recent decades were initially created by white men in the elite's moderate or liberal wing. Since these programs were first put into effect to deal with racial discrimination—mostly by white men at or near the top of corporations, universities, and other organizations—they have typically involved modest, often successful efforts to bring some people of color and white women into major institutions where they had historically been excluded. These affirmative action programs have the look of going significantly beyond equality of opportunity, but actually they have mostly just opened up opportunities to those who are quite qualified for them.

Much research demonstrates that the use of well-crafted affirmative action programs, together with designating specific organizational responsibility for them, is an effective way of diversifying workforces and other institutions. For instance, one research evaluation of corporate employment diversity efforts at the managerial level looked at several different strategies. The researchers found that typical diversity training programs were the least effective approach to increasing a corporation's percentage of black and female managers. Mentoring and networking programs also showed less significant effects in increasing managerial diversity than did organizational programs accenting "accountability, authority, and expertise (affirmative action plans, diversity committees and taskforces, diversity managers and departments)." Concrete plans and real managerial accountability are very important in making some lasting changes in management diversity. Even so, the study found that the best affirmative action programs had modest effects on corporate diversity.[41]

From the viewpoint of even the more supportive whites, government affirmative action and similar remedial policies were designed to be modest and temporary, and to get the job opportunity game to work better in the private and public sectors for Americans of color. In recent years most critics of affirmative action seem to have forgotten that it was originally created by white male officials as a modest response to pressures from black and other protesters seeking more substantial societal changes in the 1960s era. Not surprisingly, thus, only a few affirmative action and other antidiscrimination programs have seriously challenged white male domination of historically white institutions.

White Conservative Strategies Persist

The white conservative political resurgence since the 1980s has periodically involved attacks on these and other antidiscrimination programs. The conservative ideological attack, with its continuing denial of significant societal racism, its assertion of white innocence, and its romanticizing of the racist past, has frequently been accompanied by political actions that have moved the U.S. government and private organizations away from attempts at racial desegregation and other necessary racial change.

Conservative intellectuals have helped in getting conservative politicians elected and in preparing backtracking legislation, and they have participated actively in shaping and manipulating the views and inclinations of the general public by serving as op-ed writers in major newspapers, appearing as experts on major news programs and influential talk shows, and writing best-selling books. Recall the extensive development of conservative theories about black Americans (for example, Chapter 3, pp. 73–91).[42]

Conservative commentaries drawing on the "IQ" test literature continue to plague the scientific community and the public discussion. Recall that the distinguished scientist James Watson has argued that conventional "IQ" test data demonstrate that blacks are less intelligent than whites. Watson has also hypothesized that, because a little research suggests that melanin (which creates skin color) extracts enhance sex drive, dark-skinned people must have a greater sex drive than lighter-skinned people. This unreflective white-framed approach to the biology of "race" is an old approach that most scientists used in the overtly racist, early decades of the twentieth century. In recent decades, however, the overwhelming majority of physical and social scientists have abandoned this blatant biological racism.[43]

Since the 1970s, as part of the conservative resurgence against government actions to reduce racial inequalities, powerful whites in government and business have cut back or ended numerous antidiscrimination programs. For example, most U.S. companies now do little significant training of their white and other employees for interracial cooperation and management.[44] In addition, since the 1970s white conservatives have filed major lawsuits, including those that have resulted in Supreme Court decisions dismantling affirmative action programs, such as the 1989 *Croson* decision on business set-asides noted in Chapter 5. Recent cases have continued to weaken antidiscrimination programs in areas such as education and voting rights. Decided by a conservative-controlled Supreme Court in the early 2000s, two major University of Michigan cases (*Gratz v. Bollinger* and *Grutter v. Bollinger*) effectively limited attempts in higher education to improve lagging diversity in colleges and universities. The high court significantly limited the use of remedial action using racial characteristics that was aimed at diversifying college admissions, although it did allow them to be used alongside numerous other factors in carefully crafted admissions procedures. However, in a major 2013 case, *Fisher v. University of Texas*, the conservative majority on the Court further limited this modest use of a race-conscious factor in admissions by requiring college administrators to exhaust all other alternatives for increasing student racial diversity before using it. Ignoring the fact that most colleges have tried other, usually unsuccessful approaches to increase student racial diversity, the Court's decision likely ended most significant affirmative action efforts in higher education.[45]

Over recent decades a conservative Supreme Court has also rejected the argument, well documented in social science research, that institutional racism is the immediate context and shaper of individual racism. The Court's conservatives have argued that the civil rights created by the Fourteenth Amendment to the U.S. Constitution are only for individuals and cannot be used to destroy long-established institutional discrimination. Since the 1980s, a string of cases from this conservative high court have treated the white interest in keeping white privilege and power as much more important than the interests of Americans of color in eradicating systemic racism.[46]

Indeed, federal judges have often ignored existing research data. Take the common claim that affirmative action in the area of college scholarships has greatly hurt white students because students of color get a huge and unfair share of them. Yet recent analyses show that among full-time undergraduates in four-year colleges and universities, students of color are about one-third of applicants for grants and scholarships, but get only about one-quarter of private scholarships. "Caucasian students receive more than three-quarters (76%) of all institutional merit-based scholarship and grant funding, even though they represent less than two-thirds (62%) of the student population."[47] An overwhelming majority of grants and fellowships are available for whites. Another recent social science study found that white undergraduates with solid financial support for college costs from their affluent families were much more likely than similar students of color to get *additional* college scholarship support.[48] Preferential treatment for whites has long been central, institutionalized, and legitimate. It is action to remedy longstanding discrimination against Americans of color that has been controversial and difficult to implement.

Generating Significant Organizational Change

In recent years many analysts, especially conservative analysts, have regularly suggested that affirmative action and other programs of government intervention against discrimination have not brought the significant changes promised, should be cataloged as failures, or violate merit procedures. However, some important programs of remedial action have brought substantial organizational changes and increased respect for merit. Consider the substantial efforts at job and other racial desegregation in the U.S. Army. Today the Army, which has the largest proportion of black personnel in the military, is probably the most desegregated of the larger historically white institutions. The proportion of black Americans among Army officers has been shown to be significantly higher than it is among executives in most large corporations. Today, thousands of black officers constitute the largest group of black executives in any historically white organization. African Americans also make up a disproportionate percentage of the important sergeant ranks in the Army, a proportion higher than that for comparable supervisors in most other U.S. workplaces.[49]

How was this desegregation of an organization with a long history of well-institutionalized segregation accomplished? The explanation lies in the fact that the armed forces were ordered to desegregate by President Harry Truman in 1948. Linked to this is the fact that the Army is an authoritarian organization that has in recent decades punished overt discrimination by white personnel and rewarded officers who worked for significant desegregation. The Army has required courses on racial, ethnic, and gender issues, and diversity in units is often taken into account in personnel decisions. Interestingly, the Army approach accents *merit* procedures. To meet the problem of enlistees without the skills necessary to move up the ranks—a common problem for civilian employers as well—the Army has developed a strong array of compensatory education programs. Rather than lower standards, the Army has often set up programs to bring personal skills to levels necessary for satisfactory performance and promotion. These educational programs are usually well crafted and relatively brief, and have generally been successful in providing many black personnel and other personnel of color with the skills necessary to meet military entrance and promotion standards. Given real opportunities, black Americans have excelled in the job structure of a historically white institution. In addition, the U.S. military requires significant diversity training for officers and enlisted personnel. There are also spin-off effects from the military desegregation: The most racially integrated towns and cities in the United States are generally near military bases.[50]

Army programs demonstrate that much more can be done to reduce and remedy historic discrimination. In the enforcement of antidiscrimination laws and the desegregation of everyday operations, military leaders and ordinary personnel have often accomplished much more than white executives and managers in most other government agencies, in large corporations and most other businesses, or in most unions. Nonetheless, much remains to be done. Military surveys show there is still much subtle and covert discrimination, and some blatant discrimination, in various military branches.[51]

Significant efforts are also being made to bring organizational change in other sectors of society. For example, in a 2012 study of racial barriers faced by administrators of color and other non-traditional administrators at major universities, the senior administrators Edna Chun and Alvin Evans have laid out well major recommendations for institutional change in universities. Among these are numerous recommendations that apply to an array of public and private organizations:

> Increase representational diversity by hiring women, minority, and LGBT administrators in positions of *line* authority, including executive positions traditionally held by white males;

> Vest diverse administrators with *appropriate* authority and resources commensurate with the level of their position and ensure comparability in similar level positions;

> Monitor employment patterns by organizational area and supervisory purview for hiring, promotion, compensation, evaluation, and termination decisions in terms of *adverse impact* upon diverse administrators.

> Eliminate *"wired searches"* [predetermined searches] or waivers and strengthen diversity recruitment; ensure diversity of search committees.[52]

These are just a few of their perceptive suggestions for large-scale organizational change. They conclude their research-based book thus: "Recognition and celebration of the talents of all members of the university community will strengthen the creation of a climate of respect, dignity, and empowerment that supports the attainment of Inclusive Excellence."[53]

Antiracist Strategies Today

As we have seen previously, the social context can restrict or encourage the possibility that whites (and others) will take action against systemic racism and for a society that is more humane, egalitarian, and just. Historical conditions and the existing social structure set limits on what individuals can do, but they are not all-determining. Today, even within a society thoroughly grounded in white racism, a significant number of whites are working actively with Americans of color to destroy that racism in their own lives and in the larger society.

Some Strategies in Dealing with Individual Whites

At lecture sessions I have done over the decades, some whites ask, usually in frustration and after they have become more aware that racial hostility and discrimination are commonplace: "What can I do to bring change? I am only one individual." The answer to this may lie in the old idea that one person, whatever her or his status, can help to topple an oppressive system if action is taken at the right place and time. One person's actions can make a real difference. Consider the European Holocaust. It might not have happened if a modest number of individuals had taken action to stop it at the right point in time.

Zygmunt Bauman has suggested that,

> Evil is not all powerful.... The testimony of the few who did resist shatters the authority of the logic of self-preservation. It shows it for what it is in the end—a choice. One wonders how many people must defy that logic for evil to be incapacitated.[54]

This is the important practical question. During the 1950s–1960s civil rights movement only a modest percentage of black Americans, and a very small percentage of most other groups, ignored the logic of self-preservation and actively participated in the organized protests against Jim Crow. Today, likewise, we need more people who will ignore self-preservation and act to disrupt individual and group framing and actions that reinforce the persisting racial hierarchy.

One barrier for most whites is their significant lack of empathy for the situations of those across the color line. Racism requires in its oppressors and discriminators a lack of recognition of the humanity of the racialized others. Systemic racism, thus, involves the social alexithymia discussed previously. Being an oppressor in a racist society typically requires a significantly reduced ability to understand or relate to the experiences, such as recurring pain, of those regularly targeted by racist framing, hostility, and discrimination.

Whites who change in this regard seem to develop through at least three stages: *sympathy*, *empathy*, and *autopathy*. The initial stage, sympathy, is important but limited. It typically involves a willingness to set aside some racist stereotypes, images, and hostility, and the development of a friendly if variable interest in what is happening to the racialized others. Numerous whites have moved into this stage since the 1960s civil rights movement. Empathy is a much more advanced stage, in that it requires a developed ability to routinely reject numerous distancing stereotypes and other racial framing, plus a sustained capacity to see and feel some of the pain of those in the oppressed group. Autopathy is yet a third and more advanced stage. Autopathic understandings and feelings occur when a white person has intentionally put herself or himself, if partially, into the racist world of the oppressed—and not only receives racist hostility from other whites but also personally feels some pain that comes from being enmeshed in racist conditions central to the lives of oppressed others. This case of feeling racism's pain more directly often comes when whites are close friends, lovers, parents, or other relatives of blacks or other people of color who are direct and daily targets of racism. Accounts by white parents of children of color sometimes reveal the great autopathic pain the former frequently endure as they confront the racism faced by their children.[55]

Today the challenge for those seeking to expand antiracist strategies and actions includes the creation of conditions where more whites will have to confront the reality of the everyday pain that systemic racism has caused Americans of color, including those with whom they come into regular contact. A large-scale educational effort—one that is candid about the past and present reality of white-racist framing and practices—seems required if more than a handful of whites are to move into these important stages of empathy and autopathy.

The Role of Education

Over more than four decades of teaching experience with thousands of students, I have found that, until whites have substantial instruction in the history and contemporary reality of racial oppression, most reject the important understandings and interpretations they need to be supportive of major changes in our racist system. Undoubtedly, changing the centuries-old white racial frame and actions generated by it will require much effort, including improved educational strategies. Today, few Americans have had even a brief Stereotyping 101 or Racism 101 course in their educations, from kindergarten to college or graduate school.[56] This has had a serious impact on whites' and others' knowledge of our racist history and contemporary racial realities.

Recent psychological research has shown whites' knowledge of historical racism is related to their ability to understand contemporary racism. Comparing black college students with white students, one study found that whites "perceived less racism in both isolated incidents and systemic manifestations of racism." White students did worse on a measure of historical knowledge than the black students. Not surprisingly, among these whites denial of contemporary racism was also found to be linked to their ignorance of the history of racism.[57]

By means of well-constructed Racism 101 courses, whites, and many others, can become much more aware of the reality of the conventional white-racist framing deeply imbedded in their minds. They can be taught the importance of reframing away from this old white racial frame to an operational liberty-and-justice framing of society. Generating a sincere acceptance of this liberty-and-justice frame, and increasing action out of it, will likely require an expanded process of renewed education in which white individuals and their networks move toward understanding how our system of white privilege and power was created, and how whites maintain it today. Such education needs to probe deeply into the deeply racist character of society and requires purposeful unlearning of the mythology whites have used to paper over the continuing reality of racial discrimination. Collective forgetting of society's racialized history, and their family's racialized history, is central to the way in which most whites have dealt with U.S. racism. Some antiracist educators have developed innovative Racism 101 strategies to bring home the reality of this racialized history. One effective strategy involves getting white and other students in a course to study and trace out their own family's history of developing and passing along assets and wealth over the last several generations. One teacher has noted that

> uncovering and reflecting on specific examples of unjust impoverishment and unjust enrichment in their personal family histories had a profound impact on many students. Many white students acknowledged being able to see and understand how racism and white privilege operated in their own lives in ways that had not been able to before.[58]

Recently, the Southern Poverty Law Center published a report evaluating the educational standards for teaching about the civil rights movement in all states and the District of Columbia. They found the typical efforts on the part of (mostly white) legislators and educators in the *majority* of states were to downplay, ignore, or superficially review this important rights movement and its racist context:

> Too often, we found, the movement, when it is given classroom time, is reduced to lessons about two heroic figures—Martin Luther King and Rosa Parks—and four words, "I have a dream." We found that only a handful of states required educators to pay significant attention to the movement and the lessons it can teach about citizenship. Over 30 states required minimal or even no instruction; many had standards that barely went beyond a superficial treatment of events and leaders. Overall … in almost all states, there is tremendous room for improvement.[59]

For those interested in significantly remedying the extensive ignorance of a great many Americans, and especially most white Americans, this important report laid out model curriculum standards for teaching accurately, richly, and rigorously about civil rights and the pathbreaking civil rights movement.

Some Impacts of Education

Learning more about the harsh reality of U.S. history—about its oppression, brutality, and unjust impoverishment for Americans of color, and its unjust enrichment and privileges for whites—is likely to be critical to the goal of increasing the number of whites (and others) who will actively join antiracist efforts at local and national levels.[60] As of now, this important educational project is clearly in an early stage. One optimistic finding from recent research is that even modest educational steps can make some difference. Some psychological research has demonstrated that diversity videos and courses can have some positive effects on the awareness of racism and privilege among white students and on their inclination to participate in antiracist actions. One recent study examined the impact of a short video showing the extent of white racism today on the racial views of the white college students who viewed it. Compared with a control group, those who watched the video "showed significant increases in racial awareness (i.e., decrease in racial colorblindness), White empathy, and White guilt, at posttest." The overall impact was modest, however, for there were no significant differences between the two groups in racial prejudice. Still, educational videos can "serve as a powerful and practical teaching and learning resource in counseling-related coursework."[61]

Another study involved two groups of white children aged 6–11. Each group was given six 20-minute daily history lessons providing biographical information on historically important African Americans. One group got biographies with explicit discussions of racial discrimination faced by the person under consideration, while the other group got the biographies without references to discrimination. Before and after the lessons, researchers gave these white children an evaluative scale designed to measure positive and negative views of black and white Americans. The children who had the brief racial discrimination lessons had significantly more positive attitudes and less negative attitudes about black Americans than the group that had not gotten such lessons. The children getting the discrimination lessons also revealed in testing that they were more inclined than the others to racial fairness and, among older children, had more racial guilt.[62] Such research suggests that even brief historical lessons about discrimination may have some modest positive effects on whites' racial attitudes, including activation of their sense of responsibility for a racist society.

The usefulness of white racial guilt has been debated, but a few studies suggest it may have positive effects. Research on white college students has shown that the extent of their feelings of guilt about apparently racist views predicts their interest in participating in prejudice-reducing behavior.

In one study those with more racial guilt were more likely to desire to participate in reading prejudice-reducing articles and in "rectifying the transgression that originally produced the guilt."[63] Another recent study of new college students who were relatively unaware of racism found that their participation in diversity courses and activities increased their sense of white racial guilt. Diversity courses not only accelerate "academic and social growth of white students but also ... encourage positive changes in emotions about racial issues."[64] From these researchers' perspective, the generation of the emotion of racialized guilt can conceivably play a beneficial role in stimulating action against racism.

In addition, stimulating critical thinking about one aspect of U.S. racism can stimulate critical thinking and reframing in other areas. In another study researchers using a "white privilege attitudes scale" demonstrated that white empathy for, and understanding of, the racist conditions faced by Americans of color increase as white understandings critical of white privilege increase—in this case on attitudinal items measuring awareness of white racial privilege, willingness to confront it, and remorse over it.[65]

Teaching people in one racial group how to see complexity and nuances in people in other groups may be another useful step in breaking down some racial framing. In one Canadian study psychological researchers showed 264 photos of Chinese, black, and white male faces to 20 whites. After they had been trained for hours in seeing subtle differences in these particular faces, the volunteers were less likely to associate negative words like "hate" with black faces than before the training. Training in seeing facial differences might reduce some racial profiling by police and other officials: "It's beneficial even if it doesn't affect their unconscious bias because it's still good to have them tell individuals apart better than before, and a side benefit might be that it affects how much they stereotype."[66] One problem in the interactions associated with everyday racism is the way in which members of one group, especially the dominant group, operate out of a racial framing that sees little difference in racial out-groups, indeed a framing that often insists "they all look alike."

Yet other social science research has examined which strategies and experiences break down racial isolation in high school and college settings. The character of interracial contacts, including friendships, is important. One research study found that positive interracial experiences in desegregated high school settings, such as significant interracial friendships, increased the likelihood of having meaningful interracial friendships later on in college.[67] Another important study of white college students who had same-race or other-race roommates for several months found that those with other-race roommates ended up with more diverse friends, viewing diversity as more important, and being more comfortable with interracial interactions than white students with same-race roommates.[68] In addition, a study at eight University of California campuses asked students about how they "gained a deeper understanding" of the views of students who differed from them in religious beliefs, nationality, race and ethnicity, sexual orientation, and political opinions. Researchers found that discussions that *improved* student understandings "more commonly occurred (about 60% reporting frequent) where the topic was race/ethnicity and nationality—student differences that were more apparent because of visual differences or accent." The students themselves made this connection between changed views and visible group characteristics. The reality of racial–ethnic diversity in organizational settings like this can have, under the right circumstances (for example, ongoing equal-status contacts), some positive effects on what people learn and understand about those unlike themselves.[69]

Throughout a number of recent studies, thus, we observe the impact of diverse race–ethnic experiences and equal-status contacts on the racial views of whites. Consider another illuminating research project with policy implications. Researchers recently compared white college students who scored high on antiracist measures with students who did not score in the antiracist range. The more antiracist white students had more diversity experiences in growing up and on campus, and in the testing they showed more empathetic concern about racism issues and more awareness of the concerns of students of color. The researchers suggest a practical implication:

> White antiracist role models are critical in helping White individuals to understand the insidiousness of racism and the importance of White people challenging racism.... White antiracist students could serve as discussion facilitators, teaching assistants, residence hall assistants, and paraprofessionals to raise other White students' awareness of racial issues.[70]

In practice, administrators and faculty leaders at universities and other organizations seeking to deal forcefully with racism issues might well make more extensive use of antiracist whites in antiracism and serious diversity efforts.

Interracial Organizations Working against Racism

Group action against racism is essential. Antiracist action began in the first centuries of this country's development. Multiracial groups have periodically helped to bring social changes, as the 1840s–1850s antislavery abolitionists and 1950s–1960s civil rights activists demonstrated. Some whites have given their lives for antiracist movements. In October 1859, John Brown, a white abolitionist, led a band of whites and blacks in an attempt to seize weapons at a federal arsenal at Harper's Ferry, with the goal of arming enslaved black Americans and facilitating rebellion against slavery's oppression. Today, one necessary step is for all levels of antiracist education to offer courses discussing the actions of black and white activists like John Brown. Radical abolitionists constituted one of the first multiracial groups to struggle vigorously against systemic racism. Brown's lucid comment on his sentence of death for his efforts indicates commitment to racial justice:

> Now, if it is deemed necessary that I should forfeit my life for the furtherance of the ends of justice, and mingle my blood further with the blood of my children and with the blood of millions in this slave country whose rights are disregarded by wicked, cruel, and unjust enactments,—I submit, so let it be done![71]

Since the antislavery efforts of the diverse Harper's Ferry band in 1859, a long line of whites, blacks, and others of color have worked together, often against enormous opposition, to bring expanded liberty and justice to this country. Recall the creation of the NAACP in the early 1900s, an organization seeking to fight racial segregation. For many years this organization, which has constantly worked against systemic racism, has had blacks and whites in its leadership and membership. It celebrated its one-hundredth anniversary in 2009, with President Barack Obama as keynote speaker and with a racially diverse audience. Its chair, the celebrated civil rights activist Julian Bond, made clear in interviews that the social justice and racial equality goals of the organization had not been met, and that much work on discrimination and inequality lay ahead.[72] We should note that not only the NAACP efforts, but also other organizational efforts in the black-led civil rights movement of the 1950s and 1960s, involved many participants from an array of racial and ethnic groups, including numerous whites. This movement had significant success in bringing down official Jim Crow segregation. In a social system like ours there seem to be only a few high leverage points from which to precipitate lasting changes, and U.S. history suggests that large coalitions of black and nonblack Americans working against systemic racism can create such high leverage points for significant progressive change in society.

In recent decades many antiracist whites have helped to organize or have joined in grassroots organizations working against racism. For example, dozens of groups called the Institutes for the Healing of Racism regularly hold seminars and dialogues on issues of racism in various cities. These multiracial groups work locally to heighten the awareness of racism, educate citizens about how to fight racial hostility and discrimination, and provide dialogue across local racial-group boundaries. They have dealt openly with racist framing and institutional racism in their own lives and communities. The associated National Resource Center for Racial Healing has trained more than 1,500 antiracism activists.[73]

Typical of the range of current antiracist organizations are the People's Institute for Survival and Beyond (PI) and Antiracist Action (ARA). Located in New Orleans and created by black activists, PI is a community-oriented group that sets up "Undoing Racism" workshops to train people in community and non-profit organizations. These multiracial workshops—which have trained thousands of people, many of them whites, since the 1980s—are designed to help community activists and concerned officials in organizations better understand racism, power inequalities, and cultural diversity and to show how to "undo racism" in their lives, organizations, and communities. Taking a somewhat different tack, the often substantially white ARA groups have forcefully protested white-supremacist and other racist groups and worked against government racism in cities in the United States and Canada. For example, their Copwatch programs attempt to reduce police brutality by such actions as having members take video devices into the streets to record police actions in dealings with citizens of color.[74]

While objectives and tactics have varied, numerous other organizations have pressed for changes in systemic racism over recent decades. A brief sampling includes the Dismantling Racism Program of the National Conference (St. Louis), the Anti-Racism Institute of Clergy and Laity Concerned (Chicago), the Northwest Coalition against Malicious Harassment, the Southern Empowerment Project, the Committee against Anti-Asian Violence, and the Antiracism Study Dialogue Circles Metamorphosis (ASDIC) program. Based in Minnesota, ASDIC activists have used well-crafted dialogue and study workshops to stimulate awareness of racism, antiracist discussions, and change efforts in their communities. This multiracial group has successfully worked on an array of important educational and action goals, which include educating and empowering local people of diverse backgrounds to speak out on community patterns of white racism and helping them to protest for a more just and democratic society, locally and nationally. ASDIC programs provide models for other antiracist groups. The group has utilized quality racial-equity curriculum materials tailored for specific community groups and has generated networking "capital" among change agents working against racism in midwestern communities. ASDIC has facilitated more than one hundred workshops and dialogue circles with more than 1,800 community participants in antiracist activism—teachers, students, non-profit and government staff, members of religious organizations, and others. ASDIC's antiracist curriculum has been offered as for-credit college courses. ASDIC has also worked with other organizations in setting up Overcoming Racism conferences that provide educational and other support for antiracism trainers and organizations.[75]

Note too that serious racial dialogue groups like those of ASDIC are being used in other educational settings as an important step in antiracist action. For example, in college courses some social justice educators have incorporated sustained "Intergroup Dialogue" segments in which white students and students of color are provided with important information about societal power and privilege and pressed to think very deeply and critically about this society's racist structures.[76]

Unmistakably, an important step in a broad antiracist strategy for the U.S. would be to expand greatly the number and size of antiracist efforts and organizations and connect them into an effective national association working against systemic racism. Today, broad multiracial coalitions working against racial oppression seem very necessary. Coalitions have periodically been attempted, and successful. For instance, since the 1980s the Reverend Jesse Jackson, a black civil rights leader, has worked with people from numerous racial and ethnic groups, including many whites, to build the Rainbow Coalition (later Rainbow PUSH). This influential organization, based in Chicago, has pressed since the 1980s for social justice goals such as: better jobs and government job creation; more extensive government efforts against racism, sexism, and homophobia; and government efforts to protect the environment. For decades now, the organization has helped to win progressive electoral battles in several states; it supported Jesse Jackson's pioneering bids for the U.S. presidency in 1984 and 1988. Most recently, the organization has continued its open-umbrella coalition approach and focused major organizational efforts on persisting unemployment and poverty, home foreclosures, health care problems, voter registration, corporate inclusion, and higher-education issues facing Americans of color.[77]

A Democratic Constitutional Convention: An Idea Whose Time Has Come?

In 1787, some 55 white men met in Philadelphia and wrote a Constitution for what was seen as the first democratic nation. They met at the end of a revolutionary struggle and articulated their perspective using language about human equality and freedom. However, they had a very restricted view of those grand ideas. This Constitutional Convention did not include white women, African Americans, or Native Americans, who then made up a substantial majority of the population. Nor did it include representation for white men with little property. The representatives of less than 5 percent of the population framed a new constitution that has governed, with some amendments, the United States since the eighteenth century. The document created by these propertied white men generally reflected their racial, class, and gender interests. While some of these interests encompassed the desires of all Americans to be free of the tyrannies of Europe—such as the constitutional prohibition of aristocratic titles and of a state religion—it took strong protests from ordinary Americans before even a Bill of Rights was added by the elite to their new Constitution.[78]

The 1858 Constitution

Not one of the original Constitutional Convention's delegates saw African Americans and Native Americans as human beings whose views, interests, and perspectives should be seriously considered. How then should African Americans and Native Americans, whose ancestors were present in large numbers in the country but excluded at the convention and whose enslavement was ratified by the Constitution, regard the document? Why should they accept the authority of a Constitution their ancestors played no part in making? As I see it, this undemocratic Constitution and its often racially biased tradition of pro-white interpretation over the intervening centuries should be replaced, for this tradition has constrained progressive change toward racial and other equality and justice for too long. All attempts to fully eradicate systemic racism since the late 1700s have been constrained by this document and interpretations of it by the mostly white judges and members of Congress holding office since that time. Significant attempts at societal change—scattered court decisions knocking down some discrimination and new civil rights laws—have been made within this white-framed and white-dominated societal context and, thus, have come slowly and with enough deficiencies, such as weak or no enforcement, to ensure that the underlying system of racial oppression has not been eliminated. The U.S. democratic project yet remains to be fully accomplished.

Only one racially diverse group of Americans has, to my knowledge, tried to formulate and implement an antiracist constitution and declaration of independence. On May 8, 1858, more than a year before the previously mentioned Harper's Ferry raid, John Brown and his allies, black and white, met in Chatham, Canada, to formulate a new constitution to govern the revolutionaries fighting for liberty for enslaved Americans—a constitution looking forward to a new antiracist nation of the United States. A total of 12 white Americans and 33 black Americans (some having fled to Canada) were present at this authentic liberty convention. The preamble to the pathbreaking provisional constitution they created read as follows:

> Whereas slavery, throughout its entire existence in the United States, is none other than a most barbarous, unprovoked and unjustifiable war of one portion of its citizens upon another portion ... in utter disregard and violation of those eternal and self-evident truths set

forth in our Declaration of Independence: therefore, we, citizens of the United States, and the oppressed people who, by a recent decision of the Supreme Court, are declared to have no rights which the white man is bound to respect, together with all other people degraded by the laws thereof, do, for the time being, ordain and establish ourselves the following provisional constitution and ordinances, the better to protect our persons, property, lives, and liberties, and to govern our actions.[79]

Their radical declaration of independence further insisted "that the Slaves are, & of right ought to be ... free." Their new constitution and declaration of independence appear to be the only ones in U.S. history to be prepared by the representatives of oppressed African Americans, with their interests in liberty and justice substantially in mind.[80]

A New U.S. Constitutional Convention

Over recent decades, the U.S. government has a history of pressuring certain undemocratic countries to develop democratic constitutional conventions or commissions and, thus, democratic constitutions. For example, in 2005 numerous U.S. officials put great pressure on the new Iraqi officials who replaced U.S.-deposed dictator Saddam Hussein to develop a constitutional commission that would represent all the people of Iraq and create a democratic constitution. U.S. officials insisted that all major religious and ethnic groups in Iraq have representation, that women be represented, and that women's rights, minority rights, and religious rights be recognized in the new constitution. Among the 55 members of this constitutional commission were indeed male and female representatives of most major groups in Iraq. The final Iraqi Constitution, approved in a national referendum, describes the country as a "democratic, federal, representative republic" and a "multiethnic, multireligious country." It specifically lists an array of protected human rights, among them equality before law, equal opportunity, privacy, right to counsel, presumption of innocence, freedom of speech and press, the right to vote, economic and cultural liberty, the right to work, ownership of personal property, and a dozen more human rights. Significantly, this innovative constitution explicitly bans racial discrimination and prohibits groups from propagating racism.[81]

In stark contrast, however, the United States has *never* had such a constitutional convention or commission that represented all (or even much) of the population, nor has it developed a U.S. Constitution with nearly as large an array of explicit human rights protections as this Iraqi constitution. It is hard to see how the United States can insist on being the world's premier democracy without having its own political constitution made in at least as democratic a fashion as the U.S.-pressured Iraqi Constitution.

Given this historical background, it seems time for the United States to have another constitutional convention, one that fairly represents all Americans. The old racialized foundation of the U.S. sociopolitical system needs to be replaced if the persisting realities of racial hostility and discrimination are to be thoroughly removed, just as the sinking foundation of a dilapidated old building must be replaced. A new constitutional convention is required not only to address issues of human rights and restitution for racially oppressed groups, but also to ensure that the governing document of the new multiracial democracy is produced by representatives of all the people. The egalitarian and democratic ideas associated with the U.S. Bill of Rights and civil rights laws could well be points for important discussion at this new convention. However, as I see it, no existing U.S. laws should automatically be part of a new constitution because the meaning of these laws usually rests on their interpretation by the current, mostly white-dominated, judiciary.

What would be a more adequate set of starting points in beginning the debate on a constitution for a true multiracial democracy? The new convention might use the United Nation's Universal Declaration of Human Rights and related human rights documents that have expanded that declaration, including those on women's rights. First ratified in 1948 by the United Nations, this important international declaration today represents a growing consensus across the globe on what human rights are essential for a healthy society (see below, pp. 310–311). Without collective and governmental respect for a broad array of fundamental human rights there can be no real democracy. Thus, the official call for the new constitutional convention might indicate a grounding of its discussions in a mutual respect for the broad human rights of all Americans and in a mutual respect for the plurality of U.S. cultures and heritages.

Some experienced civil rights scholars and leaders have opposed the idea of a new constitutional convention because they fear the white majority there might even roll back existing civil rights protections. For example, the constitutional scholar Roy Brooks has criticized this idea of a new convention because it "would open debate and reconsideration of the existing document, and the consequences could be dire."[82] He and others fear that in a society where many whites are still operating out of a white-racist framing such a new convention might be dominated by whites who would restrict existing rights such as free speech and reproductive rights.

These fears might be reasonable if the new convention were to be dominated just by white men of a conservative bent. However, in my hypothetical scenario the convention would *not* take place unless those who write the new constitution are fully representative of *all* sectors of the population. No other arrangement will create the necessary conditions for full and open debates on matters of concern to all the people. If the convention were to be held today, this stipulation would mean that white men would be about 31 percent of the delegates, instead of the 100 percent representation they had at the first convention. In addition, that group would now include a much more diverse array of white men than at the first convention. In addition, about 37 percent of the delegates would be Americans of color; women of all backgrounds would constitute a little more than half of the delegates. These changes alone would make a contemporary convention dramatically different in representation, and likely discussion, from the 1787 convention.

Some readers may wonder if the average citizen or politician, who may be relatively ignorant of complex political and legal matters and with U.S. history, would have the ability to deal intelligently with issues of government as complex and difficult as those faced by a new constitutional convention. One partial solution for this would be to require a process of intensive, open, and critical political education for all delegates, indeed perhaps for the entire population. Prior to calling an official convention, those committed to the creation of a full democracy might press for trial conventions to test how such a truly representative convention might operate in dealing with decisionmaking processes, human rights, and controversial political issues. Indeed, there could be a practice convention in each region, which might well generate important political debates in every area. The final convention might then have its agenda shaped by the collective wisdom and decisions emanating from these regional deliberations.

A truly representative assembly would ensure that, for the first time in U.S. history, the white majority hears much discussion of, and faces pressure to take seriously, the group interests and rights of Americans of color. This assembly will necessarily be diverse enough that many decisions on key constitutional provisions will likely have to be negotiated among the diverse contending groups. Constitutional decisions will require a consideration of the originally excluded interests of white women and Americans of color, as well as of the more recently asserted interests of gay, lesbian, bisexual, and transgender (GLBT), disabled, and other Americans. As with the first convention, the debates will be revealing and educational, for delegates and the country as a whole. These debates would likely remove the smokescreen disguising the current undemocratic reality of U.S. society and show unequivocally how racial, class, gender, heterosexist, and other forms of exploitation and discrimination operate to the detriment of a great many Americans. A true democracy is one in which all people not only are represented but also have fair input into the creation and operation of its laws and political institutions. As now structured, with antique and undemocratic institutions such as a U.S. Senate elected on the basis of territory not population and an unelected Supreme Court, the U.S. political system is less democratic than numerous European political systems.[83] Of course, a new constitutional convention would be only a first step. A truly democratic constitution becomes the political foundation on which to build and operate an array of effective democratic institutions and policies. Today, as in the past, many of our major institutions are far from democratic and representative. For example, as of 2013 only 112 Americans have ever served as very powerful Supreme Court justices, who among other things interpret the constitutionality of congressional lawmaking. Ninety-seven percent have been white, and 95 percent have been white men. Given this biased demographic reality, the dominance of a strong white racial frame in many court decisions over more than two centuries is unsurprising.

For all its possible difficulties, a new constitutional convention seems required not only to guarantee full human rights for previously excluded Americans but also to insure that the foundational document of this country is made by the representatives of all Americans. Such a convention is also an important part of a reinvigorated antiracist strategy to build a truly just and egalitarian foundation for the United States. Once those who have never actively participated in U.S. politics see that their true representatives have been involved in making the founding document, commitment to and involvement in the new democracy will likely increase substantially. A strongly and truly democratic constitution—with broad citizen participation in its associated institutions and recurring citizen activism on behalf of its asserted human rights—seems the only real guarantee of full liberty, equality, and social justice for the United States.

Restitution and Reparations for Racism

As yet, no major group of white Americans has taken on the responsibility to call for reparations for the past and continuing negative impact of slavery, segregation, and contemporary racism on African Americans. For the most part, white leaders and rank-and-file whites have rejected proposals for large-scale reparations for those Americans of color who have suffered from systemic racism. Recall the 2009 apology from the U.S. Senate for slavery and Jim Crow segregation. (The U.S. House passed a similar resolution in 2008.) This modest apology included a disclaimer barring black Americans from seeking government reparations for centuries of oppression. An anemic apology like this operates, in effect, to downplay the current negative consequences of this oppression.

Once there is a new democratic constitution in place, a comprehensive antiracist strategy would require an early addressing of reparations for the damage done by centuries of white-imposed oppression to African

Americans and other Americans of color. Let us now consider here some of the arguments over such reparations for African Americans, the group most often discussed in this regard.

Arguments against Reparations

Today, as in the past, most whites reject the idea that whites should have to pay with strong antidiscrimination, affirmative action, and reparative programs for the persisting negative consequences brought on African Americans by the legacies of three and a half centuries of slavery and Jim Crow segregation. A common reaction is, "Slavery happened centuries ago" and "Let bygones be bygones."

This view is documented in research on current white opposition to affirmative action. For example, in one recent study white respondents were given a hypothetical scenario with a white person having a *slightly* higher merit score than a black person applying for a job, but with the black person being hired. Evaluating this situation, most whites were opposed to the qualified black person being hired. They used reasoning like "merit should be foremost," "the past is the past," and "two wrongs don't make a right." However, on other survey questions these whites gave abstract support for doing something about the difficult societal situation faced by black Americans, but this support gave way when white applicants had slightly better conventional test scores. Most did not think that the recent racist past should affect, even a little, employment decisions in the present.[84]

In many whites' view of this society the unjust enrichments gained by whites over earlier centuries should just be forgotten. Collective forgetting is one way in which most handle the tension between the values of liberty and justice and the long history of racial oppression. However, there are major problems in the argument that whites today should not be accountable for what their ancestors did, as many say, "hundreds of years ago." Indeed, slavery ended about 150 years ago, and today many black Americans are only a few generations removed from their enslaved ancestors. In addition, the near-slavery of Jim Crow segregation only came to an end in the late 1960s, well within the lifetimes of many white and black Americans today.

Many whites are inconsistent in regard to what parts of past U.S. history they wish to be acknowledged, and what parts they wish to ignore or forget. In the thinking of most, the actions of our founders and later political leaders that have benefited whites are given great weight and legitimacy. Such actions include the making of a U.S. Constitution and subsequent court decisions that interpreted it in the interest of whites. In contrast, according to the prevailing view, racially oppressive actions by the same white founders and later leaders should be forgotten or forgiven by those whose ancestors were severely victimized by these leaders' oppressive actions. Not surprisingly, a majority of whites do not view earlier structures of oppression as relevant to present-day inequalities. Nonetheless, these whites will insist that black Americans and other Americans of color accept the U.S. Constitution and the laws created by whites as fully binding on them, even though they had no say in the laws' creation. The legal scholar Richard Delgado has summarized this point well in the form of a comment from a black professor in a constructed dialogue: Most whites insist that blacks "owe obligations arising out of that social contract, but no obligation is owed to us arising from the abuse we suffered in connection with it."[85]

Furthermore, some analysts have argued that reparations would not be fair for whites whose ancestors immigrated to the U.S. after slavery. However, this common view overlooks the massive discrimination faced by black Americans under Jim Crow segregation for a century after slavery, as well as contemporary discrimination. Much antiblack discrimination has been carried out, or colluded in, by later white immigrants and their descendants. In addition, these whites, like those whose ancestors came earlier, were substantially enriched by a great array of white "affirmative action" programs after World War II (see below). Yet other anti-reparations arguments by conservatives include the argument that African Americans are "better off" in the United States, even with enslavement, than they would have been in Africa. Among other problems, however, this view conveniently ignores the extensive European imperialism and intensive colonization that have long devastated and impoverished much of Africa, political–economic operations and consequences still evident across Africa today. It is likely that Africans would be prosperous today if they had not lost tens of millions of mostly younger people over centuries to the Atlantic slavery system and if they had maintained full control over their mineral and other valuable resources that have been lost to Western imperialism.[86]

The Strong Case for Restitution and Reparations

In the Charter of the Nuremberg Tribunal—in which the U.S. government was centrally involved and which was convened to deal with the German Nazi war crimes after World War II—"crimes against humanity" were defined as "murder, extermination, enslavement, deportation, and other inhumane acts committed against any civilian population ... whether or not in violation of the domestic law of the country where perpetrated."[87] As we showed in previous chapters, white Europeans and Americans have a long tradition of such crimes against humanity. Large-scale enslavement and extensive oppression of Africans across the Atlantic basin for centuries were, and remain, one of the most serious "crimes against humanity."

Most whites have benefited from centuries of racial oppression and the transmission of racial privileges and/or substantial amounts of ill-gotten wealth from earlier oppression to later generations. Enslaved Africans and African Americans created much wealth and capital that spurred the economic development of southern U.S. areas, as well as the Industrial Revolution in the U.S. and Europe. "Western production levels were transformed," the scholar Ali Mazrui informs us. "But so were Western living standards, life expectancy, population growth, and the globalization of capitalism. How do we measure such repercussions of slavery?"[88] The current prosperity, relatively long life expectancies, and relatively high living standards of whites as a group in the U.S., as well as in the West generally, are substantially rooted in the agony, exploitation, and impoverishment of those colonized and enslaved, as well as in the oppression and misery of their descendants under legal segregation and contemporary discrimination. As we have shown throughout this book, over centuries white Americans as individuals, families, and communities have done much damage to African Americans. This damage is not just in the past, for African Americans today suffer from many psychological, economic, political, and other social costs that are the consequences of past and present white racism.

Researchers Jonathan Kaplan and Andrew Valls have suggested that one can base a strong case for black reparations just on the reality and impact of blatant housing discrimination over the decades of the Jim Crow era—discrimination that often persists in a less overt form in our era. For a lengthy period extreme racial segregation in housing was forced or reinforced by federal laws and government regulations mandating discrimination against Americans of color. Whites who implemented the huge government homeownership programs after World War II, such as the Federal Housing Administration (FHA) and Veterans' Administration (VA) programs, built blatant racial discrimination into their operation. The FHA program had an underwriting manual that strongly encouraged racially exclusionary housing covenants for new subdivisions, and the VA housing program had similar blatantly discriminatory regulations. White members of Congress made sure these large-scale programs were run by local white officials whose racist views affected decisions about housing loans for Americans of color. Not until the 1980s were all aspects of this operational discrimination fully removed. Even then, much housing discrimination by local government officials and private individuals has continued by informal means. Housing discrimination was not officially banned until the 1968 Civil Rights Act and its later amendments were passed.[89]

Significantly, government housing legislation passed after World War II enabled a very large number of white families to move into the middle class in the decades since that war—with the resulting substantial build-up of housing equities being a major source of resources and wealth many whites have passed to children and grandchildren. In contrast, because of substantial government-supported discrimination in housing, as well as in other institutional areas, African American families were usually unable to secure adequate housing and to build up similar housing equity and related resources for children and grandchildren. The currently huge wealth gap between white and black Americans is substantially the result of such government-supported blatant discrimination in the recent and distant past. Thus, one can today quantify some of what is owed to many still-living older black Americans who suffered for years under government-supported blatant housing and other racial discrimination.[90]

This housing example effectively counters some whites' arguments that racial oppression was in some far distant past and that it is not possible to identify perpetrators or victims for significant compensation. It also shows some problems with a related argument some whites have made against reparations. They argue that institutional discrimination against African Americans is too impersonal for the development of concrete remedies. In several federal court cases, white judges have asserted the view that, while there may be societal discrimination, no one can determine who in particular is responsible and who has benefited. However, the housing example is one where one can often identify who in particular was responsible and who in particular was harmed—and what the significant long-term costs actually were, and still are today.

Recall that in traditional Western law the concept of unjust enrichment includes not only receiving benefits that justly belong to another but also the obligation to make full *restitution* to the harmed victims. Numerous court decisions have provided remedies measured more by the gain to a culpable defendant than by a victimized plaintiff's loss. The defendant must give up the unjust enrichment, including substantial gains often made from it.[91] However, the law on such remedies has traditionally ignored group claims against unjust enrichment, and systemic racism involves unjust injuries to a very large group by the dominant benefiting group. An antiracist strategy might well extend the remedies law to such socially imposed conditions of group oppression. Whites whose families have been in North America for generations, which is the majority, generally benefit today from significant racial advantages their ancestors gained, often including gains under slavery and/or Jim Crow segregation. A majority have benefited from economic, political, and educational discrimination that favored their ancestors—and still favors them today (see Chapter 7, pp. 207–216). As with individual remedies, group remedies should encompass stopping the unjust extraction of benefits now and in the future as well as making restitution to the victim group for past discriminatory actions. Restitution and reparations are inadequate without stopping the racialized processes that distribute, maintain, and increase the ill-gotten gains for present and future generations of whites.

A few federal judges have recognized the principle of large-scale restitution as relevant to eliminating the effects of past discrimination. In *Larry Williams et al. v. City of New Orleans et al.*, appellate justice John Wisdom argued that the U.S. Congress that crafted the antislavery (Thirteenth, Fourteenth, Fifteenth) amendments to the U.S. Constitution and a major civil rights act after the Civil War intended to grant the federal government power

> to provide for remedial action aimed at eliminating the present effects of past discrimination against blacks as a class ... the thirteenth amendment is an affirmative grant of power to eliminate slavery along with its "badges and incidents" and to establish universal civil freedom. The amendment envisions affirmative action aimed at blacks as a race. When a present discriminatory effect upon blacks as a class can be linked with a discriminatory practice against blacks as a race under the slavery system, the present effect may be eradicated under the auspices of the thirteenth amendment.[92]

Given this important historical argument, one can understand why many whites wish to *break* the historical link to our large-scale past oppression. A full recognition of that historical linkage creates great pressure for significant white compensation and restitution for African Americans in the present.

Government Restitution and Reparations

Most white Americans appear to consider significant reparations for group-based damages suffered by black Americans to be a radical and undesirable public policy. However, white political leaders, white judges, and ordinary whites have on occasion accepted the principle of reparations for past damages done to certain groups. U.S. courts have required corporations to compensate the deformed children of mothers who took harmful drugs during their pregnancies without knowing the drug's side-effects. The courts held that such harm done to later generations was foreseeable by the corporate executives at that earlier point. The argument that those executives are now gone was not allowed to get the corporations off the hook. Harmed children received significant compensation even though the damage from corporate decisions became evident years later. This compensation principle is similar to the one asserted by those arguing for reparations for African Americans, whose current socioeconomic conditions often reflect significant damage done by earlier generations of whites.[93]

Significantly, the U.S. government has justifiably been active since World War II in efforts to pressure the German government to make large-scale reparations to Jewish and other victims of the Nazi Holocaust, even though no one making the reparations was part of earlier Nazi governments. Occasionally, U.S. political leaders have recognized a reparations principle in regard to discriminatory action taken against U.S. citizens. Belatedly, the federal government agreed to pay modest reparations to Japanese Americans wrongfully imprisoned in U.S. internment camps during World War II. In 1987 Congress passed a law containing an apology to these Japanese Americans and providing $1.2 billion in concrete reparations for past racial discrimination.

With actions like this in mind, Roy Brooks has argued that to redress its role in the brutal enslavement and segregating of African Americans, the U.S. government must not only provide an official apology but also support that apology with substantial reparations. This is an *atonement* formula: "Apology and reparation—plus forgiveness leads to racial reconciliation." Interestingly, other governments have made strong apologies for involvement in racial oppression, including the apology by the post-war German government to Jews who survived the Holocaust and the apology of the South African government for apartheid. In several cases significant reparations for past government crimes have also been provided. A formal U.S. government apology has begun to "set the record straight" on the impact of slavery and Jim Crow, but only concrete reparations will transform the "rhetoric of the apology into a meaningful, material reality."[94]

Specific Proposals for Reparations

From the earliest days of abolitionist activity in the eighteenth and nineteenth centuries black leaders and their white allies argued that abolition of slavery and citizenship for African Americans were not enough. At an 1865 Republican convention, one white congressional leader, Thaddeus Stevens, called for taking of 400 million acres from former slaveholders and providing that to freed African Americans to work. Another white abolitionist, Senator Charles Sumner (Massachusetts), also called for land grants to those recently enslaved. Legal equality alone would not eradicate the "large disparities of wealth, status, and power."[95] In the years 1866–1867 reparations legislation was brought before Congress, but failed. After the southern oligarchy of former slaveholders resumed control in the 1870s, little was heard on the matter of such compensation for slavery. A century passed, and then since the 1960s civil rights movement the idea of reparations has had a resurgence. Dr. Martin Luther King, Jr. called for significant compensation for slavery, segregation, and contemporary discrimination.[96]

Over recent decades activists, scholars, and a few politicians have developed campaigns for reparations. Thus, in 1994 Nation of Islam leaders petitioned the United Nations for reparations for antiblack racism. In 1992 experts selected by the Organization of African Unity developed a campaign for African reparations from Western countries (for colonialism) like those provided by the German government to Holocaust survivors. In 1996 the British House of Lords had a debate on the impact of slavery on Africa and Africans, with a few members proposing reparations for African countries from colonizing nations. Lord Anthony Gifford defended the idea that international law requires those who commit crimes against humanity, including enslavement, to make reparations to their victims or their descendants. There is no statute of limitations for such crimes against humanity, so the still-harmed contemporary descendants of earlier victims of oppression deserve substantial reparations.[97]

Such a serious debate needs to be held in the U.S. Congress. Every year since 1989 Congressman John Conyers, Jr. (Michigan) has introduced a bill in Congress to set up a commission to investigate the continuing impact of slavery on black Americans and examine the possibility of reparations for slavery and its lasting impact. A key feature of the commission would be to educate the public, especially the white public, on the racist realities of U.S. history. While Conyers has been unable to secure hearings, he has gotten cosponsors and continued to work for public discussion of reparations for systemic racism.[98]

In the case of African Americans, reparations might take several interrelated forms. One type of action would be the gradual transfer of an appropriate amount of compensating wealth from white communities to black communities, a transfer linked to particular remedial goals. The National Coalition of Blacks for Reparations in America has sought $400 million in reparations—not just individual compensation but provision of group programs enabling black communities to prosper collectively. One way to make substantial restitution is to provide well-funded and extensive government support programs, over generations, at local and state levels for upgrading the education, job training, housing opportunities, and incomes of black Americans as individuals. A similar program could provide government resources to significantly upgrade major public facilities, including schools, in all black communities. Other actions would guarantee representative political participation in all local, state, and national legislatures, so that black Americans could have an appropriate voice in government decisions. Such programs would be critical steps in a comprehensive strategy designed to restore African Americans to the place they would have been, had not trillions of dollars in wealth and uncounted other resources been taken from them by means of slavery, Jim Crow segregation, and contemporary discrimination.[99]

Opponents of reparations have argued that there is no money available on such a scale. However, recent government expenditures demonstrate that the issue is not principally the amount of money. The federal government quickly found more than a trillion dollars to bail out private financial and related institutions in the 2008–2010 economic recession, with little difficulty. The government has found trillions for military defense programs and overseas actions later judged to be unnecessary. Given such huge expenditures, the federal government, which was heavily involved in creating and maintaining the slavery and Jim Crow systems, can likely find the substantial amount of money needed to meet this country's moral and restorative obligations to long-oppressed African Americans, Native Americans, and other Americans of color.

Note too that well-planned and well-distributed reparations and other restoration programs may be a better government option than the intentionally limited remedial programs of the past, such as affirmative action, which was initially the creation of white elites responding to civil rights protests. Substantial economic reparations can more easily be seen as direct compensation for great economic damages suffered at the hands of whites over centuries—and not as a government "handout," a common view whites have of current remedial programs.[100]

Building a Real Democracy

Apparently, few white Americans have envisaged for the United States the possibility of a truly just and egalitarian multiracial democracy grounded solidly in respect for a full array of human rights. Certainly, the white founders did not conceive of such a possibility, even in the long run. Nor did later leaders such as Presidents Abraham Lincoln, Woodrow Wilson, Franklin D. Roosevelt, and Dwight D. Eisenhower envision that type of multiracial democratic future. Most contemporary white political leaders also do not seem to have that fully democratic future in mind.

Nonetheless, over the next few decades the dramatic demographic shift toward a U.S. population majority of Americans of color will likely bring much pressure for important societal changes in the direction of expanded democracy. Over coming decades Americans of color will doubtless strive for much greater input into staffing and decisionmaking in white-dominated economic, political, and other institutions. They will have a growing ability to protest racial discrimination and racial inequalities. As the U.S. and the world change demographically and in political-economic ways, whites everywhere will probably face ever-greater pressures to create and participate in sociopolitical systems that move greatly in the direction of being non-racist, socially just, and more egalitarian.

An International Standard for Expanded Rights

As another phase in a comprehensive racial-change strategy, Americans might be pressed to think futuristically in terms of what an authentic multiracial democracy might be like. To evaluate the U.S. system and suggest a replacement, we might begin by drawing on the international rights perspective in the Universal Declaration of Human Rights—a perspective that views every person as having a broad range of basic rights by virtue of being human. The idea that human rights *transcend* the boundaries and authority of any society or government was early articulated by Thomas Jefferson and his fellow revolutionaries. Today, we need to extend this idea well beyond what the elitist white male founders envisioned. The international perspective on human rights was greatly strengthened by the Nuremberg trials of Nazi government officials after World War II. These trials established the principle that "crimes against humanity" are condemned by human principles higher than the norms and laws of any nation-state.[101]

The struggle to deal with the Nazi Holocaust, together with ongoing struggles for human rights by people in many countries—including African Americans in the U.S.—led to this pathbreaking Universal Declaration of Human Rights. It was adopted in 1948 by the United Nations General Assembly. This important international agreement stipulates in Article 1 that "all human beings are born free and equal in dignity and rights," and in Article 7 that "all are equal before the law and are entitled without any discrimination to equal protection of the law." Article 8 further asserts, "Everyone has the right to an effective remedy ... for acts violating the fundamental rights," and Article 25 states that these rights extend to everyday life: "Everyone has the right to a standard of living adequate for the health and well-being of himself and his family, including food, clothing, housing." Since 1948 numerous international covenants on economic, social, and political rights have been signed by most United Nations members, and agencies like the U.N. Commission on Human Rights have been established to monitor human rights globally. Recall that the 1969 U.N. International Convention on the Elimination of All Forms of Racial Discrimination (CERD) requires governments to make illegal the dissemination of racial-superiority ideas and organizations set up to promote discrimination. This convention, first ratified by some nations in the 1960s, was ratified by the United States only in 1994. Today CERD commits the U.S. and other governments to "adopt all necessary measures for speedily eliminating racial discrimination in all its forms and manifestations." These agreements provide some legal support for implementation of the human rights principles of the Universal Declaration of Human Rights. However, top U.S. officials have not yet undertaken to live up to this international obligation to rid the United States of all forms of racial discrimination.[102]

In the 1970s two additional agreements—the International Covenant on Economic, Social and Cultural Rights (ICESCR) and the International Covenant on Civil and Political Rights (ICCPR)—were approved by many countries and added to the Universal Declaration of Human Rights to create an International Bill of Human Rights. While the ICESCR was signed by the U.S. government in 1979, it has *not* yet been ratified by the U.S. Senate. The Senate ratified the ICCPR in 1992, but with 14 reservations, declarations, and understandings—so many that much of that Covenant was thereby invalidated for the United States. Nonetheless, these United Nations covenants represent major international responses to, as Blau and Moncada suggest, "genocide, oppressive labor practices, the antiapartheid movement, national independence movements, liberation movements of colonized people, and atrocities committed against civilians" and to the "civil rights movement in America, the feminist movement, and the newly empowered voices of indigenous groups and landless peasants."[103] Even without full U.S. participation, these agreements signal a very important and increasing international consensus on the human rights necessary for a healthy society.

International Pressure for Change

Since its adoption the Universal Declaration of Human Rights (UDHR) has been used in crafting international agreements, and provisions have become part of international law. Originally implemented to spell out the meaning of "human rights" and "fundamental freedoms" in the U.N. Charter, it is binding on countries like the United States that became U.N. members. Legal scholars view this document as the "foundational international instrument of the human rights movement."[104] Most international documents on human rights at least allude to this important declaration. Court systems in numerous nations have cited the declaration—on occasion in overturning patterns of discrimination. At least 69 national constitutions take note of the UDHR.[105]

U.S. judges and other government officials have made much less use of the declaration than those in other countries. Indeed, much of the U.S. judicial and political leadership has been lacking in commitment to much of the international human-rights perspective. Louis Henkin, a leading international legal scholar, has noted that the U.S. government "has not been a pillar of human rights, but a 'flying buttress'—supporting them from the outside, but declining itself to accept the obligations of the human rights regime."[106] One of the ironies of U.S. constitutional history is that for some years countries with emerging democracies often drew on the U.S. Constitution and its rights tradition as a model for their constitutions, yet in recent decades this has no longer been the case. One recent legal analysis shows that the United States is today "increasingly out of sync with an evolving global consensus on issues of human rights."[107] Instead, numerous countries are looking to the rights-related provisions of international human rights documents and other constitutional documents, such as the Canadian Charter of Rights and Freedoms, for human rights models.

The comprehensive human rights perspective expressed in these U.N. documents draws not only on progressive human rights traditions of Europeans but also from the human rights perspectives of Native, African, Latino, and Asian Americans, and of other peoples around the globe. U.N. human rights agreements strongly affirm that human beings have rights independent of particular governments and press governments to incorporate fundamental human rights into everyday operations. They provide an internationally legitimated standard that can be used to judge systemic racism everywhere, including in the United States. As noted above, they can be the basis for significant discussion if the United States has a new democratic constitutional convention. Implementing this egalitarian standard of human interaction by new institutionalized arrangements to effect real democracy could dramatically restructure or eliminate current racist institutions in the United States.

Major change away from our racist institutions will require much more than one-way integration of racially subordinated people into existing white-dominated institutions. A multifaceted restructuring, mutual integration, and mutual adaptation are critical—among European Americans, African Americans, and all other Americans of color. Dr. Martin Luther King, Jr. once spoke of the movement of African Americans to be "creative dissenters who will call our beloved nation to a higher destiny," and not just to seek to integrate "into existing values of American society."[108] A democratically restructured society will require new human rights commitments, which could lead to this higher societal destiny.

Certain human needs seem universal: the need for personal self-respect, for substantial control over one's life, for significant group self-management, and for access to life's material necessities. Significantly, the U.S. Constitution has no economic bill of rights, even though civil rights and labor leaders have pressed to expand U.S. rights in this direction since the 1960s. Conservative interests have fought any such expansion. Significantly, in his 1944 State of the Union address, the revered World War II era president Franklin D. Roosevelt did press for such an "Economic Bill of Rights."[109] Roosevelt conceived of an expanded bill of rights that would include economic and social rights for all regardless of race, class, or religion. In a complete democracy, as he stated the matter, there would need to be full respect for the diversity of individuals, communities, and cultures.

Links with Other Antioppression Efforts

Ultimately, a truly robust democracy is impossible without an elimination of major types of human oppression. Significant destruction of systemic racism, once begun, is likely to be corrosive of other types of oppression. In this relatively short book, even as I have tried to dig deeply into one major type of oppression, I have periodically discussed, albeit too briefly, connections between racial, class, and gender oppressions. Numerous scholars and activists have noted interconnections between these types of oppression. Sandra Harding has argued that "We should think of race, class and gender as interlocking; one cannot dislodge one piece without disturbing the others."[110] Not only racist structures, but capitalistic, sexist, heterosexist, ageist, and bureaucratic–authoritarian arrangements will have to be dismantled in this country if the lives of individuals and the functioning of communities are to be truly democratic and rid of antihuman oppression. Historically, Marxist analysis and activism have played perhaps the greatest role in generating protest movements against oppression over the last century. Labor movements, many inspired by Marxist class analysis, have brought improvements to the lives of workers in numerous countries. Labor progressives have long argued that a full-fledged economic democracy is a requisite step in destroying the class structures of economic oppression.[111]

Historically, there are strong similarities and linkages between antiracist struggles and class struggles in the United States. Ordinary workers, including white workers, are still greatly exploited by the capitalist class. White and other workers usually have little role in how their workplaces are run, and always have little role in how the general capitalistic economy operates. However, as we have seen in earlier chapters, the white elite has worked hard to secure the acceptance of the existing racial and class hierarchies by white workers by offering them the "public and psychological wage of whiteness." As a result, white workers as a group have had more socioeconomic privileges and opportunities than black workers and many other workers of color. A successful antiracist coalition across the color line will need to deal with the majority of white workers' commitments to white racial framing, privileges, and practices. Ultimately, many aspects of societal oppression will have to be dealt with, including not only antiblack and other racist framing and actions among white male and female workers but also sexist framing and actions among men and heterosexist framing and actions among heterosexual Americans.[112]

There are still multiple societal oppressions, and no one analysis can adequately deal with most or all of these major oppressions. The research evidence I have presented throughout this book shows unmistakably that systemic racism remains central to the U.S. foundation. A better and comprehensive understanding of this racism's history, framing, character, operation, and maintenance is essential to making sense of this society generally and to destroying persisting racial oppression. Having set this task, by no means do I downplay the importance of analyzing and eradicating the other types of oppression central to U.S. society, including class exploitation, sexism, and heterosexism.

Over the last century there has been some conflict between those in one group struggling against a particular type of societal oppression and those in another group contending against yet other societal oppression, and so far there has been relatively little joining together in more general antioppression efforts and coalitions. Yet at the heart of each of these societal movements for change seem to be certain paramount issues that can be accented by all those seeking to build successful coalitions. Perhaps the most important idea held in common is that of ridding the society of oppressive domination by one group over another, together with the related idea of meaningful democracy and self-determination to the fullest extent possible for every group. With great effort in organizing, perhaps this shared vision of a country ultimately free of such societal oppression can be used to build successful intergroup coalitions.

Conclusion

Antiracism is more than a theoretical framework organizing, explaining, and interpreting the realities of systemic racism. Now and in the past, active antiracism has encompassed an array of individual and group strategies to eradicate individual and systemic racism. Many have studied racial oppression, but the point is to eradicate it.

The eradication of systemic racism requires more than removing a few racial inequalities. Steps in the direction of removing discrimination and inequalities are very important and improve people's lives. However, a substantial reduction in, or full eradication of, systemic racism will require uprooting and replacing the existing hierarchy of racialized power and privilege. A developed antiracist strategy will need to move beyond reforms in current institutions to complete elimination of existing systems of racialized power.[113]

Historically, sooner or later, oppression leads to conflict, and major conflict frequently leads to significant change. Most progressive developments in human rights in U.S. and global history have come after large-scale protests, people's movements, civil disobedience, open conflict, and/or societal revolutions. Theorists and activists committed to an antiracist, liberty-and-justice framing of society cannot prove there will be societal change again, but can act on the assumption it is likely.

Why should whites support major changes in the racist system? One reason is general but essential: Whites have a moral obligation to take action, as individuals and as a group, to overturn the oppressive and systemic racism they and their ancestors have created, and make meaningful the liberty-and-justice framing of society they often loudly proclaim. Indeed, the activist-scholar Paulo Freire has argued that not only are those who are oppressed significantly dehumanized, but also those doing the oppression have dehumanized *themselves* and blocked a society's path to social justice and greater humanization of all.[114]

There are also practical, small-scale benefits for whites as individuals. One study of 50 white students found that interracial interactions were especially difficult for those with strong prejudices. Interactions with people of other racial groups resulted in very prejudiced whites being more likely than other whites to perform poorly on color/word-matching tasks.[115] Educational efforts that break down an individual's racist framing and its prejudices may give him or her better interactive skills in interracial interactions in an ever-diversifying United States.

There are significant group advantages. Systemic racism has created major racial inequalities in education and job skills, which affect not only those racially subordinated but the country as a whole. Brookings Institution analysts have noted that racial disparities in educational attainment do not just affect certain Americans of color, but greatly threaten the country's "future economic growth, as well as the broader promise of upward mobility in American society."[116] In a situation where highly educated workers are badly needed, society benefits when more people gain strong "human capital." Some years ago, the brilliant social scientist, W. E. B. Du Bois, argued that systems of oppression that exclude some people miss out on "vast stores" of human wisdom. When Americans of color are oppressed in this country's institutions, not only do they suffer greatly, but the white-controlled institutions and whites within them often suffer significantly if unknowingly. Excluding Americans of color has meant excluding much knowledge, creativity, and understanding from society generally. A society that ignores great stores of human knowledge and ability irresponsibly risks its future. This problem can regularly be seen in white policymakers' often poor decisions on many domestic issues, as well as in their frequently poor decisions about U.S. foreign policy, such as ill-advised military invasions overseas.[117]

If there is no real societal change in the near future, pressures for change will increase dramatically as whites become an ever-smaller minority of the population over the twenty-first century. As Abraham Lincoln once predicted, a "house divided against itself cannot stand." At the time, Lincoln's metaphor accented the centrality and contradictions of slavery. We can extend it to the reality of a country still inegalitarian and racially divided because of "slavery unwilling to die." The question hanging over white Americans is this: do they wish to face increased societal conflicts for themselves, their children, or their grandchildren? During the 1960s civil rights movements numerous leaders of color and a few white leaders pointed out that without social justice there can be no lasting public order. Without social justice the United States will never achieve a truly democratic and stable social order.

African Americans remain at the center of the system of racial oppression, and their antiracist counter-framing and consciousness have substantial potential for continuing challenges to our racist order. Fortunately for U.S. progress on multiracial democracy, African Americans have developed large-scale change movements a few times in history, and smaller-scale movements numerous times, and there will doubtless be more such movements in the future. As a group, African Americans have not retreated to an enervating pessimism but have slowly pressed onward. Many continue to participate in civil rights, civic, and religious organizations working to eradicate racism, to get civil rights laws enforced, and to secure better living conditions for all Americans. Historically, this country has seen periods when black American protests have changed what the white elites and public see as in their own best interests.[118] This was true during the abolitionist period from the 1830s to the 1860s and again during the civil rights movements and rioting of the period from the 1950s to the early 1970s. Perhaps it can be so again.

In addition, the major efforts of African Americans to free themselves from societal oppression have often stimulated other Americans of color to do the same. Inspired by black efforts, or acting on their own, the latter have frequently reacted strongly to the white discrimination that targets them. Today, there are numerous antiracist and civil rights groups, including the American Indian Movement, the Mexican American Legal Defense and Education Fund, the Puerto Rican Legal Defense Fund, the Japanese American Citizens League, the Asian American Legal Defense Fund, and the Organization of Chinese Americans. These and other similar groups are working now for change in systemic racism. To take just one example, today Native American activists are organizing local protest movements and fighting numerous legal battles to force the federal government to honor its hundreds of legal treaties. Moreover, the groups listed above are joined by an array of other organizations pressing for social justice, including women's rights organizations and GLBT organizations. One major challenge for U.S. progressives today is to build united coalitions against the numerous types of long-established oppression.

The world of which the U.S. is but one part is dramatically changing. Numerous social contradictions have emerged out of the global racial order originally created to legitimate the imperialistic aspirations and colonial expansion of European countries. These international dynamics created social and political structures that, then as now, have created and imbedded a strong racist framing with its negative images and ideologies of recurring racial subordination. International relations, global markets, global financial institutions, and multinational corporations—along with shifts in new technologies—are all racialized, with white perspectives and the European and U.S. corporate class usually at their core. For centuries Eurocentric institutions have been globalizing, dominant, and resistant to change. Today, however, there is substantial ferment against social oppressions across the globe. Over the next century neither the U.S. nor the world is likely to stay the same. Over that century many groups and countries will likely move farther out from under the often racialized dominance of white Americans and Europeans. People of color and those who question oppression everywhere are regularly organizing for change. In recent years we have seen strong antiracism movements in South Africa and Brazil, and progressive movements by workers of color and others in numerous countries such as South Africa, Brazil, Venezuela, China, and Nigeria. In numerous European countries, racially oppressed groups are protesting systemic racism there as well.

Today, people of African descent remain the globe's largest racially oppressed group, a group now resident in many countries. In the 1980s and 1990s we saw a systemically racist society, the multiracial Republic of South Africa, move from white to black political control and begin to change the rest of its social and economic structure of racism (apartheid). Few analysts predicted such a sea change, and even though South Africa still faces serious challenges before it attains full political and economic democracy, it has changed faster than many had predicted. The possibility of a global democratic order rid of white racism remains only a dream, but the South African revolution shows that it is a powerful dream. More changes in the world's racist system will likely come as the human spirit conquers continuing realities of oppression, however daunting they may be. The chair of the Special United Nations Committee against Apartheid once expressed this futuristic hope: The "world can never be governed by force, never by fear, never by power. In the end what governs is the spirit and what conquers is the mind."[119]

Notes

Preface

1 Janet Kornblum, "Richards: 'I Lost My Temper Onstage,'" *USA Today*, November 20, 2006, www.usatoday.com/life/people/2006–11–20-michael-richards_x.htm (accessed September 4, 2009); Allen Salkin, "Comedy on the Hot Seat," *New York Times*, December 3, 2006, www.nytimes.com/2006/12/03/fashion/03comedy.html (accessed September 4, 2009).

2 "Imus Called Women's Basketball Team 'Nappy-headed Hos,'" *MediaMatters*, April 7, 2007, http://mediamatters.org/items/200704040011 (accessed November 7, 2008); on surveys, see "Race and Ethnicity," www.pollingreport.com/race.htm (accessed February 27, 2009).

3 Jane H. Hill, *The Everyday Language of White Racism* (Malden, MA: Wiley-Blackwell, 2008), pp. 134–157.

4 Paul M. Sniderman and Thomas Piazza, *The Scar of Race* (Cambridge, MA: Harvard University Press, 1993), pp. 175; Dinesh D'Souza, *The End of Racism: Principles for a Multiracial Society* (New York: Free Press, 1995), pp. 70–87.

5 "President-Elect Obama: the Voters Rebuke Republicans for Economic Failure," *Wall Street Journal*, November 5, 2008, http://online.wsj.com/article/SB122586244657800863.html (accessed December 28, 2008).

6 C. L. R. James, *American Civilization*, ed. Anna Grimshaw and Keith Hart (Cambridge, MA: Blackwell, 1993), p. 201.

7 James Madison, quoted in Michael P. Rogin, *Fathers and Children: Andrew Jackson and the Subjugation of the American Indian* (New York: Knopf, 1975), p. 319.

8 See Hope Yen, "Rise of Latino Population Blurs US Racial Lines." *The Olympian*, March 17, www.theolympian.com/2013/03/17/2465772/rise-of-latino-population-blurs.html (accessed March 18, 2013).

9 On international human rights, see Ron Schmidt, *Language Policy and Identity in the United States* (Philadelphia: Temple University Press, 2000); and Will Kymlicka, *Contemporary Political Philosophy: An Introduction*, 2nd edn. (Oxford: Oxford University Press, 2001).

1 Systemic Racism: A Comprehensive Perspective

1 National Archives and Records Administration, *Framers of the Constitution* (Washington, DC: National Archives Trust Fund Board, 1986).

2 Max Farrand, ed., *Records of the Federal Convention of 1787*, vol. 1 (New Haven, CT: Yale University Press, 1911), p. 486.

3 Herbert Aptheker, *Early Years of the Republic: From the End of the Revolution to the First Administration of Washington (1783–1793)* (New York: International Publishers, 1976), pp. 74–95.

4 Ibid., pp. 55–57.

320 · Notes

5 William Lee Miller, *Arguing about Slavery: The Great Battle in the United States Congress* (New York: Knopf, 1996), p. 21.

6 Farrand, *Records*, vol. 1, 587; William M. Wiecek, *The Sources of Antislavery Constitutionalism in America, 1760–1848* (Ithaca, NY: Cornell University Press, 1977), p. 15.

7 James Madison, Alexander Hamilton, and John Jay, *The Federalist Papers*, ed. Isaac Kramnick (New York: Viking Penguin, 1987). This quote is from number 54, italics added.

8 James Madison, quoted in Michael P. Rogin, *Fathers and Children: Andrew Jackson and the Subjugation of the American Indian* (New York: Knopf, 1975), p. 319. See also Paul Jennings, "A Colored Man's Reminiscences of James Madison," *White House History* 1 (1983): 46–51.

9 W. E. B. Du Bois, *The Suppression of the African Slave Trade to the United States of America, 1638–1870* (New York: Schocken Books, 1969), pp. 54–62; Donald Robinson, *Slavery in the Structure of American Politics* (New York: Norton, 1979), p. 71.

10 Robert A. Rutland, ed., *The Papers of George Mason: 1725–1792*, vol. 3 (Chapel Hill: University of North Carolina Press, 1970), pp. 965–966.

11 Paul Finkelman, "Slavery and the Constitutional Convention," in *Beyond Confederation: Origins of the Constitution and American National Identity*, eds. Richard Beeman, Stephen Botein, and Edward C. Carter (Chapel Hill: University of North Carolina Press, 1987), p. 225.

12 Aptheker, *Early Years of the Republic*, p. 93.

13 Donald E. Lively, *The Constitution and Race* (New York: Praeger, 1992), pp. 4–5. Lively draws on research by William M. Wiecek.

14 F. Nwabueze Okoye, "Chattel Slavery as the Nightmare of the American Revolutionaries," *William and Mary Quarterly 37* (January 1980): 13.

15 John Dickinson, *Letters from a Farmer in Pennsylvania to the Inhabitants of the British Colonies* (Philadelphia, 1768), p. 38, quoted in Okoye, "Chattel Slavery as the Nightmare of the American Revolutionaries," p. 3. Emphasis in original.

16 Benjamin B. Ringer, *"We the People" and Others* (New York: Tavistock, 1983), pp. 130–131.

17 Quotes are from William Lloyd Garrison, "A Compact with Hell," in *The United States Constitution*, eds. Bertell Ollman and Jonathan Birnbaum (New York: New York University Press, 1990), p. 96.

18 Dennis Cauchon, "For Founding Fathers, Slave Ownership Common; Practice Went Unquestioned by Many Admired Historical Figures," *USA Today*, March 9, 1998, p. 8A.

19 Herbert Aptheker, *The Unfolding Drama: Studies in U.S. History*, ed. Bettina Aptheker (New York: International Publishers, 1978), p. 100.

20 William M. Wiecek, "The Origins of the Law of Slavery in British North America," *Cardozo Law Review* 17 (May 1996): 1791.

21 "1000 Commemorate One Va. Man's Freeing of Slaves 72 Years Early," *Marietta Times*, July 29, 1991, p. A1; Andrew Levy, *The First Emancipator: Slavery, Religion, and the Quiet Revolution of Robert Carter* (New York: Random House, 2007).

22 Aptheker, *Early Years of the Republic*, p. 93.

23 W. E. B. Du Bois, *The World and Africa* (New York: International Publishers, 1965 [1946]), p. 23.

24 Frederick Douglass, "The Color Line," *North American Review* (June 1881), as excerpted in *Jones et ux. v. Alfred H. Mayer Co.*, 392 U.S. 409, 446–47 (1968). Emphasis added.

25 W. E. B. Du Bois, *Darkwater* (1920), as reprinted in *The Oxford W. E. B. Du Bois Reader*, ed. Eric J. Sundquist (New York: Oxford, 1996), p. 504.

26 Ida B. Wells-Barnett, *The Red Record: Tabulated Statistics and Alleged Causes of Lynching in the United States* (published by author, 1895), Kindle loc. 1361–1364. The short phrases are from Ida B. Wells-Barnett, *A Red Record*, in Patricia Madoo Lengermann and Jill Niebrugge-Brantley, eds., *The Women Founders: Sociology and Social Theory, 1830–1930* (New York: McGraw-Hill, 1998), p. 177. I am influenced here by Tommy J.

Curry, "The Fortune of Wells: Ida B. Wells-Barnett's Use of T. Thomas Fortune's Philosophy of Social Agitation as a Prolegomenon to Militant Civil Rights Activism," *Transactions of the Charles S. Peirce Society* 48 (2012): 456–482.

27 Oliver C. Cox, *Caste, Class, and Race* (Garden City, NJ: Doubleday, 1948), p. 344.

28 Kwame Ture [Stokely Carmichael] and Charles V. Hamilton, *Black Power: The Politics of Liberation in America* (New York: Vintage, 1967). See also Bob Blauner, *Racial Oppression in America* (New York: Harper and Row, 1972).

29 Du Bois, *The World and Africa*, p. 37.

30 See Theodore Cross, *The Black Power Imperative: Racial Inequality and the Politics of Nonviolence* (New York: Faulkner, 1984), p. 510; Patricia Williams, *The Alchemy of Race and Rights* (Cambridge, MA: Harvard University Press, 1991), p. 101; Ian Ayres and Fredrick E. Vars, "When Does Private Discrimination Justify Public Affirmative Action?" *Columbia Law Review* 98 (November 1998): 1598–1610; Richard Delgado, *The Coming Race War?* (New York: New York University Press, 1996), pp. 104–105.

31 James A. Ballentine, *Ballentine's Law Dictionary*, ed. William S. Anderson, 3rd edn. (San Francisco: Bancroft-Whiteney, 1969), p. 1320.

32 "Abraham Lincoln's Second Inaugural Address," wikisource, http://en.wikisource.org/wiki/Abraham_Lincoln%27s_Second_Inaugural_Address (accessed July 1, 2009).

33 Philomena Essed, *Understanding Everyday Racism* (Newbury Park, CA: Sage, 1991), p. 37; Bertell Ollman, *Alienation: Marx's Conception of Man in Capitalist Society*, 2nd edn. (Cambridge: Cambridge University Press, 1976).

34 I am influenced here by Catharine A. MacKinnon, *Toward a Feminist Theory of the State* (Cambridge, MA: Harvard University Press, 1989), pp. 3–5.

35 Melvin M. Leiman, *The Political Economy of Racism: A History* (London: Pluto Press, 1993); William Julius Wilson, *The Declining Significance of Race: Blacks and Changing American Institutions* (Chicago: University of Chicago Press, 1978); Jim Sleeper, *The Closest of Strangers: Liberalism and the Politics of Race in New York* (New York: Norton, 1990); William Julius Wilson, *More Than Just Race: Being Black and Poor in the Inner City* (New York: W. W. Norton, 2009).

36 Michael Omi and Howard Winant, *Racial Formation in the United States: From the 1960s to the 1990s*, 2nd edn. (New York: Routledge, 1994), p. 48.

37 Robert Miles, *Racism* (London: Routledge, 1989). For detailed critical analysis of formation theory, see Joe R. Feagin and Sean Elias, "Rethinking Racial Formation Theory: A Systemic Racism Critique, *Ethnic and Racial Studies* 36 (2012): 1–30.

38 Jorge Klor de Alva, Earl Shorris, and Cornel West, "Our Next Race Question: The Uneasiness Between Blacks and Latinos," in *Critical White Studies: Looking Behind the Mirror*, eds. Richard Delgado and Jean Stefancic (Philadelphia: Temple University Press, 1997), p. 485.

39 Dole comments on *Meet the Press*, NBC Television, February 5, 1995.

40 I am indebted to Sidney Willhelm for discussion here.

41 Iris Young, *Justice and the Politics of Difference* (Princeton, NJ: Princeton University Press, 1990), p. 52.

42 Bureau of Labor Statistics, *Labor Force Characteristics by Race and Ethnicity, 2011* (Washington, DC: U.S. Department of Labor, 2012), pp. 1–4.

43 Personal email communication, July 11, 2013. See Jennifer C. Mueller, "The Social Reproduction of Systemic Racial Inequality," unpublished PhD dissertation, Texas A&M University, 2013.

44 Signe-Mary McKernan, Caroline Ratcliffe, Eugene Steuerle, and Sisi Zhang, *Less than Equal: Racial Disparities in Wealth Accumulation* (Washington, DC: Urban Institute, 2013), p. 5.

45 Joe R. Feagin and Clairece Y. Feagin, *Racial and Ethnic Relations*, 9th edn. (Upper Saddle River, NJ: Prentice Hall, 2011), Chapters 3–4; Karen Brodkin, *How the Jews Became White Folks: And What that Says about Race in America* (New Brunswick, NJ: Rutgers University Press, 1998).

46 Edward Ball, *Slaves in the Family* (New York: Ballantine Books, 1999), p. 14.

47 Martin J. Katz, "The Economics of Discrimination: The Three Fallacies of Croson," *Yale Law Journal* 100 (January 1991): 1041–1044; Melvin L. Oliver and Thomas M. Shapiro, "Creating an Opportunity Society," *American Prospect* 18 (May 2007), pp. A27–A28.

48 Jeffrey M. Timberlake, "Racial and Ethnic Inequality in the Duration of Children's Exposure to Neighborhood Poverty and Affluence," *Social Problems* 54 (August 2007): 319–342.

49 Joe R. Feagin, Kevin Early, and Karyn D. McKinney, "The Many Costs of Discrimination," unpublished paper, University of Florida, 1999.

50 W. E. B. Du Bois, *Black Reconstruction in America 1860–1880* (New York: Atheneum, 1992 [1935]), p. 700.

51 Theodore Allen, *The Invention of the White Race: Racial Oppression and Social Control* (London: Verso, 1994), pp. 19–21.

52 Ibid., p. 143; Du Bois, *Black Reconstruction in America 1860–1880*, p. 27.

53 Louise Michele Newman, *White Women's Rights: The Racial Origins of Feminism in the United States* (New York: Oxford University Press, 1999), pp. 179–185; bell hooks, *Feminist Theory: From Margin to Center* (Boston: South End Press, 1984), pp. 6–51.

54 Joe R. Feagin, *The White Racial Frame: Centuries of Racial Framing and Counter-Framing*, 2nd. edn. (New York: Routledge, 2013).

55 Leslie Houts Picca and Joe R. Feagin, *Two Faced Racism: Whites in the Backstage and Frontstage* (New York: Routledge, 2007), pp. 5–6.

56 Du Bois, *Darkwater* (1920), as reprinted in *The Oxford W. E. B. Du Bois Reader*, pp. 497–498.

57 See Ronald T. Takaki, *Iron Cages: Race and Culture in Nineteenth Century America* (New York: Oxford University Press, 1990), pp. 4–15.

58 Benjamin Franklin, "Observations Concerning the Increase of Mankind, Peopling of Countries, Etc." (1751), as quoted in *Benjamin Franklin: A Biography in His Own Words*, ed. Thomas Fleming (New York: Harper and Row, 1972), pp. 105–106. I use modern capitalization.

59 See Robert S. Feldman, *Social Psychology* (Englewood Cliffs, NJ: Prentice Hall, 1995), p. 94.

60 Oliver C. Cox, *Elements and Social Dynamics* (Detroit: Wayne University Press, 1976), pp. xxxi, 393.

2 Slavery Unwilling to Die: The Historical Development of Systemic Racism

1 "Charles Joyner on the Middle Passage," PBS, www.pbs.org/wgbh/aia/part1/1i3067. html (accessed July 6, 2009).

2 United Nations, "Convention on the Prevention and Punishment of Genocide," *The United Nations and Human Rights, 1945–1995* (New York: United Nations Department of Public Information, 1995), p. 151.

3 David E. Stannard, *The American Holocaust: Columbus and the Conquest of the New World* (New York: Oxford University Press, 1992); Charles W. Mills, *The Racial Contract* (Ithaca, NY: Cornell University Press, 1997), pp. 98, 155.

4 William T. Hagan, *American Indians* (Chicago: University of Chicago Press, 1961), p. 14. See also pp. 12–15. An earlier version of this is in Joe R. Feagin and Clairece B. Feagin, *Racial and Ethnic Relations*, 9th edn. (Upper Saddle River, NJ: Prentice Hall, 2011), chapters 7 and 8.

5 They are quoted in Michael P. Rogin, *Fathers and Children: Andrew Jackson and the Subjugation of the American Indian* (New York: Knopf, 1975), p. 319; Winthrop D. Jordan, *White Over Black: American Attitudes Toward the Negro, 1550–1812* (Chapel Hill: University of North Carolina Press, 1968), pp. 239–241.

6 Benjamin B. Ringer, *"We the People" and Others* (New York: Tavistock, 1983), pp. 134–138.

7 *Dred Scott v. John F. A. Sandford*, 60 U.S. 393, 403–404, 408 (1857).

8 Ringer, *"We the People" and Others*, p. 36.
9 Robin Blackburn, *The Making of New World Slavery: From the Baroque to the Modern, 1492–1800* (London: Verso, 1997), p. 10.
10 A. Leon Higginbotham, Jr., *Shades of Freedom: Racial Politics and the Presumptions of the American Legal Process* (New York: Oxford University Press, 1996), pp. 14–51.
11 Forrest G. Wood, *The Arrogance of Faith: Christianity and Race in America from the Colonial Era to the Twentieth Century* (New York: Knopf, 1990), p. xviii.
12 Higginbotham, *Shades of Freedom*, p. xxiii; Lawrence M. Friedman, *A History of American Law* (New York: Simon & Schuster, 1973), pp. 72–76, 192–200; Herbert Aptheker, *American Negro Slave Revolts* (New York: International Publishers, 1943), pp. 53–78.
13 Thomas Jefferson, as quoted in Peter M. Bergman, *The Chronological History of the Negro in America* (New York: Harper & Row, 1969), p. 52.
14 Walter Johnson, "Slavery, Reparations, and the Mythic March of Freedom," *Raritan* 27 (2007): 41–67; M'Baye Gueye, "A Continent of Fear," *UNESCO Courier* 47 (1994): 16. On numbers, see Philip D. Curtin, *The African Slave Trade: A Census* (Madison: University of Wisconsin Press, 1968); Joseph E. Inikori, ed., *Forced Migration* (New York: Africana Publishing, 1982), pp. 19–33.
15 Blackburn, *The Making of New World Slavery*, p. 19; Herbert Aptheker, *The Colonial Era* (New York: International Publishers, 1959), pp. 18–39.
16 Ronald Segal, *The Black Diaspora* (New York: Farrar, Straus and Giroux, 1995), pp. 58–59; Kenneth S. Greenberg, (Princeton, NJ: Princeton University Press, 1996).
17 Peter J. Parish, *Slavery: History and Historians* (New York: Harper and Row, 1989), p. 129; see also pp. 126–132.
18 Elizabeth Fox-Genovese, *Within the Plantation Household: Black and White Women of the Old South* (Chapel Hill: University of North Carolina Press, 1988), p. 24.
19 See Kenneth Stampp, *The Peculiar Institution: Slavery in the Ante-Bellum South* (New York: Vintage Books, 1956); Robert W. Roel and Stanley Engerman, *Time on the Cross: The Economics of American Negro Slavery* (Boston: Little, Brown, 1974).
20 Lorenzo J. Greene, *The Negro in Colonial New England* (New York: Atheneum, 1969), pp. 68–69.
21 Ronald Bailey, "The Other Side of Slavery," *Agricultural History* 68 (spring 1994): 36.
22 James W. Loewen, *Lies My Teacher Told Me: Everything Your American History Textbook Got Wrong* (New York: The New Press, 1995), p. 135.
23 A. Leon Higginbotham, Jr., *In the Matter of Color* (New York: Oxford University Press, 1978), pp. 63–70, 144–149. An earlier discussion is in Joe R. Feagin, "Slavery Unwilling to Die: The Background of Black Oppression in the 1980s," *Journal of Black Studies* 17 (December 1986): 173–200. See also Ringer, *"We the People" and Others*, p. 533.
24 Olaudah Equiano, "The Interesting Narrative of the Life of Olaudah Equiano," in *Afro-American History*, ed. Thomas R. Frazier (New York: Harcourt, Brace & World, 1970), pp. 18–20. There is debate on the Equiano biography, but not Middle Passage conditions. See Adam Hochschild, *Bury the Chains: Prophets and Rebels in the Fight to Free an Empire's Slaves* (Boston: Houghton Mifflin, 2006).
25 Stephanie Smallwood, *Saltwater Slavery* (Cambridge, MA: Harvard University Press, 2007), p. 68.
26 William Wells Brown, *From Fugitive Slave to Free Man*, ed. William L. Andrews (New York: Mentor Books, 1993 [1847]), p. 30.
27 See T. Lindsay Baker and Julie P. Baker, eds., *The WPA Oklahoma Slave Narratives* (Norman: University of Oklahoma Press, 1996).
28 David Brown and Clive Webb, *Race in the American South: from Slavery to Civil Rights* (Gainesville: University of Florida Press, 2007), p. 138. See also Patricia Morton, "Introduction," in *Discovering the Women in Slavery*, ed. Patricia Morton (Athens: University of Georgia Press, 1996), pp. 7–8.
29 Patricia J. Williams, *The Alchemy of Race and Rights* (Cambridge, MA: Harvard University Press, 1991), pp. 154–156.

30 Melton A. McLaurin, *Celia: A Slave* (Athens: University of Georgia Press, 1991).
31 Hemings was half-sister of Jefferson's wife. Jerry Fresia, *Toward an American Revolution: Exposing the Constitution and Other Illusions* (Boston: South End, 1988), pp. 1–2; Dinitia Smith and Nicholas Wade, "DNA Evidence Links Thomas Jefferson to Slave's Offspring," *Gainesville Sun*, November 1, 1998, p. 4A; Henry Wiencek, *Master of the Mountain: Thomas Jefferson and His Slaves* (New York: Farrar, Straus, & Giroux, 2012), pp. 2–20 and passim.
32 James Parton, quoted in Paul Finkelman, *Slavery and the Founders: Race and Liberty in the Age of Jefferson* (Armonk, NY: M. E. Sharpe, 1996), p. 143.
33 Jordan, *White Over Black*, p. 153.
34 S. E. Anderson, *The Black Holocaust* (New York: Writers and Readers Press, 1995), pp. 156–158.
35 I am indebted here to discussions with Holly Hanson. See John Thornton, *Africa and Africans in the Making of the Atlantic World, 1400–1680* (New York: Cambridge University Press, 1992), pp. 5–9; Molefi Kete Asante, "The Wonders of Africa," post to Discussion List for African American Studies (H-Afro-Am), November 1999.
36 W. E. B. Du Bois, *Darkwater* (1920), as reprinted in *The Oxford W. E. B. Du Bois Reader*, ed. Eric J. Sundquist (New York: Oxford, 1996), p. 504.
37 W. E. B. Du Bois, *Black Reconstruction in America 1860–1880* (New York: Atheneum, 1992 [1935]), p. 10.
38 See John Willinsky, *Learning to Divide the World: Education at Empire's End* (Minneapolis: University of Minnesota Press, 1998), p. 191.
39 Rafael Tammariello, "The Slave Trade," *Las Vegas Review-Journal* (February 8, 1998): 1E.
40 J. H. Parry and P. M. Sherlock, *A Short History of the West Indies*, 3rd edn. (New York: St. Martin's Press, 1971), pp. 110–111. See also William M. Wiecek, *The Sources of Antislavery Constitutionalism in America, 1760–1848* (Ithaca, NY: Cornell University Press, 1977), pp. 15–16.
41 William M. Wiecek, "The Origins of the Law of Slavery in British North America," *Cardozo Law Review* 17 (May 1996): 1739; Eric Williams, *Capitalism and Slavery* (Chapel Hill: University of North Carolina Press, 1994 [1944]), pp. 98–107; Douglass C. North, *The Economic Growth of the United States, 1790–1860* (Englewood Cliffs, NJ: Prentice Hall, 1961), pp. 38–45; Blackburn, *The Making of New World Slavery*, chapter 12; Anderson, *The Black Holocaust*, p. 19; Barbara L. Solow and Stanley L. Engerman, "British Capitalism and Caribbean Slavery: The Legacy of Eric Williams: An Introduction," in *British Capitalism and Caribbean Slavery: The Legacy of Eric Williams* (Cambridge: Cambridge University Press, 1987), pp. 8–9.
42 Williams, *Capitalism and Slavery*, p. 52. See also Wilson E. Williams, *Africa and the Rise of Capitalism* (New York: AMS Press, 1975 [1938]), pp. 23–25.
43 Solow and Engerman, "British Capitalism and Caribbean Slavery," pp. 5–7; Ronald Bailey, "'Those Valuable People, the Africans,'" in *The Meaning of Slavery in the North*, eds. David Roediger and Martin H. Blatt (New York: Garland, 1988), p. 11.
44 Fred Bateman and Thomas Weiss, *A Deplorable Scarcity: The Failure of Industrialization in the Slave Economy* (Chapel Hill: University of North Carolina Press, 1981); Stanley Lebergott, *The Americans: An Economic Record* (New York: Norton, 1984); Robert S. Browne, "Achieving Parity Through Reparations," in *The Wealth of Races: The Present Value of Benefits from Past Injustices*, ed. Richard F. America (New York: Greenwood Press, 1990), pp. 201–202.
45 North, *The Economic Growth of the United States, 1790–1860*, p. 63.
46 Bailey, "'Those Valuable People, the Africans,'" p. 14; see also p. 19. I draw here on North, *The Economic Growth of the United States, 1790–1860*, p. 63; and Ronald T. Takaki, *Iron Cages: Race and Culture in Nineteenth-Century America* (New York: Oxford University Press, 1990), p. 78.
47 North, *The Economic Growth of the United States, 1790–1860*, p. 41; Takaki, *Iron Cages*, p. 77; Browne, "Achieving Parity Through Reparations," p. 201; Segal, *The Black Diaspora*, pp. 56–58.

48 Ali A. Mazrui, "Who Should Pay for Slavery? Reparations to Africa," *World Press Review* 8 (August 1993): 22. I also draw on North, *The Economic Growth of the United States, 1790–1860*, p. 122.

49 Herbert Aptheker, *The Unfolding Drama: Studies in U.S. History*, ed. Bettina Aptheker (New York: International Publishers, 1978), p. 84; Segal, *The Black Diaspora*, p. 58.

50 Fritz Hirschfeld, *George Washington and Slavery: A Documentary Portrayal* (Columbia: University of Missouri Press, 1997), p. 236. I also draw here on pp. 16, 37, 49, 68–69.

51 Takaki, *Iron Cages*, pp. 43–54.

52 Edmund S. Morgan, *American Slavery, American Freedom: The Ordeal of Virginia* (New York: Norton, 1975), p. 5. See Derrick Bell, "White Supremacy in America: its Legal Legacy, its Economic Costs," in *Critical White Studies: Looking Behind the Mirror*, eds. Richard Delgado and Jean Stefancic (Philadelphia: Temple University Press, 1997), p. 596.

53 *Merriam-Webster's Collegiate Dictionary*, 10th edn. (Springfield, IL: Merriam-Webster, 1993), p. 901. See Jack Niemonen, "The Role of the State in the Sociology of Racial and Ethnic Relations: Some Theoretical Considerations," *Free Inquiry in Creative Sociology* 23 (May 1995): 28.

54 William Lee Miller, *Arguing about Slavery: The Great Battle in the United States Congress* (New York: Knopf, 1996), p. 13; Loewen, *Lies My Teacher Told Me*, pp. 143–146.

55 Aptheker, *The Unfolding Drama*, p. 83.

56 John Hope Franklin, *From Slavery to Freedom*, 4th edn. (New York: Knopf, 1984), pp. 250–253.

57 Stetson Kennedy, *After Appomattox: How the South Won the War* (Gainesville: University Press of Florida, 1995), p. 3. See Cedric J. Robinson, *Black Movements in America* (New York: Routledge, 1997), pp. 86–88.

58 Kennedy, *After Appomattox*, pp. 3–4.

59 Civil Rights Cases, 109 U.S., 62–63 (1883).

60 Ruth Thompson-Miller and Joe R. Feagin, "The Reality and Impact of Legal Segregation in the United States," in *Handbook of the Sociology of Racial and Ethnic Relations*, eds. Hernán Vera and Joe R. Feagin (New York: Springer Science, 2007), pp. 455–464; John W. Cell, *The Highest State of White Supremacy: The Origins of Segregation in South Africa and the American South* (Cambridge: Cambridge University Press, 1982), pp. 168–170.

61 *Plessy v. Ferguson*, 163 U.S. 537, 552–553, 563 (1896).

62 Trudier Harris, *Exorcising Blackness: Historical and Literary Lynching and Burning Rituals* (Bloomington: Indiana University Press, 1984), p. 7.

63 The quotes are from Nedra Tyre, "You All Are a Bunch of Nigger Lovers," in *Red Wine First* (New York: Simon & Schuster, 1947), pp. 120–122, as quoted in Harris, *Exorcising Blackness*, p. 10.

64 Sidney Willhelm, personal communication, July 1998; Melvin L. Oliver and Thomas M. Shapiro, *Black Wealth/White Wealth: A New Perspective on Racial Equality* (New York: Routledge, 1995), pp. 14–15.

65 Oliver and Shapiro, *Black Wealth/White Wealth*, p. 14.

66 Du Bois, *Black Reconstruction*, p. 602.

67 Trina Williams, "The Homestead Act—Our Earliest National Asset Policy," paper presented at the Center for Social Development's symposium, "Inclusion in Asset Building," St. Louis, Missouri, September 21–23, 2000.

68 Pete Daniel, *The Shadow of Slavery: Peonage in the South, 1901–1969* (Urbana: University of Illinois Press, 1972), p. ix; Feagin, "Slavery Unwilling to Die," pp. 173–200.

69 John Egerton, *Speak Now against the Day: The Generation before the Civil Rights Movement in the South* (Chapel Hill: University of North Carolina Press, 1994), pp. 29–30.

70 Ringer, *"We the People" and Others*, p. 535.

71 Bob Blauner, *Racial Oppression in America* (New York: Harper and Row, 1972), p. 64.

72 Arthur I. Waskow, *From Race Riot to Sit-In, 1919 and the 1960s* (Garden City, NJ: Doubleday, 1966), pp. 209–240; David Chalmers, *Hooded Americanism: The History of the Ku Klux Klan* (Durham, NC: Duke University Press, 1987 [1965]), pp. 200–250.

73 Gunnar Myrdal, *An American Dilemma*, vol. 1 (New York: McGraw-Hill, 1964 [1944]), p. 240.

74 Harvard Sitkoff, *A New Deal for Blacks: The Emergence of Civil Rights as a National Issue* (New York: Oxford University Press, 1978), pp. 37–38.

75 C. G. Wye, "The New Deal and the Negro Community," *Journal of American History* 59 (December 1972): 630–640; Nancy J. Weiss, *Farewell to the Party of Lincoln: Black Politics in the Age of FDR* (Princeton, NJ: Princeton University Press, 1983), p. 119.

76 David Brown and Clive Webb, *Race in the American South: from Slavery to Civil Rights* (Gainesville: University of Florida Press, 2007), pp. 193–196.

77 Ibid. See Richard Wright, *Black Boy* (New York: HarperCollins, 1993 [1944–1945]), p. 231.

78 W. E. B. Du Bois, *Black Reconstruction in America, 1860–1880* (New York: Atheneum, 1992 [1935]), p. 700.

79 William H. Harris, *The Harder We Run: Black Workers since the Civil War* (New York: Oxford University Press, 1982), pp. 124–131.

80 Ibid., p. 131.

81 Sidney M. Willhelm, *Who Needs the Negro?* (Cambridge, MA: Schenkman, 1970); Sidney M. Willhelm, *Black in a White America* (Cambridge, MA: Schenkman, 1983). I also draw on Willhelm's presentation at Syracuse University, June 10, 1998.

82 *Jones et ux. v. Alfred H. Mayer Co.*, 392 U.S. 409, 442–443 (1968).

83 Ibid., pp. 446–447.

3 The White Racial Frame: A Social Force

1 Thomas Jefferson, *Notes on the State of Virginia*, ed. Frank Shuffelton (New York: Penguin, 1999 [1785]), pp. 147–148.

2 W. E. B. Du Bois, *Dusk of Dawn: An Essay Toward an Autobiography of a Race Concept* (New Brunswick, NJ: Transaction Books, 1984 [1940]), p. 144.

3 Karl Marx and Friedrich Engels, *The German Ideology*, ed. R. Pascal (New York: International Publishers, 1947), p. 39.

4 Kenneth O'Reilly, *Nixon's Piano: Presidents and Racial Politics from Washington to Clinton* (New York: Free Press, 1995), p. 11.

5 Oliver C. Cox, *Caste, Class, and Race* (Garden City, NJ: Doubleday, 1948), pp. 331–334; Joe R. Feagin and Clairece B. Feagin, *Racial and Ethnic Relations*, 9th edn. (Upper Saddle River, NJ: Prentice Hall, 2011).

6 Ronald T. Takaki, *Iron Cages: Race and Culture in Nineteenth-Century America* (Oxford: Oxford University Press, 1990), pp. 11–14.

7 Marimba Ani, *Yurugu: An African-Centered Critique of European Cultural Thought and Behavior* (Trenton, NJ: Africa World Press, 1994), pp. 348, 482–484; Edward W. Said, *Orientalism* (New York: Vintage Books, 1979), pp. 6–7.

8 Takaki, *Iron Cages*, pp. 12–14.

9 James Fenimore Cooper, *The Last of the Mohicans* (1826), as quoted in Emily Morison Beck, ed., *John Bartlett's Familiar Quotations*, 15th edn. (Boston: Little Brown, 1980), p. 463.

10 Winthrop D. Jordan, *White Over Black: American Attitudes Toward the Negro, 1550–1812* (Chapel Hill: University of North Carolina Press, 1968), pp. 18–19.

11 A. Leon Higginbotham, Jr., *Shades of Freedom: Racial Politics and the Presumptions of the American Legal Process* (New York: Oxford University Press, 1996), p. 119.

12 Jordan, *White Over Black*, p. 12. I draw on Michael Banton, *Racial and Ethnic Competition* (Cambridge: Cambridge University Press, 1983), pp. 37–38.

13 Jordan, *White Over Black*, p. 96. See also pp. 94–96.

14 Manning Marable, *Black American Politics* (London: New Left Books, 1985), p. 5; Higginbotham, *Shades of Freedom*, p. 11.

15 Tomás Almaguer, *Racial Fault Lines* (Berkeley and Los Angeles: University of California Press, 1994), p. 28; Takaki, *Iron Cages*, pp. 30–34.

16 William M. Wiecek, "The Origins of the Law of Slavery in British North America," *Cardozo Law Review* 17 (May 1996): 1777; see also Edmund S. Morgan, *American Slavery, American Freedom: The Ordeal of Virginia* (New York: Norton, 1975), pp. 3–20.

17 See Frances Lee Ansley, "Stirring the Ashes: Race, Class and the Future of Civil Rights Scholarship," *Cornell Law Review* 74 (September 1989): 993.

18 Samuel Hopkins, quoted in Jordan, *White Over Black*, p. 276; emphasis added.

19 A. Leon Higginbotham, Jr. and Barbara K. Kopytoff, "Racial Purity and Interracial Sex in the Law of Colonial and Antebellum Virginia," *Georgetown Law Journal* 77 (August 1989): 1671.

20 Benjamin Franklin, quoted in Takaki, *Iron Cages*, p. 50; see also Claude-Anne Lopez and Eugenia W. Herbert, *The Private Franklin: The Man and His Family* (New York: Norton, 1975), pp. 194–195.

21 George Frederickson, *The Black Image in the White Mind* (Middletown, CT: Wesleyan University Press, 1971), p. 282.

22 Joel Kovel, *White Racism: A Psychohistory*, rev. edn. (New York: Columbia University Press, 1984), pp. xli–xlvii.

23 Cox, *Caste, Class, and Race*, p. 332.

24 See Lewis R. Gordon, *Her Majesty's Other Children: Sketches of Racism from a Neocolonial Age* (Lanham, MD: Rowman & Littlefield, 1997), p. 55.

25 Audrey Smedley, *Race in North America* (Boulder, CO: Westview Press, 1993), p. 303.

26 Jan N. Pieterse, *White on Black: Images of Africa and Blacks in Western Popular Culture* (New Haven, CT: Yale University Press, 1992), p. 41.

27 Jefferson, *Notes on the State of Virginia*, pp. 145–148.

28 Benjamin Schwarz, "What Jefferson Helps Explain," *Atlantic Monthly*, March 1997, n.p., quoted from www.theatlantic.com.

29 Immanuel Kant, *Gesammelte Schiften*, as quoted in Emmanuel C. Eze, "The Color of Reason: The Idea of 'Race' in Kant's Anthropology," in *Postcolonial African Philosophy: A Critical Reader*, ed. Emmanuel C. Eze (Oxford: Blackwell, 1997), pp. 130, 118.

30 Ibid., p. 118.

31 William H. Tucker, *The Science and Politics of Racial Research* (Urbana: University of Illinois Press, 1994), pp. 8–9; Ivan Hannaford, *Race: The History of an Idea in the West* (Baltimore, MD: Johns Hopkins University Press, 1996), pp. 205–207.

32 Smedley, *Race in North America*, p. 26.

33 Fredrickson, *The Black Image in the White Mind*, p. 48.

34 Pieterse, *White on Black*, p. 60. The quote is from p. 34.

35 Arthur de Gobineau, *Selected Political Writings*, ed. M. D. Biddiss (New York: Harper & Row, 1970), p. 136.

36 Tucker, *The Science and Politics of Racial Research*, p. 23. See also Allan Chase, *The Legacy of Malthus: The Social Costs of the New Scientific Racism* (New York: Knopf, 1977), pp. 91–94.

37 *Dred Scott v. John F. A. Sandford*, 60 U.S. 393, 407–408 (1857).

38 Abraham Lincoln, "The Sixth Joint Debate at Quincy, October 13, 1858," in *The Lincoln–Douglas Debates: The First Complete, Unexpurgated Text*, ed. Harold Holzer (New York: HarperCollins, 1993), p. 283.

39 Andrew Johnson, quoted in Ani, *Yurugu*, p. 299.

40 James Brooks, quoted in Tucker, *The Science and Politics of Racial Research*, p. 25.

41 *Plessy v. Ferguson*, 163 U.S. 537, 560 (1896).

42 Ian F. Haney Lopez, *White by Law: The Legal Construction of Race* (New York: New York University Press, 1996), pp. 1–7, 203–227.

43 Charles Darwin, as quoted in Frederickson, *The Black Image in the White Mind*, p. 230.

44 M. G. Delaney is cited in Stephen Jay Gould, *Hen's Teeth and Horse's Toes* (New York: Norton, 1983), pp. 21–22. See Joe R. Feagin, *Subordinating the Poor: Welfare and American Beliefs* (Englewood Cliffs, NJ: Prentice Hall, 1975), pp. 35–36; Frederick L.

Hoffman, "Vital Statistics of the Negro," *Arena* 5 (April 1892): 542, cited in Frederickson, *The Black Image in the White Mind*, pp. 250–251.

45 John Higham, *Strangers in the Land* (New York: Atheneum, 1963), pp. 96–152; Tucker, *The Science and Politics of Racial Research*, p. 35.

46 Carl C. Brigham, *A Study of American Intelligence* (Princeton, NJ: Princeton University Press, 1923), pp. 124–125, 177–210.

47 Madison Grant, *The Passing of the Great Race* (New York: Charles Scribner's Sons, 1916).

48 Lothrop Stoddard, *The Rising Tide of Color: Against White World-Supremacy* (New York: Scribner's, 1920), p. 3.

49 Tucker, *The Science and Politics of Racial Research*, p. 93.

50 Theodore Cross, *Black Power Imperative: Racial Inequality and the Politics of Nonviolence* (New York: Faulkner, 1984), p. 157.

51 Magnus Hirschfeld, *Racism*, trans. and ed. Eden and Cedar Paul (London: Gollancz, 1938). The book was originally published in German in 1933.

52 Warren G. Harding and Calvin Coolidge, quoted in Tucker, *The Science and Politics of Racial Research*, p. 93.

53 Rudyard Kipling, "The White Man's Burden," in *Rudyard Kipling's Verse: Inclusive Edition 1885–1926* (New York: Doubleday, Doran and Co., 1929), pp. 373–374.

54 Theodore W. Allen, *The Invention of the White Race* (New York: Verso, 1994), pp. 21–50, 184; Cox, *Caste, Class, and Race*, pp. 575–576, 578.

55 David R. Roediger, *The Wages of Whiteness: Race and the Making of the American Working Class* (London: Verso, 1991), p. 127.

56 Federal Communications Commission, "Report on Ownership of Commercial Broadcast Stations," November 14, 2012, pp. 3–7; S. Derek Turner and Mark Cooper, "Out of the Picture: Minority and Female TV Station Ownership in the United States," *freepress* 2006, www.freepress.net (accessed February 26, 2009); S. Derek Turner, "Off the Dial: Female and Minority Radio Station Ownership in the United States: How FCC Policy and Media Consolidation Diminished Diversity on the Public Airwaves," *freepress* 2007, www.freepress.net (accessed February 26, 2009); David K. Shipler, "Blacks in the Newsroom," *Columbia Journalism Review* (May/June 1998): 26–29; Robert M. Entman *et al.*, *Mass Media and Reconciliation: A Report to the Advisory Board and Staff, The President's Initiative on Race* (Washington, DC, 1998).

57 Edward Herman, "The Propaganda Model Revisited," *Monthly Review* 48 (July 1996): 115; Sidney Blumenthal, *The Rise of the Counter-Establishment* (New York: Times Books, 1986), pp. 4–11, 133–170; Peter Steinfels, *The Neoconservatives: The Men Who Are Changing America's Politics* (New York: Touchstone, 1979), pp. 214–277.

58 Franklin D. Gilliam, Jr. and Shanto Iyengar, "Prime Suspects: The Effects of Local News on the Viewing Public," University of California at Los Angeles, unpublished paper, n.d.

59 Richard Cohen, "Ignorant, Apathetic and Smug," *Washington Post*, February 2, 1996, p. A19; Bobbie Harville, "History: Knowledge is Lacking; Americans' Understanding of the Country's History is Thin, a New Survey Reveals," *Dayton Daily News*, July 14, 1996, p. 15A.

60 James W. Loewen, *Lies My Teacher Told Me: Everything Your American History Textbook Got Wrong* (New York: The New Press, 1995).

61 Qingwen Dong and Arthur Phillip Murrillo, "The Impact of Television Viewing on Young Adults' Stereotypes Towards Hispanic Americans," *Human Communication* 10 (2007): 33–44.

62 Lerone Bennett, *Confrontation: Black and White* (Baltimore, MD: Penguin, 1965), pp. 187–188.

63 John H. Franklin, *From Slavery to Freedom*, 4th edn. (New York: Knopf, 1974), p. 421; Derrick Bell, "*Brown v. Board of Education* and the Interest Convergence Dilemma," *Harvard Law Review* 93 (1980): 518.

64 *Brown v. Board of Education of Topeka*, 347 U.S. 483 (1954).

65 Thomas Ferguson and Joel Rodgers, *Right Turn: The Decline of the Democrats and the Future of American Politics* (New York: Hill and Wang, 1986), pp. 55–56.

66 Samuel P. Huntington, "The Erosion of American National Interests," *Foreign Affairs* (September/October 1997): 28.

67 *Report of the National Advisory Commission on Civil Disorders* (Washington, DC: U.S. Government Printing Office, 1968), pp. 1, 5.

68 Ferguson and Rodgers, *Right Turn*, pp. 65–66.

69 *City of Richmond, Virginia v. J. A. Croson Co.*, 488 U.S. 469 (1989); see also *Adarand Constructors, Inc. v. Pena*, 515 U.S. 200 (1995).

70 Barbara J. Flagg, "'Was Blind But Now I See': White Race Consciousness and the Requirement of Discriminatory Intent," *Michigan Law Review* 91 (1993): 953; Wendy Moore, *Reproducing Racism* (Lanham, MD: Rowman & Littlefield, 2008).

71 Larry T. Reynolds, *Reflexive Sociology: Working Papers in Self-Critical Analysis* (Rockville, MD: Rockport Institute Press, 1999), pp. 141–145.

72 Arthur R. Jensen, "How Much Can We Boost IQ and Scholastic Achievement?" *Harvard Educational Review* 39 (1969): 1–123; Richard J. Herrnstein and Charles Murray, *The Bell Curve: Intelligence and Class Structure in American Life* (New York: Free Press, 1994), pp. 295–316; Jean Stefancic and Richard Delgado, *No Mercy: How Conservative Think Tanks and Foundations Changed America's Social Agenda* (Philadelphia: Temple University Press, 1996), p. 34.

73 Merlin Chowkwanyun, "Race Is Not Biology: How Unthinking Racial Essentialism Finds Its Way into Scientific Research," *The Atlantic*, May 23, 2013, www.theatlantic.com/health/archive/2013/05/race-is-not-biology/276174/ (accessed June 4, 2013); Elspeth Reeve, "The Heritage Foundation's Immigration Guru Wasn't Just Racist —He's Wrong," *Atlantic Wire*, May 8, 2013, www.theatlanticwire.com/politics/2013/05/heritage-foundation-jason-richwine/65005/ (accessed June 4, 2013).

74 "Nobel Winner in 'Racist' Claim Row," CNN.com, October 18, 2007, http://edition.cnn.com/2007/TECH/science/10/18/science.race/index.html?iref=mpstor yview (accessed January 20, 2009).

75 Jessie Daniels and Amy J. Schulz, "Constructing Whiteness in Health Disparities Research," in *Health and Illness at the Intersections of Gender, Race and Class*, eds. A. J. Schulz and L. Mullings (San Francisco: Jossey-Bass, 2006), pp. 89–127. See also Chowkwanyun, "Race Is Not Biology."

76 Daniels and Schulz, "Constructing Whiteness in Health Disparities Research."

77 Daniel P. Moynihan, *The Negro Family: The Case for National Action* (Washington, DC: U.S. Government Printing Office, 1965), p. 5.

78 Ellen K. Coughlin, "Worsening Plight of the Underclass Catches Attention," *Chronicle of Higher Education*, March 1988, p. A5. See Joe R. Feagin and Leslie Inniss, "The Black Underclass Ideology in Race Relations Analysis," *Social Justice* 16 (winter 1989): 12–34.

79 Juan Williams, *Enough: The Phony Leaders, Dead-End Movements, and Culture of Failure that Are Undermining Black America—and What We Can Do About It* (New York: Three Rivers Press, 2007); Bill Cosby and Alvin F. Poussaint, *Come On People: On the Path from Victims to Victors* (New York: Thomas Nelson, 2007).

80 Anthony Farley, "The Black Body as Fetish Object," *Oregon Law Review* 76 (fall 1997): 522–526.

81 Joe R. Feagin and Eileen O'Brien, *White Men on Race* (Boston: Beacon, 2003); Rhonda Levine, "The Souls of Elite White Men: White Racial Identity and the Logic of Thinking on Race," paper presented at annual meeting, Hawaiian Sociological Association, February 14, 1998.

82 Glenn Adams, Teceta Thomas Tormala, and Laurie T. O'Brien, "The Effect of Self Affirmation on Perception of Racism," *Journal of Experimental Psychology* 42 (2006): 616–626. Italics added.

83 "President-Elect Obama: The Voters Rebuke Republicans for Economic Failure," *Wall*

Street Journal, November 5, 2008, http://online.wsj.com/article/SB122586244657
800863.html (accessed December 28, 2008).

84 Lisa B. Spanierman *et al.*, "White University Students' Responses to Societal Racism: A
Qualitative Investigation," *The Counseling Psychologist* 36 (November 2008), p. 860.

85 Jane H. Hill, *The Everyday Language of White Racism* (Malden, MA: Wiley-Blackwell,
2008), p. 180. See also pp. 134–157.

86 Hernán Vera and Andrew Gordon, *Screen Saviors: Hollywood Fictions of Whiteness*
(Lanham, MD: Rowman & Littlefield, 2003); Cedric J. Robinson, *Black Movements in
America* (New York: Routledge, 1997), p. 12.

87 Hernán Vera and Andrew Gordon, "Sincere Fictions of the White Self in the American
Cinema: 1915–1998," unpublished paper, University of Florida, 1998.

88 Dinesh D'Souza, *The End of Racism: Principles for a Multiracial Society* (New York: Free
Press, 1995), p. 113.

89 Jon Hubbard, *Letters to the Editor: Confessions of a Frustrated Conservative* (Bloomington, IN: iUniverse, 2009), pp. 183–189.

90 Kristin Collins, "Plantation Tours Downplay Slavery: Study," *Chicago Sun-Times*,
February 11, 2009, www.suntimes.com/news/nation/1424984,w-plantations-slavery-
joellane-museum021109. article (accessed March 13, 2009). The South Carolina
government brochure is *South Carolina: Smiling Faces, Beautiful Places*, n.d.

91 Jacqueline Soteropoulos, "Skeptics Put Cops on Trial: The American Public Isn't Giving
Government or Police Officers the Blind Trust it Once Did," *Tampa Tribune*, April 17,
1995, p. A1. I draw on Nick Mrozinske, "Derivational Thinking and Racism," unpublished research paper, University of Florida, fall 1998.

92 Mrozinske, "Derivational Thinking and Racism." The search algorithm did not allow
for the word "whites" alone because this picks up individual surnames.

93 Edward Ball, *Slaves in the Family* (New York: Ballantine Books, 1999), p. 13.

94 Feagin and O'Brien, *White Men on Race*.

95 Patrick Buchanan, as quoted in Clarence Page, "U.S. Media Should Stop Abetting Intolerance," *Toronto Star*, December 27, 1991, p. A27.

96 Patrick Buchanan, as quoted in John Dillin, "Immigration Joins List of 92 Issues,"
Christian Science Monitor, December 17, 1991, p. 6.

97 Patrick J. Buchanan, "A Brief for Whitey," March 21, 2008, www.buchanan.org
(accessed March 31, 2008).

98 Peter Brimelow, *Alien Nation: Common Sense about America's Immigration Disaster*
(New York: Random House, 1995), pp. 10, 59. See also VDARE.COM, http://en.wiki-
pedia.org/wiki/VDARE (accessed April 30, 2009).

99 Huntington, "The Erosion of American National Interests," p. 28. See Arthur Schlesin-
ger, Jr., *The Disuniting of America: Reflections on a Multicultural Society* (New York:
Norton, 1991), pp. 13, 124–125.

100 Frank Furedi, *The Silent War: Imperialism and the Changing Perception of Race* (New
Brunswick, NJ: Rutgers University Press, 1998), p. 1.

101 George Lakoff and M. Johnson, *Metaphors We Live By* (Chicago: University of Chicago
Press, 1980), p. 158.

4 Contemporary Racial Framing: White Americans

1 J. L. Eberhardt, P. A. Goff, V. J. Purdie, and P. G. Davies, "Seeing Black: Race, Crime, and
Visual Processing," *Journal of Personality and Social Psychology*, 87 (2004): 876–893.

2 Herbert Blumer, "Race Prejudice as a Sense of Group Position," *Pacific Sociological
Review* 1 (spring 1958): 3–7.

3 Gordon Allport, *The Nature of Prejudice*, abridged edn. (New York: Anchor Books,
1958), p. 10. See Teun A. van Dijk, *Discourse, Racism and Ideology* (La Laguna: RCEI
Ediciones, 1996), pp. 49–50.

4 David R. Roediger, *The Wages of Whiteness: Race and the Making of the American
Working Class* (London: Verso, 1991), pp. 96–121.

5   Surveys are cited in Richard Morin, "Unconventional Wisdom: New Facts and Hot Stats from the Social Sciences," *Washington Post*, April 6, 1997, p. C5.

6   William Brink and Louis Harris, *The Negro Revolution in America* (New York: Simon & Schuster, 1964), pp. 140–143; see also William Brink and Louis Harris, *Black and White* (New York: Simon & Schuster, 1966), pp. 109, 136.

7   For surveys, see Howard Schuman, Charlotte Steeh, and Lawrence Bobo, *Racial Attitudes in America: Trends and Interpretations* (Cambridge, MA: Harvard University Press, 1985), pp. 71–162; Herbert H. Hyman and Paul B. Sheatsley, "Attitudes Toward Desegregation," *Scientific American* 211 (July 1964): 16–22; Glenn Firebaugh and K. F. Davis, "Trends in Antiblack Prejudice, 1972–1984: Region and Cohort Effects," *American Journal of Sociology* 94 (1988): 251–272.

8   Lincoln Quillian, "New Approaches to Understanding Racial Prejudice and Discrimination," *Annual Review of Sociology* 32 (2006): 299–328.

9   See John F. Dovidio *et al.*, "Stereotyping, Prejudice, and Discrimination: Another Look," in *Stereotypes and Stereotyping*, eds. C. Neil Macrae, Miles Hewstone, and Charles Stangor (New York: Guilford, 1995), pp. 276–319.

10   See Andrew Scott Baron and Mahzarin R. Banaji, "The Development of Implicit Attitudes: Evidence of Race Evaluations from Ages 6 and 10 and Adulthood," *Psychological Science* 17 (2006): 52–53; John F. Dovidio, John C. Brigham, Blair T. Johnson, and Samuel L. Gaertner, "Stereotyping, Prejudice, and Discrimination: Another Look," in *Stereotypes and Stereotyping*, eds. C. Neil Macrae, Miles Hewstone, and Charles Stangor (New York: Guilford, 1995), pp. 276–319; Sonja M. B. Givens and Jennifer L. Monahan, "Priming Mammies, Jezebels, and Other Controlling Images: An Examination of the Influence of Mediated Stereotypes on Perceptions of an African American Woman," *Media Psychology* 7 (2005), pp. 102–103.

11   Eduardo Bonilla-Silva and Tyrone A. Forman, "'I Am Not a Racist But…': Mapping White College Students' Racial Ideology in the U.S.A.," *Discourse and Society* 11 (2000): 51–86.

12   Brittany C. Slatton, *Mythologizing Black Women: Unveiling White Men's Racist and Sexist Deep Frame* (Boulder, CO: Paradigm Publishers, 2013), p. 63.

13   Nilanjana Dasgupta, Debbie E. McGhee, Anthony G. Greenwald, and Mahzarin R. Banaji, "Automatic Preference for White Americans: Eliminating the Familiarity Explanation," *Journal of Experimental Social Psychology* 36 (2000): 316–328. This research is summarized in Shankar Vedantam, "Many Americans Believe They Are Not Prejudiced: Now a New Test Provides Powerful Evidence that a Majority of Us Really Are," *Washington Post Magazine*, January 23, 2005, p. W12.

14   Baron and Banaji, "The Development of Implicit Attitudes," pp. 52–53.

15   Mark Potok, "The Year in Hate and Extremism," *Intelligence Report* (SPLC), Spring 2013, www.splcenter.org/home/2013/spring/the-year-in-hate-and-extremism#.UZEEncpYxhE (accessed May 13, 2013).

16   Leslie Houts Picca and Joe R. Feagin, *Two Faced Racism: Whites in the Backstage and Frontstage* (New York: Routledge, 2007). See Joe R. Feagin, Hernán Vera, and Pinar Batur, *White Racism: The Basics*, 2nd edn. (New York: Routledge, 2001), pp. 186–253.

17   Slatton, *Mythologizing Black Women*, p. 69. I am also indebted to Christiana Otto for discussions here.

18   General Social Survey, National Opinion Research Center, Chicago, 1994. For current examples, see Jackie Gilbert, Norma Carr-Ruffino, John M. Ivancevich, and Millicent Lownes-Jackson, "An Empirical Examination of Inter-Ethnic Stereotypes: Comparing Asian American and African American Employees," *Public Personnel Management* (summer 2003): 252–265.

19   Sut Jhally and Justin Lewis, *Enlightened Racism* (Boulder, CO: Westview Press, 1992), p. 95. See also pp. 96–110.

20   Thomas F. Pettigrew, "The Ultimate Attribution Error: Extending Allport's Cognitive Analysis of Prejudice," *Personality and Social Psychology Bulletin* 5 (1979): 461–476.

I draw on the research summary in Robert S. Feldman, *Social Psychology* (Englewood Cliffs, NJ: Prentice Hall, 1995), pp. 91–92.

21 Patricia Hill Collins, *Black Feminist Thought: Knowledge, Consciousness, and the Politics of Empowerment* (Boston: Unwin Hyman, 1990), p. 67. I draw here on Yanick St. Jean and Joe R. Feagin, *Double Burden: Black Women and Everyday Racism* (Armonk, NY: M. E. Sharpe, 1998), chapters 3–4.

22 See Jan N. Pieterse, *White on Black: Images of Africa and Blacks in Western Popular Culture* (New Haven, CT: Yale University Press, 1992).

23 Slatton, *Mythologizing Black Women*, p. 45 and passim.

24 Joya Misra, Stephanie Moller, and Marina Karides, "Envisioning Dependency: Changing Media Depictions of Welfare in the Twentieth Century," *Social Problems* 50 (2003): 482–504. See also Derrick Z. Jackson, "Unspoken During Race Talk," *Boston Globe*, December 5, 1997, p. A27.

25 Slatton, *Mythologizing Black Women*, p. 73.

26 Joshua J. Dyck and Laura S. Hussey, "The End of Welfare as We Know It? Durable Attitudes in a Changing Information Environment," *Public Opinion Quarterly*, November 22, 2008, advance access online version, http://poq.oxfordjournals.org/cgi/content/abstract/nfn053v1 (accessed May 11, 2009).

27 Anthony E. O. King and Terrence T. Allen, "Personal Characteristics of the Ideal African American Marriage Partner: A Survey of Adult Black Men and Women," *Journal of Black Studies* 39 (2009): 570–588. The quote is from the abstract.

28 Diane Roberts, *The Myth of Aunt Jemima: Representations of Race and Region* (New York: Routledge, 1994), p. 5.

29 Marci Bounds Littlefield, "The Media as a System of Racialization: Exploring Images of African American Women and the New Racism," *American Behavioral Scientist* 51 (January 2008): 675–685; Slatton, *Mythologizing Black Women*; Patricia Hill Collins, *Black Sexual Politics* (New York: Routledge, 2005); and Joe R. Feagin and Melvin P. Sikes, *Living with Racism: The Black Middle-Class Experience* (Boston: Beacon Press, 1994).

30 "Candidate Apologizes for 'Buckwheat' Remark," WDSU.com, November 12, 2007, www.wdsu.com/news/14573933/detail.html (accessed April 11, 2008).

31 St. Jean and Feagin, *Double Burden*, pp. 90–91.

32 Adia Harvey Wingfield, *Doing Business with Beauty: Black Women, Hair Salons, and the Racial Enclave Economy* (Lanham, MD: Rowman & Littlefield, 2008).

33 Kamesha Spates, *What Don't Kill Us Makes Us Stronger: African American Women and Suicide* (Boulder, CO: Paradigm Publishers, forthcoming).

34 Louwanda Evans, *Cabin Pressure: African American Pilots, Flight Attendants, and Emotional Labor* (Lanham, MD: Roman & Littlefield, 2013), p. 24.

35 See Mark Warr, "Dangerous Situations: Social Context and Fear of Victimization," *Social Forces* 68 (1990): 905–906.

36 Earl Warren, quoted in Theodore Cross, *Black Power Imperative: Racial Inequality and the Politics of Nonviolence* (New York: Faulkner, 1984), pp. 157–158.

37 Will Weissert, "Federal Judge Accused of Making Racial Comments," Associated Press, June 4, 2013 www.chron.com/default/article/Federal-judge-accused-of-making-racial-comments-4576503.php (accessed June 10, 2013).

38 "Bennett under Fire for Remarks on Black Crime," CNN.com, September 30, 2005, www.cnn.com/2005/POLITICS/09/30/bennett.comments/index.html (accessed January 20, 2009).

39 "Remarks by the President on Trayvon Martin," July 19, 2013, www.whitehouse.gov/the-press-office/2013/07/19/remarks-president-trayvon-martin (accessed July 22, 2013).

40 For example, Dinesh D'Souza, *The End of Racism: Principles for a Multiracial Society* (New York: Free Press, 1995), pp. 245–272.

41 Joe R. Feagin and Hernán Vera, *White Racism: The Basics* (New York: Routledge, 1995), p. 159.

42 Lev S. Vygotsky, *Mind in Society: The Development of Higher Psychological Processes*, eds. M. Cole, V. John-Steiner, S. Scribner, and E. Souberman (Cambridge, MA: Harvard University Press, 1978). I draw here on Steven Shaffer, "Resurrecting the Linguistic Relativity Hypothesis," www.scshaffer.com/files/scsshaffer-lrh.pdf (accessed February 6, 2006), pp. 2–17.

43 P. R. Klite, R. A. Bardwell, and J. Salzman, "Local TV News: Getting Away with Murder," *Press/Politics* 2 (1997): 102–112; Franklin D. Gilliam, Jr. and Shanto Iyengar, "Prime Suspects: The Effects of Local News on the Viewing Public," unpublished research paper, University of California (Los Angeles), n.d.

44 Heinz Endowment, *Portrayal and Perception: Two Audits of News Media Reporting on African American Men and Boys* (Pittsburgh: Heinz Endowment, 2011), p. 4. See also Dana Mastro, Maria Knight Lapinski, Maria A. Kopacz, and Elizabeth Behm-Morawitz, "The Influence of Exposure to Depictions of Race and Crime in TV News on Viewer's Social Judgments," *Journal of Broadcasting and Electronic Media* 53 (2009): 615–635.

45 Travis L. Dixon and D. Linz, "Overrepresentation and Underrepresentation of African Americans and Latinos as Lawbreakers on Television Shows," *Journal of Communication* 50 (2000): 131–154; Travis L. Dixon and D. Linz, "Television News, Prejudicial Pretrial Publicity, and the Depiction of Race," *Journal of Broadcasting and Electronic Media* 46 (2002): 112–136. I also draw on Mary Beth Oliver, "African American Men as 'Criminal and Dangerous': Implications of Media Portrayals of Crime on the 'Criminalization' of African American Men," *Journal of African American Studies* 7 (2003): 6–7.

46 Oliver, "African American Men as 'Criminal and Dangerous,'" pp. 8–9.

47 Travis L. Dixon, "Crime News and Racialized Beliefs: Understanding the Relationship Between Local News Viewing and Perceptions of African Americans and Crime," *Journal of Communication* 58 (March 2008): 106–125.

48 Eberhardt *et al.*, "Seeing Black: Race, Crime, and Visual Processing," pp. 876–893.

49 Katheryn Russell, *The Color of Crime: Racial Hoaxes, White Fear, Black Protectionism, Police Harassment, and Other Macroaggressions* (New York: New York University Press, 1998), pp. 69–93 and passim.

50 Gilliam and Iyengar, "Prime Suspects," p. 17; Mastro *et al.*, "The Influence of Exposure to Depictions of Race and Crime," pp. 615–635.

51 Bruce Western, *Punishment and Inequality in America* (New York: Russell Sage Foundation, 2006). See Robert B. Hill *et al.*, *Research on the African American Family: A Holistic Perspective* (Westport, CT: Auburn House, 1993).

52 See Manning Marable, "Incarceration vs. Education: Reproducing Racism and Poverty in America," *Urban Habitat*, fall 2008, www.urbanhabitat.org/node/2808 (accessed June 29, 2009).

53 James A. Rada, "Color Blind-Sided: Racial Bias in Network Television's Coverage of Professional Football Games," *Howard Journal of Communications* 7 (July–September 1996): 234–236; James A. Rada and K. Tim Wulfemeyer, "Color Coded: Racial Descriptors in Television Coverage of Intercollegiate Sports," *Journal of Broadcasting and Electronic Media* 49 (2005): 65–85. The quote is on p. 80.

54 Andrea M. Eagleman, "Stereotypes of Race and Nationality: A Qualitative Analysis of Sport Magazine Coverage of MLB Players," *Journal of Sport Management* 25 (2011): 156–168.

55 Abby L. Ferber, "The Construction of Black Masculinity: White Supremacy Now and Then," *Journal of Sport and Social Issues* 31 (2007): 22.

56 See Charles Gallagher, "Miscounting Race: Explaining Whites' Misperceptions of Racial Group Size," *Sociological Perspectives* 46 (2003): 381–396; see also Priscilla Labovitz, "Just the Facts," *New York Times*, March 25, 1996, p. A2.

57 Charles A. Gallagher, "Living in Color: Perceptions of Racial Group Size," unpublished research paper, Georgia State University, 1999.

58 Picca and Feagin, *Two Faced Racism.*

59 Tim Cox, "Rights Groups Cautious about 'Odd Couple' Appearances," United Press International, November 22, 1988.

60 Kenneth O'Reilly, *Nixon's Piano: Presidents and Racial Politics from Washington to Clinton* (New York: Free Press, 1995), pp. 6–7; Bruce Oudes, ed., *From: The President: President Nixon's Secret Files* (New York: Harper and Row, 1989), p. 451.

61 Claudio E. Cabrera, "Judge Admits Sending Racist Email about Obama," *The Root*, March 1, 2012, www.theroot.com/racist-obama-emails-judge-richard-cebull (retrieved March 2, 2012); "Orange County GOP Official Refuses to Resign over Racist Email," *Los Angeles Wave*, wire services, April 16, 2011, www.wavenewspapers.com/news/orange-county-racist-ape-chimp-email-gop-republican-obama-davenport-119993794.html (retrieved February 10, 2012).

62 These examples are from http://novusordo.com, as cited in Margaret Ronkin and Helen E. Karn, "Mock Ebonics: Linguistic Racism in Parodies of Ebonics on the Internet," *Journal of Sociolinguistics* 3 (August 1999): 360–380.

63 Seth Stephens-Davidowitz, "The Effects of Racial Animus on a Black Presidential Candidate: Using Google Search Data to Find What Surveys Miss," unpublished research paper, Harvard University, June 9, 2012.

64 Jane H. Hill, *The Everyday Language of White Racism* (Malden, MA: Wiley-Blackwell, 2008), especially pp. 134–157; Rosalind Chou and Joe Feagin, *The Myth of the Model Minority* (Boulder, CO: Paradigm Books, 2008), chapter 1.

65 Rosina Lippi-Green, *English with an Accent* (New York: Routledge, 1997), p. 201.

66 See Adia Harvey Wingfield and Joe R. Feagin, *Yes We Can: White Racial Framing and the 2008 Presidential Campaign* (New York: Routledge, 2010), especially chapters 1–5.

67 I draw from *Merriam-Webster's Collegiate Dictionary*, 10th edn. (Springfield: Merriam-Webster, 1993), pp. 118, 1348; and Robert B. Moore, "Racist Stereotyping in the English Language," in *Racism and Sexism: An Integrated Study*, ed. Paula S. Rothenberg (New York: St. Martin's Press, 1988), pp. 270–271.

68 Thomas Greenfield, as quoted in Moore, "Racist Stereotyping in the English Language," p. 273.

69 Joanna Russ, *How to Suppress Women's Writing* (Austin: University of Texas Press, 1983), pp. 17–25. I am indebted to Nick Mrozinske for this point.

70 Toni Morrison, *Playing in the Dark: Whiteness and the Literary Imagination* (New York: Vintage Books, 1992), pp. 63–65.

71 No name was given. The spelling and punctuation are per the original letter.

72 "Baseball Committee Formed to Investigate Racist, Ethnic Remarks Made by Cincinnati Reds Owner," *Ethnic NewsWatch*, December 9, 1992, p. 1.

73 Damon Williams, *Strategic Diversity Leadership: Activating Change and Transformation in Higher Education* (Sterling, VA: Stylus, 2013), p. 115, 157. See also Leslie Carr, *"Colorblind" Racism* (Thousand Oaks, CA: Sage, 1997).

74 James R. Kluegel and Eliot R. Smith, *Beliefs about Inequality* (New York: Aldine de Gruyter, 1986), pp. 186–187.

75 Pew Research Center, "Blacks See Growing Values Gap between Poor and Middle Class: Optimism about Black Progress Declines," November 13, 2007, www.pewsocialtrends.org/2007/11/13/blacks-see-growing-values-gap-between-poor-and-middle-class/ (accessed September 13, 2013).

76 "Race and Ethnicity," www.pollingreport.com/race.htm (accessed February 27, 2009).

77 All the surveys are reported in "Race and Ethnicity," www.pollingreport.com/race.htm (accessed February 27, 2009).

78 Joe R. Feagin, *The White Racial Frame: Centuries of Racial Framing and Counter-Framing*, 2nd. edn. (New York: Routledge, 2013), pp. 89–162; and Eduardo Bonilla-Silva, *Racism without Racists*, 4th edn. (Lanham, MD: Rowman & Littlefield, 2013).

79 Feagin and Vera, *White Racism*, pp. 160–161.

80 Bonilla-Silva, *Racism without Racists*; George V. Gushue and Madonna G. Constantine,

"Colorblind Racial Attitudes and White Racial Identity Attitudes in Psychology Trainees," *Professional Psychology: Research and Practice* 38 (2007): 321–328.

81 Jerome M. Culp, Jr., "Water Buffalo and Diversity: Naming Names and Reclaiming the Racial Discourse," *Connecticut Law Review* 26 (fall 1993): 209.

82 Patricia G. Devine, "Stereotypes and Prejudice: Their Automatic and Controlled Components," *Journal of Personality and Social Psychology* 56 (1989): 15–16. I draw on the summary of Devine's work in Feldman, *Social Psychology*, p. 97.

83 David O. Sears, "Symbolic Racism," in *Eliminating Racism*, eds. Phyllis A. Katz and Dalmas A. Taylor (New York: Plenum, 1988), pp. 55–58; Lawrence Bobo, "Group Conflict, Prejudice, and the Paradox of Contemporary Racial Attitudes," in *Eliminating Racism*, eds. Katz and Taylor, pp. 99–101; Michael Hughes, "Symbolic Racism, Old-Fashioned Racism, and Whites' Opposition to Affirmative Action," in *Racial Attitudes in the 1990s: Continuity and Change*, eds. Steven A. Tuch and Jack K. Martin (Westport, CT: Praeger, 1997), pp. 73–74.

84 Lawrence Bobo, James R. Kluegel, and Ryan A. Smith, "Laissez-Faire Racism: The Crystallization of a Kinder, Gentler, Antiblack Ideology," in *Racial Attitudes in the 1990s: Continuity and Change*, eds. Steven A. Tuch and Jack K. Martin (Westport, CT: Praeger, 1997), pp. 25, 39.

85 See surveys reported at www.pollingreport.com/race.htm (accessed June 29, 2009); Quillian, "New Approaches to Understanding Racial Prejudice and Discrimination," pp. 299–328.

86 Sidney Verba and Gary R. Orren, *Equality in America: The View from the Top* (Cambridge, MA: Harvard University Press, 1985), p. 63.

87 Public Religion Research Institute, "Monthly Religion News Surveys," May 2013, http://publicreligion.org/research/2013/05/may-2013-religion-politics-tracking-survey/ (accessed June 9, 2013).

88 Quoted from the survey report at "Race and Ethnicity," www.pollingreport.com/race.htm (accessed February 27, 2009).

89 Matthew Smith, "Bridging the Gulf Between Blacks and Whites," *Pittsburgh Post-Gazette*, April 7, 1996, p. A1; and Jeffrey M. Jones, "Race, Ideology, and Support for Affirmative Action: Personal Politics Has Little to Do with Blacks' Support," Gallup Poll, August 2005, www.gallup.com (accessed May 27, 2008).

90 Robert J. Blendon *et al.*, "The Public and the President's Commission on Race," *Public Perspective* (February 1998): 66.

91 Christine Reyna, P. J. Henry, William Korfmacher, and Amanda Tucker, "Examining the Principles in Principled Conservatism: The Role of Responsibility Stereotypes as Cues for Deservingness in Racial Policy Decisions," *Journal of Personality and Social Psychology* 90 (2005): 109–128.

92 Ruth Frankenberg, *White Women, Race Matters* (Minneapolis: University of Minnesota Press, 1993), pp. 228–229; Karyn D. McKinney, *Being White: Stories of Race and Racism* (New York: Routledge, 2005).

93 Survey results are cited in Blendon *et al.*, "The Public and the President's Commission on Race," p. 66.

94 Quoted in "Whites Suffer More Racism Than Blacks: Study Shows White American People Believe They Are More Discriminated Against," *Daily Mail*, May 24, 2011, www.dailymail.co.uk/news/article-1390205/Whites-suffer-racism-blacks-Study-shows-white-people-believe-discriminated-against.html (accessed June 9, 2013). The study is Michael Norton and Samuel R Sommers, "Whites See Racism as a Zero-Sum Game that They Are Now Losing," *Perspectives on Psychological Science* 6 (2011): 215–218.

95 Marimba Ani, *Yurugu: An African-Centered Critique of European Cultural Thought and Behavior* (Trenton, NJ: Africa World Press, 1994), p. 294.

96 See Theodor W. Adorno *et al.*, *The Authoritarian Personality* (New York: Harper, 1950), pp. 248–279; Thomas F. Pettigrew, *Racially Separate or Together?* (New York: McGraw-Hill, 1971), pp. 131–135.

97   John D. Foster, *White Race Discourse: Preserving Racial Privilege in the Post-Racial Society* (Lanham, MD: Lexington Books, 2013), p. 7.

98   John Briggs and F. David Peat, *Turbulent Mirror: An Illustrated Guide to Chaos Theory and the Science of Wholeness* (New York: Harper & Row, 1990), p. 154.

99   Maurice Halbwachs, *On Collective Memory*, ed. and trans. L. Coser (Chicago: University of Chicago Press, 1992), pp. 38, 52. See also Picca and Feagin, *Two Faced Racism*, chapter 1.

100 Feldman, *Social Psychology*, p. 399.

101 Feagin and Vera, *White Racism*, p. 149. The poll is by CBS polls, as reported at http://db.cbs.com/prd1 (accessed May 1999).

102 Bonilla-Silva, *Racism without Racists*.

103 The quote is from a research summary by Siri Carpenter, "Buried Prejudice: The Bigot in Your Brain," *Scientific American* (May 2008), www.sciam.com/article.cfm?id=buriedprejudice-the-bigot-in-your-brain (accessed June 1, 2008). See also Vygotsky, *Mind in Society*; Steven Shaffer, "Resurrecting the Linguistic Relativity Hypothesis," www. scsshaffer.com/files/scsshaffer-lrh.pdf (accessed February 6, 2006), pp. 2–17.

104 Debra Van Ausdale and Joe R. Feagin, "Using Racial and Ethnic Concepts: The Critical Case of Very Young Children," *American Sociological Review* 61 (October 1996): 779–793. See also Jean Piaget, *The Moral Judgment of the Child* (Glencoe, IL: The Free Press, 1932).

105 Jessie Daniels and N. Lalone, "Racism in Video Gaming: Connecting Extremist and Mainstream Expressions of White Supremacy," in *Race, Gender, Class in Video Gaming*, eds. David Embrick and András Lukács (Lanham, MD: Lexington Press, 2012), p. 86. See also pp. 83–97.

106 Daniels and N. Lalone, "Racism in Video Gaming," pp. 89–93.

107 Ibid. I draw here on discussions with Jessie Daniels.

108 Joseph Carroll, "Who Are the People in Your Neighborhood? South Reports Highest Proportion of Blacks; West Reports Highest Number of Hispanics, Recent Immigrants," Gallup Poll, July 2005, www.gallup.com/poll/17293/Who-People-Your-Neighborhood.aspx (accessed March 2, 2009); William H. Frey, "Census Data: Blacks and Hispanics Take Different Segregation Paths," Brookings Institution, December 16, 2010, www.brookings.edu/research/opinions/2010/12/16-census-frey (accessed June 10, 2013).

109 Isabel Wilkerson, "The Tallest Fence: Feelings on Race in a White Neighborhood," *New York Times*, June 21, 1992, section 1, p. 18.

110 Heidi McGlothlin and Melanie Killen, "Intergroup Attitudes of European American Children Attending Ethnically Homogeneous Schools," *Child Development* 77 (September/October 2006): 1375–1386. See also Jim Sidanius, Felicia Pratto, and Lawrence Bobo, "Racism, Conservatism, Affirmative Action, and Intellectual Sophistication," *Journal of Personality and Social Psychology* 70 (1996): 487.

111 Gizelle Anzures *et al.*, "Own- and Other-Race Face Identity Recognition in Children: The Effects of Pose and Feature Composition," *Developmental Psychology* (forthcoming). On the out-group homogeneity effect, see also Christian A. Meissner, John C. Brigham, and David A. Butz, "Memory for Own- and Other-race Faces: A Dual-Process Approach," *Applied Cognitive Psychology* 19 (2005): 545–567.

112 Cara A. Talaska, Susan T. Fiske, and Shelly Chaiken, "Legitimating Racial Discrimination: Emotions, not Beliefs, Best Predict Discrimination in a Meta-Analysis," *Social Justice Research* 21 (2008): 263–296.

113 Laurie A. Rudman and Richard D. Ashmore, "Discrimination and the Implicit Association Test," *Group Processes and Intergroup Relations* 10 (2007): 359–372.

114 Russell H. Fazio *et al.*, "Variability in Automatic Activation as an Unobtrusive Measure of Racial Attitudes: A Bona Fide Pipeline?" *Journal of Personality and Social Psychology* 69 (1995): 1025–1026.

115 Bridget C. Dunton and Russell H. Fazio, "An Individual Difference Measure of Motivation to Control Prejudiced Reactions," *Personality and Social Psychology Bulletin* 23 (March 1997): 316–326.

116 Richard J. Barnet and John Cavanagh, *Global Dreams: Imperial Corporations and the New World Order* (New York: Touchstone, 1994), p. 138. I draw on Joe R. Feagin and Pinar Batur-Vanderlippe, "The Globalization of Racism and Antiracism: France, South Africa and the United States," unpublished manuscript, University of Florida, 1996; and Robert W. McChesney, "The New Global Media: It's a Small World of Big Conglomerates," *The Nation*, November 29, 1999, www.hartfordwp.com/archives/29/053.html (accessed July 3, 2008).

117 Jeffrey K. Lyons, "Media Globalization and Its Effect upon International Communities: Seeking a Communication Theory Perspective," *Global Media Journal* 4 (fall 2005), http://lass.calumet.purdue.edu/cca/gmj/fa05/gmj-fa05-lyons.htm (accessed May 14, 2009); Anup Shah, "Media Conglomerates, Mergers, Concentration of Ownership," *Global Issues*, www.globalissues.org/article/159/media-conglomerates-mergers-concentration-of-ownership (accessed June 10, 2013).

118 Pinar Batur-Van der Lippe, "Centering on Global Racism and Anti-Racism," *Sociological Spectrum* 19 (1999): 467–484.

119 Yarrow Dunham, Andrew S. Baron, and Mahzarin R. Banaji, "From American City to Japanese Village: A Cross-Cultural Investigation of Implicit Race Attitudes," *Child Development* 77 (2006): 1268–1281; Yuki Fujioka, "Television Portrayals and African American Stereotypes: Examination of Television Effects When Direct Contact is Lacking," *Journalism and Mass Communication Quarterly* 76 (spring 1999): 52–75.

120 Hsiao-Chuan Hsia, "Imported Racism and Indigenous Biases: The Impacts of the U.S. Media on Taiwanese Images of African Americans," paper presented at meeting of American Sociological Association, August 5–9, 1994, Los Angeles.

121 Alexis Tan, Lingling Zhang, Yungying Zhang, and Francis Dalisay, "Stereotypes of African Americans in China and Media Use," paper presented at the Annual Meeting of the Association for Education in Journalism and Mass Communication, Washington, DC, August 8, 2007.

122 Nestor Rodriguez, personal communication with the author.

5 Racial Oppression Today: Everyday Practice

1 The study was done by Marianne Bertrand and Sendhil Mullainathan and is summarized in David Wessel, "Racial Discrimination: Still at Work in the U.S.," *Wall Street Journal Online*, at www.careerjournal.com/myc/diversity/20030916-wessel.html (accessed May 26, 2005). See Pamela Mendels, "Up for Evaluation," *Newsday*, June 13, 1995, p. 6.

2 See Kwame Ture [Stokely Carmichael] and Charles Hamilton, *Black Power* (New York: Random House, 1967); the older approach is in Gordon Allport, *The Nature of Prejudice*, abridged edn. (New York: Anchor Books, 1958).

3 Philomena Essed, *Understanding Everyday Racism* (Newbury Park, CA: Sage, 1991), p. 50.

4 International Convention on the Elimination of All Forms of Racial Discrimination, www.hrcr.org/docs/CERD/cerd3.html (accessed September 13, 2013).

5 Amani Nuru-Jeter *et al.*, "'It's The Skin You're In': African-American Women Talk about Their Experiences of Racism," *Maternal and Child Health Journal* 13 (2009): 32. See also pp. 33–39.

6 Joe R. Feagin and Melvin P. Sikes, *Living with Racism: The Black Middle-Class Experience* (Boston: Beacon Press, 1994), p. 54.

7 John O. Calmore, "To Make Wrong Right: The Necessary and Proper Aspirations of Fair Housing," in *The State of Black America 1989* (New York: National Urban League, 1989), p. 89.

8 The lead researcher was Kerry Kawakami. I draw on summaries in "Racism: What We Say Doesn't Match What We Do," www.msnbc.msn.com/id/28563183/ (accessed June 29, 2009); and in "Study Finds Gap Between What We Say, Do About Racism," www.freep.com/article/20090108/NEWS07/90108092/1118/RSS (accessed March 13, 2009).

9 Leslie Houts Picca and Joe R. Feagin, *Two Faced Racism: Whites in the Backstage and Frontstage* (New York: Routledge, 2007).

10 Joe R. Feagin, Hernán Vera, and Nikitah Imani, *The Agony of Education: Black Students at White Colleges and Universities* (New York: Routledge, 1996); Joe R. Feagin and Karyn D. McKinney, *The Many Costs of Racism* (Lanham, MD: Rowman & Littlefield, 2003; and Joe R. Feagin, *Systemic Racism: A Theory of Oppression* (New York: Routledge, 2006).

11 "Views of Law Enforcement, Racial Progress and News Coverage of Race," Pew Research Center, March 30, 2012, www.people-press.org/2012/03/30/blacks-view-of-law-enforcement-racial-progress-and-news-coverage-of-race/ (accessed June 11, 2013).

12 Gallup Organization, *Blacks and Whites Still Perceive Local Treatment of Blacks Differently* (Princeton, NJ: Gallup Organization, 2003), www.gallup.com/poll/8476/BlacksWhites-Still-Perceive-Local-Treatment-Blacks-Differently.aspx (accessed January 18, 2008); Gallup Organization, *Black–White Relations 2001 Update* (Princeton, NJ: Gallup Organization, 2001), pp. 1–24, at www.gallup.com/poll/9901/BlackWhite-RelationsUnited-States-2001-Update.aspx (accessed May 15, 2009).

13 Gene Demby, "New Survey Takes a Snapshot of the View from Black America," NPR, www.npr.org/blogs/codeswitch/2013/06/04/188301149/new-survey-takes-a-snapshot-of-the-view-from-black-america (accessed June 11, 2013).

14 Josephine Louie, "We Don't Feel Welcome Here: African Americans and Hispanics in Metro Boston," Harvard University Civil Rights Project, research report, April 25, 2005, pp. i–iii.

15 Michael Omi and Howard Winant, *Racial Formation in the United States* (New York: Routledge, 1986); Joe R. Feagin and Sean Elias, "Rethinking Racial Formation Theory: A Systemic Racism Critique, *Ethnic and Racial Studies* 36 (2012): 1–30.

16 The National Commission on the Voting Rights Act, *Protecting Minority Voters: The Voting Rights Act at Work 1982–2005* (Washington, DC:, Lawyers' Committee for Civil Rights under Law, 2006); Chandler Davidson, Tanya Dunlap, Gale Kenny, and Benjamin Wise, *Republican Ballot Security Programs: Vote Protection or Minority Vote Suppression—or Both?* Report to Center for Voting Rights and Protection, September 2004; Roy L. Brooks, Gilbert Paul Carrasco, and Michael Selmi, *The Law of Discrimination: Cases and Perspectives* (New Providence, NJ: LexisNexis, 2012), pp. 650–651.

17 Chandler Davidson, "The Historical Context of Voter Photo ID Laws," *PS: Political Science and Politics* 42 (January 2009): 93–95.

18 Davidson *et al.*, *Republican Ballot Security Programs;* see also National Commission on the Voting Rights Act, *Protecting Minority Voters.*

19 Chandler Davidson, Tanya Dunlap, Gale Kenny, and Benjamin Wise, "Vote Caging as a Republican Ballot Security Technique," *William Mitchell Law Review* 34 (2008): 533–562.

20 *Shelby County, Ala. v. Holder*, 2013 BL 167707 (U.S. June 25, 2013).

21 *City of Richmond, Virginia v. J. A. Croson Co.*, 488 U.S. 469 (1989).

22 Michel Rosenfeld, "Decoding Richmond: Affirmative Action and the Elusive Meaning of Constitutional Equality," *Michigan Law Review* 87 (June 1989): 1762.

23 *City of Richmond, Virginia v. J. A. Croson Co.*, 488 U.S. 469, 503 (1989).

24 Martin J. Katz, "The Economics of Discrimination: The Three Fallacies of Croson," *Yale Law Journal* 100 (January 1991): 1044.

25 *City of Richmond, Virginia v. J. A. Croson Co.*, 488 U.S. 469, 552–553 (1989).

26 Jerome McCristal Culp Jr., "Understanding the Racial Discourse of Justice Rehnquist," *Rutgers Law Journal* 25 (spring 1994): 604. See Matthew Smith, "Bridging the Gulf between Blacks and Whites," *Pittsburgh Post-Gazette*, April 7, 1996, p. A1.

27 *Parents Involved in Community Schools v. Seattle School District No. 1*, 551 U.S. 701, 803 (2007). See also pp. 835, 868. This case was heard in connection with *Meredith v. Jefferson County Board of Education*. See Joe R. Feagin, *White Party, White Government: Race, Class, and U.S. Politics* (New York: Routledge, 2012), pp. 138–140.

28 Gary Orfield, John Kucsera, and Genevieve Siegel-Hawley, *E Pluribus ... Separation: Deepening Double Segregation for More Students* (Los Angeles: UCLA Civil Rights Project, 2012), pp. 7–9.

29 Gunnar Myrdal, *An American Dilemma*, vol. I (New York: McGraw-Hill, 1964 [1944]); Joe R. Feagin and Harlan Hahn, *Ghetto Revolts* (New York: Macmillan, 1973).

30 Gallup Organization, *A Downturn in Black Perceptions of Racial Harmony* (Princeton, NJ: Gallup Organization, 2007), www.gallup.com/poll/28072/Downturn-Black-Perceptions-Racial-Harmony.aspx (accessed January 18, 2008); Gallup Organization, *Black–White Relations 2001 Update* (Princeton, NJ: Gallup Organization, 2001), pp. 1–24.

31 Kim Lersch and Joe R. Feagin, "Violent Police–Citizen Encounters: An Analysis of Major Newspaper Accounts," *Critical Sociology* 22 (1996): 29–49.

32 ACLU, "Racial Profiling Alert," www.aclu.org/racialjustice/racialprofiling/index.html (accessed May 15, 2009).

33 Jeffrey Fagan, Executive Summary [expert witness report], "Stop and Frisk: Updated Data Confirms Earlier Findings of Rights Violations," Center for Constitutional Rights, 2012. See also the research of Harry Levine in "Racial Disparity and Trickery in Marijuana Arrests," CUNY website, www1.cuny.edu/mu/podcasts/2010/07/29/racial-disparity-and-trickery-in-marijuana-arrests (accessed June 17, 2013).

34 ACLU, "Racial Profiling Alert," April 2006, www.aclu.org/racialjustice/racialprofiling/2 8283res20060401.html (accessed May 15, 2009).

35 ACLU, "Landmark Settlement Reached with Maryland State Police in 'Driving While Black' Case," www.aclu.org/racialjustice/racialprofiling/34753prs20080402.html (accessed May 15, 2009).

36 Michael R. Cogan, "The Drug Enforcement Agency's Use of Drug Courier Profiles: One Size Fits All," *Catholic University Law Review* 41 (1992): 943–946; David Harris, *Driving While Black: Racial Profiling on Our Nation's Highways* (New York: American Civil Liberties Union, 1999), as cited at www.lwvcincinnati.org/publications/Driving_While_Black.html (accessed February 2, 2006).

37 Keith Rushing, "Cardin Introduces the End Racial Profiling Act of 2013," Rights Working Group, May 24, 2013, www.rightsworkinggroup.org/content/cardin-introduces-end-racial-profiling-act-2013 (accessed June 14, 2013).

38 "U.N. Expert Calls on U.S. to Address Ongoing Issues of Racism," May 8, 2008, http://news.prnewswire.com/DisplayReleaseContent.aspx?ACCT=ind_focus.story&STORY=/www/story/05–08–2009/0005022751&EDATE= (accessed May 15, 2009).

39 Ian Ayres and Joel Waldfogel, "A Market Test for Race Discrimination in Bail Setting," *Stanford Law Review* 46 (May 1994): 993. See also p. 994; Johanna H. Foster, "Striving for Equity in Criminal Justice: An Analysis of Variability of Bail Bonds in the Tenth Judicial District of North Carolina," Master's paper, University of North Carolina (Chapel Hill), 2005.

40 Ezekiel Edwards, Will Bunting, and Lynda Garcia, *The War on Marijuana in Black and White* (New York: American Civil Liberties Union, 2013), pp. 3–9.

41 Ibid., pp. 3, 8.

42 David L. Lewis, "Bias in Drug Sentences," *National Law Journal* (February 5, 1996): p. A19.

43 Julie Rawe, "Congress's Bad Drug Habit," *Time*, November 19, 2007, p. 60; and Devlin Barrett, "Attorney General Wants Review of Cocaine Sentences," *Washington Post*, www.boston.com/news/nation/washington/articles/2009/06/24/attorney_general_wants_review_of_cocaine_sentences/ (accessed September 13, 2013).

44 "Minorities Dominate Federal Death Penalty Prosecutions," Death Penalty Information

Center, www.deathpenaltyinfo.org/federal-death-penalty#statutes (accessed June 17, 2013). See also G. Ben Cohen, and Robert J Smith, "The Racial Geography of the Federal Death Penalty," *Washington Law Review* 85 (2010): 425–492.

45 Glenn L. Pierce and Michael L. Radelet, "The Impact of Legally Inappropriate Factors on Death Sentencing for California Homicides, 1990–1999," *Santa Clara Law Review* 46 (2005): 1–49.

46 Amnesty International, *United States of America: Rights for All* (London: Amnesty International Publications, 1998), pp. 3, 109–110; Susan Estrich, *Real Rape* (Cambridge, MA: Harvard University Press, 1987), p. 107; Michael J. Carter, "Charges of Racism Offer New Evidence," InterPress Service, www.ipsnews.net/news.asp? idnews=42514 (accessed March 19, 2009). The Houston research was conducted by Scott Phillips.

47 Richard C. Dieter, *Struck by Lightning: The Continuing Arbitrariness of the Death Penalty Thirty-Five Years after Its Re-instatement in 1976* (Washington, DC: Death Penalty Information Center, 2011); "Innocence Project," Wikipedia, http://en.wikipedia.org/wiki/Capital_punishment_in_the_United_States#endnote_2 (accessed July 14, 2013).

48 David A. Love, "The Racial Bias of the US Death Penalty," *The Guardian*, January 3, 2012, at www.nodeathpenalty.org/news-and-updates/racial-bias-us-death-penalty (accessed July 16, 2013).

49 Amnesty International, *United States of America: Rights for All*, p. 110; see also Love, "The Racial Bias of the US Death Penalty."

50 William E. Martin and Peter N. Thompson, "Judicial Toleration of Racial Bias in the Minnesota Justice System," *Hamline Law Review* 25 (winter 2002): 235–270.

51 Roger Boesche, "How White People Riot: Quietly, at the Ballot Box," *Baltimore Sun*, October 15, 1995, p. 3F.

52 Feagin and Hahn, *Ghetto Revolts*, pp. 78–81.

53 FBI, *Hate-Crime Statistics, 2011* (Washington, DC: U.S. Department of Justice, 2012).

54 The quote is from "For the Record," *Intelligence Report* (SPLC), Spring 2013, www.splcenter.org/home/2012/spring/for-the-record#.UZJVB8pYxhE (accessed May 13, 2013).

55 Thomas Fields-Meyer *et al.*, "One Deadly Night: Deep in the Woods of East Texas, James Byrd Died a Terrible Death, Leaving a Town and a Nation in Shock," *People*, June 29, 1998, p. 46; Howard Chua-Eoan and Hilary Hylton-Austin, "Beneath the Surface: A 'New South' Town is Haunted by 'Deep South' Ghosts—And a Fresh, Ugly Murder," *Time*, June 22, 1998, p. 34. The *New York Times* article is dissected in Les Payne, "Exploitation and Dismissal of a Victim," *Newsday*, June 21, 1998, p. B6.

56 Gary Harki, "Six Arrested, Charged in Woman's Weeklong Torture," *Charleston Gazette*, September 11, 2007, p. 1A.

57 Sophia Hong, "New Noose Incident in Hempstead Town Building," *Newsday*, January 11, 2008, p. A22.

58 Paul Vitello, "Few Answers about Nooses, but Much Talk of Jim Crow," *New York Times*, October 21, 2007, www.nytimes.com/2007/10/21/nyregion/21noose.html?ex=1350705600&en=2b dea5e2571dfa16&ei=5124&partner=permalink&exprod=permalink (accessed May 17, 2009).

59 "Hate Map," Southern Poverty Law Center, 2013, www.splcenter.org/get-informed/hate-map (accessed June 16, 2013); Klanwatch Project, *False Patriots: The Threat of Antigovernment Extremists* (Montgomery: Southern Poverty Law Center, 1996), pp. 3–5.

60 "Hate and Extremism," Southern Poverty Law Center, www.splcenter.org/what-we-do/hate-and-extremism (accessed May 14, 2013); Southern Poverty Law Center, "Hate Group Numbers up by 54% since 2000," www. splcenter.org/news/item.jsp?aid=366 (accessed June 19, 2009).

61 "David Duke Holds Memphis News Conference," http://whitereference.blogspot.com/2008/11/dr-david-duke-holds-memphis-news.html (accessed December 26, 2008). On vandalism, see Greg Mitchell, "Racial Incidents and Threats against Obama Soar," November 15, 2008, www.huffingtonpost.com/greg-mitchell/racial-incidents-and-thre_b_144061.html (accessed December 29, 2008).

62 Jessie Daniels, *Cyber Racism* (Lanham, MD: Rowman & Littlefield, 2009), pp. 5–6; Sonia Scherr, "Hate Groups Claim Obama Win Is Sparking Recruitment Surge," Hatewatch, November 6, 2008, www.splcenter.org/blog/2008/11/06/hate-groups-claimobama-win-is-sparking-recruitment-surge (accessed December 26, 2008). I am indebted here to discussions with Daniels.

63 Jessie Daniels, "Race, Civil Rights, and Hate Speech in the Digital Era," in *Learning Race and Ethnicity: Youth and Digital Media*, ed. Anna Everett (Cambridge, MA: MIT Press, 2008), p. 129.

64 Alexander Tsesis, *Destructive Messages: How Hate Speech Paves the Way for Harmful Social Movements* (New York: NYU Press, 2002); Jennifer M. Pendleton, "Review of Destructive Messages," *Harvard Human Rights Journal* 16 (spring 2003): 312–314.

65 Jessie Daniels, "Race and Racism in Internet Studies: A Review and Critique," *New Media Society*, December 10, 2012, http://nms.sagepub.com/content/early/2012/12/06/1461444812462849 (accessed May 6, 2013).

66 James Wright, "Black Republicans Ponder Their Future," *Afro Newspapers*, November 24, 2008, http://blackpoliticsontheweb.com/2008/11/23/black-republicans-ponder-their-future/ (accessed September 13, 2013); Alexander Burns, "Steele: 'How Do You Like Me Now?'" *Politico*, January 30, 2009, http://dyn.politico.com/printstory.cfm?uuid=2A1BA222–18FE-70B2-A83323D0DB01F7E4 (accessed February 9, 2009).

67 Max Blumenthal, *Republican Gomorrah: Inside the Movement that Shattered the Party* (New York: Nation Books, 2010), Kindle DX locations 4816–4817.

68 Terence Fitzgerald, "Change? Don't Count on It: American Racism is on Full Display," *RacismReview*, racismreview.com (accessed April 5, 2011); Terence Fitzgerald, "Politically Recycling the Great Divide," *RacismReview*, October 20, 2008, www.racismreview.com/blog/2008/10/20/politically-recycling-the-great-divide/ (accessed April 10, 2011); Jim Brunner "Snohomish County GOP Pulls '$3 Bills' Smearing Obama from Fair Booth," *Seattle Times*, August 27, 2008, http://seattletimes.nwsource.com/html/localnews/2008140846_fair27m0.html (accessed April 26, 2011). For detailed analysis, see Joe R. Feagin, *White Party, White Government: Race, Class, and U.S. Politics* (New York: Routledge, 2012), pp. 142–190.

69 Quoted in Amy Goodman, "Former McCain Supporter: McCain Is 'Unleashing the Monster of American Prejudice,'" *Democracy Now*, October 13, 2008, www.alternet.org/rights/102837/former_mccain_supporter%3A_mccain_is_%22unleashing_the_monster_of_american_prejudice%22/?page=2 (accessed April 25, 2011).

70 Devin Burghart, "Tea Party Nation Warns of White Anglo-Saxon Protestant 'Extinction'" IREHR, March 29, 2011, www.irehr.org/issue-areas/tea-parties/19-news/76-tea-party-nation-warns-of-white-anglo-saxon-protestant-extinction (retrieved April 15, 2011).

71 Devin Burghart, Leonard Zeskind, and the Institute for Research and Education on Human Rights, *Tea Party Nationalism*, August 2010, www.teapartynationalism.com (retrieved April 15, 2011); and Kate Zernike, *Boiling Mad: Inside Tea Party America* (New York: Henry Holt Times Books, 2010), passim.

72 Ed Kilgore, "Cracker to Cracker," *Washington Monthly*, May 13, 2013, www.washingtonmonthly.com/political-animal-a/2013_05/cracker_to_cracker044789.php (accessed June 6, 2013).

6 More Racial Oppression: Other Institutional Sectors

1 John R. Logan and Brian Stults, *The Persistence of Segregation in the Metropolis: New Findings from the 2010 Census: Census Brief Prepared for Project US2010* (Providence, RI: Brown University, 2011), pp. 2–3.

2 Ibid., p. 21.

3 Jorge de la Roca, Ingrid Gould Ellen, and Katherine O'Regan, "Race and Neighborhoods in the Twenty-first Century: What Does Segregation Mean Today?" unpublished research paper, New York University, March 2013, p. 18.

4 Logan and Stults, *The Persistence of Segregation in the Metropolis,* p. 23; John R. Logan, Brian J. Stults, and Reynolds Farley, "Segregation of Minorities in the Metropolis: Two Decades of Change," unpublished research paper, Center for Social and Demographic Analysis, University of Albany, 2004, p. 11; Richard D. Alba, John R. Logan, and Brian J. Stults, "How Segregated Are Middle-Class African Americans?" *Social Problems* 47 (November 2000): 543–558.

5 *Jones et ux. v. Alfred H. Mayer Co.,* 392 U.S. 441–443 (1968).

6 Ibid., p. 445 (1968). See also Joe R. Feagin, "Excluding Blacks and Others from Housing: The Foundation of White Racism," *Cityscape* 4 (1999): 79–91.

7 Stephen G. Meyer, *As Long As They Don't Move Next Door: Segregation and Racial Conflict in American Neighborhoods* (Lanham, MD: Rowman & Littlefield, 2000), p. 8.

8 U.S. Housing Scholars and Research and Advocacy Organizations, *Residential Segregation and Housing Discrimination in the United States: Report to the U.N. Committee on the Elimination of Racial Discrimination* (Washington, DC: Poverty and Race Research Action Council and National Fair Housing Alliance, 2008); Farai Chideya, *The Color of Our Future* (New York: William Morrow, 1999), p. 132. See also Douglas S. Massey and Nancy A. Denton, *American Apartheid: Segregation and the Making of the Underclass* (Cambridge, MA: Harvard University Press, 1993).

9 "The Multi-City Study of Urban Inequality," *Russell Sage Foundation Newsletter,* fall 1999, p. 2; Margery Austin Turner, Raymond J. Struyk, and John Yinger, *Housing Discrimination Study: Synthesis* (Washington, DC: U.S. Government Printing Office, 1991), pp. ii–viii; Fair Housing Action Center, Inc., "Greater New Orleans Rental Audit," New Orleans, 1996; San Antonio Fair Housing Council, "San Antonio Metropolitan Area Rental Audit 1997," San Antonio, 1997. See also Fair Housing Council of Greater Washington, as reported in Caroline E. Mayer, "Minorities Said to Face Bias in House Hunting; Study Finds Blacks, Hispanics Treated Worse," *Washington Post,* April 9, 1997, p. C9; U.S. Housing Scholars and Research and Advocacy Organizations, *Residential Segregation and Housing Discrimination in the United States.*

10 Shanna L. Smith, National Fair Housing Alliance, "Testimony Before the House Financial Services Committee, Subcommittee on Housing and Community Opportunity," February 28, 2006, www.house.gov/financialservices/media/pdf/022806ss.pdf. (accessed May 18, 2009).

11 Margery Austin Turner *et al., Housing Discrimination against Racial and Ethnic Minorities 2012* (Washington, DC: U.S. Department of Housing and Urban Development, 2013), pp. 1–5.

12 Adrian G. Carpusor and William E. Loges, "Rental Discrimination and Ethnicity in Names," *Journal of Applied Social Psychology* 36 (April 2006): 934–952.

13 Vincent J. Roscigno, Diana L. Karafin, and Griff Tester, "The Complexities and Processes of Racial Housing Discrimination," *Social Problems* 56 (February 2009): 49–69. The quote is on p. 67.

14 Stacie B. Royster, "Lawyers' Committee Applauds HUD's Release of Proposed Regulation Concerning Disparate Impact Claims under the Fair Housing Act," November 17, 2011, www.lawyerscommittee.org/newsroom/press_releases?id=0182 (accessed June 17, 2013). See also Gregory D. Squires, "The Disparate Impact Rule Works," *American Banker,* February 22, 2013, pp. 9–10.

15 Martin D. Abravanel and Mary K. Cunningham, *How Much Do We Know? Public Awareness of the Nation's Fair Housing Laws* (Washington, DC: U.S. Department of Housing and Urban Development, 2002), p. 20.

16 See Stephen Thernstrom and Abigail Thernstrom, *America in Black and White: One Nation, Indivisible, Race in Modern America* (New York: Simon & Schuster, 1997).

17 Maria Krysan and Reynolds Farley, "The Residential Preferences of Blacks: Do They Explain Persistent Segregation?" *Social Forces* 80 (March 2002): 937–980.

18 Meyer, *As Long As They Don't Move Next Door,* pp. 219–220; Krysan and Farley, "The Residential Preferences of Blacks," pp. 937–980.

19 Shanna L. Smith and Cathy Clous, "Documenting Discrimination by Homeowners Insurance Companies through Testing," in *Insurance Redlining: Disinvestment, Reinvestment, and the Evolving Role of Financial Institutions*, ed. Gregory D. Squires (Washington, DC: Urban Institute Press, 1997), pp. 106–117; John Goering and Ron Wienk, "An Overview," in *Mortgage Lending, Racial Discrimination, and Federal Policy*, eds. J. Goering and R. Wienk (Washington, DC: Urban Institute Press, 1996), pp. 16–19.

20 Gregory D. Squires, personal communication; see Sunwoong Kim and Gregory D. Squires, "The Color of Money and the People Who Lent It," *Journal of Housing Research* 9 (1998): 271–284.

21 Trevor Delaney, "Subprime Lenders Under Fire," *Black Enterprise* (October 2007): 31–32; Vikas Bajaj and Ford Fessenden, "What's Behind the Race Gap?" *New York Times*, November 4, 2007, p. 16.

22 Delaney, "Subprime Lenders Under Fire"; Bajaj and Fessenden, "What's Behind the Race Gap?"

23 "NFHA Condemns Racist Bloomberg Businessweek Magazine Cover," press release, March 1, 2013. The release cites Shanna L. Smith, CEO of NFHA.

24 Joe Sims, "How Racism Sparked Capitalism's Financial Crisis," *People's Weekly World Newspaper*, www.pww.org/article/articleview/14364 (accessed March 19, 2009).

25 National Fair Housing Alliance, *The Banks are Back—Our Neighborhoods are not Discrimination in the Maintenance and Marketing of REO Properties* (Washington, DC: National Fair Housing Alliance, 2012), p. 3. See also pp. 2–5.

26 Joe R. Feagin and Robert Parker, *Building American Cities* (Englewood Cliffs, NJ: Prentice Hall, 1990), chapter 5; Leland T. Saito, *The Politics of Exclusion: The Failure of Race Neutral Policies in Urban America* (Palo Alto, CA: Stanford University Press, 2009).

27 National Fair Housing Alliance, *Fair Housing Enforcement: Time for a Change*, May 1, 2009, Washington, DC; National Commission on Fair Housing and Equal Opportunity, Report, 2008, as summarized in Gary Orfield, *Reviving the Goal of an Integrated Society: A Twenty-first-Century Challenge* (Los Angeles: UCLA Civil Rights Project, 2009), p. 5.

28 National Fair Housing Alliance, *Fair Housing in a Changing Nation: 2012 Fair Housing Trends Report* (Washington, DC: National Fair Housing Alliance, 2012), pp. 1–12; and an email communication with Shanna L. Smith, National Fair Housing Alliance, June 17, 2013.

29 Feagin and Parker, *Building American Cities*, chapter 8; Huiping Li, Harrison Campbell and Steven Fernandez, "Residential Segregation, Spatial Mismatch and Economic Growth across US Metropolitan Areas," *Urban Studies* (May 2013): 1–19.

30 Yves Zenou, "Spatial versus Social Mismatch," *Journal of Urban Economics* 74 (2013): 113–132.

31 "The Multi-City Study of Urban Inequality," pp. 1–3, and its supplement.

32 Li *et al.*, "Residential Segregation, Spatial Mismatch and Economic Growth across US Metropolitan Areas," pp. 1–19.

33 James H. Johnson, Jr., Grover C. Burthey, III, and Kevin Ghorm, "Economic Globalization and the Future of Black America," *Journal of Black Studies* 38 (2008): 883–899; see also Sidney M. Willhelm, *Black in a White America* (Cambridge, MA: Schenkman, 1983), p. 345.

34 Equal Employment Opportunity Commission, "Race-Based Charges: FY 1997–FY 2012," www.eeoc.gov/eeoc/statistics/enforcement/race.cfm (accessed July 11, 2013); Josephine Louie, "We Don't Feel Welcome Here: African Americans and Hispanics in Metro Boston," Harvard University Civil Rights Project, research report, April 25, 2005, pp. i–iii.

35 Alfred W. Blumrosen *et al.*, *Employment Discrimination Against Women and Minorities in Georgia* (Newark, NJ: Rutgers University S. I. Newhouse Center for Law and Justice, 1999).

36 Stevie Watson, Osei Appiah, Corliss G. Thornton, "The Effect of Name on

Pre-Interview Impressions and Occupational Stereotypes: The Case of Black Sales Job Applicants," *Journal of Applied Social Psychology* 41 (2011): 2405–2420. The quote is from p. 2414.

37 Devah Pager, "The Mark of a Criminal Record," *American Journal of Sociology* 108 (March 2008): 937–975. I also draw on David Wessel, "Racial Discrimination: Still at Work in the U.S.," *Wall Street Journal* Online, at www.careerjournal.com/myc/diversity/20030916-wessel.html (accessed May 26, 2005); and Devah Pager and Lincoln Quillian, "Walking the Talk: What Employers Say versus What They Do," *American Sociological Review* 70 (June 2005): 355–380.

38 Marc Bendick, Jr., "Situation Testing for Employment Discrimination in the United States of America," *Revue Horizons Stratégiques, Centre d'Analyse Stratégique*, July 2007, pp. 6–18.

39 Margaret M. Zamudio and Michael I. Lichter, "Bad Attitudes and Good Soldiers: Soft Skills as a Code for Tractability in the Hiring of Immigrant Latina/os over Native Blacks in the Hotel Industry," *Social Problems* 55 (November 2008): 573–589.

40 Marc Bendick, Jr., "Race–Ethnic Employment Discrimination in Upscale Restaurants: Evidence from Paired Comparison Testing," Bendick and Egan Economic Consultants, Washington, DC, February 2009; Marc Bendick Jr., Rekha Eanni Rodriguez, and Sarumathi Jayaraman, "Employment Discrimination in Upscale Restaurants: Evidence from Matched Pair Testing, *Social Science Journal* 47 (2010): 802–818; Jennifer Lee, "Racial Bias Seen in Hiring of Waiters," *New York Times*, March 31, 2009, http://cityroom.blogs.nytimes.com/2009/03/31/racial-bias-seen-in-hiring-of-waiters/?hp (accessed April 7, 2009).

41 Brian D. Volz, "Race and the Likelihood of Managing in Major League Baseball," *Journal of Labor Research* 34 (2013): 30–51; Erica R. Smith, "The Rooney Rule: Affirmative Action Policy and Institutional Discrimination in the National Football League," unpublished PhD dissertation, University of Miami, 2008; John N. Singer, C. Keith Harrison, and Scott J. Bukstein, "A Critical Race Analysis of the Hiring Process for Head Coaches in NCAA College Football," *Journal of Intercollegiate Sport* 3 (2010): 270–296; Barry Bozeman and Daniel Fay, "Minority Football Coaches' Diminished Careers: Why is the 'Pipeline' Clogged?" *Social Science Quarterly* 94 (March 2013): 29–58. I am indebted to Michael Regan for these references.

42 Kwame Agyemang and Joshua DeLorme, "Examining the Dearth of Black Head Coaches at the NCAA Football Bowl Subdivision Level: A Critical Race Theory and Social Dominance Theory," *Journal of Issues in Intercollegiate Athletics* 3 (2010), p. 35.

43 Scoop Jackson, "African-American Agents, and Us," ESPN.com, February 9, 2012, http://espn.go.com/espn/commentary/story/_/page/jackson-120209/progress-slow-african-american-sports-agents| (accessed June 7, 2013).

44 Mikaela J. Dufur and Seth L. Feinberg, "Race and the NFL Draft: Views from the Auction Block," *Qualitative Sociology* 32 (2009), p. 68. See also pp. 60–69.

45 William C. Rhoden, *Forty Million Dollar Slaves: The Rise, Fall, and Redemption of the Black Athlete* (New York: Three Rivers Press, 2007). The quote is from the cover text.

46 Kevin B. Blackistone, "The Whitening of Sports Media and the Coloring of Black Athletes' Images," *Wake Forest Journal of Law and Policy* 2 (2012): 215–225.

47 "Locked Out: The Lack of Gender and Ethnic Diversity on Cable News Continues," *Media Matters*, May 7, 2007, http://mediamatters.org/reports/200705070003 (accessed May 26, 2009).

48 Marc Bendick Jr., *Discrimination Against Racial/Ethnic Minorities in the United States: Empirical Findings from Situation Testing* (Geneva: International Labor Organization, 1996), p. 24.

49 Zenou, "Spatial versus Social Mismatch," pp. 113–132.

50 Nancy DiTomaso, *The American Non-Dilemma: Racial Inequality without Racism* (New York: Russell Sage, 2013), pp. 64–66; Nancy DiTomaso, "How Social Networks Drive Black Unemployment," *New York Times* blog, May 5, 2013, http://opinionator.blogs.

nytimes.com/2013/05/05/how-social-networks-drive-black-unemployment/?nl=today
sheadlines&emc=edit_th_20130506 (accessed May 6, 2013).

51 Donald Tomaskovic-Devey, M. Thomas, and K. Johnson, "Race and the Accumulation of Human Capital across the Career: A Theoretical Model and Fixed-effects Application," *American Journal of Sociology* 111 (2005): 58–89.

52 Deirdre A. Royster, *Race and the Invisible Hand: How White Networks Exclude Black Men from Blue-Collar Jobs* (Los Angeles: University of California Press, 2003).

53 Christopher M. Boulton, "Rebranding Diversity: Colorblind Racism Inside the U.S. Advertising Industry," unpublished PhD dissertation, University of Massachusetts, 2012.

54 Marc Bendick, Jr. and Mary Lou Egan, "Research Perspectives on Race and Employment in the Advertising Industry," Bendick and Egan Economic Consultants, Inc., Washington, DC, January 2009, p. 1.

55 Ibid., p. 1.

56 Marc Bendick, Jr., Mary Lou Egan, and Louis Lanier, "The 'Business Case for Diversity' and the Pernicious Practice of Matching Employees to Customers," paper presented at Tenth International Human Resource Management Conference, Santa Fe, NM, June 2009, p. 12. Italics added. See also Stuart Elliott, "Advertising: A Lawyer's Call for a Greater Black Presence in Agencies," *New York Times*, January 8, 2009, www.nytimes.com/2009/01/09/business/media/09adco.html?_r=1 (accessed April 7, 2009).

57 Marc Bendick, Jr., Mary Lou Egan, and Suzanne Lofhjelm, "Workforce Diversity Training: From Anti-Discrimination Compliance to Organization Development," *Human Resource Planning* 24 (2001): 10–25.

58 Jason K. Dempsey and Robert Y. Shapiro, "The Army's Hispanic Future," *Armed Forces and Society* 35 (2009), p. 553. See also Gary Langer, "Racial Discrimination: An Army Survey," ABC News, January 6, 2009, http://abcnews.go.com/blogs/politics/2009/01/racial-relation (accessed June 21, 2013).

59 Lawrence Bobo and Susan A. Suh, "Surveying Racial Discrimination: Analyses from a Multiethnic Labor Market," unpublished research report, Department of Sociology, University of California at Los Angeles, August 1, 1995.

60 Ryan A. Smith, *Changing the Face of Public Service Leadership: A Research Report and Call To Action* (New York: National Urban Fellows, 2010), pp. 19–21, 43.

61 Donna Chrobot-Mason, Belle Rose Ragins, and Frank Linnehan, "Second Hand Smoke: Ambient Racial Harassment at Work," *Journal of Managerial Psychology* 23 (2013): 470–491.

62 Marc Bendick, Jr., Mary Lou Egan, and Suzanne Lofhjelm, *The Documentation and Evaluation of Anti-Discrimination Training in the United States* (Geneva: International Labour Organization, 1998), p. 9.

63 Smith, *Changing the Face of Public Service Leadership*, p. 19.

64 Benjamin P. Bowser, *The Black Middle Class: Social Mobility—and Vulnerability* (Boulder, CO: Lynne Rienner Publishers, 2007), p. 140.

65 Jesse Washington, "Study: Networking Hinders Black Women Executives," Associated Press, January 7, 2009, www.foxnews.com/wires/2009Jan07/0,4670,BlackWomenExecutives,00.html (accessed March 19, 2009).

66 See, for example, Bendick *et al.*, *The Documentation and Evaluation of Anti-Discrimination Training in the United States*, p. 9.

67 Edna Chun and Alvin Evans, *Diverse Administrators in Peril: The New Indentured Class in Higher Education* (Boulder, CO: Paradigm, 2012). See also Alvin Evans and Edna Chun, *Creating a Tipping Point: Strategic Human Resources in Higher Education* (San Francisco: Jossey-Bass, 2012).

68 Edna Chun and Alvin Evans, *The New Talent Acquisition Frontier: Integrating HR and Diversity Strategy in the Private and Public Sectors and Higher Education* (Sterling, VA: Stylus, 2013), p. 128.

69 George F. Dreher and Taylor H. Cox, "Race. Gender and Opportunity: A Study of

Compensation Attainment and the Establishing of Mentoring Relationships," *Journal of Applied Psychology* 81 (1996): 297–308.

70 Derrick Bell, "Property Rights in Whiteness—Their Legal Legacy, Their Economic Costs," in *Critical Race Theory: The Cutting Edge*, ed. Richard Delgado (Philadelphia: Temple University Press, 1995), p. 75.

71 Cited in Tim Wise, "Commentary," http://academic.udayton.edu/race/01race/white10. htm (accessed November 24, 2004).

72 The Bureau of Labor Statistics data are summarized in Orfield, *Reviving the Goal of an Integrated Society*, p. 5; see also Bendick and Egan, "Research Perspectives on Race and Employment in the Advertising Industry," p. 1.

73 See Tomaskovic-Devey *et al.* "Race and the Accumulation of Human Capital Across the Career," pp. 58ff.

74 Magnus Lofstrom and Timothy Bates, "African Americans' Pursuit of Self-Employment," *Small Business Economics* 40 (2013): 73–86.

75 Thomas M. Shapiro, *The Hidden Cost of Being African American: How Wealth Perpetuates Inequality* (New York: Oxford University Press, 2004), p. 31; Jennifer C Mueller, "The Social Reproduction of Systemic Racial Inequality" unpublished PhD dissertation, Texas A&M University, 2013.

76 Martin J. Katz, "The Economics of Discrimination: The Three Fallacies of *Croson*," *Yale Law Journal* 100 (January 1991): 1044. For recent data, see Lofstrom and Bates, "African Americans' Pursuit of Self-Employment," pp. 73–84.

77 Maria Enchautegui *et al.*, *Do Minority-Owned Businesses Get a Fair Share of Government Contracts?* (Washington, DC: Urban Institute Press, 1996), p. 51; Timothy Bates and William D Bradford, "Venture-Capital Investment in Minority Business," *Journal of Money, Credit and Banking* 40 (March–April 2008): 489–503.

78 Lofstrom and Bates, "African Americans' Pursuit of Self-Employment," p. 84.

79 Adia Harvey Wingfield, personal communication. See Adia Harvey Wingfield, *Doing Business with Beauty: Black Women, Hair Salons, and the Racial Enclave Economy* (Lanham, MD: Rowman & Littlefield, 2008); Lofstrom and Bates, "African Americans' Pursuit of Self-Employment."

80 Viviana Bompadre, "Transparent Barriers," *Kellogg Insight*, http://insight.kellogg.northwestern.edu/article/transparent_barriers/(accessed June 24, 2013).

81 Gary Orfield, John Kucsera, and Genevieve Siegel-Hawley, *E Pluribus … Separation: Deepening Double Segregation for More Students* (Los Angeles: UCLA Civil Rights Project, 2012), pp. 7–9.

82 Orfield, *Reviving the Goal of an Integrated Society*, pp. 3–6.

83 *Freeman v. Pitts*, 503 U.S. 467 (1992). See also *Board of Education of Oklahoma v. Dowell* 488 U.S. 237 (1991).

84 Zeus Leonardo, *Race, Whiteness, and Education* (New York: Routledge, 2009), p. 10.

85 Orfield, *Reviving the Goal of an Integrated Society*, pp. 3–6; "Vital Statistics," *Journal of Blacks in Higher Education* (summer 2008), www.jbhe.com/vital/60_index.html (accessed April 6, 2009).

86 New York ACORN Schools Office, *Secret Apartheid: A Report on Racial Discrimination against Black and Latino Parents and Children in the New York City Public Schools* (New York: ACORN, 1996).

87 Allison Roda and Amy Stuart Wells, "School Choice Policies and Racial Segregation: Where White Parents' Good Intentions, Anxiety, and Privilege Collide," *American Journal of Education* 119 (February 2013), p. 277. See also pp. 261–293.

88 David N. Figlio, "Names, Expectations and the Black–White Test Score Gap," National Bureau of Economic Research Working Paper, March 2005, www.nber.org/papers/w11195 (accessed May 22, 2009); "University Of Florida Economist Finds that Black Children's Names Hinder Their Educational Development," *Journal of Blacks in Higher Education Weekly Bulletin* (May 26, 2005): 1.

89 Suzanne Russell, "'White Girls Club' at Franklin H.S. Posting Racially Insensitive

Comments and Photos," *NJ News*, April 22, 2013, www.mycentraljersey.com/article/20130418/NJNEWS/304180036/-White-Girls-Club-Franklin-H-S-posting-racially-insensitive-comments-photos?nclick_check=1 (accessed May 15, 2013).

90 Helena Andrews, "'White Girls Club' Is Neither Cool Nor Clever," *The Root*, May 15, 013, www.theroot.com/views/white-girls-club-neither-cool-nor-clever?page=0,1& wpisrc=root_lightbox (accessed May 15, 2013).

91 Chris Chapman, Jennifer Laird, Nicole Ifill, and Angelina Kewal-Ramani, *Trends in High School Dropout and Completion Rates in the United States: 1972–2009* (Washington, DC: National Center for Education Statistics, 2011).

92 Tukufu Zuberi and Eduardo Bonilla-Silva, eds., *White Logic, White Methods* (Lanham: Rowman & Littlefield, 2008).

93 Richard Delgado, *The Coming Race War?* (New York: New York University Press, 1996), p. 71.

94 "Vital Statistics," *Journal of Blacks in Higher Education*.

95 Sean F. Reardon, Rachel Baker, and Daniel Klasik, *Race, Income, and Enrollment Patterns in Highly Selective Colleges, 1982–2004* (Stanford, CA: Center for Education Policy Analysis, Stanford University, 2011), executive summary, n.p.

96 Associated Press, "Racism Tears through Providence College," May 5, 2013, www.nhregister.com/articles/2013/05/05/news/doc5187266841f52505913592.txt?viewmode=fullstory (accessed May 8, 2013).

97 C. Richard King and David J. Leonard, "The Rise of the Ghetto-Fabulous Party," *Colorlines Magazine*, October 5, 2007, www.diverseeducation.com/artman/publish/article_9687.shtml (accessed May 22, 2009).

98 This list is compiled from extensive reading of the media and Tim Wise, "Majoring in Minstrelsy: White Students, Blackface and the Failure of Mainstream Multiculturalism," June 22, 2007, www.lipmagazine.org/~timwise/minstrelsy.html (accessed May 22, 2009); and from King and Leonard, "The Rise of the Ghetto-Fabulous Party."

99 Jennifer C. Mueller, Danielle Dirks, and Leslie Houts Picca, "Unmasking Racism: Halloween Costuming and Engagement of the Racial Other," *Qualitative Sociology* 30 (2007): 315–335.

100 Ibid. See Rosalind Chou, "Racist Frame Is Still Firmly in the Minds of Educated Whites," www. racismreview.com (accessed May 22, 2009).

101 Brendesha M. Tynes and Suzanne L. Markoe, "The Role of Color-Blind Racial Attitudes in Reactions to Racial Discrimination on Social Networking Sites," *Journal of Diversity in Higher Education* 3 (2010), p. 1. See Jessie Daniels, "Race and Racism in Internet Studies: A Review and Critique," unpublished research paper, New York, Hunter College, 2012.

102 Leslie Houts Picca and Joe R. Feagin, "Experiences of Students of Color," University of Dayton, unpublished research, 2009.

103 Tamara Towles-Schwen and Russell H. Fazio, "Automatically Activated Racial Attitudes as Predictors of the Success of Interracial Roommate Relationships," *Journal of Experimental Social Psychology* 42 (2006): 698–705.

104 Stacey Patton, "At the Ivies, It's Still White at the Top," *Chronicle of Higher Education*, June 9, 2013, http://chronicle.com/article/At-the-Ivies-Its-Still-White/139643/ (accessed June 11, 2013).

105 Joe R. Feagin, *The White Racial Frame: Centuries of Racial Framing and Counter-Framing*, 2nd edn. (New York: Routledge, 2013), pp. 136–137.

106 Cynthia Willming, "Leisure-travel Behaviors of College-educated African Americans and Perceived Racial Discrimination," unpublished PhD dissertation, University of Florida, 2001. I draw on the summary in Danielle Dirks and Stephen K. Rice, "'Dining while Black': Tipping as Social Artifact," *Cornell Hotel and Restaurant Administration Quarterly* 45 (February 2004): 30–47.

107 Zachary W. Brewster and Sarah Nell Rusche, "Quantitative Evidence of the Continuing Significance of Race: Tableside Racism in Full-Service Restaurants," *Journal of Black Studies* 43 (2012): 359–384.

108 See citations in Jerome D. Williams, May O. Lwin, Anne-Marie G. Hakstian, and Velma A. R. Gooding, "Assessing Perceived Discrimination in 'Brick and Mortar' Retail Settings Using a Power–Responsibility Equilibrium Framework," in *Brick and Mortar Shopping in the Twenty-first Century*, ed. Tina Lowrey (Mahwah, NJ: Lawrence Erlbaum, 2007), pp. 172–179.

109 New Jersey Citizen Action, "New Report Highlights Impact of Hidden Practice of Auto Finance Markup on New Jersey Consumers," press release, February 23, 2005, www. njcitizenaction.org/craautofinancpress.html (accessed July 15, 2013).

110 Thomas L. Ainscough and Carol M. Motley, "Will You Help Me, Please? The Effects of Race, Gender and Manner of Dress on Retail Service," *Marketing Letters* 11 (2000): 129–135. See also Anne-Marie G. Harris, "Shopping While Black: Applying 42 U.S.C. 1981 to Cases of Consumer Racial Profiling," *Boston College Third World Law Journal* 23 (2003): 1.

111 I am indebted here to discussions with Jessie Daniels.

112 Brendesha M. Tynes, Michael T. Giang, David R. Williams, and Geneene N. Thompson, "Online Racial Discrimination and Psychological Adjustment among Adolescents," *Journal of Adolescent Health* 43 (2008): 565–569.

113 Brendesha M. Tynes, Elizabeth L. García, Michael T. Giang, and Nicole E. Coleman, "The Racial Landscape of Social Network Sites: Forging Identity, Community, and Civic Engagement," *I/S: A Journal of Law and Policy* 7 (2011), pp. 71–72.

114 Tyan P. Dominguez, "Race, Racism, and Racial Disparities in Adverse Birth Outcomes," *Clinical Obstetrics and Gynecology* 51 (June 2008): 360–370; Tyan P. Dominguez *et al.*, "Stress in African American Pregnancies: Testing the Roles of Various Stress Concepts in Prediction of Birth Outcomes," *Annals of Behavioral Medicine* 29 (2005): 12–21; Tyan P. Dominguez *et al.*, "Racial Differences in Birth Outcomes: The Role of General, Pregnancy, and Racism Stress," *Health Psychology* 27 (2008): 194–203.

115 C. A. Morrison, "Pain and Ethnicity in the United States: A Systematic Review," *Journal of Palliative Medicine* 9 (2006): 1454. See also Joe R. Feagin and Zinobia Bennefield, "Systemic Racism and U.S. Health and Health Care," *Social Science and Medicine*, forthcoming, 2014; Eric L. Krakauer, Christopher Crenner, and Ken Fox, "Barriers to Optimum End-of-life Care for Minority Patients," *Journal of the American Geriatric Society* 50 (2002): 182–190. "Mental Health Care Doesn't Meet Standards, Study Finds," *Research Matters*, www. researchmatters.harvard.edu/story.php?article_id=108 (accessed May 26, 2005).

116 J. Sabin, B. A. Nosek, A. Greenwald, and F. P. Rivara, "Physicians' Implicit and Explicit Attitudes about Race by MD Race, Ethnicity, and Gender," *Journal of Health Care for the Poor and Underserved* 20 (2009): 896–913. Several studies are reported in Vanessa Housing, "Doctors in Study Prefer Whites to Blacks: UW Researchers Take a Look at Physician Biases," SeattlePI.com, October 29, 2008, http://seattlepi.nwsource.com/local/385343_doctorbias29.html?source=rss (accessed April 6, 2009).

117 Alexander R. Green *et al.*, "Implicit Bias among Physicians and Its Prediction of Thrombolysis Decisions for Black and White Patients," *Journal of General and Internal Medicine* 24 (January 2009): 137–140; L. A. Cooper *et al.*, "The Associations of Clinicians' Implicit Attitudes about Race with Medical Visit Communication and Patient Ratings of Interpersonal Care," *American Journal of Public Health* 102 (2012): 979–987.

118 Cynthia Gordy, "Troubled Waters," *Essence*, July 2007, pp. 146–176. See also Robert D. Bullard, Glenn S. Johnson, and Angel O. Torres, *Environmental Health and Racial Equity in the United States: Strategies for Building Environmentally Just, Sustainable, and Livable Communities* (Washington, DC: American Public Health Association Press, 2011).

119 Paul Mohai and Robin Saha, "Racial Inequality in the Distribution of Hazardous Waste: A National-Level Reassessment," *Social Problems* 54 (August 2007): 343–370.

120 Robert D. Bullard and Beverly Wright, *The Wrong Complexion for Protection: How the Government Response to Disaster Endangers African American Communities* (New York: New York University Press, 2012), p. 3.

121 Quoted in Benjamin B. Ringer, *"We the People" and Others* (New York: Tavistock, 1983), p. 327.

7 White Privileges and Black Burdens: Still Systemic Racism

1 Joe R. Feagin and Melvin P. Sikes, *Living with Racism: The Black Middle-Class Experience* (Boston: Beacon Press, 1994), pp. 295–296; Joe R. Feagin and Karyn D. McKinney, *The Many Costs of Racism* (Lanham, MD: Rowman & Littlefield, 2003), pp. 39–64.

2 Karyn D. McKinney, "'I Really Felt White': Turning Points in Whiteness Through Inter-racial Contact," *Social Identities* 12 (2006): 183; Joe R. Feagin and Eileen O'Brien, *White Men on Race: Power, Privilege and the Shaping of Cultural Consciousness* (Boston: Beacon Press, 2003); Joyce E. King, "Dysconscious Racism: Ideology, Identity, and the Miseducation of Teachers," *Journal of Negro Education* 60 (1991): 135.

3 McKinney, "'I Really Felt White'" p. 183 and passim; Joe R. Feagin, *The White Racial Frame: Centuries of Racial Framing and Counter-Framing*, 2nd edn. (New York: Routledge, 2013), pp. 222–224.

4 Jane Lazarre, *Beyond the Whiteness of Whiteness* (Durham, NC: Duke University Press, 1996), p. 41.

5 Nyla R. Branscombe, Michael T. Schmitt, and Kristin Schiffhauer, "Racial Attitudes in Response to Thoughts of White Privilege," *European Journal of Social Psychology* 37 (2007): 203–215. The quote is on p. 213.

6 Frances Lee Ansley, "Stirring the Ashes: Race, Class and the Future of Civil Rights Scholarship," *Cornell Law Review* 74 (September 1989): 1035.

7 See Theodore Cross, *The Black Power Imperative: Racial Inequality and the Politics of Nonviolence* (New York: Faulkner, 1984), p. 510.

8 David R. Roediger, *The Wages of Whiteness: Race and the Making of the American Working Class* (London: Verso, 1991), p. 12; see also Joe R. Feagin, Clairece B. Feagin, and David Baker, *Social Problems*, 6th edn. (Upper Saddle River, NJ: Prentice Hall, 2005), pp. 462–463, 500.

9 Trina Williams, "The Homestead Act—Our Earliest National Asset Policy," paper presented at the Center for Social Development's symposium, Inclusion in Asset Building, St. Louis, Missouri, September 21–23, 2000; Kenneth W. Smallwood, "The Folklore of Preferential Treatment," unpublished manuscript, Southfield, Michigan, 1985; Cross, *The Black Power Imperative*, pp. 515–518.

10 Irving Kristol, "The Negro Today Is Like the Immigrant of Yesterday," *New York Times Magazine*, September 11, 1966, pp. 50–51, 124–412.

11 Theodore Hershberg *et al.*, "A Tale of Three Cities: Blacks, Immigrants, and Opportunity in Philadelphia, 1850–1880, 1930, 1970," in *Philadelphia: Work, Space, Family and Group Experience in the Nineteenth Century*, ed. T. Hershberg (New York: Oxford University Press, 1981), pp. 462–464.

12 Herbert Hill, "The Racial Practices of Organized Labor—the Age of Gompers and After," in *Employment, Race and Poverty*, eds. Arthur M. Ross and Herbert Hill (New York: Harcourt, Brace & World, 1967), p. 365; Stanley B. Greenberg, *Race and State in Capitalist Development* (New Haven, CT: Yale University Press, 1980), p. 349.

13 Sophia Hong, "New Noose Incident in Hempstead Town Building," *Newsday*, January 11, 2008, p. A22; Joe R. Feagin, *Systemic Racism: A Theory of Oppression* (New York: Routledge, 2006), pp. 199–207. On the costs, see Joe R. Feagin, Kevin Early, and Karyn D. McKinney, "The Many Costs of Discrimination: The Case of Middle-Class African Americans," *Indiana Law Review* 34 (2001): 1313–1360.

14 See Cross, *The Black Power Imperative*, pp. 515–518; Melvin L. Oliver and Thomas M. Shapiro, *Black Wealth/White Wealth: A New Perspective on Racial Inequality* (New York: Routledge, 1995), pp. 36–45.

15 Ira Katznelson, *When Affirmative Action Was White: An Untold History of Racial Inequality in Twentieth-Century America* (New York: W. W. Norton, 2005), pp. 38ff.

16 Ibid., pp. 38–39; David Roediger, *Working Toward Whiteness* (New York: Basic Books, 2005).

17 Harvard Sitkoff, *A New Deal for Blacks* (New York: Oxford University Press, 1978); Joe R. Feagin, "Slavery Unwilling to Die: The Background of Black Oppression in the 1980s," *Journal of Black Studies* 17 (December 1986): 173–200; Cross, *The Black Power Imperative*, p. 515.

18 See Joe R. Feagin, *White Party, White Government: Race, Class, and U.S. Politics* (New York: Routledge, 2012), passim.

19 Crosby Burns, Kimberly Barton, and Sophia Kerby, *The State of Diversity in Today's Workforce* (Washington, DC: Center for American Progress, 2012), p. 4. See also Jesse Washington, "Study: Networking Hinders Black Women Executives," Associated Press, January 7, 2009, www.foxnews.com/wires/2009Jan07/0,4670,BlackWomenExecutives,00.html (accessed March 19, 2009).

20 Nancy DiTomaso, "How Social Networks Drive Black Unemployment," *New York Times* blog, May 5, 2013, http://opinionator.blogs.nytimes.com/2013/05/05/how-social-networks-drive-black-unemployment/?nl=todaysheadlines&emc=edit_th_20130506 (accessed May 6, 2013).

21 United for a Fair Economy Staff, *Born on Third Base: What the Forbes 400 Really Says about Economic Equality and Opportunity in America* (Boston: United for a Fair Economy, 2012), pp. 14–15.

22 *Dred Scott v. John F. A. Sandford*, 60 U.S. 393, 407 (1857). Emphasis added. On women in Fortune 500, see Burns, Barton, and Kerby, *The State of Diversity in Today's Workforce*, pp. 4–5.

23 Mary Beth Norton, *Liberty's Daughters* (Boston: Little, Brown, 1980); Edmund S. Morgan, *American Slavery, American Freedom: The Ordeal of Virginia* (New York: Norton, 1975), p. 165.

24 Carmen DeNavas-Walt, Bernadette D. Proctor, Jessica C. Smith, "Income, Poverty and Health Insurance Coverage in the United States: 2011," U.S. Census Bureau, September 2012, www.census.gov/newsroom/releases/archives/income_wealth/cb12–172.html (accessed July 3, 2013); Graduate Minority Student Project, University of California (Berkeley), "Statistics of Racism in the United States: Income, Health, and Rights," http://struggle4reparations. com/starkey/rep_sta.html (accessed May 27, 2009).

25 DeNavas-Walt *et al.*, "Income, Poverty and Health Insurance Coverage in the United States: 2011."

26 Signe-Mary McKernan, Caroline Ratcliffe, Eugene Steuerle, and Sisi Zhang, *Less than Equal: Racial Disparities in Wealth Accumulation* (Washington, DC: Urban Institute, 2013), p. 5. For earlier data and longitudinal analysis, see Thomas Shapiro, Tatjana Meschede, and Sam Osoro, *The Roots of the Widening Racial Wealth Gap: Explaining the Black–White Economic Divide* (Waltham, MA: Brandeis Institute on Assets and Social Policy, 2013).

27 McKernan *et al.*, *Less than Equal*, p. 1. I also draw on Thomas M. Shapiro, *The Hidden Cost of Being African American: How Wealth Perpetuates Inequality* (New York: Oxford University Press, 2004), p. 31.

28 Madura Wijewardena, "Understanding the Equality Index," in *The 2013 State of Black America* (New York: National Urban League, 2013), pp. 23–27.

29 Dawn Turner Trice, "Downturn has Wiped Out Gains of Last 30 years, Urban League Says," *Black Star Journal*, October 07, 2012, http://blackstarjournal.org/?p=1551 (accessed May 16, 2013).

30 James Marketti, "Estimated Present Value of Income Diverted during Slavery," in *The Wealth of Races: The Present Value of Benefits from Past Injustices*, ed. Richard F. America (New York: Greenwood, 1990), p. 118.

31 Roger L. Ransom and Richard Sutch, "Growth and Welfare in the American South in the Nineteenth Century," in *Market Institutions and Economic Progress in the New South 1865–1900*, eds. Gary Walton and James Shepherd (New York: Academic Press, 1981),

pp. 150–151; David H. Swinton, "Racial Inequality and Reparations," in *The Wealth of Races*, ed. America, p. 156.

32 William A. Darity, Jr., "Forty Acres and a Mule: Placing the Price Tag on Oppression," in *The Wealth of Races*, ed. America, p. 11. Total figures have been put at $10–24 trillion by Richard America and Jack White. See Kevin Merida, "Did Freedom Alone Pay a Nation's Debt?" *Washington Post*, November 23, 1999, p. C1.

33 Stephen J. DeCanio, "Accumulation and Discrimination in the Postbellum South," in *Market Institutions and Economic Progress in the New South 1865–1900*, eds. Walton and Shepherd, p. 105; see also pp. 103–125.

34 Swinton, "Racial Equality and Reparations," p. 157.

35 Martin J. Katz, "The Economics of Discrimination: The Three Fallacies of *Croson*," *Yale Law Journal* 100 (January 1991): 1041–1045.

36 Shapiro, *The Hidden Cost of Being African American*, pp. 30–51; Oliver and Shapiro, *Black Wealth/White Wealth*, pp. 36–50.

37 Melvin L. Oliver and Thomas M. Shapiro, "Creating an Opportunity Society," *American Prospect* 18 (May 2007), p. A27. See Shapiro, *The Hidden Cost of Being African American*, pp. 70–72; Benjamin P. Bowser, *The Black Middle Class: Social Mobility—and Vulnerability* (Boulder, CO: Lynne Rienner Publishers, 2007), p. 87.

38 Andrew Hacker, *Two Nations: Black and White, Separate, Hostile, Unequal* (New York: Scribner's, 1992), pp. 31–32.

39 Patricia J. Williams, "Alchemical Notes: Reconstructing Ideals from Deconstructed Rights," *Harvard Civil Rights and Civil Liberties Review* 22 (1987): 415.

40 Ellis Cashmore, *The Black Culture Industry* (New York: Routledge, 1997), pp. 1, 3.

41 I am indebted to here discussions with Charity Clay.

42 Martin Luther King, Jr., *Where Do We Go from Here? Chaos or Community?* (New York: Bantam Books, 1967), p. 122.

43 Joe R. Feagin, *The White Racial Frame: Centuries of Racial Framing and Counter-Framing*, 2nd edn. (New York: Routledge, 2013), chapters 6 and 7; Feagin and Sikes, *Living with Racism: The Black Middle Class Experience*.

44 Joe R. Feagin and Zinobia Bennefield, "Systemic Racism and U.S. Health and Health Care," *Social Science and Medicine*, forthcoming, 2014; Judith Lichtenberg, "Racism in the Head, Racism in the World," *Philosophy and Public Policy* 12 (spring/summer 1992): 4.

45 Ruth Thompson-Miller and Joe R. Feagin, "Continuing Injuries of Racism: Counseling in a Racist Context," *The Counseling Psychologist* 35 (2007): 106–115. See Feagin and McKinney, *The Many Costs of Racism*, pp. 46–120.

46 Claude M. Steele and Joshua Aronson, "Stereotype Threat and the Intellectual Test Performance of African Americans," *Journal of Personality and Social Psychology* 69 (1995): 797–811. See also Feagin and McKinney, *The Many Costs of Racism*, pp. 39–64; Claude M. Steele, "A Threat in the Air: How Stereotypes Shape Intellectual Identity and Performance," *American Psychologist* (June 1997): 627.

47 William H. Grier and Price M. Cobbs, *Black Rage* (New York: Basic Books, 1968), p. 4. See also Feagin and McKinney, *The Many Costs of Racism*.

48 Feagin and Sikes, *Living with Racism*, p. 294. See also Feagin and McKinney, *The Many Costs of Racism*, pp. 39–52, 142–145.

49 Alexander Thomas and Samuel Sillen, *The Theory and Application of Symbolic Interactionism* (Boston: Houghton Mifflin, 1977), p. 54.

50 Teletia R. Taylor *et al.*, "Racial Discrimination and Breast Cancer Incidence in US Black Women," *American Journal of Epidemiology* 1 (2007): 46–54.

51 Feagin and McKinney, *The Many Costs of Racism*, p. 78. See also Thompson-Miller and Feagin, "Continuing Injuries of Racism," pp. 106–115.

52 This study by Nancy Krieger is summarized in Amanda Husted, "Discrimination Can Pose Health Risk for Blacks and Homosexuals," *Atlanta Journal and Constitution* (November 1, 1994): D22. Those who reported no discrimination had blood pressure as

high as those who reported much discrimination, which Krieger interprets to mean the former are under-reporting. See Rosalind M. Peters, "Racism and Hypertension among African Americans," *Western Journal of Nursing Research* 26 (2004): 612–631.

53 Sharon B. Wyatt *et al.*, "Racism and Cardiovascular Disease in African Americans," *American Journal of Medical Science* 325 (June 2003): 315–331. Italics omitted.

54 James Oakes, *The Ruling Race: A History of American Slaveholders* (New York: Vintage Books, 1983); Kenneth M. Stampp, *The Peculiar Institution: Slavery in the Ante-Bellum South* (New York: Vintage Books, 1956), pp. 318–321; Thomas F. Pettigrew, *A Profile of the Negro American* (Princeton, NJ: Van Nostrand, 1964), p. 99; Amadu Jacky Kaba, "Life Expectancy, Death Rates, Geography, and Black People: A Statistical World Overview," *Journal of Black Studies* 39 (2009): 337–347; Donna L. Hoyert and Jiaquan Xu, "Deaths: Preliminary Data for 2011," *National Vital Statistics Reports* 61 (October 10, 2012), p. 2.

55 Rodney Coates, personal communication with the author, November 9, 1995. See also Marilyn Frye, *The Politics of Reality* (Trumansburg, NY: Crossing Press, 1983), p. 4.

56 See Feagin, *The White Racial Frame*, passim.

57 "Concurring opinion" in *Jones et ux. v. Alfred H. Mayer Co.*, 392 U.S. 409, 445 (1968).

58 Stevie Watson, Osei Appiah, Corliss G. Thornton, "The Effect of Name on Pre-Interview Impressions and Occupational Stereotypes: The Case of Black Sales Job Applicants," *Journal of Applied Social Psychology* 41 (2011): 2405–2420; Marc Bendick, Jr., *Discrimination against Racial/Ethnic Minorities in the United States: Empirical Findings from Situation Testing* (Geneva: International Labour Organization, 1996), p. 23.

59 Gunnar Myrdal, *An American Dilemma*, vol. 1 (New York: McGraw-Hill, 1964 [1944]), p. 4.

60 Oliver C. Cox, *Caste, Class, and Race: A Study in Social Dynamics* (New York: Doubleday, 1948), p. 531. See Feagin and O'Brien, *White Men on Race*.

61 William Lee Miller, *Arguing about Slavery: The Great Battle in the United States Congress* (New York: Knopf, 1996), p. 10.

62 Joe R. Feagin, *White Party, White Government: Race, Class, and U.S. Politics* (New York: Routledge, 2012).

63 James W. Button, Barbara A. Rienzo, and Ken Wald, "Politics and School Health Reform: Factors Influencing the Success of School-Based Health Care," unpublished research paper, University of Florida, 1999.

64 Huiping Li, Harrison Campbell and Steven Fernandez, "Residential Segregation, Spatial Mismatch and Economic Growth across U.S. Metropolitan Areas," *Urban Studies* (May 2013): 1–19.

65 Quoted in George J. Church, "The Boom Towns," *Time*, June 15, 1987, p. 17. This section draws on discussions with Gregory D. Squires.

66 Human Development Report Office, "United States Country Profile: Human Development Indicators," http://hdrstats.undp.org/en/countries/profiles/USA.html (accessed July 4, 2013); Social Science Research Council, "The Measure of America 2013–2014," June 19, 2013, www.measureofamerica.org/measure_of_america2013–2014/ (accessed July 4, 2013).

8 Systemic Racism: Other Americans of Color

1 Southern Poverty Law Center, *Under Siege: Life for Low-Income Latinos in the South* (Montgomery, AL: SPLC, 2009), p. 4.

2 See Yolanda Flores-Niemann, "Social Ecological Contexts of Prejudice between Hispanics and Blacks," in *Race, Ethnicity, and Nationality in the United States: Toward the Twenty-First Century*, ed. Paul Wong (Boulder, CO: Westview Press, 1999), p. 170; Eduardo Luna, "How the Black/White Paradigm Renders Mexicans/Mexican Americans and Discrimination against Them Invisible," *Berkeley La Raza Law Journal* (fall 2003), pp. 226, 230.

3 This estimate assumes a birth rate of about 40 live births per 1,000 persons under slavery for the period. Estimating this birth rate for the varying black population over

the period—the black population grew from about half a million in 1776 to about 4.2 million in 1865—one gets about six million births as a low-end estimate. I am indebted to Doug Deal for helping me estimate the six million figure.

4 I base this rough calculation on estimates of the "crude birth rate" for each year in this entire period. On Native Americans, see Vine Deloria, *Custer Died for Your Sins: An Indian Manifesto* (London: Macmillan, 1969).

5 See Ellis Cose, *Colorblind: Seeing Beyond Race in a Race-Obsessed World* (New York: HarperCollins, 1997).

6 Jorge Klor de Alva, Earl Shorris, and Cornel West, "Our Next Race Question: The Uneasiness Between Blacks and Latinos," in *Critical White Studies: Looking Behind the Mirror*, eds. Richard Delgado and Jean Stefancic (Philadelphia: Temple University Press, 1997), p. 485; Deloria, *Custer Died for Your Sins*, p. 8.

7 Ruth Frankenberg, *White Women, Race Matters* (Minneapolis: University of Minnesota Press, 1993), p. 12. See also Joe R. Feagin and Hernán Vera, *White Racism: The Basics* (New York: Routledge, 1995); Joe R. Feagin, *Systemic Racism: A Theory of Oppression* (New York: Routledge, 2006).

8 See Joe R. Feagin and Clairece B. Feagin, *Racial and Ethnic Relations*, 9th edn. (Upper Saddle River, NJ: Prentice Hall, 2011), chapters 7–11.

9 Lewis R. Gordon, *Her Majesty's Other Children: Sketches of Racism from a Neocolonial Age* (Lanham, MD: Rowman & Littlefield, 1997), pp. 5, 53.

10 Frank Wu, "Neither Black Nor White: Asian Americans and Affirmative Action," *Boston College Third World Law Journal* 15 (1995): 249–250. See Janine Young Kim, "Are Asians Black? The Asian-American Civil Rights Agenda and the Contemporary Significance of the Black–White Paradigm," *Yale Law Journal* 108 (June 1999): 2385–2413.

11 Tomás Almaguer, *Racial Fault Lines* (Berkeley and Los Angeles: University of California Press, 1994), pp. 7, 210.

12 Feagin and Feagin, *Racial and Ethnic Relations*, chapters 10–11.

13 Ronald T. Takaki, *Strangers from a Different Shore: A History of Asian Americans* (Boston: Little, Brown, 1989), p. 100. This section draws on pp. 99–104.

14 Ibid., p. 101; see *Gong Lum v. Rice*, 275 U.S. 78, 85 (1927).

15 *People v. Hall*, 4 Cal. 399 (1854). See Takaki, *Strangers from a Different Shore*, p. 102; Benjamin B. Ringer, *"We the People" and Others* (New York: Tavistock, 1983), p. 382.

16 Takaki, *Strangers from a Different Shore*, p. 101.

17 Ibid.

18 *Plessy v. Ferguson*, 163 U.S. 537, 561 (1896).

19 Claire Jean Kim, "The Racial Triangulation of Asian Americans," *Politics and Society* 27 (March 1999): 105–138.

20 Gary Y. Okihiro, *Margins and Mainstreams: Asians in American History and Culture* (Seattle: University of Washington Press, 1994), p. 34.

21 Edward K. Strong, Jr., *The Second-Generation Japanese Problem* (Stanford, CA: Stanford University Press, 1934), p. 133. See also Miriam Sharma, "Labor Migration and Class Formation among the Filipinos in Hawaii, 1940–1946," in *Labor Immigration under Capitalism*, eds. Lucie Cheng and Edna Bonacich (Berkeley and Los Angeles: University of California Press, 1984), pp. 583–593.

22 George Frederickson, *The Black Image in the White Mind* (Middletown, CT: Wesleyan University Press, 1971), p. 305.

23 *In re Ah Yup*, 1 F. cas. 223 (C. C.D.Cal. 1878); Ian F. Haney Lopez, *White by Law: The Legal Construction of Race* (New York: New York University Press, 1996), pp. 1–7, 203–227.

24 James J. Scheurich and Michelle D. Young, "Coloring Epistemologies: Are Our Research Epistemologies Racially Biased?" *Educational Researcher* 26 (May 1997): 7. See Mario de Valdes y Cocom, "Secret Daughter: The Blurred Racial Lines of Famous Families," January 1999, www.pbs.org/wgbh/pages/frontline/shows/secret/famous (accessed June 30, 2009).

25 John C. Calhoun, quoted in Frederickson, *The Black Image in the White Mind*, p. 136.

26 Abel G. Rubio, *Stolen Heritage* (Austin, TX: Eakin Press, 1986).

27 Joan Moore, *Mexican Americans*, 2nd edn. (Englewood Cliffs, NJ: Prentice Hall, 1976), p. 108; Feagin and Feagin, *Racial and Ethnic Relations*, chapter 8.

28 Lopez, *White by Law*, p. 61.

29 Theodore W. Allen, *The Invention of the White Race* (New York: Verso, 1994), p. 27; Feagin and Feagin, *Racial and Ethnic Relations*, chapter 8.

30 Feagin and Feagin, *Racial and Ethnic Relations*, chapter 8; Nestor Rodriguez, personal communication with the author.

31 Oliver C. Cox, *Caste, Class, and Race: A Study in Social Dynamics* (New York: Doubleday, 1948), p. 349.

32 Roberto Suro, *Strangers Among Us: How Latino Immigration Is Transforming America* (New York: Knopf, 1998), pp. 81–82; Feagin and Feagin, *Racial and Ethnic Relations*, chapters 8–11.

33 See the white-framed arguments of Dinesh D'Souza, *The End of Racism: Principles for a Multiracial Society* (New York: Free Press, 1995), p. 300.

34 Rosalind Chou and Joe R. Feagin, *The Myth of the Model Minority* (Boulder, CO: Paradigm Books, 2008).

35 Anonymous, "If No Deal Is Struck, Four-in-Ten Say Let the Sequester Happen," Pew Center, February 21, 2013, www.people-press.org/2013/02/21/if-no-deal-is-struck-four-in-ten-say-let-the-sequester-happen (accessed July 7, 2013); and John Liu, personal communication with the author.

36 Jorge M. Chavez and Doris Marie Provine, "Race and the Response of State Legislatures to Unauthorized Immigrants," *Annals of the American Association of Political and Social Science* 623 (May 2009): 79–92.

37 Nathan Glazer, *We Are All Multiculturalists Now* (Cambridge, MA: Harvard University Press, 1997), p. 149.

38 Andrew Hacker, *Two Nations: Black and White, Separate, Hostile, Unequal* (New York: Scribner's, 1992), p. 16.

39 See Michael Lind, *The Next American Nation: The New Nationalism and the Fourth American Revolution* (New York: Free Press, 1995), pp. 115–116.

40 Ewa A. Golebiowska, "The Contours and Etiology of Whites' Attitudes Toward Black–White Interracial Marriage," *Journal of Black Studies* 38 (2007): 268–287.

41 Daphne Lofquist, Terry Lugaila, Martin O'Connell, and Sarah Feliz, *Households and Families: 2010* (Washington, DC: U.S. Census Bureau, 2012); and Wendy Wang, "The Rise of Intermarriage Rates, Characteristics Vary by Race and Gender," Pew Research Center, February 16, 2012, www.pewsocialtrends.org/2012/02/16/the-rise-of-intermarriage/2/ (accessed May 9, 2013).

42 See Milton M. Gordon, *Assimilation in American Life* (New York: Oxford University Press, 1964); Julie Montgomery, "Cyber Brides: The Internet and the Asian Commodity," unpublished master's paper, University of Florida, 1999; C. N. Le, "The Public and Private Sides of Ethnicity," www.asiannation.org/interracial.shtml (accessed June 9, 2009).

43 The survey is cited in cited in Wang, "The Rise of Intermarriage Rates." On intermarriage issues, see Erica Chito Childs, *Navigating Interracial Borders: Black–White Couples and Their Social Worlds* (New Brunswick, NJ: Rutgers University Press, 2005), p. 183.

44 Peter Brimelow, *Alien Nation: Common Sense about America's Immigration Disaster* (New York: Random House, 1995), pp. 10, 59.

45 For example, Samuel P. Huntington, "The Erosion of American National Interests," *Foreign Affairs* (September/October 1997): 28.

46 Joe R. Feagin and Danielle Dirks, "Who Is White? College Students' Assessments of Key US Racial and Ethnic Groups," unpublished manuscript, Texas A&M University, 2004. On similar findings for Canadian students, see Maurice Berger, *White Lies: Race and the Myths of Whiteness* (New York: Farrar, Straus, and Giroux, 1999), pp. 41–42.

47 Pew Hispanic Center and Kaiser Family Foundation, *2002 National Survey of Latinos* (Washington, DC: Pew Hispanic Center/Kaiser Family Foundation, 2002), pp. 31–33; and Paul Taylor, Mark Hugo Lopez, Jessica Hamar Martinez, and Gabriel Velasco, *When Labels Don't Fit: Hispanics and Their Views of Identity* (Washington, DC: Pew Hispanic Center, 2012).

48 See Rosalind S. Chou and Joe R. Feagin, *The Myth of the Model Minority: Asian Americans Facing Racism* (Boulder, CO: Paradigm Books, 2008).

49 Sharon Chang, "Mixed Race, Pretty Face," *Racism Review*, April 4, 2013, www.racismreview.com/blog/2013/04/04/mixed-race-pretty-face/ (accessed May 13, 2013); U.S. Census Bureau, "The Two or More Races Population: 2010," September 2012, www.census.gov/prod/cen2010/briefs/c2010br-13.pdf (accessed May 17, 2013).

50 William Lee Adams, "Mixed Race, Pretty Face?" *Psychology Today*, January 1, 2006 www.psychologytoday.com/articles/200512/mixed-race-pretty-face (accessed May 13, 2013).

51 Jennifer Lee and Frank D. Bean, "Reinventing the Color Line: Immigration and America's New Racial/Ethnic Divide," *Social Forces* 86 (December 2007): 577–579.

52 See Debra Van Ausdale and Joe R. Feagin, *The First R: How Children Learn Race and Racism* (Lanham, MD: Rowman & Littlefield, 2001).

53 Donna Jackson Nakazawa, *Does Anybody Else Look Like Me? A Parent's Guide To Raising Multiracial Children* (Jackson, TN: Perseus-Da Capo Press, 2004).

54 On discrimination facing groups of color, see Feagin and Feagin, *Racial and Ethnic Relations*, chapters 4–11.

55 New America Media, *Deep Divisions, Shared Destiny: A Poll of African Americans, Hispanics, and Asian Americans on Race Relations* (San Francisco: New America Media, 2007), pp. 6–8, 11.

56 Paul Taylor *et al.*, *The Rise of Asian Americans* (Washington, DC: Pew Research Center, 2012), p. 12.

57 Chou and Feagin, *The Myth of the Model Minority*. See also Min Zhou, *Chinatown: The Socioeconomic Potential of an Urban Enclave* (Philadelphia: Temple University Press, 1992); Pyong Gap Min, ed., *Asian Americans: Contemporary Trends and Issues* (Thousand Oaks, CA: Sage, 1995); Paul Ong, ed., *Economic Diversity: Issues and Policies* (Los Angeles: Leadership Education for Asian Pacifics, 1994); Cliff Cheng, "Are Asian American Employees a Model Minority or Just a Minority?" *Journal of Applied Behavioral Science* 33 (September 1997): 277–290.

58 Ryan A. Smith, *Changing the Face of Public Service Leadership: A Research Report and Call to Action* (New York: National Urban Fellows, 2010), pp. 19–21, 43.

59 Lei Lai, "The Model Minority Thesis and Workplace Discrimination of Asian Americans," *Industrial and Organizational Psychology* 6 (2013): 93–96.

60 FBI, *Hate-Crime Statistics, 2011* (Washington, DC: U.S. Department of Justice, 2012); see also U.S. Commission on Civil Rights, *Civil Rights Issues Facing Asian Americans in the 1990s* (Washington, DC: U.S. Government Printing Office, 1992).

61 Leland Saito, personal communication with the author, fall 1998. See Leland Saito, *Race and Politics: Asian Americans, Latinos, and Whites in a Los Angeles Suburb* (Urbana: University of Illinois Press, 1998), pp. 39–54.

62 Leland T. Saito, "From 'Blighted' to 'Historic': Race, Economic Development, and Historic Preservation in San Diego, California," *Urban Affairs Review* 45 (2009): 166–187; and Wendy Cheng, "'Diversity' on Main Street? Branding Race and Place in the New 'Majority-Minority' Suburbs," *Identities: Global Studies in Culture and Power* 17 (2010), pp. 471–477.

63 Taylor *et al.*, *The Rise of Asian Americans*, p. 7.

64 Ibid,, p. 4. See also Chou and Feagin, *The Myth of the Model Minority*.

65 I summarize in part from Chou and Feagin, *The Myth of the Model Minority*, chapter 1. See Center for Medicaid Services, *Medicaid Managed Care Enrollment Report: Depression Diagnoses for Adolescent Youth* (Medicaid Statistics Publications, 2002); Laura Harder, "Asian Americans Commit Half of Suicides at Cornell," *Cornell Daily Sun*, March 29,

2005, p. 1; Elizabeth Cohen, "Push to Achieve Tied to Suicide in Asian-American Women," CNN. com, www.cnn.com/2007/HEALTH/05/16/asian.suicides/index.html (accessed May 16, 2007).

66 Mark Potok, "The Year in Hate and Extremism," *Intelligence Report* (SPLC) (Spring 2013), www.splcenter.org/home/2013/spring/the-year-in-hate-and-extremism#. UZEEncpYxhE (accessed May 13, 2013).

67 Pew Research Center, *Second-Generation Americans: A Portrait of the Adult Children of Immigrants* (Washington, DC: Pew Research Center, 2013), pp. 80–81.

68 Southern Poverty Law Center, *Under Siege*, pp. 3–6.

69 Hilario Molina II, "Racializing the Migration Process: An Ethnographic Analysis of Undocumented Immigrants in the United States," PhD dissertation, College Station, Texas, Texas A&M University, 2012, n.p.

70 National Fair Housing Advocate, "Farmworkers Represented by CRLA and the County of Riverside Settle Major Fair Housing Case," www.fairhousing.com/news_archive/ releases/crla5–23–00.html (accessed March 1, 2001); Dan Rozek, "Elgin Denies Housing Bias against Hispanics," *Chicago Sun-Times*, October 3, 2000, p. 32; "Center Calls for the Rejection of Anti-Immigrant Ordinances," Southern Poverty Law Center Report, September 2006, p. 3.

71 Smith, *Changing the Face of Public Service Leadership*, pp. 19–21, 43.

72 Joe R. Feagin and José A. Cobas, *Latinos Facing Racism: Discrimination, Resistance, and Endurance* (Boulder, CO: Paradigm Publishers, 2013); Maria Chávez, *Everyday Injustice: Latino Professionals and Racism* (Lanham, MD: Rowman & Littlefield, 2011).

73 "Hispanics and Arizona's New Immigration Law," Fact Sheet, Pew Hispanic Center, April 29, 2010; and Anne-Marie Nuñez, Richard E. Hoover, Kellie Pickett, A. Christine Stuart-Carruthers, and Maria Vázquez, *Latinos in Higher Education and Hispanic-Serving Institutions: Creating Conditions for Success* (New York: Wiley, 2013), Kindle loc. 272, 649–651.

74 Southern Poverty Law Center, *Under Siege*, p. 5. The survey is cited in "Hispanics and Arizona's New Immigration Law."

75 Southern Poverty Law Center, *Under Siege*, p. 5.

76 FBI, *Hate-Crime Statistics*; and Southern Poverty Law Center, *Under Siege*.

77 Associated Press, "Teen Survivor of Hate Crime Attack at Texas Party Jumps From Cruise Ship, Dies," www.foxnews.com/story/0,2933,287721,00.html#ixzz2OwLsXdoI (accessed March 29, 2013); and Anonymous, "Luis Ramirez's Attackers Get Nine Years in Prison for Deadly Beating." http://colorlines.com/archives/2011/02/luis_ramirezs_ attackers_get_nine_years_in_prison_for_deadly_hate_crime.html (accessed March 29, 2013).

78 Edna A. Viruell-Fuentes, Patricia Y. Miranda, and Sawsan Abdulrahim, "More than Culture: Structural Racism, Intersectionality Theory, and Immigrant Health," *Social Science and Medicine* 75 (2012): 2099–2106; Michael Smart, "Racism Associated with Disturbed Sleep and Depression in Latinos, BYU Study Shows," January 30, 2006, http:// byunews.byu.edu/archive06-Jan-steffen.aspx (accessed April 6, 2009).

79 I draw here on an email conversation with Leland Saito. See Chou and Feagin, *The Myth of the Model Minority*, passim.

80 *When You're Smiling: The Deadly Legacy of Internment*, produced and directed by Janice D. Tanaka, Visual Communications, 1999.

81 Interview by Joe Feagin, fall 1998. Used by permission.

82 Chou and Feagin, *The Myth of the Model Minority*, pp. 3–23; see also Karen Pyke, "Vietnamese Parents and Their Children: Pressures of Assimilation," unpublished research paper, University of Florida, 1999.

83 Nestor Rodriguez, personal communication. See José A. Cobas, Jorge Duany, and Joe R. Feagin, eds., *How the United States Racializes Latinos* (Boulder, CO: Paradigm Publishers, 2009).

84 Jesse A. Steinfeldt, Brad D. Foltz, Jennifer K. Kaladow, *et al.*, "Racism in the Electronic

Age: Role of Online Forums in Expressing Racial Attitudes about American Indians," *Cultural Diversity and Ethnic Minority Psychology* 16 (2010), p. 362.

85 Ibid.

86 Ibid., p. 371.

87 Dan Graziano, "Owner: Redskins Will 'Never' Change," ESPN, http://espn.go.com/nfl/story/_/id/9259866/daniel-snyder-says-washington-redskins-never-change-team-name (accessed May 16, 2013).

88 The survey and Harjo quote are in David Price, "Friday's Morning Mashup," http://leeinks.weei.com/sports/tag/david-price (accessed May 16, 2013). For a list of contemporary white-racist usage of this epithet, see Suzan Shown Harjo, "Dirty Word Games," *Indian Country Today*, June 17, 2005, p. 1.

89 Jane H. Hill, *The Everyday Language of White Racism* (New York: Wiley-Blackwell, 2008), especially pp. 134–157.

90 Yen Lee Espiritu, *Asian American Panethnicity* (Philadelphia: Temple University Press, 1992); Joe R. Feagin and José A. Cobas, *Latinos Facing Racism: Discrimination, Resistance, and Endurance* (Boulder, CO: Paradigm Publishers, 2013), chapter 9.

91 Charles R. Lawrence III, "Race, Multiculturalism, and the Jurisprudence of Transformation," *Stanford Law Review* 47 (May 1995): 829.

92 Ibid.

93 Suro, *Strangers Among Us*, pp. 251–252, 254.

94 New America Media, *Deep Divisions, Shared Destiny*, pp. 6–8, 11; Paula D. McClain *et al.*, "Racial Distancing in a Southern City: Latino Immigrants' Views of Black Americans," *Journal of Politics* 68 (August 2006): 581–582.

95 McClain *et al.*, "Racial Distancing in a Southern City"; Claudine Gay, "Seeing Difference: The Effect of Economic Disparity on Blacks' Attitudes Toward Latinos," *American Journal of Political Science* 50 (October 2006), pp. 982, 990, 994–995.

96 Jack Strauss, "Allies, not Enemies: How Latino Immigration Boosts African American Employment and Wages," Immigration Policy Center, www.immigrationpolicy.org/perspectives/allies-not-enemies-how-latino-immigration-boosts-african-american-employment-and-wages (accessed June 28, 2013).

97 New America Media, *Deep Divisions, Shared Destiny*, pp. 6–8, 11.

98 Karen Pyke and Tran Dang, "'FOB' and 'Whitewashed': Identity and Internalized Racism among Second Generation Asian Americans," *Qualitative Sociology* 26 (summer 2003): 168.

99 See France Winddance Twine, *Racism in a Racial Democracy: The Maintenance of White Supremacy in Brazil* (New Brunswick, NJ: Rutgers University Press, 1998); Leone Campos de Sousa and Paulo Nascimento, "Brazilian National Identity at a Crossroads: The Myth of Racial Democracy and the Development of Black Identity," *International Journal of Politics, Culture, and Society* 19 (June 2008): 129–143.

9 Antiracist Strategies and Solutions: Past, Present, and Future

1 The full resolution is at www.opencongress.org/bill/111-sc26/text (accessed June 24, 2009).

2 Advisory Board on Race, *One America in the 21st Century: Forging a New Future* (Washington, DC: U.S. Government Printing Office, 1998).

3 Oliver C. Cox, *Caste, Class, and Race: A Study in Social Dynamics* (New York: Doubleday, 1948), p. 571.

4 Derrick Bell, *Faces at the Bottom of the Well* (New York: Basic Books, 1992), p. 12; italics omitted. See also Derrick Bell, *Race, Racism, and the Law*, 6th edn. (New York: Aspen Publishers, 2008).

5 John Briggs and F. David Peat, *Turbulent Mirror: An Illustrated Guide to Chaos Theory and the Science of Wholeness* (New York: Harper & Row, 1990), p. 177.

6 Steve H. Murdock, *An America Challenged: Population Change and the Future of the*

United States (Boulder, CO: Westview Press, 1995), pp. 33–47; U.S. Census Bureau, "An Older and More Diverse Nation by Midcentury," August 2008, www.census.gov/Press-Release/www/releases/archives/population/012496.html (accessed June 12, 2009); William H. Frey, *Melting Pot Cities and Suburbs: Racial and Ethnic Change in Metro America in the 2000s* (Washington, DC: Brookings Institution, 2011).

7 Joe R. Feagin, "The Future of U.S. Society in an Era of Racism, Group Segregation, and Demographic Revolution," in *Sociology for the Twenty-First Century: Continuities and Cutting Edges*, ed. Janet Abu-Lughod (Chicago: University of Chicago Press, 1999), pp. 199–212; U.S. Census Bureau, "An Older and More Diverse Nation by Midcentury," August 2008, www.census.gov/Press-Release/www/releases/archives/population/012496.html (accessed June 12, 2009); William H. Frey, "Diversity Spreads Out," Brookings Institution, www.frey-demographer.org/reports/Brook06.pdf (accessed June 19, 2009). See also Adia Harvey-Wingfield and Joe R. Feagin, *Yes We Can: White Racial Framing and the Obama Presidency*, 2nd edn. (New York: Routledge, 2013), chapter 10.

8 Dale Maharidge, *The Coming White Minority: California's Eruptions and America's Future* (New York: Random House, 1996), p. 11.

9 H. Robert Outten, Michael T. Schmitt, Daniel A. Miller and Amber L. Garcia, "Feeling Threatened about the Future: Whites' Emotional Reactions to Anticipated Ethnic Demographic Changes," *Personality and Social Psychology Bulletin* 38 (2102): 14.

10 William H. Frey, *The New Metro Minority Map: Regional Shifts in Hispanics, Asians, and Blacks from Census 2010* (Washington, DC Brookings, 2011), pp. 1–4; William H. Frey, "Metropolitan Magnets for International and Domestic Migrants," www.frey-demographer.org/reports/Brook3–2.pdf (accessed June 19, 2009); William H. Frey, "Domestic and Immigrant Migrants: Where Do They Go?" *Current*, January 22, 1997, n.p.

11 William H. Frey, *America's Diverse Future: Initial Glimpses at the U.S. Child Population from the 2010 Census* (Washington, DC: Brookings Institution, 2011), p. 1.

12 "President Exit Polls," *New York Times*, http://elections.nytimes.com/2012/results/president/exit-polls (accessed November 8, 2012); "President: Full Results (Exit Polls)," CNN, www.cnn.com/election/2012/results/race/president#exit-polls (accessed November 8, 2012). The Native American estimate is from Shari Valentine.

13 Quoted in Kevin Sack, "South's Embrace of G.O.P. is Near a Turning Point," *New York Times*, March 16, 1998, p. A1. I am indebted to suggestions from Chandler Davidson. See also Kevin Phillips, *The Emerging Republican Majority* (New Rochelle, NY: Arlington House, 1969).

14 See Joe R. Feagin, *White Party, White Government: Race, Class, and U.S. Politics* (New York: Routledge, 2012).

15 Paul Jenkins, "The GOP's White Supremacy," *Huffington Post*, December 28, 2008, www.huffingtonpost.com/paul-jenkins/the-gops-white-supremacy_b_153823.html (accessed December 29, 2008); James Wright, "Black Republicans Ponder Their Future," *Afro-American Newspapers*, November 24, 2008, http://news.newamericamedia.org/news/view_article.html?article_id= (accessed December 18, 2008); Matt Katz, "Party and Its Delegates Paint Pictures of Diversity," Joint Center for Political and Economic Studies, www.jointcenter.org/newsroom/in-the-news/party-and-its-delegates-paint-picture-of-diversity (accessed May 14, 2013).

16 David A. Bositis, *Blacks and the 2012 Republican National Convention* (Washington, DC: Joint Center for Political and Economic Studies, 2012); and Jackie Jones, "Black Influence on Democratic Party Is Far Greater than Republican Party," September 7, 2012, http://atlantablackstar.com/2012/09/07/black-influence-on-democratic-party-is-far-greater-than-republican-party/ (accessed May 17, 2013). See also Feagin, *White Party, White Government*.

17 See Bonnie L. Mitchell and Joe R. Feagin, "America's Racial–Ethnic Cultures: Opposition Within a Mythical Melting Pot," in *Toward the Multicultural University*, eds. Benjamin Bowser, Terry Jones, and Gale Auletta-Young (Westport, CT: Praeger, 1995),

pp. 65–86; Joe R. Feagin, *The White Racial Frame: Centuries of Racial Framing and Counter-Framing*, 2nd edn. (New York: Routledge, 2013).

18 Merton L. Dillon, *Slavery Attacked: Southern Slaves and Their Allies, 1619–1865* (Baton Rouge: Louisiana State University Press, 1990), p. 269; Herbert Aptheker, *American Negro Slave Revolts* (New York: International Publishers, 1952), pp. 162–163.

19 Robin D. G. Kelley, *Race Rebels: Culture, Politics, and the Black Working Class* (New York: Free Press, 1994).

20 Aldon Morris, *The Origins of the Civil Rights Movement: Black Communities Organizing for Change* (New York: Free Press, 1984); Joe R. Feagin and Clairece B. Feagin, *Racial and Ethnic Relations*, 9th edn. (Upper Saddle River, NJ: Prentice Hall, 2011), chapter 7. I am also indebted to comments from Aldon Morris.

21 I use quotes as reprinted in Benjamin B. Ringer, *"We the People" and Others* (New York: Tavistock, 1983), pp. 311–330. See *Brown v. Board of Education of Topeka*, 347 U.S. 483, 493 (1954) and the institutional racism case, *Griggs v. Duke Power Co.*, 401 U.S. 424 (1971).

22 Roy L. Brooks, Gilbert Paul Carrasco, and Michael Selmi, *The Law of Discrimination: Cases and Perspectives* (New Providence, NJ: LexisNexis, 2012), pp. 435–436. See also U.S. Commission on Civil Rights, *Funding Federal Civil Rights Enforcement: The President's 2006 Request* (Washington, DC: U.S. Commission on Civil Rights, 2005).

23 See Roy Brooks, *Rethinking the American Race Problem* (Berkeley and Los Angeles: University of California Press, 1990), p. 105.

24 Office of Civil Rights Evaluation, U.S. Commission on Civil Rights Redefining Rights in America, "The Civil Rights Record of the George W. Bush Administration, 2001–2004," www.thememoryhole.org/pol/usccr_redefining_rights.pdf (accessed April 12, 2005). See also Max Felker-Kantor, "'A Pledge Is Not Self-Enforcing': Struggles for Equal Employment Opportunity in Multiracial Los Angeles, 1964–1982," *Pacific Historical Review* 82 (February 2013): 63–94.

25 See "We ACT for Environmental Justice," *Third Force*, November/December 1997, 18–21; "Ex-BART Cop Arrested," *NBC Bay Area News*, http://www.nbcbayarea.com/news/local/BART-Shooting-Officer-Arrested-Taken-Back-to-Oakland.html (accessed July 21, 2009); "Police: 120 Arrested in Largest Moral Monday Protest Yet," WRAL.com, www.wral.com/naacp-120-arrested-in-latest-round-of-moral-monday-protests/12588918/ (accessed June 30, 2013); Justin Akers Chacón, "The New Immigrant Civil Rights Movement," *International Socialist Review*, www.isreview.org/issues/47/newmovement.shtml can (accessed June 30, 2013).

26 Linda Jones, "Closing the Books on Slavery? African American Groups Seek Reparations on Ancestors' Behalf," *Dallas Morning News*, June 15, 1996, p. 1C.

27 Isabel Wilkerson, "Middle-Class but not Feeling Equal, Blacks Reflect on Los Angeles Strife," *New York Times*, May 4, 1993, p. A20; Roy Brooks, *Integration or Separation? A Strategy for Racial Equality* (Cambridge, MA: Harvard University Press, 1996).

28 Marimba Ani, *Yurugu: An African-Centered Critique of European Cultural Thought and Behavior* (Trenton, NJ: Africa World Press, 1994), p. 570. See Molefi Kete Asante, *The Afrocentric Idea* (Philadelphia: Temple University Press, 1987).

29 Frantz Fanon, *Toward the African Revolution* (New York: Grove Press, 1967), p. 103.

30 Joe R. Feagin and Melvin P. Sikes, *Living with Racism: The Black Middle-Class Experience* (Boston: Beacon Press, 1994), pp. 286–287. See also Joe R. Feagin and Karyn McKinney, *The Many Costs of Racism* (Lanham, MD: Rowman & Littlefield, 2003); Ruth Thompson-Miller and Joe R. Feagin, "Continuing Injuries of Racism: Counseling in a Racist Context," *Counseling Psychologist* 35 (2007): 106–115.

31 See Feagin and McKinney, *The Many Costs of Racism*; Thompson-Miller and Feagin, "Continuing Injuries of Racism."

32 David Walker, *Appeal to the Coloured Citizens of the World*, ed. Charles M. Wiltse (New York: Hill and Wang, 1965), p. 75.

33 Anna Julia Cooper, *The Voice of Anna Julia Cooper*, eds. Charles Lemert and Esme Bhan (Lanham, MD: Rowman & Littlefield, 1998), pp. 207, 212.

34 Martin Luther King, Jr., *Where Do We Go from Here? Chaos or Community?* (New York: Bantam Books, 1967), p. 9.

35 "Blacks, Whites Differ on Government's Role in Civil Rights," Gallup.com, August 19, 2011, www.gallup.com/poll/149087/Blacks-Whites-Differ-Government-Role-Civil-Rights.aspx (accessed June 10, 2013).

36 Tyler Kingkade, "Students Split on Affirmative Action for College Admissions Ahead of *Fisher v. University of Texas* at Austin Supreme Court Case," *Huffington Post*, October 5, 2012, www.huffingtonpost.com/2012/10/05/affirmative-action-fisher-university-of-texas-at-austin_n_1942720.html (accessed June 11, 2013). The survey was done by the Berkley Center for Religion, Peace and World Affairs at Georgetown University.

37 Richard Morin, "Misperceptions Cloud Whites' View of Blacks," *Washington Post*, July 11, 2001, p. A01. For countering data, see Feagin and Feagin, *Racial and Ethnic Relations*, chapter 7; Rasmussen Reports, "What They Told Us: Reviewing Last Week's Key Polls," www.rasmussenreports.com/public_content/lifestyle/general_lifestyle/82_say_u_s_is_best_place_to_live_41_say_u_s_lacks_liberty_and_justice_for_all (accessed July 6, 2008).

38 Pew Research Center, "Blacks See Growing Values Gap between Poor and Middle Class: Optimism about Black Progress Declines," November 13, 2007, http://pewsocialtrends.org/pubs/700/black-public-opinion (accessed May 5, 2008).

39 Ralph Ellison, *Shadow and Act* (New York: Random House, 1964), p. 304.

40 Gunnar Myrdal, *An American Dilemma*, vol. 2 (New York: McGraw-Hill, 1964), p. 929. I also draw here on Walter A. Jackson, *Gunnar Myrdal and America's Conscience: Social Engineering and Racial Liberalism, 1938–1987* (Chapel Hill: University of North Carolina Press, 1990), pp. 11–15, 369–370.

41 Alexandra Kalev, Frank Dobbin, and Erin Kelly, "Best Practices or Best Guesses? Assessing the Efficacy of Corporate Affirmative Action and Diversity Policies," *American Sociological Review* 71 (August 2006): 589–617.

42 Peter Steinfels, *The Neoconservatives* (New York: Touchstone, 1979), p. 6. See also Stephan Thernstrom and Abigail Thernstrom, *America in Black and White: One Nation Indivisible* (New York: Simon & Schuster, 1999); Irving Kristol, "Thoughts on Equality and Egalitarianism," in *Income Distribution*, ed. Colin D. Campbell (Washington, DC: American Enterprise Institute, 1977), p. 42.

43 "Nobel Winner in 'Racist' Claim Row," CNN.com, October 18, 2007, http://edition.cnn.com/2007/TECH/science/10/18/science.race/index.html?iref=mpstor yview (accessed January 20, 2009); and "James D. Watson," Wikipedia, http://en.wikipedia.org/wiki/James_D._Watson#Political_activism (accessed January 20, 2009).

44 Roy L. Brooks, Gilbert Paul Carrasco, and Michael Selmi, *The Law of Discrimination: Cases and Perspectives* (New Providence, NJ: LexisNexis, 2012), pp. 435–436 and passim; Marc Bendick, Jr., Mary Lou Egan, and Suzanne Lofhjelm, *The Documentation and Evaluation of Anti-Discrimination Training in the United States* (Geneva: International Labour Organization, 1998), p. 17.

45 Susan W. Kaufmann, "The History and Impact of State Initiatives to Eliminate Affirmative Action," *New Directions for Teaching and Learning* 2007 (Fall 2007): 4–5; Caryn Meyers Fliegler, "Dim Days For Affirmative Action," *University Business* 10 (February 2007), p. 13. See *Grutter v. Bollinger*, 539 U.S. 306 (2003) and *Gratz v. Bollinger*, 539 U.S. 244 (2003); *Fisher v. University of Texas, et al.*, 81 USLW 4503 (2013).

46 Cheryl I. Harris, "Whiteness as Property," *Harvard Law Review* 106 (June 1993): 1707.

47 Mark Kantrowitz, "The Distribution of Grants and Scholarships by Race," Finaid: Student Financial Aid Policy Analysis, 2011, www.finaid.org/scholarships/20110902racescholarships.pdf (accessed April 8, 2013).

48 Jennifer C. Mueller, "The Social Reproduction of Systemic Racial Inequality" unpublished PhD dissertation, Texas A&M University, 2013.

49 Charles C. Moskos and John S. Butler, *All That We Can Be: Black Leadership and Racial Integration the Army Way* (New York: Basic Books, 1996), pp. 5–8; Mike Prior, "Sixty

Years after Integration, Opportunities Abound for Minority Soldiers," Armed Forces Press Service, July 28, 2008, www.defenselink.mil/news/newsarticle.aspx?id=50615 (accessed July 2, 2009); Nelson Lim, Michelle Cho, and Kimberly Curry, *Planning for Diversity: Options and Recommendations for DOD Leaders* (Santa Monica: RAND, 2008).

50 See Moskos and Butler, *All That We Can Be*, pp. 2, 74. Current data are in Prior, "Sixty Years after Integration."

51 Gary Langer, "Racial Discrimination: An Army Survey," ABC News, January 6, 2009, http://abcnews.go.com/blogs/politics/2009/01/racial-relation (accessed June 21, 2013); Jacquelyn Scarville *et al.*, *Armed Forces Equal Opportunity Survey* (Arlington, VA: Defense Manpower Data Center, 1999), pp. 46–50, 150–153.

52 Edna Chun and Alvin Evans, *Diverse Administrators in Peril: The New Indentured Class in Higher Education* (Boulder, CO: Paradigm, 2012), pp. 144–146. Italics added.

53 Ibid., p. 146.

54 Zygmunt Bauman, *Modernity and the Holocaust* (Ithaca, NY: Cornell University Press, 1989), p. 207.

55 I am indebted to discussions with Sharon Rush. See Sharon Rush, *Loving Across the Color Line* (Lanham, MD: Rowman & Littlefield, 2000); Jane Lazarre, *Beyond the Whiteness of Whiteness* (Durham, NC: Duke University Press, 1996).

56 I summarize the detailed discussion in Feagin, *The White Racial Frame*, chapter 9.

57 Jessica Nelson, Glenn Adams, and Phia S. Salter, "The Marley Hypothesis: Denial of Racism Reflects Ignorance of History," *Psychological Sciences* 24 (2012): 213–218.

58 Jennifer Mueller, personal communication, July 30, 2013. See Jennifer C. Mueller, "Tracing Family, Teaching Race: Critical Race Pedagogy in the Millennial Sociology Classroom, *Teaching Sociology* 41 (2013): 172–187; Jennifer C. Mueller and Joe Feagin, "Pulling Back the 'Post-Racial' Curtain: Critical Pedagogical Lessons from Both Sides of the Desk," in K. Haltinner, ed., *Teaching Race and Anti-Racism in Contemporary America: Adding Context to Colorblindness* (New York: Springer, forthcoming).

59 Teaching Tolerance Project, *Teaching the Movement: The State Standards We Deserve* (Montgomery, AL: Southern Poverty Law Center, 2012), p. 4.

60 See James W. Loewen, *Lies My Teacher Told Me: Everything Your American History Textbook Got Wrong* (New York: The New Press, 1995), p. 163; James W. Loewen, *Teaching What Really Happened: How to Avoid the Tyranny of Textbooks and Get Students Excited about Doing History* (New York: Teachers' College Press, 2009).

61 Jason R. Soble, Lisa B. Spanierman, and Hsin-Ya Liao, "Effects of a Brief Video Intervention on White University Students' Racial Attitudes," *Journal of Counseling Psychology*, 58 (2011), pp. 151 and 156. See Lisa B. Spanierman, V. P. Poteat, Y. Wang, and E. Oh, "Psychosocial Costs of Racism to White Counselors: Predicting Various Dimensions of Multicultural Counseling Competence," *Journal of Counseling Psychology* 55 (2008): 75–88.

62 Julie M. Hughes, Rebecca S. Bigler, and Sheri R. Levy, "Consequences of Learning about Historical Racism among European American and African American Children," *Child Development* 78 (November/December 2007): 1689–1705. The quote is on p. 1695.

63 David M. Amodio, Patricia G. Devine, and Eddie Harmon-Jones, "A Dynamic Model of Guilt: Implications for Motivation and Self Regulation in the Context of Prejudice," *Psychological Science* 18 (June 2007): 524–530.

64 Nathan R Todd, Paul V Poteat, and Lisa B. Spanierman, "Longitudinal Examination of the Psychological Costs of Racism Across the College Experience," *Journal of Counseling Psychology* 4 (2011), p. 518.

65 E. Janie Pinterits, V. Paul Poteat, and Lisa B. Spanierman, "The White Privilege Attitudes Scale," *Journal of Counseling Psychology* 56 (2009): 417–429.

66 As reported in C. Eugene Emery, "Brown Study Counteracts Racial Stereotypes," www.projo.com/education/content/BROWN_FACES_02–15–09_9LD9Q76_v10.1da8fe3.html (accessed April 7, 2009).

67 Elizabeth Stearns, Claudia Buchmann, and Kara Bonneau, "Interracial Friendships in the Transition to College: Do Birds of a Feather Flock Together Once They Leave the Nest?" *Sociology of Education* 82 (April 2009): 175–195.

68 Sarah E Gaither and Samuel R. Sommers, "Living with an Other-Race Roommate Shapes Whites' Behavior in Subsequent Diverse Settings," *Journal of Experimental Social Psychology* 49 (2013): 272–276.

69 "Student Experience in the Research University," University of California, http://cshe.berkeley.edu/research/seru (accessed May 22, 2009).

70 Kathleen Kordesh, Lisa Spanierman, and Helen A. Neville, "White University Students' Racial Affect: Understanding the Antiracist Type," *Journal of Diversity in Higher Education* 6 (2013), pp. 47–48.

71 Cedric J. Robinson, *Black Movements in America* (New York: Routledge, 1997), p. 63.

72 "Interview with Julian Bond," *Democracy Now*, July 21, 2009.

73 Nathan Rutstein, *From a Gnat to an Eagle: The Story of Nathan Rutstein*, ed. Carolyn Kerner Stein (Wilmette, IL: Bahai Publishing, 2008); Nathan Rutstein, *Racism: Unraveling the Fear* (Washington, DC: The Global Classroom, 1993), pp. 225–228; National Resource Center for the Healing of Racism, www.nrchr.org/index.php (accessed July 3, 2013).

74 Eileen O'Brien, *Whites Confront Racism* (Lanham, MD: Rowman & Littlefield, 2001); Michael Omi, "(E)racism: Emergent Practices of Antiracist Organizations," paper presented at American Sociological Association Meetings, San Francisco, CA, August 1998. See the websites for People's Institute at www.pisab.org (accessed July 3, 2013); and for Antiracist Action at http://antiracistaction.org (accessed July 3, 2013).

75 I draw on 2012–2013 emails and notes prepared by Herb Perkins, Bundy Trinz, Margery Otto, and Tim Johnson.

76 See Kristie A. Ford and Victoria K. Malaney, "'I Now Harbor More Pride in My Race': The Educational Benefits of Inter- and Intraracial Dialogues on the Experiences of Students of Color and Multiracial Students," *Equity and Excellence in Education* 45 (2012): 14–35; Kristie A. Ford, "Shifting White Ideological Scripts: The Educational Benefits of Inter- and Intraracial Curricular Dialogues on the Experiences of White College Students," *Journal of Diversity in Higher Education* 5 (2012): 138–158.

77 The Rainbow PUSH Coalition is described at www.rainbowpush.org (accessed July 3, 2013).

78 See Joe R. Feagin and Hernán Vera, *White Racism: The Basics* (New York: Routledge, 1995), pp. 188–191.

79 W. E. B. Du Bois, *John Brown* (New York: International Publishers, 1962), pp. 263–264.

80 Ibid., pp. 264–265. I use modern spelling.

81 See Ibrahim al-Marashi, "Iraq's Constitutional Debate," *Meria*, http://meria.idc.ac.il/journal/2005/issue3/jv9no3a8.html (accessed June 24, 2009); "Constitution of Iraq," http://en.wikipedia.org/wiki/Iraqi_Constitution (accessed June 24, 2009).

82 Brooks, *Integration or Separation*, p. 115. I am indebted here to discussions with Roy Brooks.

83 See Joe R. Feagin, "Heeding Black Voices: The Court, Brown, and Challenges in Building a Multiracial Democracy," *University of Pittsburgh Law Review* 66 (fall 2004): 57–81; Joe R. Feagin and Bernice M. Barnett, "Success and Failure: How Systemic Racism Trumped the *Brown v. Board of Education* Decision," *University of Illinois Law Review* (2004): 1099–1130.

84 Brent Barry and Eduardo Bonilla-Silva, "'They Should Hire the One with the Best Score': White Sensitivity Qualification Differences in Affirmative Action Hiring Decisions," *Ethnic and Racial Studies* 31 (February 2008): 215–242.

85 Richard Delgado, *The Coming Race War?* (New York: New York University Press, 1996), p. 10.

86 Roy L. Brooks, *Atonement and Forgiveness: A New Model for Black Reparations* (Los Angeles: University of California Press, 2004), pp. 188, 194; Joe R. Feagin, "Documenting the Costs

of Slavery, Segregation, and Contemporary Discrimination: Are Reparations in Order for African Americans?" *Harvard Black Letter Law Journal* 20 (2004): 49–80.

87 Lord Anthony Gifford, "The Legal Basis of the Claim for Reparations," paper presented to First Pan-African Congress on Reparations, Abuja, Federal Republic of Nigeria, April 27–29, 1993.

88 Ali A. Mazrui, "Who Should Pay for Slavery? Reparations to Africa," *World Press Review* 8 (August 1993): 22.

89 Jonathan Kaplan and Andrew Valls, "Housing Discrimination as a Basis for Black Reparations," *Public Affairs Quarterly* 21 (July 2007): 255–270.

90 Ibid., especially p. 268.

91 Andrew Kull, "Rationalizing Restitution," *California Law Review* 83 (October 1995): 1191–1198.

92 *Larry Williams, et al. v. The City Of New Orleans, et al.*, 729 F. 2d 1554, 1577 (1984).

93 Delgado, *The Coming Race War?*, p. 103.

94 Brooks, *Atonement and Forgiveness*, pp. xii–xiv, 142. I extend arguments in Leslie Houts Picca and Joe R. Feagin, *Two Faced Racism: Whites in the Backstage and Frontstage* (New York: Routledge, 2007), pp. 271–272.

95 Rhonda V. Magee, "The Master's Tools, from the Bottom Up: Responses to African American Reparations Theory in Mainstream and Outsider Remedies Discourse," *Virginia Law Review* 79 (May 1993): 886. Sumner is quoted at p. 887.

96 Martin Luther King, Jr., *Why We Can't Wait* (New York: Signet Books, 1963).

97 Gifford, "The Legal Basis of the Claim for Reparations."

98 See John Conyers, Jr., statements on reparations bill, http://conyers.house.gov/index. cfm/reparations (accessed July 4, 2013).

99 See their website for more detailed, savvy arguments: www.ncobra.org.

100 See Feagin, "Documenting the Costs of Slavery, Segregation, and Contemporary Discrimination," pp. 50–79.

101 Gideon Sjoberg *et al.*, "Ethics, Human Rights and Sociological Inquiry: Genocide, Politicide and Other Issues of Organizational Power," *American Sociologist* 26 (spring 1995): 11–13.

102 United Nations, *The United Nations and Human Rights, 1945–1995* (New York: United Nations Department of Public Information, 1995), pp. 33, 153–155, 219–225.

103 Judith Blau and Alberto Moncada, *Human Rights: Beyond the Liberal Vision* (Lanham, MD: Rowman & Littlefield, 2005), p. 63; "The Universal Declaration of Human Rights," http://en.wikipedia.org/wiki/Universal_declaration_of_human_rights#cite_note-1 (accessed June 26, 2009).

104 Louis Henkin, Sarah H. Cleveland, Laurence R. Helfer, Gerald L. Newman, and Diana F. Orentlicher, *Human Rights* (New York: Foundation Press, 2009), p. 216. I am indebted here to suggestions by Roy Brooks.

105 Ibid., citing Tom Ginsburg, Svitlana Chernykh, and Zachary Elkins, "Commitment and Diffusion: How and Why National Constitutions Incorporate International Law," *University of Illinois Law Review* (2008): 201, 208.

106 Henkin *et al. Human Rights*, p. 76. See also Hurst Hannum, "The Status and Future of the Customary International Law of Human Rights: The Status of the Universal Declaration of Human Rights in National and International Law," *Georgia Journal of International and Comparative Law* 25 (fall 1995/winter 1996): 287–320; "Universal Declaration of Human Rights," Wikipedia, http://en.wikipedia.org/wiki/Universal_ Declaration_of_Human_ Rights (accessed July 16, 2013).

107 David S. Law and Mila Versteeg, "The Declining Influence of the United States Constitution," *New York University Law Review* 87 (2012), p. 767.

108 Quoted in Sidney M. Willhelm, *Black in a White America* (Cambridge, MA: Schenkman, 1983), p. 352.

109 Franklin Roosevelt, "State of the Union," www.presidency.ucsb.edu/ws/index. php?pid=16518 (accessed February 28, 2005).

110 Sandra Harding, "Taking Responsibility for Our Own Gender, Race, Class: Transforming Science and the Social Studies of Science," *Rethinking Marxism* (fall 1989): 14.

111 See Melvin M. Leiman, *Political Economy of Racism* (London: Pluto Press, 1993), pp. 7–9, 313.

112 On racial lines in the feminist movement, see Louise Michele Newman, *White Women's Rights: The Racial Origins of Feminism in the United States* (New York: Oxford University Press, 1999), pp. 179–185. See also W. E. B. Du Bois, *Black Reconstruction in America 1860–1880* (New York: Atheneum, 1992 [1935]), p. 30.

113 See Michael Albert *et al.*, *Liberating Theory* (Boston: South End Press, 1986).

114 Paolo Freire, *Pedagogy of the Oppressed*, 30th anniversary edn. (New York: Bloomsbury Academic, 2000), p. 44.

115 Jennifer A. Richeson and J. Nicole Shelton, "When Prejudice Does Not Pay: Effects of Interracial Contact on Executive Function," *Psychological Science* 14 (May 2003): 287–290.

116 William H. Frey, Alan Berube, Audrey Singer, and Jill H. Wilson, "Getting Current: Recent Demographic Trends in Metropolitan America," Brookings Institution, www.brookings.edu/reports/2009/~/media/Files/rc/reports/2009/03_metro_demographic_trends/03_metro_demographic_trends.pdf (accessed June 12, 2009). The quote is on p. 21.

117 See W. E. B. Du Bois, "On the Ruling of Men," in *The Oxford W. E. B. Du Bois Reader*, ed. Eric J. Sundquist (New York: Oxford University Press, 1996), pp. 555–557. See Feagin, *The White Racial Frame*.

118 Frances Lee Ansley, "Stirring the Ashes: Race, Class and the Future of Civil Rights Scholarship," *Cornell Law Review* 74 (September 1989): 1002.

119 Quoted in Paul G. Lauren, *Power and Prejudice: The Politics and Diplomacy of Racial Discrimination* (Boulder, CO: Westview Press, 1988), p. 288.

Index

Terms in **bold** are followed by a brief definition

Custom Materials
DELIVER A MORE REWARDING EDUCATIONAL EXPERIENCE.

The Social Issues Collection

This unique collection features 250 readings plus 45 recently added readings for undergraduate teaching in sociology and other social science courses. The social issues collection includes selections from Joe Nevins, Sheldon Elkand-Olson, Val Jenness, Sarah Fenstermaker, Nikki Jones, France Winddance Twine, Scott McNall, Ananya Roy, Joel Best, Michael Apple, and more.

1 Go to the website at
routledge.customgateway.com

2 Choose from almost 300
readings from Routledge
& other publishers

3 Create your complete
custom anthology

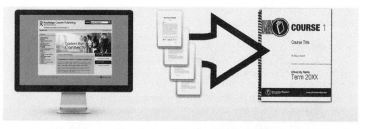

Learn more:
routledge.customgateway.com | 800.200.3908 x 501 | info@cognella.com

University Readers is an imprint of Cognella, Inc. ©1997-2013

6191439